Risky Busin

Risky Business?
Youth and the
Enterprise Culture

Robert MacDonald
and
Frank Coffield

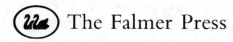 The Falmer Press

(A member of the Taylor & Francis Group)
London • New York • Philadelphia

UK   The Falmer Press, 4 John Street, London WC1N 2ET
USA   The Falmer Press, Taylor & Francis Inc., 1900 Frost Road, Suite 101,
Bristol, PA 19007

First published 1991

British Library Cataloguing in Publication Data

**Library of Congress Cataloguing-in-Publication Data
available on request**

ISBN 1 85000-897-3
ISBN 1 85000-898-1 (pbk)

Jacket design by Caroline Archer

Typeset in 10½/12 pt Bembo by
Graphicraft Typesetters Ltd., Hong Kong

*Printed in Great Britain by Burgess Science Press, Basingstoke
on paper which has a specified pH value on final paper
manufacture of not less than 7.5 and is therefore 'acid free'.*

Contents

List of Tables and Figures

List of Tables

List of Figures

List of Abbreviations

BEP	Business Enterprise Programme
CP	Community Programme
CPVE	Certificate of Pre-Vocational Education
DES	Department of Education and Science
DTI	Department of Trade and Industry
EAS	Enterprise Allowance Scheme
EATE	Enterprise Awareness in Teacher Education
EHE	Enterprise in Higher Education
ERA	Education Reform Act
ESRC	Economic and Social Research Council
ET	Employment Training
ETE	Education, Training and Employment
GGP	Graduate Gateway Programme
HIE	Highlands and Islands Enterprise
LEA	Local Education Authority *and* Local Enterprise Agency
LEC	Local Enterprise Company
LEPY	Local Enterprise Policy for Youth
MEP	Management Extension Programme
MESP	Mini Enterprise in Schools Project
MSC	Manpower Services Commission
NAO	National Audit Office
NECCA	North of England County Councils Association
NECDA	North-east Co-operative Development Agency (pseudonym)
PEP	Private Enterprise Programme
PRF	Performance Related Funding
PYBT	Prince's Youth Business Trust
RDG	Regional Development Grant
SE	Scottish Enterprise
TA	Training Agency
TC	Training Commission
TEC	Training and Enterprise Council

List of Abbreviations

TFE	Training for Enterprise Programme
TUSIU	Trade Union Studies Information Unit
TVEI	Technical and Vocational Education Initiative
TYE	Teesside Young Entrepreneurs (pseudonym)
UDC	Urban Development Corporation
VPP	Voluntary Projects Programme
YOP	Youth Opportunity Programme
YT	Youth Training
YTS	Youth Training Scheme

Preface and Acknowledgments

Our study is one of the first attempts to examine the relevance and effectiveness of enterprise initiatives for young people. The issues raised in this book concern the attempts of young women and men to establish a working life for themselves in depressed areas of the United Kingdom and are, we hope, likely to be controversial. Our greatest debt is to the people who spared the time to talk to us about their experiences in the 'enterprise culture'. We dedicate this book to them and wish them the best of luck with their risky businesses.

This work was made possible by a grant (n. XC05750014) from the Economic and Social Science Research Council (ESRC). The Research and Initiatives Committee and the School of Education at Durham University supported us financially at critical times and we are also pleased to acknowledge their help. Chapter 2 appeared in substantially the same form in *The British Journal of Education and Work* whose editor, Ian Jamieson, has kindly given us permission to reprint it here.

It remains for us to acknowledge the considerable help we have received, in organizing the research project and writing this book, from a wide range of people in the North-East. In particular we would like to thank Eric Sugden, Dennis Samways, Norma Wilburn, Tony Mason, Mike Shepherd, Liz Walker, Bob Little and the many other key professionals working on Teesside whose assistance was invaluable. We would also like to thank Robert Blackburn, Shane Blackman, Bob Coles, Gerald Grace, Bob Hollands and Jacqueline Merchant for reading and commenting on various chapters and reports. Reiner Siebert, a student from the University of Duisburg, West Germany, worked with us for three months and successfully completed the interviews with the unemployed sub-group in our sample, pursuing his interest in comparing the attitudes of unemployed youth with their apparently more enterprising peers. We wish, in addition, to record our appreciation to Lynn Carrington who willingly helped us out whenever the pressure was on, irrespective of the impact of our demands on her own time. And finally, our deepest thanks go to our Project Secretary, Ann Scott, who has shown us both what commitment to a task really means and who has, at all times, been a joy to work with.

Robert MacDonald
Frank Coffield
School of Education,
University of Durham
September, 1990

Chapter 1

Introduction: Youth and Enterprise

'Our mission is to develop an enterprise culture in the North to replace a dependency culture'.[1] This statement captures both the essence of government policy for the depressed regions and the paramount objective of the industry which has grown up to deliver enterprise to them. During the 1980s, *The Enterprise Years*, according to the title of Lord Young's autobiography (1990), thousands of millions of pounds have been spent on an ideological project to transform the culture of education, training and employment within the United Kingdom and it has been one of the policies dearest to the heart of Mrs Thatcher's Government. It is time for an independent report on what is done in the name of enterprise, what happens to young people who set up their own businesses and what wider impact such policies have had on the political and economic experiences of school-leavers struggling to find a secure toehold in the labour market.

This book, therefore, represents one of the first detailed empirical tests of the attempts to create an enterprise culture in this country. Its other major theme is the cultural and economic responses of young adults to the virtual collapse of work in localities like Teesside in the 1980s. Structural changes in the economy and in education over the past twenty years have greatly transformed the careers followed by young people as they leave school and search for jobs. The established routes, forged in the post-war political consensus and prosperity of the 1950s and 1960s, held as far as the mid-1970s, until the sudden quadrupling of oil prices led to an economic recession in Western countries. In 1975, 60 per cent of 16 year olds went from school directly into employment. By 1987 this number had shrunk to 18 per cent (Department of Education and Science 1988). Moreover, this global economic crisis had very local consequences. It sparked off massive youth unemployment, hitting the more peripheral areas of Britain, like the county of Cleveland, the hardest. Youth unemployment grew more in one year — 1980 — than in the whole of the previous decade (Raffe, 1987) and the early years of the 1980s saw the instigation of special measures to cope with the soaring numbers of teenage unemployed (and the attendant public fears of youth unrest and disaffection).

The story of the return of mass unemployment and how the Manpower Services Commission (MSC) radically reshaped education and training in Britain is a different one from the tale to be told here (see, for example: Dale, 1985; Finn, 1987; Coles, 1988; Ainley and Corney, 1990; Coles and MacDonald, 1990). All we need point to is how these hasty and much criticized government interventions into the youth labour market have been gradually revised and formalized into an evolving *system* of vocational training, ranging from the Technical and Vocational Educational Initiative (TVEI) for school pupils, through various versions of the Youth Training Scheme (YOP to YTS to YT) for school-leavers, to Employment Training (ET) for adults.

Whilst the economic recession of the 1970s inspired national programmes of educational and training reforms these have failed to exorcise the demon of unemployment for particular groups of people in particular localities. Even full participation in a succession of courses and schemes cannot guarantee jobs. As a result, the North-East has some of the best trained dole queues in the world and so far-reaching have the social and economic changes been in the past two decades that questions have been raised about the continuing adequacy of theories developed in the 1960s, when it was still possible to write books with titles like *Into Work* (Carter, 1966) and *Adolescent Needs: the Transition from School to Work* (Maizels, 1970).

Our book makes a different kind of contribution to the avalanche of reports (for example: Gleeson, 1983; Bates *et al.*, 1984; Varlaam, 1984; and Roberts, 1984) on the transitions from school which have appeared in the 1980s, reporting the rise in unemployment and its consequences for young people. Although we draw upon this now quite vast literature on youth (un)employment, training and education, and share with it a number of common concerns and approaches, we wish to highlight two trends in recent research which we particularly welcome and to which we hope to contribute.

First, we locate our work firmly within the growing tradition of research in the sociology of youth and in education (Corrigan, 1979; Connell *et al.*, 1982) which emphasizes the importance of studying 'ordinary' young people rather than exotic, unusual or unrepresentative youth groups (the Punks, Teds, Skins and so on). This broader view has developed from Willis's early ethnography of the 'lads', through Jenkins' study of 'lads, citizens and ordinary kids' in Belfast, from Coffield, Borrill and Marshall's investigation of 'growing up at the margins' to Brown's examination of the schooling of 'ordinary kids' (Willis, 1977; Jenkins, 1983; Coffield *et al.*, 1986; Brown, 1987). Phillip Brown (1987), for example, studied the 'invisible majority' of ordinary working class pupils who neither enthusiastically accepted nor vigorously rejected the school; in his own words, those 'who neither left their names engraved on the school's honours boards, nor gouged them into the top of class-room desks' (1987:1).

So although studies of youth during the 1970s (e.g. Hall and Jefferson, 1976; Willis, 1978; Hebdige, 1979) made valuable contributions to our understanding of the sub-cultural aspects of various youth groups, research developed in essentially élitist directions, paying little attention to the realities of the everyday lives of the majority of young adults. Conversely, studies of youth unemployment may have generated a wealth of information about national trends and disrupted youth transitions but few of these have seriously attempted to grasp the local or cultural meaning of these experiences. In this book we hope to go some way to combining these relatively distinct traditions of research on youth by exploring the cultural and economic responses of a wide range of ordinary young people to the structure of opportunities facing them. Moreover, we focus on one particular form of response — youth enterprise — which to date has been largely ignored by youth researchers.

A second important trend in studies of youth over the past ten years, and which reappears as a key issue in our argument, is the importance of locality. Local labour markets shape the choices available to young adults and help to structure huge regional differences between the North and South. David Ashton, Malcolm Maguire and colleagues have been particularly associated with this valuable addition to the debate:

> Thus although the economic recession has increased the level of youth unemployment nationally, school-leavers' chances of employment and 'choice' of work are still greatly influenced by the structure of their local labour market. (Ashton, *et al.*, 1982:19)

Ashton and Maguire (1986:2) have shown, for instance, that 'the chances of the sons of middle-class fathers in Sunderland finding employment were less than those of sons of lower working-class families in St. Albans'. Conventional explanations of these differences — personal attributes and social background — were clearly not as satisfactory as the character of the local labour market in affecting employment prospects. Consequently, we pay particular attention to the way youth opportunities, transitions into the labour market and aspects of the experience of enterprise are structured at an immediate, local level by Teesside's changing economy. In short, we aim to explore the cultural and economic meanings of enterprise for a broad group of young people in the locality of Teesside. Enterprise and youth, then, are the twin pillars of this book. We will now describe briefly how these two focal concerns came together into a research project.

During the mid to late 1980s, it became apparent to us that some-thing unusual was afoot in the county of Cleveland. We became aware of the emergence of a thriving enterprise industry which was offering train-ing and advice on enterprise to school-pupils, school-leavers, young adults and the community at large. At that time, Cleveland had the highest unemployment rate in mainland Britain, its economy was domin-ated by a few giants like ICI and British Steel, and, as such, it posed a particularly severe test of the Government's policy of industrial and social regeneration through enterprise. In short, if the enterprise culture could be shown to work in Cleveland, it could probably work anywhere. Local professionals compared the task to 'rowing up a waterfall'. We decided, so to speak, to kit ourselves out in waterproof clothes in order to study the boats, the rowers, and the obstacles and so chart what progress they made. Our endeavours were made possible by funding from the Econo-mic and Social Research Council (ESRC).

In 1987 the ESRC established the *16 to 19 Initiative* to address a number of questions:

> What happens to [young people] after the age of 16 in education, in work and at home? What do they feel about their opportunities and what influences the choices they make? How do they perceive the economic and political world around them and where do they see themselves fitting into it? (Bynner, 1987b:8)

The ESRC commissioned two consultants, a psychologist, Glynis Break-well, from the University of Surrey and a sociologist, Ken Roberts, from the University of Liverpool, to review the literature on the economic and political socialization of young adults; and their reports sharpened the key questions which needed to be asked about this age group.

First, how do the careers of young people in education, employ-ment, the family and leisure differ between various groups? Second, how do these different careers *interact*? For example, the family responsibilities and leisure pursuits of young women are unlikely to be the same as those of young men, whatever their qualifications and job prospects. Third, how do young people themselves 'create and sustain identities from the consistencies and contradictions that they encounter' (Roberts, 1987:23). Finally, a new synthesis between the theory and findings of sociological and psychological research was looked for in the work of the *Initiative*. The ESRC then proceeded to establish at the core of the *16 to 19 Initiative*:

> a longitudinal research project carried out by local university research teams involving 6,400 young people in four areas of the country — Kirkcaldy, Sheffield, Liverpool and Swindon. In each area two samples of 800 young people — the school-leavers (now aged 15 to 16) and the school-leavers of two years ago (now aged

17 to 18) will be followed up for two years. The first survey was carried out in April 1987 and [was] repeated in 1988 and 1989. (Bynner, 1987b:9)

The core studies, as they came to be called, will publish the first overview of their findings in a book entitled *Careers and Identities* (Bynner, 1991).

The intention of the *16 to 19 Initiative* was always to fund a number of much smaller, self-contained projects in specialized areas to prevent all their eggs being entrusted to four large baskets. A series of associated studies was therefore established into topics and samples of young people which were not adequately covered by the core studies. Projects were set up to investigate: young adults in a rural labour market; young people with special needs; family socialization; ethnic minority youth; adolescent identity; teenage 'housing careers'; and the use of video methods in the study of socialization. In addition, the Anglo-German Foundation awarded a grant for a comparative study of young people in declining labour markets (Bremen and Liverpool) and expanding labour markets (Paderborn and Swindon) in the Federal Republic of Germany and in Britain.[2]

Our Project: The Teesside 16 to 25 Initiative

We successfully applied to the ESRC for an associated study into the impact of enterprise on the education, training and employment of young adults in a depressed area of Britain (Cleveland). In more detail, the central aim of our proposed research was to study new career patterns for young people for whom traditional routes into employment had either disappeared or become severely restricted. School-leavers began to ex-perience a much wider variety of early careers; until the mid-1970s many moved straight from school into apprenticeships and jobs which often lasted into adulthood. Increasingly, some started to undergo protracted transitions into adulthood by way of government training schemes (Hol-lands, 1990) and spells in and out of employment before landing a 'real' job. Others became trapped in a succession of schemes and/or 'shit' jobs (their expression) which led nowhere; some of these slowly became part of the long-term unemployed. It was under such grim economic con-ditions that some young adults turned to explore alternatives through enterprise in self-employment, co-operatives and community projects. Others began working wherever they could, 'on the side', in 'fiddle' jobs or even travelled to find employment in southern England or abroad.

The aim of our study has been to concentrate on self-employment, enterprise schemes, co-operatives and community projects. The con-straints of a modest budget have meant, however, that the project lasted only fifteen months from October 1988 to December 1989; the total sum available and the time-scale placed constrictions on the scope of the research but, within these limits, we still managed to interview over 100 young people. We were interested in studying not just new forms of transition from school to self-employment, but also the experience of enterprise, for instance, as it related to the economic and political attitudes of our informants. The central question which we sought to answer was: what does enterprise *mean* for young people in Cleveland? Moreover, we were keen to assess the impact of enterprise courses and schemes on the local culture of work, which was itself undergoing marked changes (Beynon *et al.*, 1985). In the early stages of planning the research we developed a large number of more specific but interrelated questions, and we list the principal ones here:

1 What is the present state of, and future prospects for, the Cleveland economy? We wished to trace the historical development of local industries to deepen our understanding of current problems on Teesside and their impact on the transitions from school to (un)employment by young people.

2 What is enterprise? What definitions of it are used and what do enterprise courses consist of? How extensive is the enterprise movement and what ideology or ideologies underpin it? What is the significance of the new policies to decentralize and privatize training and enterprise to the new Training and Enterprise Councils (TECs)? What are the theoretical or practical justifications for the activities carried out in the name of enterprise? Have these activities been evaluated and have the evaluations been acted upon to improve practice?

3 What enterprise initiatives are taking place locally? How many organizations are involved, what models or enterprise do they promote and how? By whom are they funded and with what aims and objectives?

4 What kinds of young people become involved in enterprise and why do they move into self-employment in small businesses or co-operatives? How do they start up in business and what problems do they face? What kind of work do they do and under what conditions?

5 What are the implications of our findings for policy in the general areas of the education, training and (un)employment of young adults and in the more specific field of starting small businesses? To what extent has the enterprise culture taken root on Teesside?

6 Last, but by no means least, how do young adults themselves assess enterprise? How do they rate the quality of the experiences they undergo and what processes does it involve them in? How is success and failure defined in official terms and by young people themselves? What are the political and economic outlooks of

'young entrepreneurs'?[3] Are they more conservative than their peers and what do they understand by the term 'the enterprise culture'?

As is obvious from such an extensive list, we were journeying into unknown territory; there was no danger of us running out of questions but we could not be sure at the outset how many of these would be adequately answered by our study. We hope, by the end of Chapter 10, to have answered at least some of them.

We were also concerned that, despite the flow of considerable sums of public money into enterprise projects in Cleveland, few, if any, independent evaluations had been carried out. The area bristled with unexamined claims, some of which were mutually inconsistent. For instance, we were told by staff delivering the Enterprise Allowance Scheme (EAS) in the area that participants were doing just as well here as in other, more prosperous parts of the country. On the other hand, we were told by enterprise advisers that the depressed local economy, with its narrow industrial base and culture of employment (rather than enterprise), would inevitably hinder the chances of the new self-employed on the scheme. There was a clear need to put these conflicting claims to the empirical test.

Method

We employed four approaches to assess the significance of these new routes through the labour market and the cultural importance of these changes for young people:

(i)   an examination of the literature on the concept, philosophy and practice of enterprise.

(ii) an historical analysis of the Cleveland economy and the collapse of employment for young adults in the local labour market during the 1980s.

(iii) a survey and a series of interviews with key professionals involved in the enterprise industry.

(iv) qualitative interviews with over 100 young adults in Cleveland.

In our opinion, ethnography provided the approach best suited to answering the bulk of our empirical questions, that is, about the experiences of youth in the enterprise culture. Much has been written about the origins, objectives and techniques of this form of enquiry and we need only to spell out some of its general features here (see, for instance: McCall and Simmons, 1969; Filstead, 1970; Hammersley and Atkinson, 1983; Walker, 1985, for a fuller discussion).

Ethnography was initially introduced into sociological enquiry from anthropology (e.g. Malinowski, 1922) as part of a general opposition to more positivistic approaches based on surveys. As a method of research it gives pride of place to the cultures of particular groups of people in naturally occurring settings (rather than, for instance, a university psychology laboratory) and draws upon participant observation or the ethnographic interview as its main research techniques (Spradley, 1979a, 1979b; Bastin, 1985).

Ethnography aims to explore, describe and analyse the social processes underpinning experience and the meanings participants themselves attribute to their own actions. As a form of interpretive method, it aims to develop theory from the data as it is collected rather than to find evidence to support or refute hypotheses formulated in advance (Glaser and Strauss, 1967). Within the ethnographic interview the nature of the relationship established between the researcher and the group being studied is paramount (Finch, 1984; Graham, 1984). To use the words of Margaret Mead, ethnography 'does not have subjects. We work with informants in an atmosphere of trust and mutual respect' (1972:152), or so it is to be hoped. A number of our informants seemed keen to participate in the interview. It gave them the chance to share their experiences and problems with an empathetic outsider, to rehearse for themselves, often for the first time, the reasons why they had set up in business and the difficulties they now faced. Often enterprise was a lonely experience and taking part in an interview provided the opportunity for social contact and an unthreatening discussion of personal experiences. One man, Trevor, said at the end of the interview: 'I'm pleased to have taken part. If any of the comments can help some poor soul avoid the terrible year I've had, all the pitfalls . . .'.

In ethnography the informants themselves become 'the prime source of theories about their actions and thoughts' (Harré, 1980), and their explanations are appreciated without romanticizing their plight or condemning their every transgression (Cohen, 1973). Ethnographic interviewing provides 'the opportunity for the researcher to probe deeply, to uncover new clues, to open up new dimensions of a problem and to secure vivid, accurate, inclusive accounts that are based on personal experience' (Burgess, 1982, quoted in Walker, 1985:4). Ethnography makes possible the flexible study of complex situations, which need to be analyzed in their entirety rather than isolating and investigating one or two features. In short, the problem is seen as a whole rather than broken down into meaningless bits.

We attempted to follow these general principles in exploring cultures of youth and the culture of enterprise. Our main technique was the ethnographic interview; participant observation, traditionally the ethnographic method *par excellence*, was very much underused. We would have preferred in our own project to have drawn more upon observational methods and to have produced a more complete study of our informants' experiences, but the limitations placed on us by time and money meant that we could focus on only one part of their lives — the economic sphere — and so largely disregarded other important aspects such as leisure, family and sexuality. The choice of one method always involves the sacrifice of others and in seeking to talk to a reasonably large number of informants we were left with no time to develop more intensive participant observation with interesting sub-groups.

Ethnography still proved, however, to be a particularly useful way of studying the relationships between the choices individuals make and the local structure of opportunities, between biography and history, and between problems of personal experience and issues of social structure — to use C. Wright Mills' famous expression (1970). Our approach also allowed for in-depth discussions of sensitive questions (such as the amount of money young people earned or the reasons for the failure of their businesses), and it is likely to produce more convincing and valid answers than those obtained by, for example, large scale questionnaire surveys. In this respect we would claim to have moved beyond the standard research techniques (postal questionnaires and check lists), which are routinely employed by academic studies and administrative evaluations of small business.

The statistics and correlations produced by major surveys do have their advantages but they also have two serious drawbacks from our point of view. First, a well-known finding from questionnaire surveys is the link between parental experience of self-employment and those who set up in businesses themselves (see Curran, 1986, for a review). But what politicians, administrators and social scientists need is some understanding of the particular mechanisms which lie behind this relationship. No simple, direct causal link is established by research which merely confirms an association; and no amount of sophisticated statistical operations can take the debate any further. Ethnography, on the other hand, can examine a number of possible processes which help explain the relationship. In Chapter 5 we describe how levels of self-employment among the parents of our sample were lower than those found elsewhere, that parental support can take a variety of different forms and, in general, that the link between the self-employment of parents and children is more complex than any simple correlation would suggest.

We would argue that ethnographic research has a second advantage over more quantitative research. It contains 'a profoundly important methodological possibility — that of being surprised, of reaching knowledge not prefigured in one's starting paradigm' (Willis, 1980:90). In research employing only questionnaires, responses of informants are necessarily pushed into predetermined categories which may bear little relation to the complexity or originality of their experience. In this way the subjects of research become merely respondents to questions set by

Table 1.1   The Sample of Informants

Presently self-employed	50
Seriously intending to become self-employed (including in a co-operative)	12
Previously self-employed	15
Presently or previously involved in a co-operative	9
Presently or previously involved with community enterprise projects	9
Long term unemployed (and uninvolved with enterprise)	16
Total number of people interviewed	104

The numbers listed add up to more than 104, the reason for this being that some people who were interviewed fell into more than one category. For instance, a young woman intending to set up in self-employment had also participated in a community enterprise venture.

the investigator. For example, the lack of interest in politics professed by young people, which has been found by most researchers, may be partly explained by the questions asked and the narrow range of possible responses. Typically, respondents are invited to answer a question like 'How much do you think you know about politics?' by ticking one of the following 'A Great Deal' — 'Quite a lot' — 'Not much' — 'Nothing at all'. In sharp contrast, detailed discussions, which are flexible and sensitive enough to explore and challenge the views expressed, can reveal that, although young people tend to claim immediately to be politically apathetic, they can also be very sharp critics of particular government policies and they have insightful comments to make on the economic plight of their contemporaries and of their region. The ethnographic task is to develop an explanation which makes sense of this apparent contradiction and this we attempt in Chapter 9.

All research methods, however, have their strengths and weaknesses so we attempted to develop a research design which was appropriate to the questions that we addressed, as well as combining the advantages of a variety of approaches (Denzin, 1978). To help us draw a picture of the different models of enterprise which were being promoted locally, we conducted a questionnaire survey of the veritable maze of organizations, agencies and schemes which had proliferated in Cleveland to deliver enterprise. We followed this up with an extensive series of interviews with professionals involved in youth training, careers advice, enterprise training and co-operative development. These preliminary stages of research were carried out largely in order to construct a sample of informants which reflected the relative significance of the three models of enterprise (self-employment, co-operatives and community-based projects) which were in evidence in Cleveland and the results are displayed in Table 1.1.

Young entrepreneurs, however, proved to be a particularly difficult group to contact. There exists no complete central record of young people in business. For instance, Careers Offices were unable to identify young people involved in self-employment from their records. And whilst the Training Agency helped us contact some people, their files on EAS participants provided an incomplete picture of all those under-25 year olds in business (i.e. a minority start up without the assistance of the scheme). Unlike school pupils, YTS trainees or FE college students, young entrepreneurs do not congregate together in a given place at a given time. Unlike the unemployed, they do not have to visit and register with a central office. However, they share with these other categories of young people the fact that they are not a static group. People move in and out of self-employment, making contact with them even more difficult.

However, we were able to make initial contacts through the three agencies who were generally considered to be the market leaders in particular forms of enterprise development (self-employment as opposed to co-operatives, for example). Although we concentrated on three main organizations, they were by repute typical of the enterprise industry as a whole. Potential informants were selected from the client records of these organizations using fairly random strategies. For instance, we simply examined records for March 1987, 1988 and 1989 and selected alternate names to contact. At this stage, no direction was given by enterprise advisers to particular types of client. Later, poorly represented categories of informants, particularly people from Asian backgrounds and those no longer trading, were contacted with the help of the Training Agency, from the records of the EAS. The vast majority of informants were white, with only four informants being from the Pakistani culture on Teesside. Although this slightly over-represents the proportion of Pakistani people in the local population, we were still disappointed that we failed to talk to more people who could provide a perspective on 'ethnic enterprise'.

We quickly decided to extend the age range from 16–19 to 16–25 to ensure a reasonable size of sample, whose average age turned out to be 21. Chapter 5 gives details of the types of businesses which were formed, their duration and structure. All the inteviewees were resident in the county of Cleveland, with the majority coming from Middlesbrough. The second strategy of finding informants, to add to those contacts supplied by enterprise agencies, involved a 'snowballing' method whereby the first informants were asked to suggest others. About half the informants were eventually located in this second way.

Overall, we conducted in-depth interviews with over 100 young adults, who were more or less equally divided between males and females. As such the figures tend to over-represent young women who are traditionally less involved in self-employment than young men (Hakim 1988, 1989a). Our informants were from a variety of socio-economic and educational backgrounds, although the majority left school at the age of sixteen and had parents who were, or had been, employed in working-class jobs.[4]

The interviews were guided by a flexible schedule based round the main questions we wished to ask (which was piloted with young people and enterprise specialists who were not part of the main sample). Each interview began with a brief explanation of our project, its origins, funding body and objectives. All our informants were then promised confidentiality, although some asked for their real names to be used in any subsequent publication and no-one asked to be anonymous. We have, however, changed the names of all our informants and of the main organizations we worked with to ensure that no harm should come to anyone as a result of their involvement in our research. This is standard practice in ethnography and, to make identification doubly difficult, we have sometimes altered the type and location of the work undertaken by our informants, always being careful that the substitution was from the same range of occupations to prevent any qualitative change which could mislead readers. So, for example, a hairdresser from Middlesbrough became a beauty therapist from Hartlepool (or vice-versa), and a photographer from Stockton became a picture-framer from Billingham (or vice-versa). Interviews took place in their homes or business premises, in pubs or in enterprise agencies; they usually lasted for about an hour and a half, were tape-recorded and were subsequently analysed within the tradition of ethnography and grounded theory (Glaser and Strauss, 1967).[5]

We should reiterate that our project was purposively based on a small-scale, qualitative study of one aspect of youth and their transitions (i.e. through enterprise). It is the job of the *16 to 19 Initiative* as a whole to describe the career trajectories and experiences of the whole range of young people (in school, YTS, jobs, unemployment) and we recommend John Bynner's (1991) overview for those interested in comparing our group with young people in general. And although it is not usual for more qualitative studies to be too concerned about representativeness, we are aware that policy makers and practitioners are often unacquainted with the relative merits of competing research methods and tend to favour 'number crunching' studies. We feel that they have a right to ask about the data from which we draw our conclusions and we are aware that overall the strategies we developed to contact informants were open to the risk of generating a skewed sample (for instance, towards those types of entrepreneur more likely to use advice agencies). We accept that we have perhaps not completely overcome the problems of researching youth enterprise but, on the other hand, we feel that our sample has a number of strengths.

The first of which is that, in the opinion of local experts who advised young adults on starting up in business and who made strenuous efforts to enable us to reach different types of informants, the final composition of the group interviewed fairly represents the population of 'young entrepreneurs' in Cleveland. Second, the total numbers of those under twenty-five who were in receipt of EAS in Cleveland were quite small (278 in 1989). We managed to interview seventy-four people who had been running small firms or co-ops, plus twelve people who were seriously intending to set up in business (a large sample for a qualitative study *and* compared with the total population of 278 starting up in a given year) and, thus, we feel that it is likely that they reported fairly representative experiences of enterprise. On a related point, in some categories (for instance, those who set up in co-operatives), we achieved what we believe to be virtually total coverage (i.e. nearly all under-25s in Cleveland co-ops were interviewed). Third, the informants themselves tended to know the names of other young people who had taken the plunge and become self-employed and they were satisfied that we had covered the field adequately. Finally, if the sample still remains skewed, can we estimate the direction of any bias? We have probably included more of those likely to be highly committed, to make a go of their enterprise and succeed, given that we contacted so many who had used professional agencies to start up. That possible over-emphasis should be borne in mind when reading our assessment of the numbers of failures and successes in the enterprise culture.

We are in essence presenting a cross-sectional snapshot of young entrepreneurs as interviewed in Cleveland in 1989. To some degree we fail to capitalize on one of the normal advantages of ethnography, namely, the study of processes *over time*. Our study can certainly not be described as longitudinal, but its design allowed us to examine the *processes* of enterprise by interviewing informants who were at different stages of setting up or managing a business. We met some people who were planning the launch of their enterprise, while others had been self-employed for various lengths of time (from a few weeks to several years), as well as others who had gone 'bust' and so were able to reflect on their experiences. Having said this, it would, of course, have been preferable to have developed a larger sample, to have revisited all informants for follow-up discussions (only a handful were met more than once), to have developed other forms of qualitative research (especially participant observation and group discussions) and to have taken back our findings and interpretations for their consideration and comment. These are some of the limitations of the project and we must live with them.

Towards an Enterprise Culture?

The first meeting which either of us attended to discuss the setting up of the ESRC's *16 to 19 Initiative* took place near Oxford in May 1986. Since then, the significance of enterprise in British society, has, if anything, intensified. Expertise which has developed in this country in enterprise training and in setting up small firms is now being exported to Eastern Europe (*The Guardian*, 17 September 1990), and Lord Young has become an adviser on enterprise to the Hungarian Government. The prospects for young people have also become more varied and complex. The themes underpinning this book are large, topical, and pressing; they bring together theories from sociology, psychology, geography, economics and politics. And it is the answers to the political and policy questions we ask which will gradually influence the future of regions like Teesside and the position of young working-class women and men throughout the country. As John Maynard Keynes put it in a famous passage over fifty years ago:

> Practical men, who believe themselves to be quite exempt from any intellectual influences, are usually the slaves of some defunct economist. Madmen in authority, who hear voices in the air, are distilling their frenzy from some academic scribbler of a few years back. (1936:383)

The 1980s in Britain witnessed a re-awakening of fashionable but uncritical interest in some of the better known ideas of Adam Smith, whose work has been misinterpreted as unqualified support for the invisible forces of the market, for self-interest and a free enterprise economy more generally. Smith, however, expressed a deep concern for 'the education of the common people . . . in a civilized and commercial society' and concluded that: 'The expense of the institutions for education and religious instruction is . . . beneficial to the whole society, and may, therefore, without injustice, be defrayed by the general contribution of the whole society' (Smith, 1958:298).[6] His name has nevertheless been pressed into political service to lend credibility to the moral crusade to engender an enterprise culture in this country.

Our overriding aim has been to use qualitative research to test the theoretical adequacy and the practical effectiveness of current ideas in two key areas of policy: enterprise and youth. More specifically, we follow Janet Finch (1988) in claiming that ethnography has a distinctive contribution to make to the formulation of policy and theory by studying how much and what types of change have actually been achieved by the policy, in this instance, of transforming the 'dependency culture' into an enterprise culture; by identifying the unintended consequences of that policy and bringing to public attention the contradictions, tensions and incompatible aims which we have observed when the policy was implemented in a particular locality; and in using our data to question conventional wisdoms about, say, the political apathy of young adults and to move beyond them to construct more adequate and more tenable theories.

The Structure of the Book

The questions we ask and the answers we provide are presented in the book as follows. The results of our first method of enquiry into the concept and practice of enterprise are contained in Chapter 2. This chapter looks back at the riotous spread of enterprise initiatives in the 1980s and forward to the establishment and performance of the Training and Enterprise Councils (TECs) during the 1990s. The eighty-two TECs which are planned for England and Wales are presented as particularly important examples of the philosophy of enterprise as it is translated into local practice.

In Chapter 3 we look back further to the nineteenth century, in order to trace the exponential growth of Middlesbrough and the towns of Teesside through to the devastating recessions of the 1970s and early 1980s. Within the space of twenty years the boom town of the 1960s became slump city. We attempt to explain such a sudden reversal of fortunes and highlight the implications of such a depressed local labour market for young people leaving school and looking for work. The chapter ends with a critical assessment of the apparent economic recovery of the North-East during the late 1980s and 1990.

Chapter 4 is devoted to what we call the Cleveland Enterprise Industry, that collection of agencies, schemes and professionals whose task it is to rejuvenate the local economy through enterprise. By 1990, the Teesside TEC reckoned that there were 'over one hundred different agencies and organizations working with the unemployed or working to develop enterprise' (*TEC Director*, 1990:30) and that such proliferation had become 'counter-productive'. Against the back-drop of a severely depressed local labour market, we study the mushrooming and sudden contraction of the enterprise industry, identify competing models of enterprise, and examine how the national move towards an enterprise culture has fared locally in Cleveland.

In Chapter 5 we present the first part of our ethnographic investigation. The movement of young people into self-employment is a key aspect of the movement towards an enterprise culture, or so the official rhetoric goes. Here we explore, first, the motivations underlying the decisions of our informants to become 'their own boss'. We pay particular attention to the *push* of unemployment and the *pull* of entrepreneurship in the accounts collected. Second, we investigate the steps taken by young adults on the road to the enterprise culture and the problems they reported in starting up new, small businesses.

Chapter 6 explores the experiences of young men and women once businesses have been set up. We investigate the successes and failures of people running risky businesses on Teesside and the chapter ends by presenting a three-part typology of the experience of 'runners', 'fallers' and 'plodders'.[7] These themes are fleshed out in Chapter 7 where two case studies of each of these three types of experience are described in detail.

In Chapter 8 we focus on alternative forms of enterprise in co-operatives and community enterprise projects. We explore how the broader philosophy and more egalitarian politics of enterprise, for instance as manifest in the co-operative movement, are translated into the day-to-day practice of running co-ops which share all the problems described by those in more conventional small firms.

In Chapter 9 we turn our attention to the political and economic views of our informants and present a rather different argument from the standard, if not hackneyed, conclusion in the literature that young people are bored by, and alienated from, politics.

Finally, in Chapter 10 we summarize our main findings and examine how our work relates to small business research and the sociology of youth transitions. We then take the unusual step for social scientists of trying to predict the outcome of government initiatives in the areas of the education, training and employment of young adults. For reasons we explain in detail, we expect these policies to run into problems within the next few years. Having been critical, we then do not shirk the task of suggesting some alternatives which we think would stand a better chance of success.

The following chapters, therefore, move backwards and forwards from *macro* issues (for example, the attempt to revive the British economy through enterprise) to *micro* themes (like the explanations of a group of young people in Cleveland for their decision to become self-employed). Our book is a contribution to the development of ideas and to the contemporary debate at both levels, in the hope of improving the lot of all those (in Cleveland and throughout the United Kingdom), who look to the enterprise culture and who 'become their own boss' as a way of surviving in a harsh economic climate.

Notes

1 The statement was used on an overhead projector in a lecture given by Durham University Business School (DUBS) in 1989 to introduce the latest publication of DUBS on *Primary Enterprise* (1989).
2 Further information about these projects can be obtained from John Bynner, Coordinator of the Initiative, or from the research centres directly: rural labour markets (Claire Wallace, Polytechnic of the South-West); young people with special needs (Sally Tomlinson, Lancaster University); family socialization (Pat Allatt, Teesside Polytechnic); ethnic minority youth (Ken Roberts, University of Liverpool); adolescent identity (Peter Weinreich, University of Ulster), teenage housing careers (Pat Ainley, City University); the use of video methods (Glynis Breakwell, University of Surrey).

3   We use the phrase 'young entrepreneurs' as a convenient shorthand; it is not one of the phrases used by our informants and it is rather inaccurate, but useful. Similarly, as we will show in Chapter 2, the meaning of 'enterprise', 'enterprise culture' and 'dependence' are hotly debated. We are aware that there are many problems associated with all these terms and we use them without inverted commas but still critically.

4   We have tried to resist the temptation simply to categorize our informants as working class. We are sure the majority of them were, but we are equally sure that some were not. The problem of classifying youth in such terms has been very much overlooked and is discussed by one of the authors elsewhere (MacDonald 1988a, 1989). We do not want to fall into the trap of claiming that young people are 'classless' or that class is not a very significant element in their identities or the processes we describe, but simply find it difficult, for example, to unproblematically 'read off' their class from that of their parents (i.e. usually the occupation of the father). Class cultural differences were apparent in the sample. We doubt that these can be traced directly back to the job in which the father is employed.

5   The markings we use in the extracts from interviews deserve a brief explanation. When we have edited out a few words or sentences, the symbol . . . // . . . appears; square brackets [ ] contain information added by us; and . . . means a pause. *RM* refers to Robert MacDonald, who carried out all the interviews with young people, apart from those with the sub-group of unemployed people who were interviewed by Reiner Siebert (see Preface).

6   We are grateful to Malcolm McKenzie (1989) for bringing this quotation to our attention.

7   The terms 'plodding along' and 'plodders' are used here and later in the book to describe a type of *experience* of youth enterprise. These expressions should not be read as implying a deficit view of a particular type of *person*, nor as a condescending representation of young people or their comments. We could not think of a better way of expressing this type of experience and, as this image and vocabulary was drawn upon by informants to describe themselves and their experience (see Chapter 6), we have decided to retain it.

Chapter 2

The Hunt for the Heffalump Resumed: the Rise of the Enterprise Movement

> The search for the source of dynamic entrepreneurial performance
> has much in common with hunting the Heffalump. The Heffa-
> lump is a large and rather important animal. He has been hunted
> by many individuals using various ingenious trapping devices,
> but no one so far has succeeded in capturing him. All who claim
> to have caught sight of him report that he is enormous, but they
> disagree on his particularities. Not having explored his current
> habitat with sufficient care, some hunters have used as bait their
> own favourite dishes and have then tried to persuade people that
> what they caught was a Heffalump. However, very few are con-
> vinced, and the search goes on. (Kilby, 1971:1)

To study the world of enterprise is to re-enter the world of A.A. Milne,
Winnie the Pooh and Piglet, and in this chapter we resume Kilby's search
for the fabulous chimera, the Heffalump, but have to report that we had
no more success than Christopher Robin or Eeyore. We examine the
ideological project of the Conservative Government to transform Britain's economy and education by means of enterprise. The main initiatives designed to promote such a culture are described and the concept,
practice and philosophy of enterprise are explored. The chapter ends by
discussing, in detail, a particularly important example of the Government's national strategy on enterprise, namely, the establishment of the
new TECs, which mark, according to the Training Agency, 'the start of
a major revolution in the way vocational education and training is managed in this country' (*Insight*, 1990:14).

A few years ago the word 'enterprise' was fashionable: it has now
become pervasive and is in danger of becoming compulsory or at least
very difficult to avoid. When social historians come to assess Britain in
the 1980s, they are likely to emphasize this key word. It has come to
stand for a collection of political, economic and social values and,
perhaps, more than any other term it summarizes the *zeitgeist* created by

the Conservative Government during the last decade. James Hamilton Dunn, in a prophetic article written in 1977, argued that a change in the direction of British politics was seen by the New Right to require:

> the creation (or rediscovery) of what the New Right call a 'myth' or 'spirit'. In order for these myths to be accepted, politicians must appeal to the imagination of the British people . . . This new spirit can be called the spirit of enterprise. It should create greater economic freedom but it requires faith to maintain it . . . As with religious faith, the faith in the spirit of enterprise takes the shape of a way of life, which becomes the driving force of the community. (1977:226)[1]

In the words of one of the leading exponents of enterprise, Allan Gibb: 'The entrepreneur in the UK has become the god (or goddess) of current UK political ideology and a leading actor in the theatre of the "new economics"' (1987:3). The 1980s witnessed a burst of schemes, courses, agencies and publications, all specializing in the promotion of the enterprise culture. In 1989 at the national launch of the TECs, Norman Fowler, then Secretary of State for Employment, described them as a 'genuine revolution in the way Britain develops its people and stimulates business growth' (*Employment Gazette*, April 1989:155). The Training Agency (TA, 1989a:2) believes that enterprise will play an important role in 'the restructuring of the British economy, the starting of small businesses, the revival of the inner cities and the expansion of European markets in 1992'.

It is, however, Lord Young (formerly Chairman of the Manpower Services Commission and Secretary of State for Employment from September, 1985 to July, 1987) who is most identified with the policy of promoting an enterprise culture. His explanation for the decline of British industry neatly encapsulates the ruling ideology of the Conservative Government of the 1980s:

> The problems of our economy have largely stemmed from a lack of enterprise. But don't pick on the managers in British industry today. At least, they made the choice to go into industry and commerce, they took on the challenge of producing goods and services and they are fighting to create wealth and jobs. The real culprits are bedded deep in our national history and culture. (1986:25)

Of the four culprits who are mentioned by name, the first is the education system 'which had little contact and no regard for industry — which looked down on scientific and technical subjects and which disdained vocational preparation'. The other three culprits listed by Lord Young are 'a financial system ... with little concern for small businesses', a protectionist industrial system and a confrontational system of industrial relations.

The first section of this chapter critically examines the House that Lord Young has Built, and explores what is euphemistically described as 'the philosophy of enterprise', the growth of the enterprise movement and issues surrounding its meaning and role in educational and social policy.

The Rise of the Enterprise Movement

A broad enterprise movement is now in full swing and includes the following initiatives, most of which arrive with a virtually compulsory acronym attached to their official title (more detail is provided on those projects thought to be less familiar or more recent).

Technical and Vocational Education Initiative (TVEI) is now regularly included in the list of enterprise initiatives issued by the Training Agency (e.g. TA, 1989a:2). It was announced in Parliament by the Prime Minister in November 1982, and is administered by the Training Agency (formerly the Manpower Services Commission or MSC) rather than by the DES, with the objective of enriching the curriculum to help 14 to 18 year olds prepare for the world of work. The national extension of TVEI is estimated to cost about £90 million per year over the ten years of its development from the Autumn term 1987 onwards (Department of Employment *et al.*, 1986:10).

The Mini Enterprise in Schools Project (MESP) began as a national scheme in England and Wales in 1985 for 'children from any age, from primary to sixth form' to run 'a small business, making or selling products or services' (MESP, 1988). It was launched by the Industry/Education Unit of the Department of Trade and Industry under Lord Young, has been supported by the Society of Education Officers and has been backed financially by the National Westminster Bank which provides a £40 grant to every participating school and a business account combining a low interest loan of up to £50, if required. It remains to be seen whether the project develops the enterprise culture within pupils or whether 'their experience of business in school may stimulate in them a critical penetration of the exploitative relations involved in capitalist production' (Shilling, 1989:122), or indeed whether students learn, for instance, to form price-fixing cartels. Questions also need to be asked about the quality of the products offered for sale by these mini-companies. Do any of them become in any way commercially viable and, if so, what happens if they begin to pose a serious challenge to existing local firms?

Enterprise in YTS was launched by Lord Young and Geoffrey Holland (then Director of MSC) in 1986 with the aim of developing an enterprise culture among young people. The MSC responded to this initiative by setting up a series of projects to develop different approaches to the training of enterprise and their stated objective was as follows: 'By 1990 Enterprise training will be sufficiently developed to be available to all trainees in all Youth Training Schemes (YTS) as an integral part of their training' (MSC leaflet, *Enterprise in YTS*, 1987). In the same way as MESP has grown to include the promotion of mini-companies in other vocational schemes such as the Certificate for Prevocational Education (CPVE) and TVEI (see Shilling, 1989), so enterprise training is conceived by the MSC as relevant not only to YTS trainees but to a wide range of unemployed people on the New Job Training Scheme, the Community Programme and their successor, Employment Training.

Training for Enterprise Programme (TFE) aims to 'equip potential and existing entrepreneurs with the skills and knowledge successfully to launch, manage and develop a small business' (NAO, 1988:16). The number of trainees has grown very rapidly from 32 in 1977–78 to over 115,000 in 1987–88 at a cost of over £64 million. The main programmes on offer under TFE are:

1   Business Enterprise Programme (BEP): up to seven days of basic training covering the skills needed to set up and run a small business.
2   Private Enterprise Programme (PEP): a series of thirteen one-day training modules for existing businesses, for which there were 60,000 places in 1987–88.
3   Management Extension Programme (MEP): offers unemployed managers three weeks of training in small business management, followed by a secondment to a firm for up to twenty-three weeks.
4   Graduate Gateway Programme (GGP): designed to encourage graduates to consider a career in business.

In addition, there are Enterprise Introduction Days and Enterprise Rehearsal, which allow participants to try out a business idea in a commercial setting, from which they can then be transferred to the Enterprise Allowance Scheme.

Enterprise Allowance Scheme (EAS) was introduced in 1983 with 25,000 places, after pilot schemes had been tried in five areas. It expanded rapidly with 80,000 places available in 1986 and 110,000 places for 1988/89. By 1988 over 329,000 people out of work for at least eight weeks (originally thirteen weeks) had taken up the offer of £40 per week for a year at a cost to the government of £545 million (NAO, 1988:7).

EAS is defined, in a Guide issued by the Employment Service, as 'a way of helping unemployed people who want to work for themselves' and potential applicants are told that it will pay £40 a week 'on top of what you earn in the business, for up to fifty-two weeks' (EAS Guide:1). Because EAS constitutes the major vehicle for promoting enterprise through self-employment and because EAS figures so largely in the career histories of the young people whose business ventures are described in Chapters 5, 6 and 7, we thought it would be useful to explain the conditions for eligibility in some detail.

There are six conditions, all of which have to be met to claim the allowance, and the essential points are reproduced from the Guide:

1 You must be receiving unemployment benefit or income support . . .
2 You must have been unemployed for at least eight weeks . . . (Time spent on a wide range of Training Agency courses — Job Training Scheme, Community Programme, Community Industry Scheme, Employment Rehabilitation courses, Sheltered Employment, Voluntary Projects Programme, Youth Training Scheme — or being under formal notice of redundancy, may also count towards the eight week period).
3 You must be able to show you have at least £1,000 available to invest in your business in the first twelve months. This can be a loan or overdraft.
4 You must be at least 18 and under 65 years of age.
5 You must agree to work full-time in the business (at least thirty-six hours each week).
6 Your business must be approved by the Department of Employment.

Applicants are not asked to prove that their business is commercially viable (less than 4 per cent of applications are rejected, according to Finn, 1986) but it must still satisfy three further conditions to be acceptable. The business must be new, be based in Great Britain and be suitable for public support. The third condition was introduced after two young women opened a 'massage parlour' in South Wales on the EAS and their allowance was stopped for bringing the Training Agency into public disrepute.

Those who think they meet all the conditions are invited to an EAS Awareness Day where 'experienced business people will tell you what you need to think about when you start your own business' (EAS Guide:7). Those who join EAS become entitled to three free counselling sessions and are reminded that the Training Agency 'will keep in touch with you to see how you are getting on and suggest where to go for help and advice if you have any problems or difficult decisions to make' (EAS Guide:8).

In Chapter 5 young women and men in business in Cleveland report on their experiences and their views of the EAS are incorporated into an evaluation of youth enterprise in general, an assessment which also draws on studies completed by the National Audit Office (1988).

Enterprise and Education. The Department of Trade and Industry, now subtitled the Department for Enterprise, issued a White Paper in January 1988 which argued that employers have much to contribute to the development of the curriculum, the management of schools and colleges, and the promotion of enterprise activities in these institutions. The Government then set itself three objectives: to involve 10 per cent of teachers in industrial placements every year; to provide all secondary pupils with two or more weeks of work experience; and to impress on every trainee teacher 'an appreciation of the needs of employers and of the importance of links between schools and employers' (DTI, 1988, para. 4.5). These objectives could easily serve as performance indicators of the Government's willingness to fund such activities because LEAs, schools and employers have since appeared loath to move beyond the resourcing of pilot projects, pointing to the competing demands on them from the National Curriculum and Local Management of Schools.

Enterprise in Higher Education (EHE) is an initiative of the Training Agency which was introduced in December 1987 'to assist institutions of higher education to develop enterprising graduates in partnership with employers' (TA, 1989a:2). Over one hundred institutions submitted proposals for funding of up to £1 million over five years and eleven institutions (four universities and seven polytechnics) were then invited to participate in round one of the initiative; and there has since been a second round of grants awarded involving a further fifteen institutions. The main objective is that 'every person seeking a higher education qualification should be able to develop competencies and aptitudes relevant to enterprise' (TA, 1989a:5); and staff in higher education are to be involved in training programmes so that not only the curriculum is changed but also the processes of learning and teaching. The significance of EHE is that the Training Agency has been able to buy its way into the curriculum and pedagogy of higher education by using the same technique that the MSC employed with TVEI, namely, dangling large sums of money in front of institutions which had been starved of resources. As Ian Jamieson writes, universities and polytechnics have been falling over each other to ensnare themselves upon the golden hook (1989:73). It remains to be seen whether the participating institutions seize the opportunity to develop creative local programmes and abandon the deadening jargon of the

Training Agency. It may transpire that the institutions simply use the money provided by the Training Agency for developments which were already planned but shelved for lack of funds.

Enterprise Awareness in Teacher Education (EATE). This project was launched by the Department of Trade and Industry in September 1989 with the aim of acting as a catalyst to promote staff and course development focusing on enterprise, and economic and industrial awareness within institutions of initial teacher education. EATE has been funded by the DTI initially for two years with the possibility of an extension for a third year.

Evangelical Enterprise works in partnership with the DTI's Inner Cities Task Force and the Evangelical Alliance, a grouping of black churches, to provide enterprise projects to help unemployed people. In the words of Michael Hastings, Director of Evangelical Enterprise: 'Our ongoing vision is for a new and determined Christian activism that will bring healing to Inner City areas by grasping creative opportunities to help people into real work and by supporting constructive enterprise'. (quoted by J. Roberts, 1988:371).

Local Enterprise Agencies, over 400 in number, which began as a response to high unemployment, 'are non-profitmaking companies. Typically they represent a public/private partnership, are private sector led (with) the job of providing a free, confidential business advice service for unemployed people wishing to explore the self-employment option' (Grayson, 1989:534–5).

The Training and Enterprise Councils (TECs) were launched in March 1989 by the Prime Minister and the then Secretary of State for Employment, Norman Fowler. Eventually there will be 100 TECs throughout Britain, responsible for a budget of almost £3 billion annually, although the budget for each TEC is more likely to be in the range of £20 to £50 million per year. Local TECs will set up as independent companies, entering into a commercial contract with the Secretary of State for Employment to develop training and enterprise in their area. Handing over the main responsibility for training all our young people, the unemployed and all adults requiring retraining to local employers may be, as the *Unemployment Bulletin* (1989:1) argues, a smokescreen to disguise central government's retreat from funding industrial training, but the advisability of such a move needs to be examined in detail and it is discussed in the final section of this chapter.

Scottish Enterprise (SE), and Highlands and Islands Enterprise (HIE). The Training Agency in Scotland is to be replaced by these two bodies, with SE being formed from an amalgamation with the Scottish Development Agency, with an annual budget of £500 million and a staff of 1,500. According to David Raffe (1989:9):

> the most obvious difference between these proposals and the parallel creation of TECs in England is that the new Scottish bodies will have broader responsibilities . . . The word 'training' is absent from the title of the proposed local enterprise companies: they will be LECs not TECs.

The above list is by no means complete: in addition, there are programmes sponsored by the Training Agency (e.g. New Enterprise Programme, Graduate Enterprise Programme); by the Department of Trade and Industry (e.g. The Enterprise Initiative with 500 Enterprise Counsellors); by the Department of Employment (twenty-four Enterprise Zones, Enterprise Centres, Freephone Enterprise and the Regional Enterprise Unit); and by independent, national or local organizations (e.g. Young Enterprise, the Industrial Society's Enterprise Unit, the Community Enterprise Trust, British Coal Enterprise Limited and so on).

The first conclusion to be drawn from this massive investment of resources is that enterprise is not just the latest fashion or bandwagon in Conservative thinking; rather a brave new world of enterprise has been brought into being and its influence is spreading in so many directions simultaneously that few people are likely to escape whether they are children in primary school, students in university, unemployed miners or redundant executives. The intention is nothing less than to change the culture in education, training and employment from what is termed dependence to enterprise. It remains to be seen, however, whether sufficient resources have been allocated to the 'E' element of the TECs for such a profound change to be made.

As significant as the number of initiatives has been their style: under the leadership of Lord Young, programmes have been launched with all the razzmatazz normally associated with show business; an example is 'The Enterprise Express', a seven-carriage, special exhibition train which left Euston Station with a fanfare of trumpets from the band of the Royal Marines to 'spread the message of enterprise throughout the nation' (*In Business Now*, 1986:22). The BBC Radio Four programme on Enterprise also arranged for the Express to make an unscheduled stop at Borchester, the fictional market town featured in 'The Archers'.

The Concept of Enterprise

The plethora of organizations and initiatives has created, in turn, an over-abundance of competing definitions and contrasting lists of different

Figure 2.1   *Entrepreneurial Attributes*

— Initiative
— Strong persuasive powers
— Moderate rather than high risk-taking ability
— Flexibility
— Creativity
— Independence/autonomy
— Problem-solving ability
— Need for achievement
— Imagination
— High belief in control of one's own destiny
— Leadership
— Hard work

Source: Gibb (1987:6)

enterprise skills or attributes. The debates earlier this century about the nature of intelligence, where each psychologist put forward his or her own definition, are now being repeated over the word enterprise.

One of the main producers of enterprise materials has been Durham University's Business School (DUBS) which has published *Key Skills* in enterprise for 14 to 16 year olds (Johnson *et al.*, 1987a), *Key Skills* for 16 to 19 year olds (Johnson *et al.*, 1987b) and even *Primary Enterprise* (DUBS, 1989). These teaching materials, which had been bought by 'over 75 per cent of secondary schools in Britain' by 1989 (Johnson, personal communication), find their academic justification in Allan Gibb's monograph, *Enterprise Culture — Its Meaning and Implications for Education and Training* (1987). He claims that there are at least twelve entrepreneurial attributes (see Figure 2.1) but no argument is advanced to explain why these particular twelve have been chosen.

Gibb does concede that not all of the twelve 'are measurable at present, and many are controversial, in that the evidence associating them with particular forms of behaviour is as yet weak' (1987:7). Such a reasonable and qualified assertion is, however, omitted from the introductions to the resource packs on enterprise skills for schools and colleges produced under Professor Gibb's leadership. There it is claimed 'These attributes — the essence of enterprise — have been extensively researched over the years in many countries with consensus in their findings' (Johnson *et al.*, 1987:x). Although a table is produced by Johnson *et al.* to show 'how the research findings on enterprise attributes guide the educational aims' (1987:xi), there are no references to the literature which would enable such claims to be checked.

Gibb, on the other hand, does refer to American psychologists such as McClelland and Rotter to provide a theoretical justification for including, for example, in his list of attributes 'need for Achievement' and 'high belief in control of one's own destiny'. But what is missing is any evidence that links internal locus of control and all the other attributes into a unitary concept called enterprise. Readers also need to be directed to the literature (e.g. Kilby, 1971:19) which has examined the claims made by psychologists like McClelland and judged that they failed to achieve an acceptable level of empirical verification.

A reading of the original source material is even more revealing and there is space to deal with only one of the attributes of enterprise. McClelland, for example, studied the relationship between economic development and 'the need for achievement' which he defined as 'a desire to do well, not so much for the sake of social recognition or prestige, but for the sake of an inner feeling of personal achievement' (McClelland, 1971:110–12). He took as his measure of 'the need for achievement' the number of references to 'doing a good job' in children's readers from twenty-three countries around 1925 and from thirty-nine countries around 1950; and 'for a measure of economic development we relied on the amount of electricity produced in each country'. The two measures are then claimed to be statistically correlated at a highly significant level in Western, Communist and underdeveloped countries and McClelland concludes 'it is startling to find concrete evidence for psychological determination, for psychological developments which precede and presumably cause economic changes'. No argument is offered in support of the almost imperceptible slide from correlation to presumed causation. Moreover, Abercrombie *et al.* (1986:183) claim that arguments about motivation explain only part of the relationship between individualism and capitalism:

> they provide neither the necessary nor a sufficient condition for that explanation. There are other ways in which individualism and capitalism relate to one another that are not dependent on motivation. For example, there is the familiar argument of Weber and Marx that a capitalist economy will constrain individuals to behave appropriately, regardless of their beliefs and motives, if they are to survive economically.[2]

But perhaps the most serious omission from the publications on enterprise which we have examined is the failure to provide alternative views of enterprise and to admit what a hotly contested and inadequate concept enterprise has always been. Kilby (1971:6), for example, explores seven competing theories of enterprise in his book, four psychological theories (Schumpeter, McClelland, Hagen and Kunkel) and three sociological theories (Weber, Cochran and Young) and finds them all wanting. Gibb also leaves aside the 'degree to which they [the attributes] are innate or not' — but in what way could, for example, 'moderate, risk-taking ability' or any of the other culturally-laden attributes be considered 'innate'?

Instead of the consensus claimed by Johnson *et al.* (1987a), an immediate problem in identifying the core skills of enterprise is that every

27

Figure 2.2   The Core Skills

— assess one's strengths and weaknesses
— seek information and advice
— make decisions
— plan one's time and energy
— carry through an agreed responsibility
— negotiate
— deal with people in power and authority
— problem-solve
— resolve conflict
— cope with stress and tension
— evaluate one's performance
— communicate

Source: Turner (1988:15)

organization has its own list. Community Enterprise in the Curriculum (Turner, 1988) also has exactly twelve core skills but, as can be seen from Figure 2.2., only two are even loosely the same as those in Gibb's list. So the number of 'core' enterprise skills has jumped from twelve to twenty-two. The City and Guilds of London Institute (1988) talks of six main enterprise skill areas, three of which correspond with Gibb's list. Pitman's course on enterprise skills (1987) has five transferable skills, none of which are in Figure 2.1.

The Scottish Vocational Education Council's module on Enterprise Activity seeks to develop four skills, one of which 'task management skills' could generously be said to be close to 'problem-solving ability', as Gibb has it. Finally, the Royal Society of Arts (1987) has produced a profile of thirty-one sentences 'defining the skills and competencies involved in enterprise'. These range from such sophisticated skills as Number 9 'the ability to resolve conflict' and Number 15 'the ability to solve problems', on the one hand, to such routine tasks as Number 18 'open, conduct and close brief transaction by telephone' and Number 23 'use alphabetical order and index systems to locate information in dictionaries and reference books', on the other. What kind of concept is it that has, at a conservative estimate, more than fifty 'core' skills? How many peripheral skills are there likely to be? There is a close parallel here with the 'core skills' of the Youth Training Scheme. Ruth Jonathan quotes examples of these skills such as 'filling a supermarket shelf', 'sorting incoming mail' and 'counting items singly or in batches' and then adds: 'This is not "learning through doing"; it is simply "doing" and not doing anything very stimulating at that' (1987:112).

All the lists and courses mentioned in the previous paragraph are making a series of assumptions about the nature and function of knowledge which have been challenged by Ruth Jonathan (1983) and Keith Thompson (1984). Jonathan (1983:8), for instance, attacks what she describes as 'The Manpower Service model of education' for arguing that 'the process of learning matters more than the content learnt', as if 'insight that the learning process is itself important is replaced by the false claim that it is all important'. Second, 'it is quite overlooked that the very success of, say, science depends upon steeping practitioners in the content of disciplines before they are able to strike out on their own and add to that content'. Thirdly, generic, identifiable and transferable skills cannot be epistemologically divorced from content: 'What sort of questions are intelligent and what answers are sensible depends upon context'.

To sum up at this point: first, we are not dealing with a tightly defined, agreed and unitary concept but with a farrago of 'hurrah' words like 'creativity', 'initiative' and 'leadership'. Too many of the definitions tend to be circular or consist of managerial tautologies, tricked out with the rhetoric of progressive education. Part of the confusion stems from the fact that the word 'enterprise' is used in different ways, sometimes referring to an individual ability considered amenable to improvement and at other times to a form of economic activity, usually in small businesses. For example, because one can be enterprising both by making a million before one's fortieth birthday and by shepherding passengers out of a burning aeroplane does not mean that there is a generic skill of enterprise whose essence can be distilled and taught.

Second, some notions which are central to most definitions of enterprise, problem-solving for instance, have been taken from psychology and then simplified, decontextualized and invested with a significance and power which few psychologists would be prepared to support. Problem-solving is treated within the enterprise literature as if it were the highest form of thinking or as if it were to be equated with thinking itself. The more fundamental issues of finding and accurately formulating problems, or learning to live with problems which are not amenable to easy (or any) solution are nowhere discussed. Instead of an approach which seems to suggest that the student of enterprise need only apply a set of techniques (the core skills) to be guaranteed success, a more powerful and educative model of thinking could have been presented by emphasizing the critical role of argument, controversy and debate in developing the mind (see Billig, 1989:304): thinking is better viewed 'as a social, argumentative process, rather than a monologic, individual one'.

Third, as Keith Thompson (1984:204) has argued about the Education for Capability movement, the potential terms of reference of words like 'capability' or 'skills' (or 'enterprise') are so wide that to call someone 'capable' or 'skilful' (or 'enterprising') without specific context is meaningless. And yet Gibb (1987:11) redefines 'enterprise' as 'the exercise of enterprising attributes in *any* task or environmental context' (emphasis added).

Fourth, the enthusiasm for enterprise seems to be based on the mistaken notions that there is no distinction between the words 'education' and 'training' (see Dearden, 1984), or between 'vocational education' and 'vocational training' (Pring, 1987); that *how* you learn is more important than *what* you learn; and that a general, liberal education somehow excludes the practical application of knowledge. Perhaps we will need to collapse the polarities in the centuries old debate between the liberal and the vocational in favour of a liberal vocationalism (see Silver and Brennan, 1988).

Fifth, enterprise within the education for enterprise literature tends to be viewed (e.g. by Gibb, 1987) as an individual attribute and both structural factors and local economic conditions are ignored. As the National Audit Office argued in reference to new products and services offered by the Enterprise Allowance Scheme, 'success depends upon the adequacy of local demand' (1988:8).

Sixth, where is the independent and convincing evidence of the success of enterprise education or enterprise initiatives? When accountability and value for money have become such standard management tools, why have so many enterprise initiatives been 'doomed to success' from day one? The national extension of TVEI, for example, was announced in the White Paper of July 1986 (Department of Employment *et al.*, 1986:9) but the fourteen pilot projects were launched in September 1983 for four years so no summative evaluation could have been available to influence the decision to create a national scheme.

The problems with the enterprise movement do not end with the terminological mare's nest described above. Attention also needs to be paid to the key role in enterprise education which is given to skills. Maurice Holt in 1987 edited a collection of essays which exposed the fallacy of generic, transferable skills and challenged the superficial and reductionist use of the term 'skills' to analyse professional activities such as teaching (e.g. Smith, 1987). But even those contributors who had already become anxious at the current obsession with skills failed to predict how inflated the claims were to become. Witness the stance taken by Johnson *et al.* (1987:xi): 'The components of Enterprise are a mixture of attitudes, skills and motivations (in this book we describe all three as "skills")'. Complexity is dispensed with, words become interchangeable and the concept of 'skills' becomes impossibly inflated. To paraphrase Wittgenstein's famous criticism of psychology (1978:232e), in enterprise education there are experiential learning activities and conceptual confusion.

The definitional and epistemological problems surrounding the concept of enterprise tend to be dismissed by those working within the burgeoning enterprise industry who act, speak and write as if they were all using the same concept. Such intellectual confusion has not prevented the expenditure of much commendable effort and commitment in the interests of young or unemployed people but the problems of definition and the mistaken assumptions about the nature of knowledge will not simply go away. It is perfectly possible that a number of challenging and satisfying jobs have been created by means of, for instance, the Enterprise Allowance Scheme despite the linguistic and epistemological muddle, but the quantity, the quality and the durability of these jobs can only be assessed through the type of empirical research we present in Chapters 5 and 6 of this text. Nor is it any part of our argument to defend pedagogical practices in schools or in universities which may be in need of change. What is contested is the implicit assumption in say, the Enterprise in Higher Education initiative, that combining academic excellence and practical application is a new departure for engineering, law, medicine, education, or the creative arts. Just as there is nothing as practical as a good theory, there is also nothing as impractical as misunderstood or misapplied theory (see Fullan, 1982).

There have been a number of attempts (e.g. Law, 1983; Rees, 1986) to impose some order on the different shades of enterprise projects which are currently being implemented in Britain, but it would be more appropriate to discuss such typologies in Chapter 4 where we chart the growth of the enterprise industry in Cleveland. Instead, the final section of this chapter is devoted to an assessment of the likely impact of the Government's most recent and most far-reaching development of its ideological project to create an enterprise culture, namely, the establishment of the new Training and Enterprise Councils (TECs). The next ten years will show whether they prove to be an ambitious, forward-looking and productive strategy or an ill-advised, risky and unsuccessful gamble with the future prosperity of the United Kingdom.

The Decade of the TECs

As the enterprise movement has grown, so too have the responsibilities given to employers who are now becoming increasingly involved in the management of hospitals, polytechnics, universities and schools. The Government's stance can be encapsulated in the phrase 'the employers know best' about all these varied activities. The establishment of the new TECs, however, can be seen as a radical development of this policy whereby the training of young people, of the unemployed and all those in employment has been handed over to bodies controlled by industrialists; two-thirds of each TEC Board must consist of the senior managers of national or major companies at local level. The move is presented as not so much another government programme as yet another attempt to harness the energy and commitment of employers 'to help provide the country with the skilled and enterprising workforce it needs for sustained economic growth and prosperity' (TA, 1989c:3). The TECs are in essence the last desperate throw of the voluntary system of training in Britain. In more detail, TECs can be described as a national network of independent companies, led by chief executives from private industry in order to deliver training and enterprise locally. As such, the study of the Teesside TEC, which we begin in Chapter 4, is an ideal opportunity to assess how national plans at a macro level are translated into practice at a local, micro level.

The model being followed is not the German *Dual System* of vocational training but rather the American Private Industry Councils (or PICs). According to Cay Stratton, a former Executive Director of the Boston PIC who became an adviser to the Secretary of State for Employment in 1983:

> Basically I see TECs as the next generation of PICs . . . PICs are focused exclusively on training, mainly for the long-term unemployed. The strength of TECs is their very broad remit — economic growth and community regeneration — which encompasses influencing education and training and seeking inward investment. (Stratton, 1990:13)

TECs have also grown out of the importation into this country of other American initiatives like the Boston Compact, whereby employers offer jobs to young, working-class people in the inner city who achieve previously agreed standards in schools. It will be one of the first tasks for the TECs to signal to their local communities that their remit goes way beyond coping with school-leavers with few, if any, qualifications. The plan is not only for TECs to manage existing programmes (such as Youth Training (YT), Employment Training (ET), Business Growth Training, Small Firms Counselling, the Enterprise Allowance Scheme, Training Access Points, and the Training of Trainers), and to be involved in the development of TVEI and Work Related Further Education. TECs will also be charged with assessing the economic and social needs of their locality, deciding on priorities and allocating resources to stimulate local economic development. In the words of Norman Fowler, then Secretary of State for Employment: 'if we are to expect employers to take the reins locally, we must give them real powers to make real decisions'. (*Employment Gazette*, April 1989:156). Later he issued strategic guidance (TA, 1989b:6) which described the role of the TECs as follows: 'Each TEC will need to establish a clear vision of training and enterprise in the community . . . (and) develop its ideas and plans in partnership with the community, and . . . publish them widely'.

The TECs have also been set up with great speed, following their announcement in the White Paper *Employment for the 1990s*, issued at the end of 1988. By July 1990 twenty TECs had signed operational contracts, more than fifty were in the development phase and by the end of 1991 a network of eighty-two TECs is planned to cover England and Wales. The establishment of the TECs provides an opportunity to review policy and some of the key issues in this area:

A National Plan for Education, Training and Employment (ETE)? Why are all these new structures, plans and activities necessary? Together they constitute the latest attempt to provide what has been missing in Britain for the last 150 years, namely, a coherent and comprehensive national plan for education, training *and* employment (or ETE).[3] Governments of both main parties have come and gone, the main Departments of State concerned (DES, Department of Employment, DTI, and to a lesser extent the Home Office) continue to divide the responsibilities among themselves and we are still without a coordinated and widely understood policy for ETE. Since 1945 we have witnessed successive reorganizations of the education system and of the national provision of training; and during this period, industry has undergone a series of structural changes. Each of these developments, however, has taken place more or less independently, and what we have always needed is an imaginative, over-arching policy which would emphasize the vital links between education, training and employment and how various groups progress from one stage to another. Commentators tend to discuss the relationship *either* between education and training *or* between training and employment, but what we lack is the vision to create a policy which embraces all three together.

In the early 1980s the concentration of the Government was on training (YOP, YTS, Community Programme, etc.) and *only* on train-ing; as a result the unemployed of Britain became some of the most highly trained in the world. In July 1988, the Secretary of State for Education acquired numerous new *centralising* powers through the passing into law of the Education Reform Act (ERA); within six months the Department of Employment was *decentralizing* the system of training. In what ways have the ERA (1988) and the legislation establishing the TECs been planned and coordinated in advance? If such coordination had taken place, there might now be a National Curriculum for 5–18 year olds rather than for 5–16 year olds. Perhaps one can detect the vague outline of a grand design to restructure and to privatize[4] both the education and training systems (see Edwards *et al.*, 1989:220 on this point), but on the ground at local level, staff in education and in the TECs will be left to develop what links they can in very changed circumstances.[5] The leader in *The Times Educational Supplement* (16 December 1988) reflected thus on the publication of *Employment for the 1990s*: 'it is extraordinary that, having at last got round to creating a national system of *education*, the government should now abdicate all responsibility for the *training* of school leavers' (emphasis as in original).

The third corner of the triangle — employment — has been the most neglected as can be seen from the dismantling of regional policy, the unprecedented high levels of unemployment, the lack of continuing education and training for workers, the removal of young workers' pay from the protection of the Wages Councils, and the disappearance of the debate about the quality of jobs. Has society no responsibility, for instance, to those who have done everything in their power to find employment, who have conscientiously attended one training course after another and still find themselves unemployed? (see Ashby, 1989). The interim judgement is that TECs will make the creation of a national strategic plan for ETE *less* rather than more likely because their programmes are designed to be local and tactical.

The Commitment of Employers?   The establishment of TECs is a high risk strategy which hopes finally to secure the commitment of employers to training. The historic failure (Wiener, 1981) and the continuing complacency (Coopers and Lybrand, 1985) of most British employers in relation to training is well known to government because much of the recent evidence has been produced by reports commissioned by them. What has changed since the MSC passed the following judgement: 'Training is perceived by many employers as a disposable overhead dropped at the first sign of lowering profit margins'? (New Training Initiative, 1981).

Employers themselves would not care to be judged by their record of attendance at the Area Manpower Boards of the MSC, but it is still possible that the highest trade deficit in our history in 1989 will prod them into working collectively to enable them to face and begin to beat international competition (see Godley, 1989). Local pride and concern for the future prosperity of their area may provide an additional spur to action.

As it happens, the government's expenditure plans (announced in January 1990 and containing cuts of £350 million in ET and YT) will provide an immediate test of the commitment of employers and of TEC Board members. The Government's case for reducing these budgets was threefold: in the late 1980s, the number of school-leavers was falling; youth unemployment was decreasing; and the private sector should provide more funds for training. Before the first TECs were up and running, their budgets were cut between 10 and 20 per cent and complaints began to seep into the press (see *The Guardian*, 8 August 1990) about the operational controls and lack of flexibility imposed on them (see also *Working Brief*, April 1990:6). For example, 90 per cent of a TEC's budget is already allocated to YT, ET, and EAS and the resources available for local initiatives to stimulate economic growth remain pitifully small.

Representativeness and Accountability?   It is, of course, part of the official strategy for the Boards of TECs to be controlled by chief executives who tend to come from large companies; as a result the Boards contain few, if any, directors of small businesses and only token representation from trade unions, education, local government or voluntary organizations. There is a genuine (but not insurmountable) problem in an area like, say,

Oldham; it has been estimated (*Focus on Training*, October, 1989:7) that there are as many as 15,000 small enterprises 'who could benefit from the TEC but who may be too busy or preoccupied with their own immediate survival to participate'. The Board of each TEC has fifteen seats and the voluntary organizations in North-East England education and the trade unions are tending to be given one place each.

To whom will the TECs be accountable? Performance is likely to vary from those who were first to be set up to those who have still to apply for development funding. No doubt there will be knighthoods for those judged to be successful, but what is to stop a TEC responding to the shorter-term needs of local employers and sacrificing the long-term education, training and employment prospects of young people and adults? What happens to those chief executives who are unable to take a more far-sighted view? How are they to be removed from the Board? Do they simply return to their firms and another employer is chosen to rectify the damage done?

The Training Agency (*Guide to Planning*, 1989) has laid down that each TEC will be required to:

- make its three year Corporate Plan available for public inspection
- publish an Annual Report
- hold at least one public meeting each year
- be subject to independent audits by the Department of Employment and the National Audit Office.

In addition, the contract each TEC enters into with the Secretary of State will be for a finite period, its Business Plan has to be approved by the Training Agency, planning guidelines with specific objectives will be issued each year by the Department of Employment, as will performance indicators and performance related bonuses (of around 2 per cent of the total budget). This battery of control mechanisms (performance related funding or PRF) makes clear that the TECs will be accountable not so much to the local community as directly to the Training Agency and government.

Future remit?   No-one would be surprised if the TECs were to take over responsibility for the Enterprise Initiative from the Department of Trade and Industry, but in whose interest would it be for the Careers Service, for instance, to lose its independent status as honest broker between young people and employers and be answerable directly to local TECs? Are TECs more likely to look favourably on the CBI proposal to issue to all young people who leave school at 16 credits or vouchers which are cashed in when employers provide them with training?[6] Their remit *could* be extended to cover all further education, advanced as well as non-advanced. And if it includes further education, is it too speculative to suggest that higher education could be absorbed to ensure that universities and polytechnics respond appropriately to the needs of local employers and open up access to their local communities? A strategic plan which identifies skill shortages and the need to attract inward investment from high-tech firms will fairly soon have to examine the quality of the available housing stock and of the transport system; and so the remit of the TECs may grow by leaps and bounds. The above suggestions are obviously highly speculative and the outcome is more than usually difficult to predict because all three of the main political actors involved in the conception of the scheme (Fowler, Young and Baker at the Departments of Employment, Trade and Industry and Education) have all moved on. The development of a coordinated, comprehensive policy for ETE is likely to be postponed again as new Secretaries of State work to understand their new responsibilities, never mind those which transcend those of their Departments.

National, Regional and Local Levels? The Training Agency's *Guide to Planning* (1989:4) explains how the TECs will operate 'at three levels: the national level, the industry level and the local level'. Two serious problems suggest themselves right away. First, it is by no means certain that the aggregation of 100 local business plans produces an adequate response to national needs in education, training and employment, and specific shortages in, say, high technology. And if the national priorities, as laid down by the Secretary of State, are seen to conflict with the objectives of a local TEC, which will be given precedence? Second, one strategic level is missing altogether from the plan — the regional. The North-East of England, for instance, will have five TECs, each responding to the specific needs of a small, geographically-defined area (Teesside, Wearside, Tyneside, Durham and Northumberland), but who will be responsible for regional planning and for the production of structural plans to cope with the deep-seated economic inequalities within and between the regions? It would be a constructive step if groups of TECs came together to address the problems of the region in which they are situated, but years are likely to pass before they are in a position to act in such a concerted manner.

What Levers on Change? What mechanisms will the TECs employ to encourage or to enforce change? There appears to be excessive reliance on peer pressure whereby good employers are expected persistently and amiably to cajole their more recalcitrant brethren into training their own workers — or paying for others to do so. What is to happen to those employers who do not experience sudden Pauline conversions to training on the road to Moorfoot, Sheffield or to their local TEC? Those employers who exploited YTS by taking on every year a new batch of young school-leavers without employing any of them are still in existence and their attitudes have not changed. Some TECs are already discussing the inclusion of quality controls when they sub-contract training, but they may need to introduce contract compliance or local levies on companies who resist all exhortations to train their workers.

The contrast between the treatment of employers and of members of the education service is particularly marked in this regard. Why, for example, has the Government not even taken reserve powers to enforce change on employers who resist all other forms of pressure, in the way that it has been felt necessary in education to legislate the National Curriculum into existence with all the force of statutory orders? It is predicted that a future government will have to introduce legislation to enforce the commitment to training of the rogue, fly-by-night or just the uncommitted employer. Even universities and polytechnics have only recently begun to invest in the training of their own employees.

The Values of the Board?   With chief executives holding down two-thirds of the seats on the Board of every TEC, their values will prevail and so the ethos will tend to reflect in the main the views of successful, self-made, entrepreneurial, white males. How many seats will be found, for example, in the Boardroom for women or black people? Will either group believe the rhetoric of how important they are becoming in the workforce, if they are excluded? The composition of the Boards of the first thirteen TECs to assume full responsibilities has been studied by *Working Brief* (August/September 1990:4) and, out of a total of 175 Board members, seventeen (or just less than 10 per cent) are women and only one TEC has appointed a woman to chair the council. The private sector accounts for 70 per cent of Board members, local authorities 9 per cent, trade unions 5 per cent and voluntary organizations and local education authorities 3 per cent each.

What attention will be paid to the education, training and employment needs of the handicapped or of ethnic minorities or of rural communities? The Training Agency is currently engaged in piloting performance indicators for TECs, one of which concerns the provision for trainees with disabilities or special training needs, but is it conceivable that a TEC would have its contract ended or its budget cut significantly if particular targets regarding disadvantaged groups were not met? Is it realistic for ministers to expect private sector employers to make up the Government's expenditure cuts in the training budget of those with special training needs? As the *Financial Times* commented (23 May 1990), Ministers 'should recognize that companies have no commercial incentive to finance the training of disadvantaged groups such as the mentally handicapped or long-term unemployed' (quoted by White, 1990:24).

Partnership or Control?   The advent of the TECs has been cloaked in the language of partnership. But when élite groups insist on using and reusing the word 'partnership', it is reasonably certain that a major shift in power is taking place in favour of one preferred group at the expense of another. The word 'partnership', like the word 'consultation', has fallen upon hard times. The questions which need to be asked are: Who will drive this partnership? What is the relative power of the various participants? What entitlement have minorities to a hearing or to funding? What appeals procedure will there be against the decisions of the Board? As TECs are private companies, they are outside the jurisdiction of the Ombudsman or the Parliamentary Commissioner for Administration; complaints made against a TEC will be dealt with by the Chief Executive and, if necessary, the Chairman of the Board (see *Working Brief*, August/September 1990:4).

What Future for Enterprise Education?

No matter what government had been in power in the 1980s, some radical measures would need to have been taken to cope with the continuing decline of the British economy, relative to its major international competitors. This chapter has sought to raise the question of whether those which have been taken will prove to be the most appropriate, but the problems to which they are directed are not in dispute.

The wide-ranging study *Training in Britain* (TA, 1989d:55) claims that 'In 1988 one in three individuals of working age reported having no qualifications' and, perhaps more serious still, 'one-third of 19 to 34 year olds and almost one-half of those aged 35 and over could not foresee circumstances which would lead them to undertake education or training' (53). The task facing the TECs in changing the attitudes of such a substantial minority of the workforce is not to be underestimated.

Coupled with this, we need to assess the significance for the European Community of the growth in numbers of young people in developing countries. In a speech given in December 1989, Norman Fowler gave the figures as follows:

> Between now and the year 2010 the population of Western Europe will increase by 2 per cent; that of Japan by 8 per cent; that of the United States by 17 per cent; but that of the developing world by no less than 45 per cent. In that period the numbers of those aged 15 to 24 in the developing world grow by 20 per cent, and the numbers of those aged 25 to 54 by a staggering 60 per cent.

The implications for Britain were thought to be obvious: 'we must become a high productivity, high skill, high technology economy' (Norman Fowler, *op. cit.*). Our chances of achieving that goal, however, depend largely upon developing and implementing a national policy for ETE with sufficient resources to give it vibrant life.

Successive Conservative governments have sought to reverse our economic decline by replacing what they have termed the dependency culture with the enterprise culture. Enterprise has helped to provide the ideological basis for the radical changes in education, training and industrial policy. The word 'enterprise', however, is best understood *not* as a coherent set of logically related ideas but as a short-hand way of referring to a clutch of values such as individualism, self-reliance, competition, self-employment, profitability, minimal government and capitalism unfettered by rules and regulations on the American model. Ruth Levitas (1986:80) has rightly emphasized 'the two dominant strands of thought within the New Right — neo-liberal economics and social authoritarianism'.

It could, however, be retorted that, if the notion of enterprise is such a conceptual quagmire, then surely its effects are likely to be diffuse, the unintended consequences manifold and the internal contradictions an endless source of confusion? On the other hand, logical incoherence and lack of an agreed definition did not prevent concepts like 'intelligence' or 'maladjustment' from exerting a powerful (and at times baleful) influence on social policy and on the lives of millions of children.

An example of one internal contradiction within the ruling ideology of the Conservative Government is the virtual exclusion of enterprise education from either the core or the foundation subjects or even the cross-curricular issues within the National Curriculum; and not even the rather anxious attempts by the authors of *Primary Enterprise* (DUBS, 1989:3) to show how attainment targets can be met by primary pupils through enterprise activities are likely to rescue enterprise education. The subject has run up against the buffers of another strain in Conservative thinking — the traditional conception of knowledge as a body of facts (like the curriculum for Science in the National Curriculum) to be memorized and retold in examinations like A level. On the other hand, Robins and Webster (1989:191) accurately sum up the significance of enterprise education for the new groups of peripheral workers:

> it is about . . . educating the young to be 'flexible'; it is concerned with socialising school leavers at once to believe that unemployment is a result of personality defects ('IT illiterates and moaners are unemployable'), at the same time as to accept that their work experiences will be punctuated by regular periods of retraining and readjustment to technological change.

In any dispute within the Conservative Party between knowledge and skills (entrepreneurial or otherwise), high status knowledge will be reserved for those destined for high-status occupations while new, progressive-sounding courses like enterprise education which might threaten academic standards will be thought appropriate for those who are to be trained for (un)employment. For the sake of both groups, we need to collapse this dichotomy which continues to bedevil the education, training and employment of *all* our young people. Stuart Hall (1988:10) has followed Gramsci in arguing that ideologies are rarely logically consistent or homogeneous but tend to be internally fractured: 'It is because Thatcherism knows this that it understands why the ideological terrain of struggle is so crucial'. Logical contradictions within the ideology may, as Ruth Levitas argues, 'be a strength rather than a weakness, enabling the New Right to switch the grounds of its legitimations at will' (1986:11).

For ten years now the enterprise culture has been at the centre of the political stage in Britain and this chapter has sought to begin the process of evaluating what has been achieved in our name and with our money. The massive resources that have been lavished on making a success of this ideological project could have been invested in other ways: in British manufacturing industry, in regional development and in a comprehensive, national plan to create dynamic interactions between education, vocational training and employment.

In the 1990s government will look increasingly to the TECs for improvements in our economic performance because they have entrusted the task of creating a new society to the praetorian guard of the enterprise culture — the chief executives of British industry. Within ten years we shall know whether this strategy proves to be bold, forward-looking and productive or risky, retrograde and redundant.

In the following chapter our attention switches to the historical and economic context within which the transformation of the so-called dependency culture of Teesside is being attempted. According to Bob Little, the new Chief Executive of Teesside TEC, the area 'developed an "employee culture" in which people were used to taking orders rather than taking the initiative' (*TEC Director*, Issue 2:30). Increasingly, our focus will be not so much on the praetorian guard as the ordinary foot-soldiers, the young entrepreneurs of Cleveland, who are all, apparently, to become captains of industry or, at least, bosses of their own firms and guardians of their own destinies.[7]

Notes

1 We are grateful to John Ritchie's (1987) article for bringing this article and Lord Young's (1986) to our attention.

2 Ralph Glasser, for example, describes in his autobiography (p. 19) how Richard Crossman 'in his silver grey suit and dove grey silk tie' towards the end of the 1930s asked his Oxford study group on social mobility the following question: why do people work? 'To have no money, for instance, no money at all, was to them (people like Crossman) inconceivable. How

could they ask, so innocently, "why do people work"? I said, curtly "Because they'd starve if they didn't!"' (emphasis as in the original).

3 The acronym — ETE — is produced, after the fashion of the Training Agency, in the hope that it will catch on.

4 Stephen Wilks has argued (1987:9) that in Britain, especially since 1983, 'traditional industrial policy has been submerged under a new "enterprise policy" . . . The privatization argument has moved from ideology to doctrine to dogma in a very short period of time and is being pursued for its own sake'.

5 Another example of the *lack* of coordination between the DES and the Department of Employment can be seen in the establishment of the Certificate for Prevocational Education by the DES in July 1984, to counteract the march stolen on them when the MSC set up TVEI in November 1982.

6 In March 1990, the government announced the introduction of training credits for 16 and 17 year olds leaving full-time education 'to help create a more efficient and responsive market in training' (Michael Howard, Employment Secretary, *Insight*, No. 29, Summer 1990:10). The TECs were then invited to run a range of pilot schemes to cover a total of 45,000 school-leavers, and eleven pilot projects were launched in July, 1990. The history of such initiatives suggests that training credits will be generously resourced at the pilot stage, they will be judged to have been a resounding success before any evaluation has been completed and extended nationally at a much reduced level of funding.

7 We wish to acknowledge our thanks to Tony Edwards, Gerald Grace, Jackson Hall and Bill Williamson who read and commented on earlier drafts of this chapter. The argument and the mistakes, however, remain our own.

Chapter 3

The 'Infant Hercules' Comes of Age

In 1846 J.W. Ord, one of the first historians of the Cleveland district, described Middlesbrough as 'one of the commercial prodigies of the nineteenth century' and added that to a stranger to the area: 'this proud array of ships, docks, warehouses, churches, foundries, wharves etc., would seem like some enchanted spectacle, some Arabian Nights' vision, "such stuff as dreams are made of"' (Ord, 1846, quoted in Briggs 1963:250). Newcomers to today's Teesside would be hard pressed to recognize Ord's dream of Middlesbrough in the derelict industrial sites, redundant shipyards, polluted waterways and vast steel and chemical complexes which now dominate the local landscape. For Middlesbrough, and Cleveland, have shared in, and perhaps suffered most acutely, the problems of the North as a whole. The area has experienced the drastic social, economic and physical consequences of economic recession and industrial restructuring, going from boom to bust in quick time.

The social and economic history that we relate in this chapter will attempt to unravel the trends which have resulted in the spectacular transformation of the locality. Briggs, in his description of the town in Victorian times, comments: 'The real interest of Middlesbrough's nineteenth-century history lies ... not so much in the newness of the community which was created there as in the speed with which an intricate and complex economic, social and political sequence was un-folded' (Briggs, 1963:279).

We would argue that the speed and scope of social and economic change in Cleveland over the past twenty years matches that marvelled at by Briggs and earlier historians. Our first aim is to understand what has been described as the 'Quiet Revolution' (Foord et al., 1985): how the area has changed from one of economic growth with a strong tradition of primary and secondary industry and stable patterns of employment, to, in recent times, the worst area of unemployment in mainland Britain.[1]

Our second aim is to provide an analysis of the socio-economic history of Cleveland as the context for our study of youth and enterprise.

Against the background of Cleveland's changing economic fortunes young people leave school, search for work and enter adulthood. Without understanding the nature of the local economy we cannot hope to understand the structures of opportunity through which young people make the transition to adulthood.

In the first section of this chapter we will concentrate on the *growth* of the two industrial giants which lie at the heart of economic life in Cleveland: iron and steel, on the one hand, and chemicals, on the other. Secondly, we will trace the economic *decline* of the Cleveland economy over the past twenty years, again concentrating on these two industries. The grim consequences this has had for young adults in the county will be highlighted. The third section considers the most recent changes in the fortunes of the locality, improvements in the employment situation in the late 1980s and 1990s and Cleveland's prospects for the future. Finally, we will examine the more *qualitative* changes in Teesside's economic and social life that have occurred alongside the *quantitative* collapse of local employment. We pay special attention to the employment policies pursued within the major industries in the county. Together these discussions will provide the necessary context for our investigation of youth enterprise in Cleveland.

'The Youngest Child of England's Enterprise'

It is necessary right at the beginning to clarify, very briefly, a few geographical terms (see Figure 3.1). Cleveland came into existence in 1974 as a result of local government reorganization. It is a county of over half a million people located in the North-East of England between the counties of North Yorkshire, Durham and Tyne and Wear. To the north it stretches to Hartlepool, west towards Darlington in County Durham, east to the sea at Redcar and the rural areas surrounding Guisborough and south towards Loftus and Whitby. Our study has covered the whole county but, although our sample of informants were drawn from all areas of Cleveland, it is fair to say that the majority were based in Middlesbrough, and as such, in this section our remarks will concentrate on this town. Middlesbrough forms the centre not only of our study, but also the geographical heart of Teesside: the agglomeration of towns, including Stockton and Billingham, which have grown up around the River Tees, and which now, in turn, form the industrial and demographic heart of the county of Cleveland.

Middlesbrough's development and changing fortunes are central to an understanding of how Cleveland could, in the space of twenty years, switch from 'growth zone to unemployment blackspot' (Foord *et al.*, 1985). The history of Middlesbrough as a major industrial, commercial and population centre is relatively short. In 1820 Middlesbrough was still

Figure. 3.1   Map of Cleveland

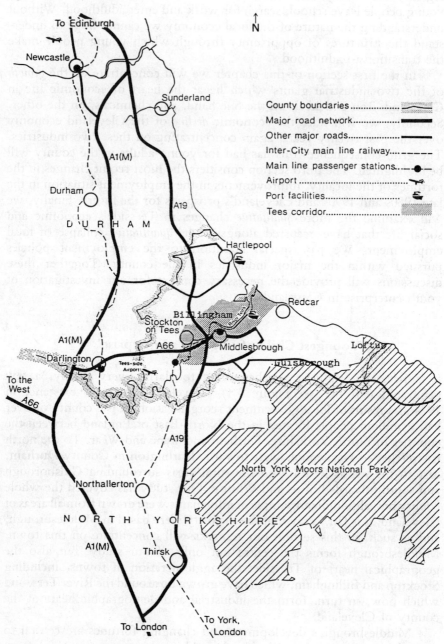

County boundaries ....
Major road network..................
Other major roads....................
Inter-City main line railway.... _ _ _ _
Main line passenger stations....●─
Airport ....✈
Port facilities...........................⇶
Tees corridor...........................

(Source: Cleveland County Council)

Table 3.1   Population Growth in Middlesbrough 1801 to 1981

1801	25
1829	40
1831	154
1841	5,463
1851	7,431
1861	19,416
1871	39,563
1881	55,934
1891	75,532
1901	91,302
1951	150,010
1961	164,760
1971	157,310
1981	150,430

(Source: Briggs, 1963 and Cleveland County Council Research and Intelligence Unit, 1988a)

only a tiny, rural village, a halfway house between the religious centres of Whitby and Durham, with a population of less than 40 people (see Table 3.1).

No other English town experienced such a remarkably swift development during the last century, moving Gladstone to comment: 'This remarkable place, the youngest child of England's enterprise . . . It is an infant, gentlemen, but it is an infant Hercules' (on visiting Middlesbrough in October 1862, quoted in Briggs, 1963:245). The growth of the town during the Victorian years of the Industrial Revolution was founded upon a dramatic shift from a local agriculturally based economy to an industrial one with a massively increased local population. Initial port facilities developed with the extension of the Stockton and Darlington railway to Middlesbrough, enabling the easier exportation of coal from the Durham area, so guaranteeing the early prosperity of the town. By 1870 the population of the town reached nearly 40,000 and large-scale housing development spread to the mud-flats and salt-marshes on both sides of the River Tees.

Iron and Steel in Cleveland

Despite the early maritime connections of the town the key to Middlesbrough's economic fortunes lay in the iron industry. The flat land on Teesside made Middlesbrough ideal for the making of iron, utilizing ore from the Cleveland Hills and coking coal from the Durham coalfield. The town continued to act as a port for the export of Durham coal, though coal trade had declined sharply by the mid-Victorian years. Much port trade was passed back to Newcastle or Hartlepool as Middlesbrough's maritime importance declined. The decline in coal was, however, completely overshadowed by the growth of the local iron industry during the

1850s and 1860s. These resources were successfully exploited by the early ironmasters who, during this period of economic upheaval and declining port trade, ensured that Middlesbrough became, not a ghost town, but a centre for quite remarkable industrial expansion.

Iron production was quickly followed by the development of steel, shipbuilding and heavy engineering and in the later part of the nineteenth century steel production began to overtake the production of pig iron in Cleveland. The early history of the town has often been written as the history of 'great men': entrepreneurs like Henry Bolckow, John Vaughan and Arthur Dorman, whose capital investment sparked the development of the industrial backbone of the area. Their early contribution is still commemorated in the street and place names of the locality ('Bolckow Street', 'Dormanstown') and in statues marking their achievement. These ironmasters were quick to expand into steel production and, by 1871, ninety blast furnaces ringed the River Tees. This boom in iron and steel demanded a massive growth in the supply of local labour. The following passage gives a flavour of the hectic development of the industry and the town:

> It is obvious, then, what a field for labour is suddenly opened up by the discovery of iron in any part of the county. The genesis of the iron-making town which follows such a discovery is breath-less and tumultuous . . . the unexpectedness of it, the change in the conditions of the district, which suddenly becomes swamped under a great rush from all parts of the country of people often of the roughest kind . . . it is, unhappily, for the most part a side issue for the workman whether he and his family are going to live under healthy conditions. The main objective of his life is to be at work; that is the absolute necessity. (Bell, 1985:2–3)

Middlesbrough must have had something of the feel of the Klondike gold rush days: Briggs described it as a 'turbulent urban frontier' (Briggs, 1963:252), as it experienced a massive influx of manual workers, with men far outnumbering women in the growing population of the town.[2] The new inhabitants were attracted from all over the British Isles by the promise of work and high wages in the booming iron and steel industry. In 1871, for example, half of the town's population were born outside Yorkshire, the county in which Middlesbrough then resided (Briggs, 1963).

The increasing scale of production of iron and steel led many previously small companies into mergers during the late nineteenth century. By 1914, three major companies were responsible for the majority of iron and steel production on Teesside: Bolckow Vaughan, Dorman Long and the South Durham Steel and Iron Company. The industry expanded further to meet national needs during the First World War but was faced with pressing problems of over capacity after 1918. New rounds of mergers and takeovers led to the amalgamation of Dorman Long and Bolckow Vaughan in 1929. The new company, retaining the names of the ironmasters Dorman and Long, employed 33,000 people and had an annual steel capacity of 1.5 million tons per annum. Dorman Long was typical of the 'coal combines' which emerged in the North-East during the inter-war years, where one company would own different branches of the production process: Dorman Long, for example, owned eight pits in Durham. Iron and steel production was relatively successful on Teesside even during these depressed inter-war years. Major international contracts, like that for the Sydney Harbour Bridge, helped secure continued production.

Uncertainties over nationalization restricted further investment and expansion of Cleveland's steel industry in the period immediately following the Second World War. The industry was briefly nationalized during the early 1950s and then experienced further expansion when this decision was reversed with the re-election of the Conservative government. The postwar period has seen increasing capital investment and modernization of furnaces and plant and increasing reliance upon richer, imported, foreign ore. The last iron stone mine in Cleveland, at North Skelton, was closed in 1964.

The industry was renationalized in 1967 from the fourteen largest steel producers in the country to form the British Steel Corporation (BSC). Production was concentrated on five integrated sites, including Teesside. Massive planned and actual investment in the industry from 1970 onwards quickly turned to retrenchment during the recession-hit late 1970s and early '80s. For instance, BSC employed 254,000 people in 1967 compared with 71,000 in 1984. In 1982 Cleveland had 55,000 unemployed people and 10 per cent of them had previously been employed by BSC (Hudson and Sadler, 1985).

The Chemical Industry in Cleveland

The roots of the chemical industry in Cleveland can be traced back to the mining and extraction of salt on Teesside in the late nineteenth century (although activity was very limited during this period and often carried out as an offshoot of iron production). Teesside really 'came of age', as Beynon *et al.* (1987) put it, with the development of the chemical industry around the Tees following the First World War.

Modern, large-scale development of chemicals began in 1918 on the North bank of the Tees at Billingham. Billingham provided accessible, expansive and flat land with adequate supplies of water, power, raw materials and labour at close hand. The merger of three companies led to the formation of Imperial Chemicals Industries (ICI) in 1926 which, in turn, led to the expansion and diversification of chemical production on Teesside (for example, into the production of fertilisers at Billingham). This period of development lasted until, and through, the Second World War and Hudson (1989) reports that ICI Billingham did much to reduce the impact of inter-war depression upon Teesside. Largely because of the growth of the chemicals complex the area suffered far less than its neighbour Tyneside. By 1945 Billingham was the largest single chemicals production complex in the world (Beynon, Hudson and Sadler, 1986).

Shortly after the Second World War, ICI developed a second major plant south of the Tees at Wilton. Again the site met all the necessary requirements for chemical industry location and by the end of the 1950s ICI Wilton was emerging as a major petrochemical complex, receiving huge capital investment. The construction of the vast plant itself made enormous demands on local labour. Local employees were supplemented by workers moving into the area and daily migrants from nearby areas. For example, during the 1950s over five hundred men were travelling each day from the small town of Whitby, some thirty miles to the south (MacDonald, 1988a). There was also an increasing demand for skilled workers to be employed by ICI at Wilton. The Hailsham Plan for the North-East (Board of Trade 1963, see Hudson, 1989) called for the modernization of the Teesside economy to be based around key industries, especially chemicals. Severe worries about labour shortage in the Teesside chemical industry led to deliberate planning embargoes on the development of alternative sources of employment for skilled manual workers in the locality (Hudson, 1989). Beynon, Hudson and Sadler note: 'in the early post-war period there was a conscious emphasis upon selectively promoting the growth of chemical capacity and employment in parts of Teesside' (1986:13).

By 1976 there were 13,000 people employed at Wilton alone. This amounted to half the national workforce in petrochemicals and plastics production. By the late 1970s, with increasing overseas competition, expansion had slowed down and the shedding of labour began.

The chemical industry has historically constituted one part of Cleveland's industrial triumvirate, the others being iron and steel production and heavy engineering. More recently the locality has experienced further capital investment in the third strand of the triumvirate — heavy engineering. It has become a centre for the construction of equipment for the extraction of gas and oil from the North Sea, which, to some extent, has offset the demise of shipbuilding in Middlesbrough (Withington, 1989) and the decline in chemicals and steel production (Sadler, 1986). Sadler argues that the region was slow to develop offshore fabrication for expanding North Sea exploration but more recently this sphere of production has provided a major boost to the local heavy engineering industry (in 1985 orders worth £87 million were placed with four Teesside yards). Today this newest industry to emerge on Teesside continues to exist, precariously, on short term orders.

The rest of the local economy, its commerce, service sectors and other industries developed around these three areas of production, and, in turn, the manufacturing industries of Middlesbrough and Teesside have been closely linked with the fortunes of the wider national and international economy. As we have outlined, Middlesbrough, and Teesside more generally, experienced a buoyant post-war economy and expansion until the 1960s and the early 1970s, with booming new investment promising prosperity for the future.

From Boom to Bust in Quick Time

Briggs' history of Middlesbrough charts the miraculous growth, optimism and prosperity of the town from the mid-nineteenth to the mid-twentieth century. Since Briggs' account appeared in 1963, commentaries on Teesside make less positive reading. In 1985 Foord *et al.* commented:

> This area has experienced a spectacular and remarkable economic collapse. The last two decades have seen Teesside transformed from an area with the greatest hopes for expansion and dynamism through massive investment in a thriving and relatively modern industrial base, to one with the highest rates of unemployment (at county level) in Great Britain. (1985:2–3)

Since the growth of the three traditionally dominant and successful industries of Middlesbrough — steel, chemicals and heavy engineering — during the 1950s, '60s and early '70s, all have undergone processes of 'rationalization' to maintain profitability, resulting in labour shedding and redundancies on a massive scale. Foord *et al.* argue that the industrial decline of Teesside is *not* typical of other industrial areas of the North. A local council report also argues that the area has been typified by high productivity and competitiveness, and by good records of industrial relations and investment (Cleveland County Council Research and Intelligence Unit, 1983). Foord *et al.* argue that consensus between national Conservative and Labour administrations during the 1950s and '60s resulted in modernization, investment and expansion in a narrow industrial base. They argue that *over-concentration*, especially on steel and chemicals, resulted in Cleveland becoming very vulnerable to economic recession (Foord *et al.*, 1985). Hudson (1989) continues this line of argument and suggests that state policies for the development and modernization of the North-East, (and Teesside was seen as a prime site for modernization within the North-East) concentrating as they did upon capital investment in a very narrow industrial base, did much to weaken the local economy:

What had seemed in the 1960s to be the great advantages con-
ferred by Teesside's unique location in corporate, national, and
regional modernisation policies, now rendered it uniquely vulnerable to changes in UK state policies . . . and the 'new' international division of labour in the late 1970s and 1980s. The vulnerability
of chemicals, oil, and steel to pressures of international competition led to serious cuts in capacity and jobs on Teesside (and still
threatens more), leading to the prospect of still further increases
in unemployment. (Hudson, 1989:352)

Investment in the three areas of heavy industry produced very little
in the way of 'spin-off' employment in manufacturing industry. In 1965,
79 per cent of manufacturing employment was in these three heavy
industries. By 1984 the figure had only fallen to 74 per cent. Investment
in existing industries had reached the point by the mid-70s where the
chemical industry was only just maintaining its aggregate number of jobs
(Foord et al., 1985). Foord et al. argue, however, that the same policy
consensus continued into this period with Cleveland as a whole being
made a Special Development Area in 1982, and thus qualifying for
the maximum amount of government aid for regional industrial
development.
During the mid- to late 1970s Cleveland was regularly receiving over
a quarter of the national total of Regional Development Grant (RDG)
payments. It should also be noted that during the period 1984 to 1987, 60
per cent of Cleveland's RDG went to ICI or BSC, companies which, as
the Trade Union Studies Information Unit (TUSIU 1987) says, were
responsible for some of the severest redundancies during the same period.
Foord et al. comment:

Regional policy had focused attention and resources on steel and
chemicals, but had signally failed to diversify the local economy
and left the area critically dependent on a group of industries
experiencing decline, corporate rationalization, internationaliza-
tion and, above all else, the shedding of jobs. In the past fifteen
years employment in manufacturing industry in Teesside has
been cut by half. (1986/7:34)

Although massive investment in the giants of Cleveland's economy
could be argued to have prevented steeper cuts in employment, it is clear
that such investment has failed to either expand or secure employment for
the workers in these industries in the long term or to safeguard the future
of some of the country's key industries on Teesside.[3] Moreover, the
channelling of regional investment to these big, capital intensive projects
where labour has been shed has denied the possibility of local economic
diversification into other industrial spheres, work consolidation or

generation programmes or the development of smaller, indigenous companies. Hudson also points to the contradiction underlying the remarkable reverse in Middlesbrough's economic fortunes:

> Of all the places in the North, Middlesbrough is most untypical. In the 1970s it was painted as the success story of industrial modernization and regional planning. Here the high level of unemployment is not the result of disinvestment and the flight of capital. Vast areas of Teesside are, indeed, an industrial graveyard, marked by acre on acre of derelict land, especially along the banks of the Tees itself. But equally there is no escaping the evidence of quite massive re-equipment and fixed capital investment in chemicals, oil and steel complexes. These industries have the most up-to-date technologies and their dominance has been sustained over a long period. Yet so severe is the competition on the international markets that even these modern plants are liable to closure. The highly visible juxtaposition of industrial dereliction and investment obscures a crucial contradiction: the massive expansion of unemployment has been brought about by fixed capital investment. (Hudson, 1986:13)

Unemployment in Cleveland

The human costs of this economic decline are made manifest in the unemployment statistics, which started to show rises in Cleveland during the mid-1970s. Between 1975 and 1986 one-quarter of all jobs in Cleveland were lost; during this same period nearly half of all those with manufacturing and construction jobs were made redundant (Cleveland County Council Economic Development and Planning Department, 1986a). Between 1981 and 1986, 14,500 jobs were lost in the county. Instead of the earlier optimistic expansion, employment in steel production on Teesside fell from 29,000 in 1971 to 7,000 in 1987. ICI employed 31,500 people in 1965. This number had been slashed to 14,500 by 1985 (Beynon et al., 1987):

> Within manufacturing the worst job losses have been in the industries which have traditionally been the major employers in Cleveland — chemicals, steel and heavy engineering. (Cleveland County Council Economic Development and Planning Department, 1986:5)

Indeed, chemicals and steel — mainstays of the local economy — shed over 50,000 jobs between them in the thirteen years to 1988, amounting to over three-quarters of total job losses in this period (Tees-side TEC, 1990). During the period 1977 to 1985 the Northern region generally had the highest regional unemployment rates in Great Britain, and five of the travel-to-work areas in the North had the highest unemployment rates in the country. Two of these are in Cleveland: Middlesbrough and Hartlepool (North of England County Councils Association, 1986).

In 1965, shortly after Briggs completed his history of Middlesbrough, the unemployment rate in the county was 1.9 per cent. Between 1974 and 1979 the unemployment rate in Cleveland doubled from 5 per cent to 10 per cent, then more than doubled again to 23 per cent by 1984 (Cleveland County Council Economic Development and Planning Department, 1986a). By September 1987 the problem of unemployment in Middlesbrough, Cleveland and the North could be represented as follows:

Middlesbrough	21.2%
Cleveland	19.5%
Northern Region	14.7%
Great Britain	10.1%

(*Source*: Cleveland County Council Economic Development and Planning Department, 1987)

The problem in trying to assess the economic outlook for, or performance of, a locality through regularly published indicators (such as these unemployment figures) is, of course, that they keep changing (our reservations about the reliability of these statistics will be discussed later). What we hope to show with the above set is the relationship between places and the ratios of unemployment, which tend to hold generally true even when the actual numbers and individual rates change. In the autumn of 1987 Middlesbrough had particularly high unemployment, higher than that for Cleveland and the Northern region as a whole and more than twice the national average. By early 1988 the figure for unemployment in Cleveland had started to fall but a recent County Council report acknowledged that 'unfortunately a significant part of the reduction is probably due to administrative changes rather than to people obtaining work' and that 'in the face of the ambiguity of that figure, it is clear that the legacy of more than seven years of very high unemployment will be difficult to overcome' (Cleveland County Council Research and Intelligence Unit, 1988:2, 4).

The downturn in the numbers of unemployed continued through the late 1980s but in April 1988 there were still 12,924 people unemployed in Middlesbrough with 637 vacancies outstanding (a ratio of over 20 people for each job). In Cleveland as a whole the ratio was 22 unemployed people for every outstanding vacancy (Cleveland County Council Research and Intelligence Unit, 1988b). These county and even town-wide estimates of unemployment disguise inequities in the burden of unemployment at even more local levels. Some areas, like Yarm, have had rates as low as 6.3 per cent, whilst others like South Bank in Middlesbrough, experienced rates of over 44 per cent (Cleveland County Council Research and Intelligence Unit, 1988c).

Hard Times for Youth

The situation facing school-leavers and young people in Middlesbrough and Cleveland during the 1980s was particularly grim. There were over 10,000 young people available for employment in October 1988 in Cleveland (i.e. those registered on YTS or unemployed with the Careers Office). At this time there were seventeen job vacancies notified to the Careers Service in the county (Cleveland County Council Careers Service, October 1988). For the 3,264 unemployed youth and YTS trainees in Middlesbrough at this time there were three jobs available through the Careers Service, a ratio of over one thousand people to every job. Whilst different months will show different numbers of notified vacancies (from 3 to 10 or 17), the basic situation remains depressingly similar. Despite apparent improvements in employment opportunities both nationally and locally, in 1988 the proportion of school-leavers entering full-time employment in Cleveland was the lowest ever recorded (approximately 6 per cent) (Cleveland County Council Careers Service, October 1988).

Changes in the benefit regulations for 16 to 18 year olds in September 1988 further worsened the experiences of young people trying to find a foothold in the labour market. Despite the formidable difficulties faced by youth in finding work in Cleveland, as revealed by these bare statistics, the Social Security Act 1988 meant that Income Support was withdrawn from unemployed 16 to 18 year olds who were now no longer 'officially' unemployed and, instead, were entitled to an eight-week 'YTS Bridging Allowance' of £15 per week.

The majority of this group are no longer counted as unemployed in the monthly official figures issued by the Department of Employment. However, data on the size of this group is still collected by the local Careers Service. In October 1988, 768 youths were in receipt of this 'allowance' in Cleveland (Cleveland County Careers Service, October 1988). The consequent work of the Careers Service locally was to place these people into YTS or employment by the time their eight-week allowance finished. However, by November 1988 there were 340 young people registered with the county's Careers Service who were no longer receiving any financial support. According to the Careers Service many of these people had previously been on YTS (Cleveland County Council

Careers Service, November 1988). This figure had risen to 472 by January 1989 (Cleveland County Council Careers Service, January 1989). In December 1988 it was estimated that there were, nationally, at least 14,000 sixteen and seventeen year olds still unemployed and yet not receiving any income (see Blackburne and Jackson, 1988).

Obviously the best option facing these newly disadvantaged young people would be to intensify the search for work, as was perhaps partly the intention behind the introduction of the new regulations. In January 1989 there were, however, only thirteen jobs notified to the Careers Service with 1,418 on *their* register of unemployed. Hard times, indeed, for youth in Cleveland.

In the late 1980s the proportion of Middlesbrough school leavers whose 'first destination' after leaving school was unemployment actually *increased* from 9.5 per cent in 1985 to nearly 15 per cent in 1988 (Middlesbrough Careers Office, 1988). The respective figures for Cleveland as a whole are 4.5 per cent and 8.4 per cent (Cleveland County Council Careers Service, October 1988). In January 1988 there were 5,616 unemployed 16 to 19 year olds in Cleveland (over 12 per cent of the county total). The continuing and declining minimal recruitment of young people by Cleveland employers is explained by two trends, according to the local Careers Service:

> The main one is the growing tendency in Cleveland for employers to recruit through YTS and the fact that the expansion in job opportunities for young people which it is claimed has occurred nationally, has not yet been experienced in Cleveland. (Cleveland County Council Careers Service, October, 1988:2)

We would argue that it is not just changes in the recruitment methods of employers which have further disadvantaged young people in this instance but the continuing parlous state of the local economy. Nationally it is claimed that approximately 70 per cent of those completing YTS enter further training, employment or education (Department of Employment, 1988a). And whilst it is claimed that 'in Cleveland YTS is undoubtedly the accepted "passport" into future employment' (Cleveland County Council Careers Service, November 1988:2) it would seem that, according to the Careers Services's own evidence, YTS fails to lead to employment for the majority of participants. A recent survey of all YTS leavers between January and February 1989 painted a worrying picture. Only 17 per cent of these YTS participants had, by the time of the survey, entered employment from the scheme (Cleveland County Council Careers Service, March 1989). The Careers Service describes this situation as 'disappointing'. Young people who have found YTS a 'passport' back to the dole queue often choose stronger words to describe the apparent failure of government training schemes (Gow and McPherson, 1980; Horton, 1985).

Of course, not all young people in Cleveland decide to leave the education system at the age of 16, though the numbers staying on are considerably lower than some nearby areas of high unemployment (Teesside TEC, 1990). Approximately 30 per cent of the 1988 minimum school-leaving age cohort continued into some form of further education (Cleveland County Council Careers Service, October 1988), reflecting an historically low staying-on rate in the North-East. It is both too early and very difficult to judge from educational statistics whether young people taking this 'career trajectory' are successful in avoiding unemployment, though we do know that only 8 per cent of 17-year-old leavers entered employment. Nearly two-thirds of leavers of this age, like the majority of 16-year-old leavers, entered YTS (Cleveland County Council Careers Service, October 1988).

The economic decline of Teesside over the past twenty years severely disrupted the movement of young people from school to work during the late 1980s. The basic figures and statistics reproduced in this section convey the collapse of work in the locality for young and old. Recent falls in the local overall unemployment rates seem *not* to have widened the opportunities for youth employment. Furthermore, aggregate declines in *national* unemployment rates disguise the continuing impact youth unemployment has on transitions in this *local* labour market.

Cleveland into the 1990s

Predictions of future prospects are, of course, notoriously unreliable and prognoses can vary quite markedly. Some official approaches have been keen to develop a positive image of the region to counter the rather dismal picture which the North-East still conjures up in many people's minds (particularly those from the South-East):

> The region's economic development agencies, the local author-
> ities, the urban development corporations, the media — the
> region's key institutions and personalities — now vigorously
> promote an image of a new 'Great North', a region under-
> going a remarkable 'renaissance.' (Robinson, 1990:4)

A brighter, more ambitious and dynamic image may, in turn, lead to greater inward investment and industrial relocation in the area, or so the argument goes. But Fred Robinson (1990:6) criticizes the 'Great North' campaigning which, he argues, uncritically promotes the region: 'The "hype" can be so positive that it omits to mention the region's high levels of unemployment, the fragility of the economy and the structural economic problems which the region must face in the future'. He argues that, although image building can be a positive step in itself, it also has its dangers: criticism, analysis and debate are stifled and seen as betraying the region and its interests; an unbalanced, narrow emphasis is placed on the most visible signs of economic rejuvenation (for instance, waterfront developments on the Tyne and in Hartlepool, the Gateshead Metro Centre, Wynyard Hall conference and leisure centre developments, the Gateshead Garden Festival) and less easily seen areas of deprivation (run down mining villages, housing estates depressed by unemployment and multiple social problems) are kept out of the glossy brochures promoting the North-East.

We would agree with most of what Robinson says of the North-East and its official, almost propagandist presentation by governmental and quasi-governmental agencies: much the same holds true for Teesside as a particular instance of the general case. Whilst Training Agency and TEC assessments of the Teesside economy tend to accentuate the positive and play down the negative, more independent, less flag-waving discussions of the Cleveland economy tend to draw attention to continuing difficulties. In the following section we attempt to weave our way through the wealth of official statistics and present what we feel to be a more balanced assessment of the Cleveland economy.

The unemployment count started to fall in 1986 and by April 1990 the numbers had fallen for forty-four consecutive months. In Cleveland the rate fell from 14.4 per cent in November 1988 to 11.2 per cent a year later; every travel-to-work area in the county experienced a decline in the unemployment rate with Middlesbrough and Hartlepool losing between one-fifth and one-quarter from their count of the unemployed. The fall in the numbers of people unemployed has also been paralleled by a growth in the numbers of employees in employment. Between June 1987 and June 1988, for instance, there was a 20,000 increase in the numbers of people in employment in the North-East.

The County Council's recent *Economic Strategy* (Cleveland County Council 1989) predicts primary sector employment will remain stable, manufacturing and construction will experience a slight upturn (though work in construction is unlikely to reach pre-recession levels), whilst the service sector is likely to continue to expand (especially if the locality has further success in attracting the relocation of government and company departments). Manufacturing in steel, chemicals and heavy engineering will continue to provide the economic backbone of the area, as rationalization programmes ease off. The Council predicts only minor and gradual employment losses in these industries (Cleveland County Council, 1989).

By the beginning of 1990 the days of massive job losses and large-scale redundancies seemed to be over. There is a more optimistic mood amongst employers (Teesside TEC, 1990) which is borne out, to some degree, by the sorts of labour market statistics we quote above. This new optimism is reflected in official assessments of the labour market and recently such publications have started to draw attention to emergent skill shortages on Teesside: a marked contrast to the previous decade in which the county was seen as an employers' market, promoting itself by high-lighting the large pool of skilled workers in the area.

Skill shortages have been compounded by the much publicized 'de-mographic timebomb' of falling numbers of 16-year-old school-leavers, predicted to fall by 28 per cent between 1988 and 1994 in the county. During the 1990s the numbers of people of working age in the county are predicted to fall by 24,000 (7 per cent) (Teesside TEC, 1990). This dramatic drop in the numbers of potential employees cannot, however, be accounted for simply by demographic changes: Cleveland still experi-ences considerable net out-migration (of approximately 4,000/5,000 annually). Those migrating from Teesside are often younger people with higher levels of skills and qualifications and, although this outflow of labour from the area can ease unemployment figures during times of recession, it can also contribute to skill shortages in more prosperous periods, particularly given the traditional lack of managerial and other non-manual workers in the county. It also increases the 'dependency ratio': the increasing number of retired people and those under 16 who are dependent upon the decreasing number of skilled, high earning workers.

A further dimension of the recovery, albeit partial as Robinson suggests, of the 'Great North' has been the apparently successful efforts (e.g. of the Northern Development Company) to attract inward invest-ment into the region from the overheated, overcrowded South of Eng-land, and particularly from overseas (Department of Employment, 1989a). The Nissan car plant is probably the most well known nationally, but other companies (e.g. Komatsu, Sanyo, Goldstar, Fujitsu) have also contributed to recent small rises in manufacturing employment in the North-East. As their names suggest, major contributors to this inward investment have been from South-East Asia, particularly Japan. With the onset of the Single European Market in 1992 many such companies are looking for a European foothold for their operations. Foreign-owned companies now account for 20 per cent of the region's manufacturing jobs (Robinson, 1990).

Together these demographic changes and upturns in the economic fortunes of the local labour market (reflecting economic improvements nationally) generally make happier reading for those concerned with Cleveland's future. The County Council, who tend to take a more re-served and balanced approach to economic forecasting than other local organizations, conclude that 'total employment is expected to rise steadily (1988–91) and job prospects are likely to improve'; they go on to say, however:

> employment rates will probably continue to lag behind national rates as a result of Cleveland's inherent industrial structure... Despite improvements, unemployment is likely to continue to fall slowly but is expected to persist at an unacceptably high level... it is unrealistic to predict any great improvements over the next few years. (Cleveland County Council, 1989:3, 4)

The economic recovery, then, is only partial and the renaissance of the North-East is some way from completion, as Robinson argues in convincing detail; he prefers the description 'stable survival' (Robinson, 1990). On a number of indicators and through a number of related, detailed arguments, the economic situation of Teesside into the 1990s, and of the North-East generally, can be shown to be a marked improvement on the previous decade, but still in a precarious and vulnerable position. Labour market statistics may not be 'damned lies', but they can be interpreted to tell quite different stories. We would suggest that the media propaganda of some developers, politicians and local personalities is perhaps more a reflection of hope, wishful thinking and bravado than in-depth, dispassionate and critical assessment of the available evidence.

Take, for example, the emphasis upon inward investment from overseas. Although the establishment of manufacturing plants from Japan, South Korea and Hong Kong have certainly helped keep up the level of jobs in this sector, overall they accounted for only 5,500 jobs in 1989 (Robinson, 1990). During the same period of this supposed influx of jobs from abroad the major overseas investor in the region, the United States of America, was withdrawing on a large scale. Employment in US firms dropped by 40 per cent, shedding over 15,000 jobs between 1978 and 1989. This, as Robinson notes, raises a serious question of commitment by overseas multinationals to the North-East. Cleveland previously suffered from being a Northern outpost of national firms based in the South of England; now, rather than a national outpost, it is a global outpost (Austrin and Beynon, 1979) with planning decisions affecting the lives of thousands of workers being taken in Tokyo and Detroit, rather than in London.

Equally serious questions are beginning to be asked of the dramatic falls in unemployment described by Department of Employment statistics. It is fair to say that unemployment quickly dropped down the agenda of issues of national, political concern (Coles and MacDonald, 1990), as the consistently improved figures were reported each month. Unemployment in the labour markets of the south is seen to be a thing of the past and of far more pressing importance (in these traditionally more prosperous areas and now, to some extent, in the North-East) are issues of skill shortage and retraining. However, we would follow Cleveland County Council in maintaining that unemployment is still a major issue, if not *the* major issue facing the locality (Cleveland County Council Research and Intelligence Unit, 1988a). Despite large drops in those counted as unemployed, in August 1990 the unemployment rate in the county was 12.8 per cent, still over twice the national average of 5.6 per cent. In badly hit areas, like Southbank in Middlesbrough, one in three males of working age were still officially unemployed. Cleveland enjoys the unenviable position of having the second highest level of unemployment of all the sixty-six counties in Great Britain (Cleveland County Council Economic Development and Planning Department, 1990d).

Still further questions can be asked of these alleged falls in unemployment. Recent reports (Robinson, 1990; The Labour Party, 1990) have seriously challenged the accuracy of Government-produced estimates of unemployment, and they call into question national policy and claims by Government to have solved the unemployment problem. We assess these arguments here because of their relevance to our present task: if it can be shown that unemployment has not been adequately described by official statistics, many of the more optimistic claims and predictions for the Cleveland economy need to be re-assessed.

The nub of the argument presented by Robinson and by the Labour Party is that systems of counting the unemployed and policies to help the unemployed (particularly Restart) have served to give a false impression of the true numbers of people out of work. Robinson's argument employs data from the North-East; for this reason we will develop our argument by drawing upon his argument and figures.

Robinson's first point is that only a small part of the decrease in unemployment can be accounted for by increases in people finding jobs; employment growth in the region has been very modest, around 40,000 since 1985 (31,000 employees and 9,000 self-employed) and does not come near to matching the large numbers which have been lost during this period (nearly 94,000). If we consider also that many of the people taking these jobs will not previously have been registered as unemployed (e.g. particularly married women not receiving benefit) and that many of these jobs are part-time (Department of Employment, 1989a), we begin to see a rather puzzling equation: a large drop in unemployment but only a relatively small rise in employment.

A major part of the lack of fit can be explained, according to Robinson, by the increasing impact of Government schemes. Between 1985 and 1988 the YTS and Community Programme grew by nearly 30,000 places in the Northern region: 'this growth obviously helps to reduce unemployment figures; indeed it has probably contributed as much to the fall in unemployment as has the increase in jobs' (Robinson, 1990:22).

A second point, more fully developed in the Labour Party report, also concerns the intervention of Government schemes, in this case, Restart. The report argues that the dramatic falls in unemployment coincided with the introduction of Restart in 1986. Restart is *officially designed* to help the long-term unemployed back into work by the provision of advice, information and counselling at six-monthly interviews. Lord Young, in his recent autobiography, describes how the Government, in the run-up to the general election of 1987, developed its unemployment strategy. He discusses candidly the 'hidden agenda' that lay behind Restart, which he describes as:

> the effect that the receipt of the letter and the invitation to attend the couselling session would have on some of the unemployed. My hunch was that there were quite a number of claimants who were either working and signing on or had just given up and were 'resting' on the register. My simple idea had been that merely the receipt of the letter would persuade some of those cheating that they had been found out. (1990:170–1)

He goes on to praise the results of early pilots of Restart and says:

> If a national scheme were operating we could expect roughly 23,000 extra to leave the register each month! That would be more than enough to completely reverse the whole direction of unemployment. I could scarcely contain myself; we had a strategy and it worked. (173)

That Restart was designed to reduce the unemployment count, rather than to help the unemployed, is a view that has long been held by many critics of Government schemes. To find confirmation of this in the autobiography of Restart's chief architect is perhaps surprising. Both Robinson and the Labour Party report develop their assessment of Restart and draw upon unpublished and complex government statistics to expose, what a Labour Party spokesperson is reported as calling, 'a massive fraud on the British public . . . one of the most elaborate conspiracies of the past ten years' (*The Guardian*, 8 June 1990). So what lay behind this alleged fraud? How is it supposed to have worked? If the unemployed have not gone into jobs, where have they all gone?

These critics of Restart point to the increasingly stringent availability-for-work tests whereby, for example, an unemployed claimant has to prove that he or she is actively looking for work every week. One of the less public aims of Restart (until Lord Young's autobiography was published) has been to police the unemployed and it is likely that *some* of those discontinuing their claims will have been making fraudulent claims. Others may not have met the criteria of the new tests because of, for instance, child-caring responsibilities which can limit the capacity to seek work actively and continually.

So where have these unemployed gone? Perhaps the most interesting and previously unreported effect (or misuse) of Restart has involved the switching of claimants to different types of benefit. The Labour Party report, drawing upon the Government's own statistics, argues that over half a million unemployed males disappeared from the count and did not reappear in the numbers of self-employed or employed. Many within this group of unemployed people, now classed as economically inactive, the report continues, have joined the ranks of those classed as long-term sick or disabled. The numbers receiving invalidity benefit increased by over half a million between 1983 and 1989 largely as a result of 'the ignorance of doctors and the eagerness of Jobcentres to get the unemployed classified as ill' (*The Guardian*, 12 January 1990, quoted in Robinson, 1990).

> The Government's rhetoric on unemployment fails to stand up to close scrutiny. On the one hand, claims that it is saving the taxpayer money by flushing out those who are not 'genuinely available for work' has been accompanied by a massive increase in those who now need to claim other forms of benefit. In its own words, it has simply replaced one form of dependency culture with another. (Labour Party, 1990:23)

A discussion paper produced by the Bank of England (1989), which both the Labour Party report and Robinson draw upon, estimates that from its introduction in 1986, Restart contributed to a fall in unemployment of approximately three-quarters of a million. If these reports are accurate, what faith can be placed in government claims that unemployment has been seriously tackled, never mind defeated or solved? If we put the hidden effects of Restart alongside the numerous other changes to counting procedures which have served to reduce the unemployment figures, are we not forced to conclude that government records of unemployment seriously underestimate the scale of the problem?[4] And if the numbers recorded as unemployed seriously underestimate the problem nationally, how much worse does this make the position of an unemployment blackspot like Teesside?

The problem of unemployment in Cleveland is not a thing of the past. The spectre of unemployment has not been banished but rather the full, gloomy picture of economic decline, as represented in monthly unemployment statistics, appears to have been hidden from public view by increasingly sophisticated methods of government accounting. Moreover, it would seem that some of the most recent predictions are pointing to a slowing down in the fall in unemployment and show that the direction of the underlying trend is once again turning upwards:[5] 'It appears that Cleveland is about to experience a resurgence of unemployment when the number of unemployed claimants has only just fallen significantly below 30,000' (Cleveland County Council Research and Intelligence Unit, 1990b:2).

So despite recent improvements in the national and local economy, which we accept have brought jobs for some of those previously out of work (Robinson suggests that in the North-East about one-third of the numbers knocked from the unemployment register refer to people getting jobs), Cleveland is still a long way from the full employment and economic recovery envisaged by some for the year 2000 (see Teesside TEC, 1990).

The narrow and vulnerable economic base of the locality and the increasing competitiveness of international markets continues to mean that the unhappy prospect of unemployment and decline still hangs over Middlesbrough and the towns of Cleveland; changes in the fortunes of the British Steel Corporation, and consequent closure, could, for instance, result in the direct and indirect loss of 14,500 jobs (Cleveland County Council Economic Development and Planning Department, 1983). Sadler reiterates the serious problem of over-reliance on investment in Cleveland's industrial triumvirate in order to secure future prosperity for the county:

> In this perhaps lies the strongest challenge to the locality's future, for the waves of investment within it have demonstrably been of shorter and shorter duration as the turnover time of fixed capital accelerated not just in individual plants but in the economy as a whole. Steel's central character in the locality lasted over 100 years, that of chemicals 50, but the offshore fabrication industry (though never in a position of such absolute dominance, highly significant relative to other industries locally) has been and (possibly) gone in less than 20 years. (1986:23)

The future shape and performance of the industries around Teesside are likely to be greatly affected by major economic developments in the early 1990s. Coming changes on the immediate economic horizon include the planned opening of the Channel Tunnel, the establishment of a Single European Market in 1992, and the widening of the European economy to include Eastern Bloc countries. These developments will emphasize the importance of British companies competing successfully in the European economy. How they affect the Cleveland economy awaits to be seen, but there are certainly local concerns that companies located in the North-East of England (just like those in Scotland and other 'peripheral' areas of the United Kingdom) will come under even greater pressure from international competitors. The area may become even more marginal to the centres of prosperity and business decision-making either in the South-East of England or towards the heart of a greatly expanded Europe (Cleveland County Council, 1989; Teesside, TEC 1990; Robinson, 1990). One strategy that has been pursued by those attempting to attract inward investment into Teesside has been to emphasize the large pool of relatively cheap, highly skilled, non-militant workers. In the near future it is likely that Cleveland's workers will face increased competition for jobs from workers in Eastern Europe, as multinationals intensify their global search for the most profitable sites for production.

Robinson and Gillespie, whilst acknowledging a slight upturn in the economic fortunes of the Northern region as a whole, also point to continuing grounds for pessimism about the future of economies like Cleveland's:

> there are current issues which currently pose threats to the region's economy, such as takeovers and mergers (Scottish and Newcastle, NEI); privatization (especially British Steel, British Coal) and further rationalizations of production (in chemicals, for example). The advent of the Single European Market will put further competitive pressures on the region's industries and stimulate takeover activity leading to cuts in capacity, while the Channel Tunnel could well add to the peripheralization of the North . . . The North's economy may well be off the 'danger list' but the convalescence is likely to be long. (1989:71)

Working Life on Teesside

Studies of the locality have emphasized the importance of moving beyond a simple rehearsal of the facts and figures of unemployment and economic decline to include analyses of the changing *nature* of work and work relationships (e.g. Hudson and Sadler, 1985). The major aim of our study is also to chart and understand *new* patterns of work in the enterprises and small businesses developed by young people in their early careers. Beynon *et al.* (1985) and Foord *et al.* (1985) stress the *casualization* of employment and work: how a culture previously constituted around employment with big firms from the 'cradle to the grave' has been replaced by one characterized by marginal, fractured ways of working. Beynon and his colleagues talk of a:

> deep, and perhaps fundamental, shift in the economy of the area, in local culture and in the general sensibilities of the place. A coherent local economy based on a combination of coal, steel,

chemicals, shipyards, and engineering ... is, today, being stretched to the limits. Teesside exemplifies the dimensions of these
changes in the most profound way. (1985:176)

Similarly, Foord *et al.* describe the changing culture of work in Cleveland
in the following way:

The avoidance of regulation and job protection in a labour market
characterized by high unemployment can be seen to mirror the
casualization of employment occurring on the periphery of the
formal sector through contract work and sub-contracting. The
formal and informal sectors should not be thought of in terms of
a stark contrast between black and white; rather the changing
security and conditions of work should be considered as con-
stituting a continuum. (1985:74–5)

The *Middlesbrough Locality Studies* (e.g. Beynon *et al.*, 1985) provide a
rich analysis of the decline of key industries on Teesside and the resultant
new working arrangements and practices. The strategies pursued by
British Steel Corporation, ICI and the newer offshore fabrication industry
in the face of increased economic pressure have provoked particularly
significant changes in working life on Teesside.

Within ICI there has been a concern to avoid enforced redundancies,
as a response to the problems of 'overmanning' and 'surplus' workforce
experienced by the company during the late 1970s and early '80s. ICI
has preferred, instead, a policy of 'resettlement', whereby, for example,
workers are encouraged to take early retirement, to establish small
businesses, to retrain or are helped to secure work on contracts overseas
(Beynon, Hudson and Sadler, 1986). The strategy of resettlement is,
itself, premised on a notion of retaining a minimum core of workers to
run the chemical plants, which is supplemented from time to time by
the hiring of marginal, sub-contracted maintenance workers (temporary,
casual staff working on contracts lasting from six weeks to six months).
This strategy was coupled with attempts in 1984 by ICI management to
make process workers take on the maintenance work usually undertaken
by skilled fitters (Beynon, Hudson and Sadler, 1986).

Sadler's study (1986) of the cultures of work in the offshore fabrication industry on Teesside tells a very similar story. Employment for
skilled men in the rig yards (which in many cases have taken over from
shipbuilding and related activities) is characterized by close supervision,
no career structure, intensive and hastened production conditions, the
sub-contracting out of great proportions of work, minimal or non-
existent industrial disputes and compliant unions and labour force. This
reworking of management–shop-floor relations has all been carried out in

the name of 'flexibility' with the background of high unemployment providing the necessary 'stick' to workers resistant to employers' 'carrots' (Sadler, 1986). The engineering of equipment for the offshore oil industry is at least as susceptible to the demands and quirks of international and national markets as ICI or BSC. Sadler argues that the price of oil on international markets has a clear, if indirect, impact on employment and working practices for workers in Teesside's remaining heavy engineering industry, and that the future of such work in the locality is very bleak: 'flexibility, both in and out of work, rules supreme. As does the price of oil' (1986:5).

Flexibility and new working arrangements in the chemical industry (Nichols and Beynon, 1977), as in the offshore fabrication industry, involve the overhauling or abandonment of long-held job demarcation guidelines in return for the continued employment of core workers. BSC, too, has not been slow to develop new patterns of work to their own advantage in Cleveland. Hudson and Sadler (1985) report several cases of newly redundant craftsmen previously employed at BSC's Hartlepool plant being re-hired as sub-contractors to do their previous work at much reduced rates of pay. The coming of unemployment, and the threat of further job losses, has provided the necessary climate for the introduction of changes in employment conditions:

> New working practices (effectively heightened management control over the labour process) and the increasing use of sub-contracting (effectively the creation of a marginalized group of occasional employees) have become rife in ICI, as in other chemical companies in the UK. These have been easier to introduce in the context of widespread capacity closures, and the threat of more — even a complete shutdown of the Wilton complex . . . it's difficult to argue when the alternative is redundancy. (Beynon, Hudson and Sadler, 1986:56)

Teesside has not historically been an area famous for militant labour opposition to attacks upon employment or working conditions (unlike Merseyside, for example). Rather, industrial harmony and consensus between capital and labour have characterized the heavy industries of the area: Hudson (1989) summarizes this situation with the local phrase 'what is good for ICI is good for Teesside'. Hudson and Sadler (1985:8) identify, in the early development of the iron and steel industry, 'an ideology accepted by both capital and labour which propounded a harmony of interests between them in the industry'.

Political and industrial quietism on behalf of the local trade union movement has helped shape current labour relations in the chemicals, iron and steel and engineering industries. Hudson comments:

As Mrs Thatcher pointed out in 1984, dockers on Teesside refused to join the national strike. She held this up as an example of how her policies were working in the North-East, but what it highlights is the compliant, non-militant traditions of trade unions on Teesside. It is this that makes the experience of the locality even more striking: if high investment and strike free industries still cannot guarantee employment, what can in a capitalist economy? (1986:13)

Beynon, Hudson and Sadler (1986) argue that the responses of ICI and BSC to increasing over-capacity of chemicals and steel on world markets have been different. ICI has been able to switch production around the globe in the continual search for profit, whereas BSC, by the fact of its national character, has been restricted to rationalization within Teesside and Britain. However, the effect of both strategies to ensure competitiveness has resulted in similar regimes of labour shedding and changes in working conditions and practices on Teesside:

> sub-contracting ultimately achieves the same objectives for capital . . . an accessible, cheap and disorganized labour force only too willing to respond to international competitive pressures within the steel industry by taking any kind of job on virtually any conditions which might emerge. Such arrangements lead easily to migratory habits in search of waged employment as some of those accustomed to steady jobs or those seeking their first job look outside the local economy. (Hudson and Sadler, 1985:44)

Moving away from Teesside to work, either daily, weekly or semi-permanently, is just as much part of the changing culture of employment in the locality as the new working practices and flexibility demanded of those workers who 'choose' to remain in this local labour market. The size of the population is declining in the North-East, particularly through demographic trends (e.g. the falling number of 16 to 19 year olds) and through net out-migration. Significantly, Cleveland's population fell by 3 per cent between 1981 and 1988, the second largest fall for any of the sixty-six counties in great Britain (second only to Merseyside, which contended with Cleveland for the title of worst unemployment county during this period) (Department of Employment, 1989b).

Summary

The purpose of this chapter has been to describe the historical and economic landscape through which young adults move in their efforts to make a living for themselves. We have shown how, in less than 150 years, Cleveland has changed from an economy glorious and thriving in its Victorian heyday, to an economy modern and shining with the 'white heat of technology' in the post-war period, to an economy which, in its recent past, has become infamous for the unemployment of its workers. We have tried to describe how this economic decline structures the opportunities faced by young people and in Chapter 5 we will show how unemployment frames attempts to develop new patterns of career in self-employment. Much of this has been in cold facts and figures; bare and lifeless measurements of the decline of an industrial town and area over nearly half a century.

Deep cultural changes, above all what has been called the casualization of work, have affected the working lives of people on Teesside. The nature of work has changed radically and swiftly to the point where short-term, temporary contracts, part-time work, migration and working away, 'fiddle' jobs, Government schemes and sub-contracted work now constitute a new way of working for many in Cleveland.

Recent economic improvements in Cleveland are precarious and it would be a brave (or foolish) person indeed who would predict the end of unemployment on Teesside. We have shown how unemployment statistics, apparently showing considerable recovery, need be interpreted very carefully: falling unemployment figures do not necessarily mean that more of the unemployed are getting jobs. Inward investment from overseas, whilst certainly bringing much needed jobs in the short-term, also brings worries about the long-term commitment of such employers to the North-East. Are such plants to become 'dispensable global outposts of multinational companies'? (Robinson, 1990:53). And, although local agencies have certainly begun to recognize the importance of economic diversification (Teesside TEC, 1990; Cleveland County Council, 1989), concern still needs to be expressed about the narrow base of local manufacturing employment. If it is true that 'what is good for ICI is good for Teesside' it must follow that what is bad for ICI is also bad for the area. The recently announced redundancy of 640 workers from the company's fertiliser plant at Billingham (*The Guardian*, 27 July 1990), following a slump in profits, can only dent further the belief that the large, indigenous chemical, steel and engineering companies can guarantee secure jobs for Teesside's workforce.

However, it is predicted by Teesside TEC (1990) that manufacturing employment will still be based on the big chemical and steel companies over the next decade. We have shown that these very companies were responsible for major decisions which proved disastrous for many of their workers and for Teesside as a whole. In the previous chapter we described the rise of the enterprise movement. It is perhaps worth noting at this point the irony that much of the Thatcher Government's drive towards enterprise has been phrased in opposition to the so-called dependency culture. It is clear from studies of state policy towards the region and its major industries (Hudson, 1989) that no-one has been more 'dependent' upon the state (e.g. upon government assistance through Regional Development Grants) than these giants of industry. Furthermore, it is, we think, rather specious and perverse to attack the unemployed for their dependency when their unemployment, it can be argued, is primarily a result of state mismanagement of the region. After all, had various governments not purposefully concentrated investment (and consequently employment) in a small number of industries on Teesside, then perhaps the area would have been better equipped to deal with the onslaught of (inter)national recession during the 1970s and '80s. Dependency upon employers (like ICI and BSC) was historically and officially encouraged in order to guarantee an adequate labour supply for these key industries (Hudson, 1989). The redundant workforce cannot be held responsible for industrial planning (resulting in massive unemployment and restructuring) pursued by their employers in tandem with national government during the post-war period (Board of Trade, 1963).

What will the last decade of the twentieth century hold for an economy like Cleveland's? Will it become a peripheral, post-industrial, twilight-zone at the edge of the old centre of a former empire, which is expected to shoulder the unequal burden of national economic decline? Or will the future see Cleveland born again from the ashes of industrial dereliction, rejuvenated by the government philosophy and policies for enterprise? Hudson argues that: ' "get on your bike", "form your own small firm", or "price yourself into a job" have become familiar themes in response to unemployment within the North-East' (1989:376).

Whilst we have noted the first response (in highlighting net out-migration from the county) and accept his third point, the second government response to local unemployment in the region forms the major focus of our study. If enterprise policies to encourage the development of small firms can succeed in Cleveland, then perhaps the future of the county will be brighter. In Chapter 2 we described the concept of enterprise and the rise of the enterprise movement nationally. In the next chapter we will turn our sights to enterprise policies and initiatives which have been developed by Teesside's own enterprise industry.

Notes

1   We must express our indebtedness to various researchers who have in the recent past undertaken detailed studies of Cleveland. We found the reports of Beynon, Sadler, Hudson, Lewis and Townsend (particularly *The Middlesbrough Locality Studies*) at the University of Durham and the work of Jo Foord, Fred Robinson and associates at Newcastle University especially valuable. We have drawn heavily upon these studies in writing this chapter: in

total they contain far more comprehensive and detailed commentary than we could hope to achieve in one chapter.

2　Nearly 100 years later, living conditions in Middlesbrough were still dominated by industry. Richard Hoggart, who worked in the town after the war, described it in the following way:

> In the late 1940s, it still had the air of having been thrown together for the benefit of industry: street after street of poor housing, a mean little centre, a dirty and smelly circulation of air, grey light above the chimney-pots; virtually no indication of a sense that people have a right to live with dignity and grace. (1990:76)

3　The recent closure by BSC of the Ravenscraig hot strip mill in Scotland, and the threatened closure of the whole plant, has renewed worries about the future of steel production, not only at that plant, but also in Teesside and the other BSC plants, especially as it has been reported that BSC are planning to expand overseas (*The Guardian*, 12 June 1990).

4　Cleveland County Council, using information provided by the Unemployment Unit, report that there has been a total of twenty-nine changes made to the method of counting the number of unemployed people in the United Kingdom in the past ten years (Cleveland County Council Economic Development and Planning Department, 1990a), and that all but one of these has served to lower the number of registered unemployed. They conclude that:

> Changes in benefit rules and the method of counting have resulted in many adults being removed from the count without any apparent change in their circumstances ... unemployment in Cleveland has fallen steadily over the past four years. Part of this reduction, perhaps 4,000 claimants [out of a fall of 27,000], can be attributed to changing definitions. (p. 4)

They add that the remainder did not necessarily find employment — this is only one possibility. Others include the increasing use of Government schemes and self-employment.

5　The numbers out of work and claiming benefit showed their biggest jump in six years in July 1990 and a recent report suggests that key economic indicators show the UK economy 'teetering on the brink of stagflation' (*The Guardian*, 20 July 1990).

Chapter 4

Cleveland's Enterprise Industry

The story told in this chapter is a remarkable one, whereby a community *in extremis* faced with the collapse of opportunities for old, middle-aged and young alike came together to forge a new identity and future for itself. With financial assistance from the Manpower Services Commission (as the Training Agency was then called), a network of community leaders was formed by the Church of England which had been actively involved through such groups as 'Church Action with the Unemployed'. The main participants were representatives from the voluntary services, the main local authority departments like Education, Social Services and Planning, local companies (who seconded staff), trade unions and individual volunteers.

A major incentive to such an extensive programme of self-help was the policy of central government which, during the same period, cut and cut again regional aid and capped the expenditure of local authorities. The message from London was summed up by the Prime Minister who, on a visit to the North-East in 1986, advised inhabitants of the region to stop complaining like 'moaning minnies'.

In this chapter we begin by describing national policies for regenerating the inner cities as they affected Teesside. Local leaders soon felt these were not sufficient to tackle the highest levels of unemployment in Britain and so increasingly they decided to take matters into their own hands by creating a number of initiatives. The consequent rise (and partial fall) of the enterprise industry in Cleveland is then traced and three competing models of enterprise are outlined. The interviews with thirty professionals specializing in the area and our survey of all the relevant enterprise agencies in the county are then discussed. We also briefly introduce the three main agencies through which we found most of our sample and explain the methodological problems we began to encounter. Finally, we examine how the plan to establish a national network of TECs is being implemented in Teesside.

National Policy: Regenerating the Inner Cities

At the forefront of the Government's drive to regenerate the inner cities are the Urban Development Corporations (UDCs) which were given powers to reclaim and assemble land for development and to use public funds to attract private investment. The first two UDCs were established in 1981 in the London and Merseyside docklands but, although they had been operating for some six years, the Department of the Environment 'did not specifically analyze their achievement and difficulties to identify any wider lessons before further UDCs were established in 1987' (National Audit Office, 1988b:5).

The UDCs in Teesside and Tyne and Wear were part of the second batch announced in 1987. But the original premise on which UDCs were based, that the local authorities were inadequate to deal with the complex problem of regeneration, naturally provoked opposition from local authorities who in their turn believed that 'UDCs are undemocratic because they are neither elected by nor accountable to local communities' (NAO, 1986:6). By the end of 1988–89 'cumulative spending on UDCs had exceeded £1 billion' (NAO, 1990:23), and the Corporation in Teesside currently has a budget of over £200 million. Its remit extends over 12,000 acres or almost nineteen square miles, by far the largest geographical area of any of the UDCs, and its objective is to secure the regeneration of this area:

> For this purpose the Corporation may acquire, hold, manage, reclaim and dispose of land, carry out buildings and other operations, provide services, roads and other infrastructure and carry on any other business necessary to achieve development. (Teesside Development Corporation, *Annual Report*, 1990:16)

These are sweeping powers in anyone's book.

The main schemes announced by the Teesside UDC include the following: clearing and preparing a 250 acre 'flagship site' for development at Teesdale (it has been called Teesdale but it is neither in nor near Teesdale which is much further up river); a European chemical centre on Teesside; the construction of a major leisure and shopping complex on the site of the former Stockton racecourse; and a £150 million project to build a marina in Hartlepool (which has been named 'Hartlepool Renaissance') which will come complete with 450 berths for leisure craft, 1,500 new homes, a hoe (as in Plymouth) and a piazza (as in Palermo). Such a development may well encourage tourism, but the question asked by McKie, Llewellyn and Pippin (1989:2) is whether it may 'exclude sections of the local community who have used this facility for many years and who can simply not afford to participate in up-market leisure activities'.

But their more serious criticism is that it is not 'the content of development projects which is contentious (e.g. certain TDC projects were originally reviewed by local authorities) but the mode of delivering a massive public subsidy to private industry' (McKie, Llewellyn and Pippin, 1989:7).

In addition to the UDC, Cleveland also has other local arrangements to coordinate the implementation of various national programmes from four different government departments, all concerned with regenerating the inner cities. These are: a City Action Team (an inter-departmental team to coordinate different programmes), two Inner City Task Forces (small scale, temporary organizations to deal with specific problems) and a Britannia Enterprise Zone (financial incentives offered to firms who relocate their business within its boundaries), as well as a City Technology College, a Compact (between schools and employers who commit themselves to providing jobs with training for young people who leave inner city schools having achieved preset targets) and two Rural Development Areas.

Let us examine the implementation of two of these projects in more detail. Riverside Park, the old Ironmasters district of Middlesbrough, was designated an Enterprise Zone in 1983. Those industries which relocated themselves within the Zone were attracted by the offer of ten years non-payment of rates, tax concessions and simplified planning procedures. But as Foord *et al.* (1985) argue, one effect has been to distort the local market for industrial land, causing many local firms to move short distances to take advantage of these benefits. They suggest that there has been no great influx of new companies or of jobs into the Middlesbrough area as a result of the Enterprise Zone.

The Macmillan City Technology College, named after Lord Stockton, opened in September 1989. It is located on the site of a school in Middlesbrough which was closed by the Cleveland Education Authority as part of the reorganization of secondary schools caused by falling numbers. City Technology Colleges (CTCs) are part of the Government's strategy to regenerate the inner cities and, when announced by Kenneth Baker (then Secretary of State for Education) at the Conservative Party Conference in 1986, it was claimed that this new concept in state secondary schools would be financed 'wholly or substantially' by business and industry, with government paying the running costs. Since then, the plans for fifteen CTCs have been accepted by the DES and four have already opened, one of which is Macmillan College. Its principal sponsors are British and American Tobacco Industries who contributed £1.4 million to the capital costs. The Exchequer's contribution, however, so far amounts to £5.6 million (written answer by John MacGregor, to Parliamentary question February 1990). In the same year, 1989, the total allocation to Cleveland County Council from the DES for capital expenditure was £3.5 million; this sum had to cover 150 nursery units and schools, 209 primary schools, 46 secondary schools, 9 sixth form colleges, 16 special schools, 29 special units and 6 colleges of further education.

One of the major outcomes of this bulky and untidy package of policy measures has been, in our view, to transfer the control and re-sourcing of economic development from the local authority to national government departments and quangos working in conjunction with private industry. The National Audit Office, after examining all the main programmes for regenerating the inner cities, concluded that there were two important sources of friction between central and local government. These were:

> local authorities believe that their role is under-valued by central government. They see themselves as increasingly marginalized ... [and] government support programmes are seen as a patch-work quilt of complexity and idiosyncrasy. They baffle local authorities and business alike. The rules of the game seem over-complex and some times capricious. They encourage compart-mentalized policy approaches rather than a coherent strategy. (NAO, 1990:33)

The Local Authority Response

Cleveland County Council has itself developed two major interlinked programmes aimed at local economic regeneration and the amelioration of unemployment: The *Unemployment Strategy* and the *Economic Strategy*. The *Unemployment Strategy* has three main themes: to address the needs of the unemployed individual more closely; to develop community action areas to encourage community development in areas of high unemploy-ment; and to improve the communication between the council and the unemployed in order to target schemes and measures more effectively (Cleveland County Council, 1987).

The *Economic Strategy* also has three main objectives or programmes. First, it is designed to encourage new enterprises, inward investment, local businesses, technology and development opportunities. Second, it is concerned to improve the training and retraining facilities within the county for individuals and local and incoming industries. Third, the strategy is aimed at improving the physical infrastructure, communica-tions and environment of the county so as to improve the commercial attractiveness of Cleveland (Cleveland County Council, 1989). The Council developed these county-wide initiatives whilst its budget was being steadily reduced by central government, which was simultaneously funding its own projects like the UDCs discussed above, outside of local authority control.

The Council claims, through a variety of schemes, to have supported or created 5,000 jobs within the county (Cleveland County Council 1989:33). The *Unemployment Strategy* included the following succinct point: 'the basic solution to the majority of the problems facing unemployed people would be the provision of permanent full-time work at an adequate rate of pay' (Cleveland County Council, 1987:6).

This may sound all too obvious a point, but unfortunately it seems to be a response which has evaded much of national policy formulation and delivery. Instead, Cleveland has become a critical site for the development and testing of the Thatcher Government's culture of enterprise. The same Council document that we quote above rehearses some of the thinking underlying the ideology of enterprise, and it does so with specific reference to Cleveland:

> One of the central issues for the unemployed, and more generally for the people of Cleveland, is dependency upon a narrow economic base and a few, large firms. This has long been an aspect of Cleveland's vulnerability. For the unemployed, already victims of this economic dependency, new aspects of social and economic dependency operate, involving the government, through social security and the MSC, and local government, through local services and concessions. This leads to a sense of powerlessness and helplessness. (Cleveland County Council, 1987:4)[1]

The Council's *Economic Strategy* recognizes the 'need to diversify the economy, to get away from the over-reliance on ICI, BSC and other major companies' (Cleveland County Council, 1989:13), and the need to develop enterprise as part of Cleveland's economic regeneration. It also recognizes, however, that many new businesses fail and that fewer than 1 per cent go on to employ over 100 people. Consequently the document details a number of activities to promote its enterprise strategy. These include: the promotion of self-employment and all types of new firm formation (including non-traditional, new ventures in co-operatives and community businesses); the provision of start-up grants, enterprise workshops and premises, and advice and assistance toward new business development.

Together these proposed activities reflect an understanding that at least part of the economic strategy of the county must be aimed at reducing the reliance on branch plants, where there is next to no local decision-making:

> Cleveland's major national and transnational firms are controlled from outside of the region. Local plants are only part of overall company operations. As a consequence, significant parts of the

74

Cleveland workforce are accustomed to operating in a large employer environment, divorced from central decision-making processes. This coupled with the perception that the organizational structure of large-scale industry can suppress individual enterprise, is often cited as an explanation for the traditionally low level of entrepreneurship and small firm formation in Cleveland. (Cleveland County Council, 1989:1).

Cleveland's industrial history and image, its lack of a motorway link and geographical distance from prosperous and developing South-East and European markets are considerable obstacles to major inward investment and industrial relocation in the area. The *Economic Strategy* stresses the importance of encouraging small, indigenous enterprises and predicts that: 'the number of people self-employed is expected to increase as the "enterprise culture" is further developed' (Cleveland County Council, 1989:4).

Despite increases in Northern self-employment between 1983 and 1986, the Northern region as a whole had, along with East Anglia, the lowest regional level of self-employment in the country (The Trade Union Studies Information Unit, 1987). TUSIU points out that the North also experienced the second worst net growth of businesses of all regions of Great Britain between 1980 and 1985. There were nearly as many business deregistrations as registrations during this period: 'This would seem to indicate that in the North many people are so desperate to leave the dole queue that they are forming small businesses that are incapable of competing and thriving' (TUSIU, 1987). The level of self-employment in Cleveland has traditionally been low with entrepreneurship and small business development very marginal aspects of local economic activity. A North of England County Councils Association (NECCA) report concluded in 1986 that:

> The North has fewer small firms and a smaller percentage of people in self-employment than any other region. With the emphasis of national policy on encouraging small firms and self-employment, the North is at a considerable disadvantage in being able to respond to any recovery in the national economy. (NECCA, 1986:3)

A recent study of self-employment as an option for Cleveland's unemployed (Cleveland County Council Research and Intelligence Unit, 1987c) generated several pertinent facts and conclusions. The survey was based on interviews with 1,636 unemployed people in the county in 1985 and probably constitutes the largest scale investigation of unemployment in Cleveland to date. Seven per cent (115) of the unemployed had been self-employed at some time, and of these sixty-two people had been self-employed during the 1980s. The report links the developments of these businesses with economic recession, and forty-nine businesses (out of the 115) had lasted for one year or less. In all, the survey found that 29 per cent of the unemployed were seriously interested in self-employment and, extrapolating from this percentage, that there were perhaps 16,000 potential small businessmen (and, we would add, women) among the unemployed locally. In Cleveland there were 12,600 self-employed people in 1984 (Cleveland County Council Economic Development and Planning Department, 1986a). However, only 18 per cent of the sample thought that self-employment was a real option for them; the main problems were identified as lack of capital, lack of knowledge of existing opportunities and few business ideas. Those respondents in the 25 to 44 age bracket were most likely to see self-employment as a real possibility. The reasons given for ceasing trading, by those who had previously been in business, could generally be traced back to the apparent shortage of markets for enterprises. The report notes: 'This indicates that many attempts at self-employment, as currently undertaken by unemployed people, are likely to fail, perhaps more in the Cleveland area than in other areas of the country' (Cleveland County Council Research and Intelligence Unit, 1987c:5). It concluded:

> The view adopted is that self-employment has only a limited contribution to make to reducing the numbers unemployed but the benefits, broadly defined, to the individual of having tried the option may be large even if the attempt fails ... although others may experience a demoralizing effect. (*op. cit.*:1)

Two relatively recent reports on the state of the Cleveland economy confirm the problems associated with developing self-employment in areas of economic decline:

> Setting up a new small business is hazardous and often leads to failure, especially in an area like Teesside. The 'enterprise culture' of self-employment which Ministers talk of can hardly be expected to develop in an area which big business and nationalised industries are abandoning. (Foord *et al.*, 1986/7:45)

> In the county of Cleveland ... it took fifteen years for 2,000 jobs to be created by small manufacturing businesses in the 1960s and 1970s; then, on one day in 1980, British Steel closed a factory employing 3,000 people. Small firms will need a good deal of jollying along if they are to replace traditional sources of employment. (*The Economist*, 13 December 1986)

A Local Enterprise Policy for Youth (LEPY)

This was the broad political picture within which community leaders watched the steady rise of job losses. There was mounting evidence that the impact of unemployment was particularly severe on young people. Out of a total population in Cleveland of 560,000 in 1987, more than 52,000 were registered as unemployed and around 21,000 of these were between the ages of 16 and 25.

The economic crisis, which we detailed in full in Chapter 3, brought together a remarkable collection of individuals and organizations under the leadership of Canon Bill Wright from the Teesside Industrial Mission. In his opinion, youth enterprise was invented in Cleveland and the model consists of three parts: teach enterprise early, before the age of 11 in primary schools; keep the momentum going after school during the Youth Training Scheme or Further Education; and develop it seriously during the ages 18 to 25 into micro-businesses in cheap units with high quality support. As he himself expressed it, 'Youth unemployment was already 15 years old in Cleveland when, in June 1979, I started working with sixth formers... and four directors of Teesside Small Business Club, looking at self-employment options' (Wright, 1986:1).

By 1983, there were seven organizations specializing in *youth* self-employment which were linked into an informal and voluntary forum with eleven *adult* self-employment agencies. With funding from the MSC under the Community Programme, three self-employment advisers were appointed to work with potential young entrepreneurs over the age of 16 and, by 1986, no less than thirty-seven organizations were specializing in this area.

The enterprise industry continued to mushroom and it was decided to hold a conference in May 1987 to try to hammer out a common policy for youth enterprise in Cleveland among all the interested parties, which by then numbered forty-five. From the minutes of that conference it is clear that competition among existing support groups had already become unhelpful and steps needed to be taken to 'make it easier for young clients to find their way through the maze' (Minutes of Youth Enterprise in Cleveland Conference, May 1987:1). As a result a progression chart 2 was produced (Figure 4.1) but it remains a moot point whether its users were thereby aided in their journey. What the chart 2 does illuminate, however, is that jobs were created for a whole new tier of bureaucrats, administrators and trainers through the spectacular growth of the enterprise industry.

The second conference, held in July 1988, attracted over eighty participants including a local MP and representatives from over fifty organizations, as well as one of the authors (FC). A part-time Youth Enterprise Liaison Officer had in the meantime been appointed to 'operate across the whole "Youth" age range (6 to 26)' (Minutes of LEPY

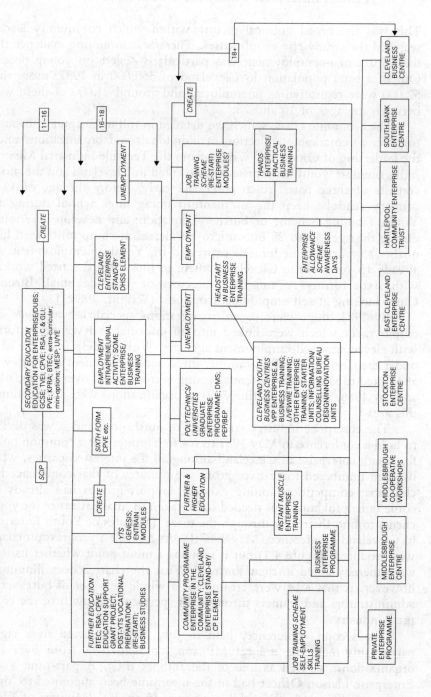

Figure 4.1   Enterprise Creation Progression Chart

Conference, 1988:1) and a Directory of over ninety local contacts for Youth Enterprise in Cleveland (Community Enterprise Trust Limited, 1988), together with a handbook of resource materials sponsored by the British Steel Corporation and entitled *Going for Enterprise* (Harrison, 1988b), had been published and were distributed to conference members.

The organizers of the Conference made clear their disappointment about the absence in 1988, as in 1987, of anyone under 25; discussions tended to be *about* young adults rather than *with* them. One speaker thought that enterprise should be presented to young people not so much as advice to 'get on your bike' but as detailed help 'to *build* your own bike.' Another contributor, a Cleveland teacher seconded to British Steel to coordinate enterprise education, was of the view that: 'it had become apparent that one of the factors holding up economic regeneration in the North-East was the need for no less than a cultural change among young people' (Harrison, 1986a:1). The aim of both conferences was to produce a Local Enterprise Policy for Youth (LEPY) and to give the agencies in Cleveland an opportunity to get together and exchange information. The latter aim was certainly achieved but participants representing so many competing interests found it difficult to get beyond the production of lists of agreed action plans and questions to be addressed.

Such extraordinarily speedy growth would have been difficult to sustain and, indeed, the pace began to slow shortly after our project began work in October 1988, with a number of rationalizations, mergers and closures. In its precipitous growth and even more sudden contraction, the enterprise industry followed the pattern set by local industry more generally.

The fifty organizations involved in youth enterprise ranged from local branches of national projects such as Business in the Community or the Industrial Society to more home grown initiatives like 'Pippatunities' (providing 'open learning facilities primarily for business and book keeping'), or Synergy ('an enterprise training agency consultancy providing staff training for Youth Enterprise Intermediaries'). To give a flavour of some of the advice begin offered, an article produced by one of these agencies, and published in the *Education for Enterprise Network* in 1988, described the task of 'facilitating enterprise' as follows:

> The three E's of enterprise facilitation are: Energetics, Energy-savers, Environment. Energetics include enthusiasm, encouragement, enjoyment, empathy . . . A list of energy-savers might include ideas generation methods, time planning techniques, action checklists, directories, simulations, and so on. Together, these energy-savers make up the facilitator's 'trick bag' to be used as tools when appropriate and relevant . . . Environment means creating an environment which allows freedom but which also has constraints and limits.

If alliteration alone could activate an area, then Teesside would have taken off some time ago.

Three Models of Enterprise

We soon felt a growing need to impose some order upon these myriad organizations, agencies and schemes, all specializing in youth enterprise. Teresa Rees (1986) has attempted to bring some sense to the different kinds of alternative employment projects, which stretch right across the whole ideological spectrum, with the following typology:

> self employment, small businesses run by young capitalist entre-
> preneurs; worker co-operatives, competing in a capitalist eco-
> nomy but operating an egalitarian management structure; and
> community businesses, offering socially useful goods and services
> to those that need them, usually without making much of a
> profit. (1986:15)

Bill Law (1983) describes the various shades of enterprise projects by saying that they can be 'blue' (self-employment or mini-companies) or 'pink' (a profit-sharing co-operative) or 'green' (concerned with a community or environmental issue). Perhaps there are also some 'rainbow' enterprises which adopt a mixed approach, combining profit-making and community involvement. But the studies which have been done in this country show that 'the majority of people who describe themselves as self-employed do not have any employees at all — not even a part-time assistant' (Hakim, 1988:429). The emphasis in most courses on enterprise remains firmly on the setting up of small businesses; alternative approaches, although sometimes alluded to in the introduction, are from then on quietly forgotten (e.g. Johnson *et al.*, 1987).

Others, however, like Dave Turner, the author of *The Enterprise Factor: Community Enterprise in the Curriculum* (1989), explicitly stress a wider range of commitments. This training package sets out to link the 'fields of community involvement and enterprise skill development' (p. 1) and employs a broad definition of the concept of enterprise which is 'relevant to all people, meaning a project, venture or undertaking' and 'aims at fostering a process of empowerment for participants which will provide skills and experiences that are relevant to the achievement of social economic and political goals' (p. 15). What may be termed the 'official' version of enterprise is, however, confined to the 'blue' corner, as can be seen from the video produced by the Training Commission on Enterprise Training in Employment Training, which defines Enterprise Training as 'training in how to start a new business, to develop that business and, of course, to make it a success'.

Instead of placing the enterprise agencies of Cleveland into discrete categories, we thought they were best portrayed as lying along a continuum. At one end, towards the right of the ideological spectrum, there were organizations in which enterprise had become interpreted as self–employment (even if their original aims embraced a broader philosophy of enterprise). These agencies offered advice, counselling, training towards business start-up and workshop space. Towards the left of the continuum could be found important, but far fewer, agencies offering advice, counselling and funding towards co-operative and community-based projects. We decided to focus our attention upon young adults involved with:

(a) enterprise as self-employment in small business;
(b) enterprise as co-operative work;
(c) enterprise as community development projects.

The balance of informants in these three categories within our sample (see Table 1.1) is a reflection of the quantity and significance of each of these interpretations of enterprise within the local economy.

Let us give an example of each of the three main types of enterprise by describing, with the use of pseudonyms, the work of one representative or leading organization of each type; we have chosen the three agencies through which we found our first informants. First, Teesside Young Entrepreneurs (TYE) was established in 1986 'to provide practical support, guidance and encouragement to young people under the age of 26 who have a desire to become self-employed or to set up their own small business'. Their headquarters contained nineteen subsidized work units, occupied on an 'easy in, easy out' licence and also provided secretarial, graphic design and photocopying services. TYE also ran a range of 'free business skills courses for young people, ranging from two days to eight weeks covering all aspects of business training. Business counselling is also offered to any young person interested in creating their own business'. Clients were referred from Job Clubs, from Restart interviews, from Enterprise Awareness Days or they simply walked in off the street.

TYE was funded on a short-term basis, by annual renewable contracts. The precariousness of their position and the complexity of their funding were features identified in other enterprise organizations in Cleveland and are obvious from an examination of their accounts in any one year. In 1987–88, for example, out of a total budget of £640,000, £614,000 (or 96 per cent) came from the public sector (Department of Environment — Urban Programme; Department of Employment — Local Enterprise Agency; Manpower Services Commission — Community Programme, Voluntary Projects Programme and Adult Training Division; Department of Trade and Industry — Task Forces and Business Improvement Scheme Grants; and Cleveland County Council). Only

£26,000 (or 4 per cent) came from four firms in the private sector, although the bigger companies in the area tended to second either bright young managers eager for new experiences or perhaps superfluous middle-aged managers for short periods of, say, two years rather than provide direct financial support.

All these grants had to be applied for, argued over and secured annually; and there was constant pressure from government departments to increase the level of revenue support from the private sector. But local firms soon became tired of the enterprise industry 'constantly holding out a begging bowl', as it was described to us. At its height, TYE had a staff complement of twenty-four which was whittled down to twelve after a traumatic merger. The local press carried the headline: 'Job Creation Agency Sacks Half its Staff'. TYE has been visited by both Mrs Thatcher and Kenneth Baker.

At the other end of the political spectrum, the North-East Co-operative Development Agency (NECDA) was set up by the County Council in 1982 to develop not only self-sustaining, individual co-operatives but a local network of support for co-operative ventures which would pursue social as well as commercial aims. For instance, NECDA offered practical help, information and advice to groups of neighbours, residents or unemployed youth who had come together to provide goods and services for their local community; it was explained to such groups that they could remain in direct control of their co-operative through worker participation in decision-making at all levels. Because workers' co-operatives are owned and run by the members working in them, the promotional literature issued by NECDA claims that they possess three advantages over the conventionally organized small business — they have a better chance of success, they are more efficient and create greater job satisfaction.

But the remit of NECDA went beyond such practical advice to include work with socially disadvantaged groups, women's groups and educational meetings in schools and colleges.[3] A further development was the adoption of a more pro-active approach based on the concept of the 'co-operative entrepreneur':

> we came to the conclusion that we are more likely to produce successful worker co-operatives by basing them around sound market gaps and key individuals, than on the expectation that ready-made groups will walk through the door of Co-operative Development Agencies with ideas around which to build viable businesses. Hence our policy is to research local, regional, and national markets for market gaps. For each gap we will then recruit a 'co-operative entrepreneur', someone with the entre-preneurial flair necessary to mould a successful business, and the

social commitment to industrial democracy. (Moreton, 1988:25, quoted by McKie, Llewellyn, and Peppin, 1989:12)

Somewhere along the continuum and to the left of the two groups already described lie organizations like Problem Solvers which favour a broadly based concept of enterprise, which they define as:

about making things happen. It refers to the willingness and ability of people to be self-determining and flexible, influencing, shaping and taking control over their own lives in any sphere, be that social, personal, economic or political. (Problem Solvers promotional material, pp. 4–5)

It was based on a 'proven model of enterprise training', namely Dave Turner's (1989) Community Enterprise ideas which had been tried out in Southern Australia and which were discussed earlier in this chapter. Problem Solvers, after a pilot stage supported by local organizations, was finally funded in 1988 by the MSC for two years with an overall budget of £1,400,000. Fifty per cent of the participants were to be unemployed, while the other fifty were to come from school, college, YTS or Employment Training: 'the main objective is to provide a mobile and flexible pool of trainers and working capital to young people and unemployed people so they can design and manage "not for personal profit" projects in their community' (LEPY, Noticeboard No. 1, Summer 1988:2). Problem Solvers aimed its programme across four sectors: industry and commerce; the public sector; the voluntary sector; and education/training, 'in order to foster the development of an enterprise culture in Cleveland'. In Chapter 8 we provide further discussion of both co-operative and community enterprise ventures.

The Local Practice of Enterprise

Not only the three agencies we have described, but all the various organizations making up the enterprise industry, failed to co-exist in harmony and mutual respect; instead, they became tough, and at times, bitter rivals in the scramble for government backing. One supporter of the broader approach put it this way in an interview with us:

From day one enterprise was hijacked by certain interests, business studies and so forth, who promoted a narrow model of enterprise, something along the mini-companies model. There is nothing wrong with that but it is always linked to the language of private enterprise, shareholders, stocks, profits and so on. There is no language or image of the political or social action possible for youth.

Added to the competition among agencies over funding, which caused its own insecurities, were the doubts and reservations expressed by certain members of staff about the enterprise mission they were engaged in which, in turn, led to internal divisions, frustrations and tensions. One senior enterprise adviser thought, for example, that it would take over fifty years to break down the dependency culture of the North-East and that the expectations of certain other organizations were unrealistic and naive. Another interviewee argued that enterprise had simply become 'a fashionable buzzword which some people had become skilful at using to attract funds for pedalling youth enterprise'. The enterprise 'bonanza' (or 'El Dorado' as it was called by another informant, a leading local educationalist) was based on a 'collusion around the simple idea that enterprise could solve difficult and real problems'. Another of the professionals in the youth training field we spoke to was worried about 'the problem of saturation, of too many one-man businesses leading to increased competition, price wars, and new firms closing down. How many car valeting services does Cleveland need?'.

Re-reading, after a year, the thirty interviews held with a wide range of professionals (Careers Officers, local authority Education Advisers, enterprise counsellors, training officers and managers), we became increasingly sympathetic to the staff of these enterprise agencies who struggled to make sense of constant changes in policy initiatives and of the ideological jargon in which such initiatives were couched. They themselves were often on contracts lasting a year or less, they had limited job satisfaction and no job security, they learned to cope with frequent changes of staff, resignations, takeovers, redundancies, rationalizations and internal politicking. On the enterprise crusade, morale was low; but they worked hard in the interests of young people because they knew that the alternative for most of them was the dole. The cynicism of one specialist in the field is caught in these remarks: 'enterprise in Cleveland is a sort of empire building. Enterprise is a hologram, it's like the Emperor's New Clothes . . . everybody is doing something, people are researching it, there must be something there, musn't there?'

In trying to understand the aims, activities and achievements of the enterprise industry in the county, we also conducted a survey of the organizations offering training, advice and activities specifically aimed at 16 to 25 year olds. What impressed us first and foremost about the replies was the ubiquitous concern to reduce the high levels of local unemployment. For example, one enterprise centre wrote as follows: 'we lean over backwards to help people to start up regardless of our view of the viability of the business'. Another theme running through many of the responses was a fierce local pride coupled with a determination that the people of Cleveland should never again be so completely at the mercy of industrial giants who could decide their economic fate. So one organization argued that 'self-employment will provide the option to broaden our business base and protect Cleveland's economy in times of recession'. All of the three models of enterprise were in evidence, from those whose 'prime interpretation of enterprise is self-employment' to those stressing co-operatives or 'the acquisition of the skills and confidence from which people may become empowered to effect the necessary initiatives... through a process of community development'. Although numbers were small, the majority were clearly supporting the narrower definition of enterprise as self-employment in small business.

When asked about their total number of clients and the number of clients per year, only one organization appeared to keep detailed and accurate records, while others provided much more ambiguous or vague answers (e.g. 'several thousand') or claimed not to know. Taken at face value, in all some 9,000 young clients were claimed to have been advised, but we could not arrive at a firm figure for the number of jobs created because so many organizations evaded the question. Whether some of the agencies were counting the very same clients is an issue we shall turn to in a moment. But what was of immediate interest was that the clear majority of these organizations had been established after 1979. What also emerges from their responses is a deep concern for their own future viability. Too many were almost totally reliant on public funding and changes in training programmes for the unemployed (say, from the Community Programme to Employment Training), thrust them into competition with each other. In addition, each change in policy resulted in new application forms, new regulations and new targets to meet.

Following this survey and interviews with professionals in the area, we targeted the three agencies which were commonly considered to be the market leaders in the promotion of the three different versions of enterprise (and which we described earlier). So far, so good; but our progress soon became impeded by a number of methodological problems.

Difficulties Encountered

Initially, we intended to focus upon 16 to 19 year olds. We very quickly realized from observations and discussions in the field that, if we maintained that narrow age focus, we would have, to quote one interviewee, 'a very quick and very short study'. In short, numbers in this age range who were involved with enterprise would be minimal. We extended the age range from 16 to 25 in order to allow us a reasonable size of sample. Additionally, the 25-year age point is one often used as a cut-off point for enterprise organizations dealing with youth enterprise (e.g. The Prince's Youth Business Trust). On a more theoretical level, we would argue that studies of youth transitions often terminate too early, at the age of 19 (see Chapter 10). So when we talk about youth, young people or young adults in this book, we mean 16 to 25 year olds.

Young businessmen and women, we were discovering, do not constitute a conveniently captive audience who are easy to contact, count and interview. Instead, we had to penetrate and comprehend the competing and rather vague claims of the enterprise agencies and move beyond them to interview people. Our progress was blocked at first by an understandable but frustrating concern of most of the agencies about the confidentiality of their clients' records. Whilst one agency would quickly and happily produce names, addresses and phone numbers of their clients, others maintained a strict embargo upon the release of such information, although we developed a strategy to circumvent this problem.[4] Even after 'giving the green light' to our research and giving the promise of access to dozens of potential informants, one critical organization hesitated for eight months (out of a fifteen-month research project) before providing basic information and a handful of potential contacts.

This problem of confidentiality was compounded by another (see Coles and MacDonald, 1990, for a fuller discussion of this point). Often it seemed that the agencies we surveyed and fostered for research purposes made quite exaggerated claims for their success in promoting the enterprise culture. Hundreds, sometimes thousands, of successful young entrepreneurs were at times alleged to have benefited from the services of some agencies. On closer inspection (when asked, for example, to 'name names') these figures often dwindled, like snow in springtime.

Two further difficulties underlie, and help to explain this. One concerns 'multiple auditing', whereby a particular young entrepreneur might be counted as a success by a number of different agencies even if their contact with the 'success story' was minimal. But why should enterprise agencies wish to over-estimate their figures?

Part of the answer, in our view, can be located in the competitive funding arrangements underpinning the growth of the enterprise industry in Cleveland. MSC/Training Agency contracts often constitute the prime source of at least initial revenue for the majority of initiatives and, critically, of the jobs of most of those working within the organizations. During 1989 we witnessed many who were employed at a variety of levels of the enterprise industry (from front-line adviser to top level management) leave as contracts came to an end and mergers and rationalization took place. For us it meant renegotiating access three times in eight months with different managers of the same organization; for them it meant losing a job. Initial multi-million pound budgets ran out and the professionals, whose task it was to introduce young adults to self-employment, were, themselves, in short-term, insecure employment. Working under such conditions, it is no surprise that tensions within particular organizations often ran high and, on occasions, a particular agency would be rocked by, for instance, the simultaneous resignation of four founder members and directors or by threats from the Training Agency or a local MP to close it down. The future of their own jobs, and the future of enterprise in Cleveland, came to depend upon renewing original sources of income, and securing fresh ones, for example, through grants for Employment Training (ET), a programme with quite different aims and objectives from some of its predecessors.

Agencies in fierce competition for contracts found themselves in the unenviable position of apparently having to claim that they had advised an ever increasing number of clients, been responsible for ever more business start ups, and that the survival rate of, and the jobs created by, these businesses had continued to climb inexorably. Applications to official funding bodies swam in self-justifying superlatives; but such a fibre-free diet is, sooner or later, bad for the health because the reports from the practitioners were becoming steadily more remote from reality. The bonanza, which came to rely too heavily on paper figures and paper achievements, could not stand much critical scrutiny and, when it came, many of the advisers and specialists in enterprise found themselves in the same boat as their clients, namely, unemployed. At the time of writing in September 1990, some of the key organizations have either disappeared from the scene, or have been merged with similar agencies, or have added to their focus on youth enterprise an interests in business start up, business relocation and business expansion more generally.

From Policy to Practice: the Local TEC

We shall return to a more detailed consideration of future prospects for the local enterprise industry in Chapter 10, but for the present a major new player has joined the already crowded stage and will play a leading role in determining the next act — the Teesside Training and Enterprise Council (TEC). The establishment of a national network of TECs was described in Chapter 2 and we can now briefly examine how policy is being implemented in one locality — Teesside. It was one of the first ten TECs to become fully operational, on 30 April 1990, following the successful submission of its Corporate and Business Plan. Its mission statement (now a compulsory item in all such official documents) announces a commitment 'to provide training, education and development programmes [notice, *not* employment] which will encourage an enterprising culture' (Teesside TEC, 1990:5).

The same message is transmitted in the list of strategic aims, the first of which is to 'create a training and enterprise environment across Teesside' and the second to 'improve the links between education and employment' (*op. cit.*:7). Considering that all TECs will depend on the quality of education in local schools as far as each new wave of workers is concerned, it is appropriate that both the County Education Officer and the Chairman of the Education Committee are both members of the Board of the Teesside TEC.

Like all other Councils, two-thirds of the Board must be leading local employers from the private sector. Senior executives from the county's major companies (e.g. ICI, British Steel and Tioxide) have joined the employers group on the Board together with representatives from medium-sized heavy engineering, construction and high-tech firms as well as local managers from a national bank, a major accountancy firm and the Port Authority.

The five Board Members selected to represent fields outside of private industry include the President of the local Chamber of Commerce and the Chief Executives of the Teesside Development Corporation and of the TEC itself, who was formerly the local area manager of the Training Agency. The remaining two places have been given to a trade unionist and a representative of the voluntary sector, who is the only woman on the Board. The TEC's development plan claimed that the composition of the Board would represent 'a spectrum of interest which covers the total community' (Teesside TEC, 1989:4). One of the main ways in which the TEC will be judged is whether it becomes 'a credible community institution; an organization that is forward-looking, open and accessible to its diverse constituencies' (Stratton, 1990:72). Preliminary indications are encouraging because the chief executive of the organization *Teesside Tomorrow*, which prepared the bid for the TEC, is on record as recognizing that 'special attention needs to be paid to how the involvement of the community can be handled and delivered' (Coldwell, 1990:76).

It is also widely acknowledged within the county that the employers on the TEC are a high powered and respected group of leading businessmen who *could* become the agents of change. The first objective of the government's plan — to attract the right calibre and level of chief executive or managing director — has therefore been achieved. Now the testing time starts: will they remain on the Board if funding by central government continues to be cut and if their powers to stimulate economic growth remain limited? The total budget for the Teesside TEC in 1989/90 is £42 million, most of which is taken up with funding Employment Training and Youth Training. The local initiative fund is tiny in comparison, at around £250,000. In a sense, then, the TECs are an outgrowth of the unemployment industry to which the ubiquitous and almost obligatory word 'enterprise' has been attached. The funds available for enterprise and business growth are frankly not serious compared to those devoted to training.

More important, however, than the composition of the Board is its corporate strategy. Though the Teesside TEC application for development funding reviewed the economy of Cleveland, it contained little critical analysis of the problems which have caused the decline of the area compared with recent, more independent studies (Foord *et al.*, 1985; Beynon *et al.*, 1985; Robinson, 1990) and our own analysis in Chapter 3. Consequently, there was little discussion of the role played by the county's big businesses, like BSC and ICI, in the production of massive local unemployment. Perhaps this is not surprising given that two Board members are senior executives from these two companies. The need for economic diversification and small business generation was noted. However, the historical failure of the giants of the Teesside economy to safeguard employment in the face of increasing international competition goes unrecognized. Instead, we find the myth repeated that economic decline and unemployment can somehow be accounted for by referring to the characteristics of the individual (unemployed) worker:

> The main thrust of the TEC's work will need to be around the development of the individual, in such a way that they can build individual enterprise and self confidence to a point where they are able to accept and accommodate change; this will be essential to face the challenge provided by the future economic growth of Teesside. The development of the community in this way will provide a basis for maximising employment opportunities in the future. (Teesside TEC, 1989:5)

The Corporate Plan of the TEC had this to say about the range of advice available to potential entrepreneurs: 'these services operate independently without any formal co-ordination, hence gaps cannot be readily identified and their effectiveness has limitations arising from confusion and lack of awareness amongst target groups' (Teesside TEC, 1990:76). The future for the enterprise industry would appear to lie in the greater collaboration, rationalization, partnerships and the creation of 'one stop shops' in order to improve access, heighten awareness, and impose some order on a rather chaotic scene. The TEC also makes it clear it intends to move as soon as possible to 'cost recovery' on enterprise activities through sales or sponsorship.

Looking back over the development of the enterprise industry in Cleveland with the benefit of hindsight it is perhaps not too surprising that it became rather uncoordinated, competitive, fragmented and uneven in quality. The attempt to find their own solution to the return of mass unemployment brought certain community leaders into a new form of association, which in turn gave rise to a new tier of professional trainers and administrators, many of whom gave unstintingly of their best to help younger generations. Commitment, altruism and creativity need, however, to be put to the test not just to ensure that public money is being spent wisely but also to safeguard the futures of young people who entrust their energy and their ideas to the enterprise movement. A more detailed assessment of the enterprise industry needs, however, to be postponed until we have presented the data we have collected on the experiences of young women and men as they establish and run businesses on Teesside.

Whatever the future pattern of enterprise agencies in the county, potential young business people are likely to be increasingly invited on to courses and encouraged to become self-employed. That, as we have seen, has been the dominant definition of enterprise and the businessmen on the Board of the TECs are likely to stress and support that version in the coming years. But why do young people decide to become self-employed? What does it entail to set up one's own business? What are the particular processes behind that simple phrase 'becoming your own boss'? These are the themes developed in the next chapter.

Notes

1 Although we would agree with the points made here about Cleveland's economic vulnerability, and we would further agree that powerlessness and helplessness are characteristics of the experience of unemployment, we would want to take issue with the view that it is 'dependency' on the state (national or local) that somehow causes these negative feelings and experiences.
2 Roger Leeming kindly gave us permission to include this chart.
3 We are grateful to Linda McKie for a copy of her joint paper with Llewellyn and Peppin (1989) on which the ideas in this section are based.
4 Briefly, this involved an enterprise agency writing to its clients asking if they did *not* wish to be contacted by us (to arrange an interview). After a given period we were then free to contact those potential informants who had not declined the opportunity to participate. This proved to be a long-winded but reasonably successful approach to constructing a sample of difficult-to-reach informants. Potential interviewees had a further chance to decline participation when they were contacted by phone, letter or personal visit to arrange a time and place for an interview.

Chapter 5

'Becoming Your Own Boss'

Becoming self-employed is perhaps the key social and economic process in the development of an enterprise culture, especially in a locality like Cleveland, or so the rhetoric goes. Any significant movement away from dependence upon either big firms for employment or welfare benefits for subsistence involves a movement towards self-employment in new, small firms. Of particular importance in the generation and the future development of a thriving local economy are the experiences of younger people of enterprise in general and their attitudes to starting businesses, in particular.[1]

The central question in this chapter is a simple one: why are these young adults in Cleveland choosing self-employment? Are they inspired to their new roles by the political ideology of enterprise? Or are they more reluctant recruits to the government's enterprise programme? Is self-employment in small business inspired by the anticipated financial rewards? Or is enterprise in a depressed area like this more a case of just getting by rather than getting on? The answers to these questions are not, however, straightforward and necessitate an exploration of the often complex and differing accounts underlying this choice. This will be followed by a discussion of the subsequent processes and problems encountered on the way to setting up in business. We shall examine the planning stages of business development, entry to the Enterprise Allowance Scheme and experiences of enterprise agencies, training courses and banks.

Unemployment and Entrepreneurship

Entrepreneurship and Early Careers

Informants were asked early in the interview about their reasons for becoming self-employed. Discussion of this topic — which developed into an exploration of the choices made by individuals — occupied a considerable part of the interview and generated a proportionate amount of detailed information about the relationship between (un)employment and entrepreneurship. Often this was in the form of an extended discussion of why certain steps were taken at certain times; in other words, how entrepreneurship related to their early careers.

Consequently, part of the task of analyzing the interviews involved plotting the *career trajectories* of informants. By this we mean that interviewees were asked about their various labour market (and, to some extent, domestic) experiences from the age of 16 to the day of the interview. For the teenage informants this was a relatively straightforward job and involved them rehearsing their steps from education (i.e. gets the order right in time) through (un)employment and government schemes over a two or three year period. Analysis of career trajectories is one of the central theoretical planks of the ESRC's *16 to 19 Initiative* (e.g. Bynner, 1987a; Roberts, 1987; Roberts and Parsell 1988). We would argue that there are, however, a number of theoretical and methodological difficulties with the notion of career trajectory generally and in relation to our work.

First, for those at the older end of the age spectrum, for instance 24- and 25-year-old informants, reconstructing personal career biographies sometimes involved detailed, lengthy and confusing discussions. A general problem of method inherent in the concept of career trajectory lies in the fact that it is often immensely difficult to identify a coherent, unitary or linear trajectory from the mess and jumble of individuals' biographies. Life is not as simple as the step-by-step model implied in this approach.

Second, some people made it clear that, although they could remember quite accurately the various 'career statuses' they had passed through, it was not easy to specify which was their *main* activity at a particular time. One informant had, at the same time, been signing on as unemployed, studying part-time at college, preparing for business start-up and working 'on the side' doing 'kissagrams' in the evening (as well as doing domestic work in the home for her boyfriend). Other research methods often used to reconstruct the career trajectories of young adults (e.g. questionnaire surveys) although eliciting 'cleaner', itemized and standardized responses, either skirt or ignore both this methodological problem and the complexity of the lives they attempt to describe.

Third, there is a problem of vocabulary when seeking to describe and analyze career histories (MacDonald, 1988a). Much of the phraseology used by sociologists and the public alike contains an almost implicit assumption of free will. Thus, terms like 'career choice', 'career opportunity' and 'decision making' suggest (wrongly) that the individual is somehow able to move through the post-school years happily and freely selecting the options most suited to him or her at various stages. This implication echoes earlier, popular models of occupational choice which suggested that the role of careers guidance was to match the school-leavers' expectations, skills and attributes with an appropriate job in the labour market (Ginzberg *et al.*, 1951). Though this perspective has, with the impact of mass unemployment in the 1970s and 1980s, now become virtually redundant, the vocabulary of occupational choice still remains.

Fourth, this vocabulary suggests that post-school educational and economic experiences fit together in a linear and positive way with the individual moving upwards and onwards with each successive step through the labour market. The very notion of career is based upon an incremental improvement up the ladder of jobs. Thus, the language of 'progression', 'career' and 'trajectory' is employed. But we would argue that the 'choices' made and the 'paths' weaved through the labour market are severely hemmed in by local social and economic conditions which structure and fence in the opportunities of people, especially in a county like Cleveland, and many of our informants were aware that they had made little progress with their 'careers'.[2]

A final problem with the concept of career trajectory, especially as employed by those who rely on questionnaire surveys, is that it can too easily become a tool for causally relating the socio-economic characteristics of respondents to their later career destinations (MacDonald 1989). In this way career trajectories are 'explained' and determined by factors such as the social class of fathers and school qualifications (e.g. Jones *et al.*, 1988), with little regard to the active cultural role played by people in the construction of their own individual biographies.

For these reasons care needs to be taken in the reconstruction of career trajectories from 'raw' ethnographic data and in the subsequent analyses. Throughout this book career trajectories are used only as descriptions, not explanations, of the activities of young people in the labour market. The reasoning and explanations of people themselves, as uncovered through ethnographic investigation, will always be given primacy over the bare bones of statistical mappings. So, given these theoretical and methodological difficulties, why bother with the complex job of unravelling career trajectories? Because the study of career trajectories still has its uses. Quite simply, analysis of the experiences preceding and following enterprise activities can illuminate the experience of enterprise itself. For instance, unemployment, as we will show, is perhaps the single most important 'social fact' in describing and discussing entry into entrepreneurship.

Responses to the question of why people became self-employed can be characterized as falling along a continuum with clearly differing explanations at either extreme. *Either* unemployment, with its negative social, psychological, cultural and material deprivations, *or* self-employment, with its imagined advantages over employment, were the two critical factors underpinning responses lying at the polar extremes of this continuum. In short, either unemployment *pushed* or self-employment *pulled* people toward starting up in business. As we say, these are the most explicit elements in the decision-making and explanations of young entrepreneurs, and characterize the two extreme 'ideal types' of the continuum.

Escaping Unemployment

The following passage is from an interview with Jack, from Stockton, who was unemployed at the time of interview and had also been out of work when he decided to try self-employment as a fine artist:

RM: So why did you think about self-employment?

Jack: The sole reason was I was applying for jobs and I just couldn't get any. I was trying all over the country. I had this talent and I thought well I might as well use it rather than be on the dole.

RM: How many applications did you make?

Jack: You're talking nearly 100. It gets a bit depressing after a while. I knew a lad who wrote away for 140 jobs in one week and he only got two letters back — politely saying 'no' . . . I didn't think it [Jack's business] was going to pay off. It would have worked for as long as I had the £40 EAS. A lot of people I know in Stockton went on the EAS for that reason.

RM: Just to get the £40?

Jack: Yes, and so they were employed for a year rather than being on the dole.

RM: Having said that, though, at least you had a business idea that you wanted to develop, didn't you? It wasn't just keeping off the dole? Or was it?

Jack: Well, if it had worked out I would have gone for it all the more. Nobody likes to say they are on the dole so they take the EAS and make the extra money so that they can keep in employment. Having said that some of them do actually go in for it and they really want to have their own business for the rest of their lives.

Jack's comments encapsulate the idea that self-employment was seen, by many, as a way of escaping unemployment at least for a while. Entry to the EAS, which we will discuss in more depth later in this chapter, was *seen* as guaranteeing an income of £40 per week (though practice sometimes proved different, as we will show in Chapter 6), and was providing gainful activity which was preferred to a continued life on the dole.[3] Having a good business idea or wanting to be your own boss were not the main determinants behind business start up. These came second, if at all, to the 'sole reason' of avoiding unemployment.

Comments such as these from Jack should not be interpreted as him wanting to avoid working. Quite clearly he had been looking hard for employment and if his embryonic business as an artist had proved viable he suggests he would have pursued it with renewed vigour. In short, just because unemployment provided negative reasons for business start-up this does not mean that young entrepreneurs had a negative attitude to their businesses. We shall argue in the next chapter that, whatever the reason for becoming self-employed, informants had an overwhelmingly diligent attitude to making a success of their venture.

Donna, from Billingham, had had a succession of part-time, temporary, casual jobs and government schemes since leaving school. She was unemployed for eight months following the Community Programme (CP) scheme, during which time she researched and planned the development of a small catering co-operative with her friend Belinda. The co-operative enterprise lasted for eleven months, following which she secured further temporary jobs. Donna's reasons for starting the co-operative were much the same as Jack's reasons for becoming self-employed:

RM: What was it about self-employment that was attractive to you?

Donna: It was a job. I wasn't — if someone had said here's a job, I would have took that. It was just that it was a way of working that's all. I mean you said that some people become self-employed because they don't like working for other people or they want to be their own boss. I've worked for lots of people. I'm quite happy working for employers . . . do you see what I mean, it was just a job, you know.

Unemployment, then, was critical in the decision to start up in business. Many reported the negative social and psychological consequences associated with worklessness (e.g. see Jahoda, 1979; Warr, 1983; Fineman, 1987; Banks and Ullah, 1988). The pressures of unemployment provided a direct and sole impetus to some, like Jack and Donna, to 'become their own boss'. In Donna's words 'it was a way of working, that's all'. One enterprise adviser informed us that in a training session he asked how many of the eighteen participants would take a job working for an employer if one was offered. Sixteen of the group said they would. For informants in this category self-employment, at least in the early decision-making and planning period, meant work, a job, and was attractive for this reason alone.

Unemployment in Early Careers

Examination of the early career of all those seventy-four who had at some time been self-employed or in a co-operative reveals that unemployment is highly significant in their biographies in a number of ways. Nine out of ten of these informants had experienced at least one spell of unemployment of two months or more since leaving school. For some, unemployment was the natural state of post-16 life. For one informant, Trevor, a 22 year old from Middlesbrough, unemployment accounted for four of his six years in the labour market.

For others unemployment had been largely avoided and only featured as a short stop-gap before becoming self-employed. A period of unemployment with benefit, for eight weeks, is one of the criteria for entry to the EAS, and it could be argued, therefore, that it is not surprising that unemployment features heavily in the labour market profiles of this sample. Accordingly the career 'statuses' of informants *immediately prior* to setting up in business were examined to explore the relationship of unemployment, of varying durations, to this process.

Over 40 per cent (or thirty-three) of the group who had been self-employed had experienced *over* two months unemployment prior to starting up in business. The mean duration of this particular spell of unemployment preceding business start-up was just over twelve months. Thus EAS regulations, to the effect that would-be young entrepreneurs must be unemployed for eight weeks, cannot explain the lengthy unemployment experienced prior to start-up by nearly half of this sub-section of the sample.

In addition, another sixteen people set up in business immediately following a government scheme; predominantly this meant Community Programme, but two young men became self-employed following the completion of their YTS schemes. The regulations for entry to EAS interpret participation on these schemes, and Employment Training, as time unemployed and thus the eight-week-unemployed with benefit requirement is waived. CP schemes in Cleveland often, it seems, included elements about becoming your own boss. As well as encouragement to become self-employed, CP participation, in a small number of cases, provided the additional advantage of access to resources and facilities useful in the business planning and start-up stages (e.g. stationery, telephones, office space and information). One or two of these informants had been 'employed' on CP schemes as enterprise advisers immediately prior to becoming self-employed themselves. They had stepped from jobs as enterprise theorists into the market place as entrepreneurs.

Fourteen people (out of seventy-four) had spent two months or less unemployed immediately before starting their enterprise. As we have said, it is not surprising that some had this relatively short period on the dole, due to EAS regulations. It is perhaps informative to look at the career statuses of this group prior to being unemployed. Eight had come from courses of non-advanced further education, seven of whom had been following courses of training and education of direct relevance to their business enterprise. For example, Heather, from Middlesbrough, had left school, taken a course in hairdressing at college, and spent two months unemployed before starting her own business as a mobile hair-dresser. A number of people mentioned that their college courses had actually included a component on enterprise skills and business start-up. Five out of this group of fourteen had been in employment before a two-month spell of unemployment; three of whom had been in employment with a direct relevance to their subsequent enterprises. An example of this career pattern was Terry's case, a 23 year old from Middles-brough, who following government schemes and two years' employment as a joiner, was unemployed for two months in his (unsuccessful) attempt to join the EAS before becoming self-employed.

The point to be made here is that, for the majority of this small group, unemployment prior to setting up in business appears to have been largely voluntary and required as a necessary stop-gap due to the requirements of the EAS. Additionally a majority of this small group described self-employment as an almost 'natural' occupational step, often taken by workers in their trade, due to the low wages paid by employers (for instance in hairdressing salons).

Most of these fourteen people had learnt a skill in their previous employment or in college which they later transferred into a business enterprise with the aid of the EAS. Of those who entered self-employment straight from employment (eleven), and hence without the assistance of the EAS, all but one had been employed in firms of the same type as their own. Within our sample the move from enterprise-related training or employment was a minority experience, but one which has been reported as a significant route into entrepreneurship. An American study found that a very high proportion of new small businesses were set up in a field of activity in which the business person had previous employment experience or training (Mayer and Goldstein, 1961, reported in Stanworth et al., 1989).

A close examination of the career trajectories of informants illustrates that unemployment is a particularly important key to unravelling the decision-making process prior to setting up in business. For the majority unemployment was a dominant fact of post-16 life and, as shown by the comments of Jack and Donna, was acknowledged as central in under-standing their reasons for becoming self-employed. For a smaller number of people, for instance those who entered the enterprise culture directly or indirectly from employment or college courses, unemployment seems to be less directly significant. Even with this group, however, who have largely avoided going on the dole for any great length of time themselves, unemployment looms in the background and casts a shadow over all their career decisions.

Becoming Your Own Boss

In this section we will consider the other extreme of the continuum of reasons for self-employment: the positive attractions of becoming your own boss. The attractions it held for people were varied and included freedom, independence and self-achievement. For many these advantages, coupled with the imagined material benefits accruing to their individual efforts (i.e. the money), constituted the reasons for becoming your own boss.

Very few of the sample seemed to become entrepreneurs in order to put their *particular* business idea into practice. Original business ideas were scarce and only one or two people actually mentioned the details of their proposed business as a reason for their starting up. Most businesses, as we describe in the next chapter, were not in any way out of the ordinary and involved very common, traditional activities.

Trudi, who had been self-employed for over two years following a short period in higher education, several jobs and two months' unemployment, described her decision to start an agency offering business services, as follows:

> I think it is better in self-employment no matter what, and I think
> I would have always gone along those lines because of the person
> I am . . . I like to do my own thing. I like to go my own way. I
> don't like to be tied down. I also found out that, no matter what,
> actually working with a boss — I couldn't trust another boss.
> Three months I had no wages. I don't think I could ever go
> through that again so trustingly.

Here Trudi expresses the desire to have autonomy and freedom in her working life and she suggests that this is almost an integral aspect of her personality. Trudi seems to be describing some of the classic elements of the elusive 'entrepreneurial personality' (see Chell 1986, for a critical review). A perceived disincentive to working for an employer in the future stems from her previous experience of labour going unrewarded as an employee.

Stewart was a 22 year old who had a two-year-old business importing and selling Turkish rugs. He had had a couple of jobs since leaving school at the age of 16 and he had been on YTS. He had also been self-employed in a different type of business when he was 18 which lasted nearly a year. This was followed by four months' employment, which he in turn left to become self-employed again.

RM: And what made you give self-employment another try?

Stewart: It is what I enjoy actually. I don't get enough satisfaction working for other people. I've got to have good challenges all the time, otherwise I'm not interested. So, therefore, I can create my own challenges and do it myself, that's all I want to do... //... Assessing why I am in self-employment — it's really that I can't work with other people.

For Stewart the initial attraction of self-employment largely rested upon the continuous challenges it offered, which he felt were lacking in the working life of an employee. In describing the reason to start up in business in these terms — by reference to the nature of self-employed work and his personal predilection for independence and meeting challenges and problems himself — Stewart's reasoning comes close to that of Trudi, and provides a final example of self-employment for self-employment's sake.

The Push of Unemployment and the Pull of Business

The accounts we have presented in these opening sections lie at the extremes of the continuum of reasons for business start-up. Most cases, however, lie towards the centre and draw upon both unemployment and entrepreneurship as factors in describing the motivations behind deciding to become self-employed.

This first extract from an interview with Tessa and Margaret, who were 20 and 19 years old respectively, and who had a fashion design and manufacturing business in Hartlepool, explores the process of leaving school, searching for jobs and starting up in business:

RM: Is there high unemployment in the area?

Margaret: Yes. You leave school and it's the dole or YTS. That's how bad it is. They won't even take people for jobs now because they say they can get them from YTS.

Tessa: I've been on the dole, for a year, one of my sisters has been on the dole for three years. You've really got to give yourself a kick up the backside to get going. We had to be on the dole to get the EAS and we actually spent two years planning this.

RM: Have you got any idea what the percent unemployed is?

Tessa: A lot!

Margaret: We used to go down the Job Centre. You needed to be the brainiest person in Hartlepool to get a job, which I definitely wasn't! Or you needed years and years of experience. It's a vicious circle. First I went for a receptionist job. I didn't want to know but I thought if it's the only job I can get, I'll do it. I didn't want to go on the dole. I didn't want to go on YTS when I'd been to college. And there was Boro Textiles for the money.

RM: Was self-employment really what you wanted to do or was it a case of the only thing going? I don't want to put words in your mouth...

Margaret: Two answers. At first there was nothing else to do — why not? Then while we were doing the research and the business plan we enjoyed it that much we thought we might as well give it a go. If anybody had offered me a job then, I would have thought hard and felt I would probably rather be in my own business.

Tessa: We got really enthusiastic about it.

Tessa and Margaret's comments show how the process of starting up in business is shaped by the restricted structure of opportunity in the local labour market. Unemployment is a fact of life for school-leavers and reduces their options to YTS (which Tessa had participated in) or, at that time, early entry to a life on the dole. YTS was seen as unattractive by Margaret because she felt she had studied enough at college to deserve employment, which she managed to get in the form of a receptionist's job. Neither this nor Margaret's later employment with a local textile firm were viewed with any great joy or sense of achievement. Unemployment and the lack of decent jobs was the first reason for them setting up in business. The second reason, as they state, was that, following the planning stages of business start-up, self-employment had become an attractive proposition in its own right.

Imran, a 23 year old from Middlesbrough, again identifies two reasons for becoming self-employed:

RM: So why did you decide to go for self-employment?

Imran: Two basic reasons. First, very simple, I couldn't get another job. Secondly, I think it is in my nature. I don't like to be under somebody. I don't mind working hard and doing long hours, or working under pressure as long as it's not from another person as my boss... So it's a bit of both really, because basically I don't have any other option.

The final passage in this section is taken from an interview with Joanne, 22, Middlesbrough who ran a knitwear shop:

RM: When you were thinking about setting up in business, were you looking around for other jobs?

Joanne: The simple fact was that I was looking around for a job and the nearest I could get was a CP scheme. I was applying for jobs all the time on the CP scheme. It was always a case of too old, too young, not enough experience. I thought there's no way I'm going to get a job by somebody else employing me . . . I was looking around for almost any job. It would be better than being on the dole. It drives me around the bend. But saying that I wouldn't take a job as a cleaner or anything like that. I felt that I'd spent my time at college and school getting all my exams . . . I'd had knitting as a hobby before the CP scheme and people started saying 'Ooh! I like your jumper, will you make me one?' I thought I could take this up as a business. The idea appealed to me of being my own boss where I could make up my own mind and I could do the work and I could get the wages at the end of the day.

Few jobs, an eagerness to work and a growing realisation that self-employment not only meant work, but also that it held a number of positive attractions which made it in some ways preferable to employment, were relevant in the process of deciding to set up in business for not only Joanne, but for the majority of informants in our study.

Other Explanations

There were, however, other important reasons for starting in business which did not fall as neatly into the typology we have developed so far. The cases we will deal with in this section provide a different perspective upon the processes of business formation. We have grouped them into three types: enterprise as a career stop-gap; enterprise as an outcome of a hobby or of family commitments; and, enterprise as a reaction to racism.

Two young entrepreneurs in separate businesses, and one of their partners who was not interviewed, became self-employed largely as a way of passing a finite period of time before taking another step in their career histories, in both cases the start of vocational college courses. The following passage is typical of this theme. It is from an interview with Mark, who was in a business partnership providing audio-visual and photographic services:

So we didn't get into college, neither of us didn't. So the next thing we thought we would do, or our parents thought it would be best for us to do, was with the aid of the EAS to set up in business for a year and then when it came round again to apply for college courses again. Rather than have done nothing over a year, we could say we have had our own business, so at least we would have something to say.

Enterprise in this and a small number of other cases meant a beneficial stop-gap assisting future employment and educational career plans. Related to this account, and to a number of others collected, is another slightly different reason for becoming self-employed which deserves mention.

Several informants had developed their businesses from earlier hobbies, leisure interests and pastimes. We have shown how vocational courses and employment in a particular area of work often led to later enterprises in that same field. These themselves were often pre-dated by a hobby or general interest in that type of work. When unemployment loomed or when business became an attractive idea, these personal interests were translated from a simple pastime of their youth into a way of making a living as they struggled to get by in adulthood. This was true, for example, for Joanne in her clothes business and Jack the artist from Stockton, whom we quoted earlier.

A further motive underpinning the move into self-employment can be described as a domestic one. Some informants, mainly women, drew attention to the relative attraction of business ownership in terms of how it fitted with their family responsibilities. Lillian had a child who was almost two years old and lived with her boyfriend in Middlesbrough. From leaving school through to her early twenties, when her baby was born, she had been employed. For five months she had been operating a business, again extending an earlier skill/hobby, as a freelance photographer:

RM: Tell me how you came to think of self-employment? You had just had a baby. Why did you think about self-employment?

Lillian: Because it would be really difficult for me to work all the time and I'm better off being my own boss. At the time I'd been doing, well looking after Janie, so I thought what can I do? I'd figured I'd do what I'm doing. It meant I could work from home and I didn't have rigid hours to stick to, so that Janie could be with me. That was basically it. I went on an Awareness Day and it was really easy . . . // . . . within the week I'd started, ready for the Christmas rush.

Lillian chose to become self-employed for reasons which, in the main, relate to her position as a mother, that is, as a worker in the domestic economy. Having her own business, with flexible hours and a base at home, allowed her to maintain these commitments whilst at the same time allowing her to keep a foot in the external labour market. Later, when Janie was older, Lillian hoped to return to her career. For the time-being, self-employment provided an enjoyable activity, some (usually very limited) financial reward and the opportunity to care for her child whilst still working. This theme was one developed by only a handful of informants but it is one that we feel is important as these few cases throw some light upon the impact of gender upon decisions to become self-employed.

Carter and Cannon, drawing upon a more extensive examination of sixty female entrepreneurs, argue that some women 'felt that employment did not allow the flexibility to pursue careers and have children. Business ownership was seen as a way of fulfilling both' (1988:47). Their informants defined success less in terms of business profits and more in terms of the way self-employment met personal needs, like the desire for independence at different times in their lives.

Entrepreneurship is a step taken more often by men than women, but it has also been shown that the numbers of women entering self-employment have been growing over the past ten years (Bevan *et al.*, 1989; Allen and Truman, 1990). The role of self-employment, underwritten by support from the EAS, in providing flexible (part-time) work in the early careers of young mothers is not one that should be overlooked and is, *perhaps*, one that should be encouraged, given the usual difficulties for young mothers in finding attractive work whilst at the same time caring for children. Relatedly, it may be the case that this sort of working could reduce the material dependence of married women houseworkers upon their spouses. Briefly, the meaning of enterprise was imbued with this further gender dimension. One young woman said:

> I wanted to be independent. Not just get married and have a husband who looked after me and just sat on my bum all day with kids around me . . . I'll have that one day and having a business like this is always something you can come back to . . . //
> . . . I'm not going to give up my business for any man. I'm too selfish. This is my baby. It's grown from nothing and nobody's going to get it off me.

This idea, that enterprise provided an element of a flexible *career* for young women, which allowed young women to return to valued work after family responsibilities had become less pressing, was one that was again mentioned by only a few informants. It is no less interesting for that. Cromie and Hayes (1988:87), following a more direct study of female entrepreneurship, conclude that 'business proprietorship might represent an effective method of overcoming some of the employment difficulties faced by women'. They also conclude that this was especially true for women with children and that the numbers of women self-employed were increasing for just such reasons.

This is not to say that there are no problems for women embarking upon the enterprise path. In Chapter 6 we will show that they faced formidable difficulties similar to those encountered by the men in the sample. Scase and Goffee (1987) and Carter and Cannon (1988), however, draw attention to the greater difficulties facing women in raising finance. The problem of appearing credible to (allegedly) sexist, sceptical bank managers was also discussed by some of the young women in our sample (see Chapter 6).

Of course, gender as a social fact influencing career decisions is of significance for men as well women. It is because women's work has traditionally been centred on the home that exceptions to this pattern become more interesting or problematic in both popular and sociological discourse. Accounts from men which incorporated a discussion of family and domestic careers were accordingly few in number. Those we collected tended to describe how increasing financial pressures from growing families had lent weight to their decision to reap the rewards for their own endeavours by becoming their own boss. Rather than using self-employment as a form of part-time employment permitting work in the home, these men used it as a way of making more money by increasing their labours through self-employment. In other words, self-employment redoubled young fathers' efforts in the labour market, but it provided only partial access to employment outside the home for young mothers.

The final part of this section will deal with enterprise as a response to racism. A small number (four) of people interviewed about their enterprises were from the Pakistani culture in Cleveland. Not surprisingly these people were the only ones to include racism as a factor in their decisions to start up in business.

There is a popular stereotype which portrays Asian adults as industrious, striving business owners running, typically, small manufacturing, catering or retail outlets (see Jones and McEvoy, 1986, for a critique). They are seen as the archetypal small scale entrepreneur. The view is that Asians are much more likely to go into business for themselves than whites. Curran (1986:21) suggests that 'popular views almost certainly represent a gross exaggeration' and he argues that the proportion of people from ethnic minorities becoming self-employed is probably no greater than the proportion of indigenous whites following this path. Nevertheless, it is still possible that entrepreneurs from ethnic minorities are motivated by quite different factors. Curran draws upon the work of Jenkins (1984) to explain the relationship of ethnic minorities to business ownership.

Jenkins' model suggests that there are three explanations for the participation of ethnic minorities in business: the *economic opportunity* model which argues that Asians, for instance, enter into business for much the same reasons as non-Asians but exploit a particular market area in doing so; the *culture* model which suggests that some ethnic groups have a predisposition towards enterprise; and the *reaction* model which describes the formation of ethnic businesses in terms of a reaction to the racist exclusion of non-whites from particular sectors of the labour market. It is likely, as Curran argues also, that these three explanations are not mutually exclusive. Certainly in the few accounts we gathered there were elements of all three, even if the evidence is weighted most strongly towards the last explanation. In general, through the four cases, discussions of how British Pakistani people moved into business (as a response to racial discrimination in the labour market) were embedded in a broader description of the influence of parental ethnic culture. Although all four mentioned societal racism as a factor in their decision-making, all four were generally supported in their business plans by their families. All had family or friends who were self-employed and family contacts in the Asian community were used to promote their businesses.

Before looking at one account we need to remind ourselves that the number of cases we are dealing with is very small and we cannot hope to do more than suggest some themes which are congruent with current research literature on ethnic enterprise. On the other hand, all of the four people interviewed who were from the Pakistani culture drew attention to issues of racism and ethnicity in their accounts.

The long passage we present is from an interview with Ranjeet, aged 19, who had recently opened a small shop on a housing estate in Middlesbrough. The interview took place there and contains contributions from her father who came in at one point:

RM:	Do you think more people from the Asian community set up businesses — why do you think that is?
Ranjeet:	I don't know. I think it's equal, isn't it? Near enough.
Father:	The one straight answer is, well as far as I'm concerned, is that there is no alternative. They just can't get jobs. My daughter [Ranjeet] has a number of qualifications, stayed on at school for two years and has all the qualifications and can't get a job.
Ranjeet:	Yes, it's difficult. You know what you're up against.
RM:	What's that?
Ranjeet:	Well there might be 20 people [going for a job] so you are one against 20.
RM:	What sort of jobs have you been applying for?
Ranjeet:	Mainly secretarial work.
RM:	And you thought at the time that you didn't get the jobs because you were Pakistani?

Ranjeet: You could tell from the places you were writing to. I could literally tell they were going to reject me ... the smaller places. I know it's difficult to get a job at somewhere like ICI because they recruit within the factory first, but at least they have the decency to write back to you. And then you just get other people where you get a straight rejection from, and you could tell, you know, the sorts of high street shops where they don't want an Asian girl working — you can just tell that's why they rejected you.

RM: Another Pakistani chap was saying that was part of it, but also that because his parents were self-employed this had been a reason influencing him?

Father: Well, that's the easy option, the easy way of looking at it. People come up to me and ask 'Why have all these Asian people got all the corner shops?' The answer is they couldn't get a decent job. You can blame the politicians for that — the white people's jobs came first. It is there, racism, it is there. It's always been there and it always will be there. That's why people have corner shops, that's why people struggle along because they've got to survive. If I had a good job, I wouldn't have to do this all the time [at this point Ranjeet's father leaves the shop].

RM: Do you agree with all that?

Ranjeet: My dad has got strong views (laughs) ... but he might have strong views, but he's right. It is difficult ... // ... I mean I'm not being disrespectful to English people but it really is a lot harder for Asian people to get jobs. Twice as hard. I mean when I came back from Pakistan I was working temporary and I must have sent hundreds of letters out. I must have had a big bag full of rejects.

RM: The other thing that people say is that Asians have all the shops 'cos they work harder?

Ranjeet: Well we have to, don't we?

Ranjeet's account, supplemented by her father's contribution, seems to support in the main what Jenkins would call the reaction model. Certainly Ranjeet's father supported the view that ethnic enterprise was largely a response to racist employment practices. This was a common theme in the accounts gathered from other British Pakistani informants. Ranjeet herself felt she had been excluded, through racial discrimination, from jobs in the labour market and self-employment was viewed as a strategy (like some of our non-Asian informants) for avoiding unemployment and developing a working life. To use Ranjeet's words, Asian people had to work harder (simply in order to overcome the obstacles in their way and establish themselves with a job).

Getting Started

In this section we will turn our focus from the initial reasons *why* people start up in business to a discussion of *how* they plan and start businesses.

Preparing for Enterprise

Overwhelmingly people spent a great deal of time and effort preparing their enterprises. Their motivation prior to starting (i.e. the relative weight of unemployment and entrepreneurship as elements in their decisions to become self-employed) bore little relation to the work done on business preparation once the initial steps towards enterprise had been taken. This held true for the motivation of young entrepreneurs when actually running businesses, as we shall see in the next chapter. Sometimes the time spent preparing beforehand was determined by the processes and operations of enterprise agencies as well as by their own choice.

Alex was a young woman who used to be involved in a design cooperative in Cleveland. Like all the small sample of informants who had set up co-ops, she and her co-workers had prepared their businesses under the auspices of North-Eastern Co-operative Development Agency (NECDA) (see Chapters 4 and 8):

> *RM:* How long did it take you to set up after leaving college?
> *Alex:* About six months. We spent a lot of time doing market research, just working out costs — incomings, and really attempting a cash-flow prediction for one or two years. Trying to work out how we would operate with each other and who would do what. It took a lot of time. Because we were working with NECDA, they wanted a booklet covering everything that would be involved in setting up. It took a long time, which was a good thing. But to be honest it doesn't have anything to do with the way you actually work once you start. Even the cash-flow — you'll be way out. It's like the Army. For the first six weeks they really put you through it and those who can't go through those six weeks drop out and I think it's that kind of process. The Agency puts you through it to see how determined you are. If you're not determined, you won't finish. You'll get to the point where you're sick and fed up and you'll give up ... // ... so we ended up getting the support of the Agency, they thought we would be viable so they put the money up as loan to pay back. That's how we got on the EAS.

The preparatory stages for this co-operative were overseen and guided by NECDA which was typical, as we have said, of all co-operatives in our study. This process bore resemblance, in some ways, to the type of help received by the sole traders from more common business enterprise agencies (such as Teesside Young Entrepreneurs). In this case, however, NECDA provided a more thorough form of guidance and supervision for the embryonic co-op and demanded the completion of various tasks such as detailed business plans and market research. In return NECDA was in the position to provide grants and loans from its own resources to assist new co-operatives which were under its wing. NECDA also often proved very helpful to young entrepreneurs in the later and final stages of enterprises. Belinda and Donna, whom we discussed earlier, ran a co-operative which closed down after ten months with £7,500 in outstanding debts. NECDA both oversaw the administration of the business closure and covered these debts (either by writing off their own financial investment or paying the bills of other creditors).

Mary and Jane, both 22 year olds from Middlesbrough, ran a knitwear production and retailing business. They too had found the process of becoming your own boss a more complicated and time-consuming one than first imagined. They had taken a three-year college course, in crafts and design, before trying to start up:[4]

Mary: After college we were straight on the dole for a year . . . we thought we'd get started much earlier . . . we were working out what we wanted to do. We were under the impression that we could walk straight out and into the bank and get £1,000, and you couldn't.

Jane: We went to a bank and told him what we would like to do and what his advice would be. He thought we were actually asking him there and then for a £1,000 each for the EAS. He said that he would give us £500 each but that we would have to find £500 each. So we had to go away and try and find £1,000. We went back a year later and said right there you are, fair enough.

RM: Where did you get the money?

Jane: It's confidential! (laughs) We did these party plans when we were on the dole and got it from there.

RM: You were working hard then at home?

Jane: Oh yes, the unemployment people sent us on these Restart interviews — I had to go to college one day a week to do a maths course and a health and safety at work course just to keep them happy, so they didn't think I was sitting on my bum all day. I had been to college for three years and it wasn't as if I was thick and just sitting on my backside —

trying to explain to them that we were doing work at home but not selling anything, just building up to the first stage. They were on my back all the time. They sent for me over and over again. I've had two Restarts and got out of two (laughs).

Mary: I only had to go to two because I said I'd go to college. But I really had to convince them. The person I had [at the Restart interview] was one of those in a suit, snotty-nosed saying 'she's a little scum-bag, just come out of college and sitting around doing nothing'. She said I should make use of my time, as if I was lying in bed all the time! They don't realise how much there is to go into all this. We were building up stock and earning money for the EAS. Preparing for it . . . //
. . . we went back to the bank manager [nearly a year later] when we had earned about £900 and he gave us an overdraft for the rest to get on to the EAS . . . I suppose we could have just borrowed the £1,000 for a week like some people do, but we wouldn't have been happy about that. We wouldn't have felt confident about it. We needed the money as it turned out 'cos business is so slow at the moment.

These extracts illustrate how difficult it was for some of the informants to become self-employed. A central problem was the money needed to qualify for the EAS. What this passage also illustrates is the determination of informants to pursue their plans for self-employment despite being set back for a great deal of time by lack of initial capital (in this case at least a year). Mary and Jane needed relatively small amounts of money to leave the ranks of the unemployed and start their business. The decision of the bank manager to demand an equal financial input from them was quite a common one for this sample, and also is common practice in business more generally. However, it was a decision which forced these two people to continue their reliance upon unemployment benefits for a year whilst they dodged the attentions of Restart officers and earned money 'on the side' in order to earn the requisite £1,000.

Several informants had similar experience of Restart interviews which were felt to be unnecessary and annoying intrusions into their personal lives and presented a series of complicating hurdles to be cleared on the path to establishing a working life through enterprise. Overwhelmingly, people wanted jobs and did not enjoy worklessness and in this sense Restart was seen in a very poor light. One person had to attend four interviews in his spell of unemployment which he saw not as encouragement or help to find work (in his view he was never offered a decent job), but rather as a time-consuming obstacle in the way of his ambitions to leave the dole through self-employment.

One of the main and implicit purposes of Restart, we would suggest, is to police unemployed claimants with the aim of identifying and penalizing those who may be involved in unreported, unpaid work 'on the side'. As they themselves said, Mary and Jane were engaged in this activity but this should not be understood as 'fiddling'. Certainly these two informants would have preferred not to have been on the dole and were keen to get their business started. The form of working that we have described was not motivated by wishes for an easy, idle sort of life supported by the efforts of others through welfare, but rather by a quite contrary concern to make a living for themselves directly through their own enterprise. Their behaviour could be interpreted not so much as evidence of the dependency culture as of rather desperate and enterprising attempts to assert some independence and dignity in the face of economic adversity.

Similarly, in practice, a very small number of young entrepreneurs (three) started working in their embryonic businesses whilst officially being unemployed (and in receipt of benefit). This is a risky business as it runs contrary to both social security and EAS regulations. This form of enterprise temporarily supported by unemployment benefits served a number of functions for new businesses. It allowed people the chance to 'test the waters' — to see if their business idea stood a realistic chance in the local economy before diving in at the deep end of enterprise through business ownership. Markets could be investigated, services and products refined, working practices tried and customers and clients fostered, before the safety net provided by unemployment benefits was thrown away. In this way new, young businesses could be built up and permitted a greater chance of survival by the 'abuse' of welfare benefits. This is what Scase and Goffee (1987) refer to as 'the scratching phase' of early business start-up.

Terry, the joiner already quoted in this chapter, tells an interesting and complicated story of his relationship with the local employment and benefit authorities. He had decided to start working for himself after seeing the profits his previous employer had been making. Though he stayed with his boss, Terry started doing jobs for his first clients at weekends, which he found earned him the same as his weekly wage. He gradually built up his own reputation and customer base. Unfortunately, Terry was made redundant by his employer. At this point Terry signed on for, and started receiving, unemployment benefit. He also continued to do individual jobs:

> and it was all hunky-dory for about three months — then all of a sudden the DHSS started following me and asking me questions . . . // . . . I'd finished with Bill [his employer] but I was still working at the weekends and was hoping that it might spread through the week. I was claiming dole but that's the way

any new business would start. Any sort of trade type business. You know, if somebody is in demand at the weekend they usually leave work and go on the dole for a few weeks. Especially with the EAS you had to be on the dole for a minimum of, I think it was thirteen weeks at that time [now eight weeks], before you were eligible. So that meant for three months I had to be fiddling . . . I had every intention of starting my own business.

Terry then told me about his experience of 'dole hassle'. Several times when he went to sign on at the Unemployment Benefit Office he found himself the subject of intense scrutiny by the staff. He was finally confronted with direct and clear evidence that he had been doing unreported work as a joiner (apparently resulting from an anonymous tip-off), was read his rights and that he was entitled to a solicitor. Terry duly took legal advice which amounted to guidance to delay responding to DHSS letters and always report when he had worked. This time delay would take him through to the necessary number of weeks (in receipt of benefit) to be eligible for the EAS. At this point Terry was then informed that he had been working too many hours to be entitled to benefit and that he would have to work less and continue to sign on for another two months. Terry followed this course of action and again (two months later) applied for the EAS. He was turned down again because this time he was deemed not to be starting a new business. Terry was one of the few informants who described this pattern of (failed) entry to EAS and eventual (successful) business start up. Thus, EAS entry requirements can sometimes conflict with more informal strategies for going self-employed.

Despite the particular nature of the difficulties experienced by Terry, it still holds true that the length of time between previous employment status and business start-up was generally considerable. A pattern of quite long periods of planning, preparation and fund-raising for businesses was frequently reported by young entrepreneurs. For example, Hamish, a young man from Middlesbrough, planned his shop for two years, during which time he was unemployed and had various temporary jobs. The obstacles they faced along the path to the enterprise culture were in some cases daunting, yet they were overcome, largely by their persistence in carrying through their plans, and despite the initial (negative) motivations pushing informants to become self-employed.

Part of the reason for apparently lengthy periods of business planning was that some informants were involved in applying for loans and grants from organizations like the Prince's Youth Business Trust and the Department of Trade and Industry (e.g. Regional Development Grant). Sometimes these loans/grants were needed for the business to get going and so start-up was dependent upon the successful completion of various tasks (e.g. the presentation and revision of elaborate business plans). This in itself was reported as a lengthy process, and several months usually elapsed before successful applicants received their grants/loans (indeed, some businesses actually started up, traded and folded before promised funds were allocated).

'You've Got the Enterprise, We've got the Allowance Scheme'

The Enterprise Allowance Scheme constitutes the major programme for developing enterprise (as self-employment) among young adults (see Chapter 2). The main problems for potential young entrepreneurs wishing to join the EAS can be the financial contribution expected and spending eight weeks in receipt of benefit. In the following examples we will look at the first of these issues in more depth.

Joanne found it difficult to raise the finance for the EAS:

RM: What about the £1,000 to get on the EAS?

Joanne: That was a lot of hard work, I can tell you, because I was
         unemployed, I didn't have a house [to offer as security]. I
         was living with my parents. So there was no bank to back
         me with a £1,000 loan. So my parents and grandparents
         scraped together what little savings they had and we got an
         overdraft of £400.

Obviously not having £1,000 to hand was an immediate problem for the majority of our informants. Some worked to raise the capital (like Mary and Jane earlier) whilst others, like Joanne, borrowed from hard-up relatives and friends. For most this was experienced as a difficult but not insurmountable problem and ways were found to pass this test of eligibility. One method, which, as judged by the number of times it was mentioned, has attained the level of common cultural practice, involves the borrowing of £1,000 from a bank on a very short-term basis. Informants approached bank managers, who were also apparently accustomed to this practice, to arrange a loan for, say, a week, with the £1,000 then being paid back plus interest and bank charges. In this way banks made a small but easy profit and young entrepreneurs gained access to the scheme without having to pass perhaps the trickiest test of having £1,000 to invest. This strategy works because EAS officials only require that the money be accessible at one particular time — at the entry stage. Often this was just a paper transaction with the banks only promising to provide the specified amount if required. Many young entrepreneurs, then, never have the £1,000 in their accounts and at their disposal.

Having said this, however, it was not a universal banking practice as shown by Mary and Jane's case. The willingness of banks to fund young businesses varied in some cases, we would argue, according to perceived social and situational factors. Some young women reported that they felt that older, male bank managers did not take their proposals seriously and showed little understanding of their aims and ambitions. Margaret and Tessa, the young designers from Middlesbrough, felt that their bank manager thought he was being 'pestered by little girls' and they had great difficulty raising the £1,000. Lesley, a beauty therapist, said that her bank manager asked, as his first question, 'What's beauty therapy?' and that he treated it as 'a silly, little girly thing'.[5]

Certainly it is difficult, methodologically, to assess these reports. They arose, however, unprompted in discussions with a significant minority of our sample. Others were much more successful in gaining support from banks and were not forced to jump through a laborious and frustrating series of sexist hoops.

One 25-year-old, male, university graduate was successful in securing a loan of over £10,000 from a bank at his first attempt. The way he discussed this success was striking in its contrast to the experiences of the young women above. What we may be glimpsing here is the power of social inequalities (in this case the triple disadvantages of being young, working-class and female) impinging upon the process of business start-up through the traditional attitudes of (middle-aged, middle-class, male) bank managers. It is difficult to prove that ageism, sexism and class prejudice are at work here, but we report the comments as they were passed to us and add that it would perhaps be surprising if bank managers were universally comfortable in accepting this new and unusual type of business person.

One critical factor involved in the process of start-up which we have not confronted directly concerns the family background and family attitudes of young entrepreneurs. A common research finding has been that parental experience of self-employment is a critical factor influencing young people towards entrepreneurship (Hough, 1982; Curran, 1986; Goldthorpe et al., 1987, Curran and Burrows, 1988; Stanworth et al., 1989; Rees and Thomas, 1989). However, what has not been uncovered, to our satisfaction, has been the reasons behind the apparent correlation between parents' self-employment and that of their children. Ethnographic approaches employing qualitative methods are more likely than questionnaire survey approaches to be able to explain the link. Our informants were asked about their parents' occupations, experience of self-employment and attitudes to their (children's) career decisions. Parental self-employment was far less common in this sample than in other studies of entrepreneurs. Less than 10 per cent said they had a mother or father who was or had been self-employed. This compares with a comparable figure of 43 per cent in a recent survey of factors behind entrepreneurship in London (Blythe et al., 1989a).

This is perhaps not surprising given the nature of the local economy and traditions of employment in big companies. What this draws attention to is the importance of analyzing the effect of local labour markets on patterns of youth labour market activity (Ashton, Maguire and Garland, 1982; Ashton, Maguire and Spilsbury, 1988; Coles, 1988). The difference between our findings in respect of parental self-employment and those from national studies (or of other labour markets) illustrate that the crushing impact of unemployment upon youth opportunities in this locality has upset common and widely reported, traditional patterns of movement into self-employment. Here the enterprise culture can draw upon a much wider constituency of potential (unemployed) recruits, many of whom, by the very nature of the culture of work in Cleveland, will not have any previous family experience of self-employment. Indeed, a stronger correlation was found between parental unemployment (rather than self-employment) and young people in business.

This is not to say that family background and parental attitudes are not important in the processes we have been describing. Rather, the influences are more subtle than correlations drawn from quantitative surveys. Of most importance was the degree of willingness and ability of families to support the activities of their entrepreneurial offspring. The extent to which this is possible is, of course, at least indirectly related to the position of the family's adult workers in the labour market. It goes without saying that some families in Cleveland are poorer than others and are therefore less able to contribute, for instance, to the £1,000 for EAS. On the other hand, two of the young male shop-owners in our sample had had their outlets bought for them (or, in another instance, had the first six months rent and rates paid) by their comparatively well-off parents. Parental support also involved, in a handful of cases, offering the family home as security for their sons' (i.e. sons, not daughters) bank loans (sometimes running to over £10,000).

Possibly the most common and most important way in which parents supported young entrepreneurs was in the provision of material help *in kind*. Very often this manifested itself in the provision of free, or very cheap, board and lodging for their sons and daughters as they tried to establish themselves in business. Some parents would offer help with occasional transport or give pocket money to their children if they hit particularly barren patches with their new business. Having stressed the material contributions of parents we recognize that, of course, it is unlikely that this would have been forthcoming had not parents emotionally supported their children's career decisions. In other words, it seemed that, where it was mentioned by informants, their parents were not opposed to their plans to become self-employed, and that material help flowed from this general attitudinal support. Scase and Goffee (1987) have also drawn attention to the impact of business start-up upon the families of entrepreneurs. Their sample of informants was generally older than ours (and apparently all male) and consequently they refer to the considerable commitment of entrepreneurs' wives and children to the new business.

Despite the problems we have outlined, and with the general backing of parents, most of the young entrepreneurs used the EAS. An interesting group did not (eleven). These were the people who felt that entry to the scheme was not worth the hassle involved (for instance, proving eight weeks unemployment and securing appropriate benefit), especially given the pressing demands of enterprises which were busy from the earliest days. Six people reported that they did not go on the scheme because they could not afford to lose the business they had attracted by embarking upon the process of entry to the EAS. It is perhaps surprising that more did not participate given the scheme's aim to help only those who would not otherwise become self-employed.

Getting Help

The process of starting up businesses typically began with the decision to become self-employed followed by the joining of the EAS which, in turn, was followed by attendance at courses of varying length in business and enterprise skills. Some of these have been mentioned in Chapter 2 but it is probably useful to describe briefly the arrangement of courses most frequently encountered by our sample.

The only compulsory training in business enterprise for these young entrepreneurs was the EAS Enterprise Awareness Day, and for very many this was their sole source of business advice and information.[6] To be eligible to join EAS one must have attended an Awareness Day in the previous six months. The day consists of advice and training in the basics of business management: cash-flows, book-keeping, advertising, insurance, etc. This is all very important for the intending entrepreneur but the Awareness Day suffers from being simply that: only a day. As we found in talking to participants, much of the content was too shallow, too rushed or too general to be of much apparent use. Following this day, EAS officials did keep in contact with the new business by means of one or two visits to their homes or business premises. (These checks proved to be, however, cursory in nature, as we will describe in Chapters 6 and 10).

The other main form of training received was that delivered by local enterprise agencies through schemes like the Business Enterprise Programme (BEP), the Private Enterprise Programme (PEP) or the Voluntary Projects Programme (VPP). The content of these courses is much the same as the Enterprise Awareness Day. We have already described the web-like character of the enterprise industry in Chapter 4. Courses like these are part of the front-line of the promotion of the enterprise culture in the county. They are generally run by, and in, the enterprise agencies we have described and take the form of small classes lasting anything from two days to eight weeks. These are free to participants and as such differ from the more specialized courses in, for instance, book-keeping run (sometimes as evening classes) by enterprise agencies. The local Polytechnic also runs similar specialized short courses.

Something of a pattern could be identified in the process of getting advice and guidance. This would begin with attendance at the Awareness Day, from which participants would be recommended to seek further help from enterprise agencies such as Teesside Young Entrepreneurs (TYE). This help tended to be in the form of initial interviews with an enterprise counsellor who could then pass the client on to other staff in the agency who ran one of the above short courses. Counsellors and advisers would be available to provide help to the new business person once their enterprise was up and running. Entrepreneurs could drop in to a number of agencies in the county where they could receive one-to-one counselling about their businesses. Usually this was reported as useful, if rather time-consuming and remote from their enterprises. Some complained that they had received 'bad advice', for instance, a handful said that they felt they had been misinformed about particular application procedures, or had their applications for grants mishandled by particular enterprise advisers, or had not been informed about particular grants.

Craig and Sandra ran a cabinet-making business in the county. They had not gone on the EAS but had received help from a local youth enterprise agency:

Craig: They're brilliant, TYE, well Martin [one of the adviser] was.

Sandra: Everything's free. You've got to pay with some of these organizations, you know, for the sessions and the typing and things like that. At TYE everything is free and you can go there any time you want.

Craig: When you're setting up, you need someone like that. Either that or you need someone who is in business themselves and they know everything. I knew a lot of people in business but they wouldn't have known all the little details like TYE. That's all they specialize in . . // . . . it made us more aware of all the grants that were open to us. We didn't know we were entitled to any. He told us what they were and who to contact.

The experience of enterprise advisers and agencies reported by Sandra and Craig was not uncommon. Many felt *generally* happy with the help that they had received from workers in this field, especially when guidance and information led to the securing of grants or loans to assist business start-up. Usually responses to our questions about getting help from enterprise agencies were phrased, as with this case, in terms of individual advisers (being particularly helpful or unhelpful). The fact that this advice and help was given free was crucial to the vast majority of young entrepreneurs who could afford little in the way of (what they regard as) extra costs.

Other responses were less enthusiastic and pointed, often with considerable business sense and insight, to the shortcomings in the enterprise industry. Others still made specific criticism of organizations and individuals. We shall concentrate on the type of comment which illuminates general issues common to the sample. Fraser had previously been self-employed:

RM: They were useful [TYE]?
Fraser: Yeah . . . [but] I feel they should monitor people's businesses more — them actually coming to see you rather than you having to go to see them all the time and maybe more technical knowledge which was what I needed. TYE can always give you advice on business generally but I wanted something in my specific field . . . they could perhaps get people to work indirect for them so, say, if someone comes in who wants to be a printer, or has got a problem as a printer, they can be directed by TYE to them.

That enterprise agencies concentrate on business start-up and do not pay enough attention to business development and support was a point made by a number of informants apart from Fraser. His second point, that practical expert advice on specific business areas was not readily available, was another frequent complaint. Stewart, the Turkish rug importer, made the following astute points:

They never really follow you up. They never really say 'How are you doing? Are there any problems?' They leave it very much to you which I think is wrong. I think all the businesses should be followed up at least on a quarterly basis. It is very easy for someone who is in business to forget about all the things that are troubling them and just go on doing things the same way. At the end of the day they end up in a big heap, not knowing what to do and somebody has to pick up the pieces and it is usually TYE. That's what tends to happen in my experience — they tend to set you up at the beginning and then pick up the pieces at the end. Whereas, if they followed you through from the beginning then I don't think they would have as many failures as they have had . . . // . . . there are a lot of businesses which have been set up and they work on government assistance for maybe the first

twelve months and struggle on for the next year, maybe see it
through the second year and then they get bored with it, sick of it
or they tend to just wither away and die. I honestly can't see the
point of that. If you are going to put a business on the rails and
set somebody up and going they should have as much backing as
you can possibly give them. I know it takes time, that sort of
follow up, but I don't think organizations like TYE are actually
getting a lot of business successes because of it. They should
concentrate their efforts more.

Another area of questioning about the types of help new entrepreneurs received concerned the content of business enterprise courses.
Following our investigation of Cleveland's enterprise industry (see Chapter 4) and the variety of concepts of enterprise circulating, we were
particularly interested to examine the forms of enterprise being encouraged and the political complexion of the content of enterprise advice.
Consequently, informants were asked about the type of information
and advice passed on to them, the relative emphasis (if any) placed
upon different business structures (e.g. sole tradership, partnerships,
co-operatives, limited companies) and the frequency of advice about
areas which are less oriented toward business profits (e.g. trade union
membership, Health and Safety regulations, employment conditions
and workers' rights).

The following passage is from an interview with Roger who, after
graduating from university, had found it difficult to find work at home in
Cleveland. He now ran a service business connected with the music and
entertainment industry:

When I went along to the Awareness Day and did the course at
TYE it struck me the amount of people there whose ideas were
appalling and they were going to start and they did start. Really,
basically, they're just encouraging them to get off the dole. When
they were asked what would make their product sell, they were
just going to undercut. You can't keep doing that for very long. I
think people were starting, you know, with the idea of cheap
labour. I think that's the sad thing for me about EAS in this
area . . . // . . . and I went along to TYE and they put me on an
eight-week VPP course . . . some parts were good — I learnt
about book-keeping which is pretty necessary. There was a lot
about selling things — like double-glazing — the hard sell! And a
part about how to sack someone. You know, people going into
self-employment and the first thing they learn is how to sack
someone! . . . // . . . at the end of the course they asked us to write
down any criticisms and I wrote down that there was nothing to
do with the other side of things. You know, workers' rights,

health and safety, trade unions. I've always been interested and gone into things from the other side — NUPE and health and safety. Unions were never mentioned once while I was there. Quite disturbing really.

Admittedly, Roger's description is unusual in its fairly overt political criticism of some of the processes of business start-up. Although a good number of informants certainly did point to the effect of EAS upon unemployment statistics (see Chapter 9), few developed this explicitly into an attack upon either the nature of small business profitability (in Roger's terms, upon cheap labour, unfair competition and potential displacement of already existing employment) or the content of business start-up courses. Although this is an exceptional case it does elucidate the general nature of business advice to young entrepreneurs in this sample, as stated by enterprise professionals, as observed in enterprise training courses and as described, less critically, by other informants.[7]

Business Grants and Loans

Young entrepreneurs sometimes received more tangible help in the form of business grants and loans. We have already discussed how the £1,000 hurdle could block the path to the EAS and entrepreneurship. Approximately one-third of the self-employed sample had managed to secure other sorts of financial backing for their enterprises. In the main these were from three sources: government grants (mainly from the DTI); grants of loans from national or local charities (e.g. Livewire, Prince's Youth Business Trust); and bank loans.

Government grants generally fell into two types, both from the DTI: those through what was the Department's Regional Development Grant (RDG) system and those through the Inner City Task Forces. RDGs were obtained by a good proportion of our sample, before they were phased out in 1988 (see Wren, 1989). These provided a grant of several thousand pounds for the creation of new jobs and for the purchase of necessary manufacturing equipment. Through this scheme some of our informants were able to qualify for a £3,000 grant for creating a job (i.e. their own). An equal amount was available for every further job created (i.e. their employees). RDGs obviously provided a great source of capital for new businesses and were much appreciated by the informants lucky enough to qualify. More recently this scheme has been replaced by the DTI's Enterprise Initiative which is seemingly much less generous in its approach to entrepreneurs of this type. Fewer of our sample received grants (up to the value of £1,000 in one case) or loans from Inner City Task Forces (these were in place in both Middlesbrough and Hartlepool). These were administered under fairly 'soft' and generous conditions. Unfortunately, many of the group had not heard of the availability of this extra source of funding.

The main problem with the RDG was the length of time it took for grant applications to be processed and funds to be paid out. Many complained about delays. The process of securing this source of funding required the submission, consideration, revision and re-submission of detailed business plans — a time-consuming process, especially when people's efforts were primarily directed toward the day-to-day running of businesses. One woman, Lynne, largely explained the failure of her business and its dramatic consequences in terms of the tardiness of RDG payments (see Chapter 6 for more details of this case). Several informants had waited over twelve months since the start of their business, and application, before receiving the money. Admittedly when cheques for as much as £3,000 did arrive the money was very welcome, as it often roughly coincided with the withdrawal of the EAS £40 per week (after twelve months). Some informants used this money to pay off earlier bank loans (e.g. for the £1,000 EAS requirement) or as collateral to secure further bank loans.

There were two other main sources of grants used by these young business people: the Prince's Youth Business Trust (PYBT) and Livewire. The first is a national charity which exists to help disadvantaged young people into business by providing grants (up to £1,000) and 'soft' loans (up to £3,000). Fewer of our informants received this than received RDG. 'Young' is defined by PYBT as being aged 18 to 25, but 'disadvantaged' is apparently, a less certain category. Discussions with enterprise advisers did not clarify this and it remained unclear whether, for instance, a female graduate would qualify (being disadvantaged by her gender, but advantaged by her education). Some informants reported being ineligible for PYBT funding on the grounds of their parents' occupational class. Nevertheless, when PYBT grants or loans were received they were again welcomed gratefully, with only a few complaints arising about this topic in interviews (again in relation to the submission requirements and delay involved).

Livewire is another national organization, but in this case with strong North-Eastern links. It again aims to help young people start up in business by providing advice and help from a personal enterprise adviser. It also holds an annual competition in which young entrepreneurs submit their business plans. Prizes for the best plans amount to £50,000 in total. A fair proportion of our informants in Cleveland were aware of Livewire and several had entered Livewire competitions, sometimes very successfully.

The final source of financial help for young businesses was, of course, the banks. Earlier we spelled out some of the difficulties *some* people had in getting the necessary £1,000 loan or overdraft for EAS entry from banks. For others, it was a much simpler and easier process.

We suggested that issues of class culture and gender were playing a part when bank managers decided to whom to grant loans. The same situation held true for larger loans and overdraft facilities. Several businesses seemed severely undercapitalized, to borrow the financial term, and operated on absolutely minimal amounts of money. Though it was difficult, and occasionally insensitive, to investigate informants' financial standing in any great depth, what did emerge was that monetary reserves, in terms of money in bank business accounts or overdraft facilities, were usually extremely low and could commonly be counted in two or three figures. An informant in a computer-related company proudly told me that he had £9.43 in reserve. Many of these young entrepreneurs were far from wealthy and had experienced considerable periods of unemployment — these were probably important factors in the reasoning of bank managers. Many of our informants must have seemed a risky investment. It would seem that our informants, in the main, did not have the right sorts of cultural capital to attract necessary business capital. This problem of the wariness of banks to fund non-traditional entrepreneurs has been reported elsewhere. Nabarro *et al.* (1986:5) in their study of enterprise policies and the unemployed identified 'discrimination against the less conventional entrepreneur', and Scase and Goffee argue that:

> women, young people and ethnic minorities, in particular can have great difficulty in raising finance, partly because their credibility and track record is regarded by many bankers as precarious. But all too often such opinions are based on rigid preconceptions rather than any real experience of lending money to these people. (1987:165)

Coupled with the reluctance of banks to provide capital, however, was the attitude of informants themselves to seeking loans. They too felt this was a risky business and many preferred to run their enterprises on a shoestring rather than be indebted to banks in the long term. Working-class culture on Teesside, rooted in the historical, local experiences of poverty and unemployment, stresses getting by, thrift and fear of debt. This was reflected in the attitudes of many of these young entrepreneurs to approaching banks for business capital. In one of the small number of qualitative assessments of the EAS, Gray and Stanworth found that very few of their Tyneside informants received initial financial backing from a bank and much fewer than in other areas were able to draw upon informal networks of family and friends for early capital investment (Gray and Stanworth, 1986). Informants in Rees and Thomas's (1989) case study of potential economic entrepreneurship amongst redundant Welsh coal-miners also identified the financial risks involved as one of the main factors dissuading them from starting businesses.

Our argument here is supported by the comments of the group of unemployed people (twelve) we interviewed (see Preface). They identified the following factors as the major reasons for their not considering self-employment a realistic option: their poverty (our term); lack of confidence and experience in business and money matters; lack of a skill or trade; and, fear of failure and running into debt with banks. For them starting up in business was a frightening and strange step to take. It sometimes held something of an abstract, dreamy attraction but was for them, living the day-to-day reality of unemployment in Teesside, thought to be impossible. Most did not know anyone who was self-employed and there was a general ignorance of the help offered through the local enterprise industry (for example, it was surprisingly common for unemployed informants not to have heard of the EAS). When the EAS was suggested as a possible route into business, the £1,000 necessary for entry was seen as an almost insurmountable hurdle ('I've never had £100, never mind £1,000!').

That apart, the small number of entrepreneurs whom we might classify as being generally successful did run their businesses with considerable financial help from the banks (often amounting to several thousand pounds investment). Clearly the attitude of banks to young entrepreneurs, and vice versa, deserves further attention by enterprise practitioners and policy-makers, and the subject of financial support for new businesses is one to which we will return in Chapter 10.

Summary

The movement of people into self-employment and new, small businesses is a process which has excited theoretical speculation from a variety of academic standpoints and has produced a considerable body of empirical literature. Traditionally a psychological perspective has held sway in small business research.

This approach attempts to identify largely psychological, motivational factors underlying individual decisions to form businesses (e.g. McClelland, 1961; Kets de Vries, 1977; Bonnett, 1990; Brockhaus, 1982, provides a useful summary). Research has been typified by the search for traits which constitute the 'entrepreneurial personality'. The quest for the psychic root of enterprise has, however, been argued to be inexact, outmoded, overly individualistic and supported only equivocally by empirical research (e.g. Chell 1986; Curran 1986; Stanworth *et al.*, 1989). Gibb and Ritchie (1982:30) conclude that:

> the weight of previous research emphasises that no one single social or psychological quality can itself hope to illustrate and account for variations of motives, skill and ambitions that individuals bring to the task of starting their own business.

Despite modifications (e.g. Stanworth *et al.*, 1989), this avenue of small business research, we would argue, still excludes numerous and highly significant economic, social, political and historical factors pertinent to the process of starting up in business. Little attention has been paid to, for instance, the role played by locality, class culture, gender, age or prevailing political ideology, in decisions to move into self-employment.

Although the tradition of (psychological) small business research on entrepreneurship has been directed toward largely individualistic explanations, more recent sociological literature has attempted to understand enterprise and self-employment within a broader analysis of Britain's changing economy and working culture. Here the growing prevalence of self-employment is seen as part of the increasing casualization and flexibility of work organization (Hakim, 1989a, 1989b), and/or an outcome of the recent small business revivalism and political attempts to encourage an enterprise culture (Burrows and Curran, 1989; Coles and MacDonald, 1990). Sociological interest in the dynamics of self-employment and small firm development has become invigorated (Burrows and Curran, 1989), though the subject still remains a poor relation in employment research. As Hakim puts it 'self-employment is one of the Cinderellas of labour market research, only recently invited to the ball' (1988:421). Burrows and Curran suggest that this can be explained by the economic forecasting of sociology's 'founding fathers' — from Marx, Durkheim and Weber alike — who predicted the inevitable industrial domination of big corporations and monopolies in late capitalist societies. Small firms and one-person businesses have been equated traditionally with much earlier phases of capitalist development.

Hakim has argued that the move to self-employment constitutes the most significant element, at least in quantitative terms, of this changing culture of work (Hakim, 1987a). The numbers of people self-employed grew rapidly during the 1980s in Britain, from about 2 million at the start of the decade to 3 million in 1989 (Hakim, 1989a). Each of the intervening years saw a rise in self-employment of 136,000 people, on average, claims Hakim (from Labour Force Survey data). Most of the growth has consisted of one-person 'micro-businesses' without employees (like the majority of our informants). About two-thirds of the self-employed work alone without any, even part-time, employees (Hakim, 1988). The self-employed now constitute over 12 per cent of the British workforce and this figure is predicted to grow (Hakim, 1988). This dramatic shift towards self-employment cannot be easily explained by the individualistic models which have dominated small business research.

Consequently, this remarkable growth in the quantitative significance of self-employment has generated much interested speculation about the causes and nature of this form of work in the late-twentieth-century British economy (see Chapter 10). The conventional, full-time, permanent, paid job is argued to be in decline. Rising self-employment is understood as part of the increasing casualization and flexibility of the labour market. It is conceptualized, for instance, as a response to changes in employment practices (e.g. the shift from the use of 'core' workers to more 'peripheral', often sub-contracted labour) and political policies, rather than as an outcome of personal motivations.

These two contrasting strands of literature — entrepreneurial personality theory and debates about the economic and cultural organization of work and employment — constitute the major approaches to investigating the movement of people into self-employment. We have introduced them here in order to locate our research within the context of these debates and we return to them in the final chapter. As it happens, each perspective (the traditional psychological and the recent sociological) attempt to answer slightly different questions. The former is largely ahistorical and asocial and has been concerned to explain why some people are/become entrepreneurs and others are/do not. This is not our intention in this chapter; rather, we identify more with the latter approach which has been inspired by an interest in the current small business revivalism and political promotion of the enterprise culture by the Thatcher government (Ritchie, 1984; Burrows and Curran, 1989).

Our project is not designed to investigate 'the entrepreneurial personality' but changing cultures of work in modern Britain in the late 1980s and 1990s. Thus, the question we asked is why, in a culture like Cleveland's, do young adults become self-employed?

To answer this question we have analyzed ethnographically accounts of motivations underlying business start-up. A major part of our task was to investigate the relationship between individual choices (e.g. to be self-employed) and the structure of opportunities facing youth in Cleveland. We explored the earlier careers (the career trajectories) of informants to examine the influence of a depressed local labour market upon decisions to move into self-employment. The individual biographies described are, of course, unique and are at least partly influenced by the psychological predispositions of particular informants. More importantly for us, however, they are also shaped by more social factors and constrained by the restricted economic opportunities faced, not just by individuals but collectivities of people. In this way, by locating individual decisions to become self-employed within the socio-economic conditions of the locality, and by situating them within a historical and political understanding of the changing culture of work, we hope to contribute to more sociological analyses of enterprise.[8]

We have argued that the shared experience of unemployment, for young people and adults alike in the county, was critical in understanding why people moved into self-employment. Quantitatively, unemployment featured strongly in our informants' early careers. Nine out of ten people had experienced unemployment since leaving school and nearly half of the self-employed informants had been unemployed for over two months immediately prior to start-up (with the mean duration of this period of unemployment being one year). Additionally, a significant route into self-employment was from government schemes, which were often considered by informants to be nothing more than a temporary respite from the dole.

Other studies of entry into entrepreneurial activities confirm the relationship between unemployment and self-employment. Allen and Hunn (1985) report that nearly 60 per cent of entrants to the EAS had been unemployed for six months or over in 1985 (and well over one-quarter had been unemployed for over a year). Studies of the move from redundancy to enterprise (Johnson and Roger, 1983; Lee, 1985; Rees and Thomas, 1989) have identified unemployment as a key explanatory variable in understanding why redundant workers had set up in business.

The idea that self-employment is increasingly being used as a response to restricted employment opportunities, especially, perhaps, in areas with the highest unemployment like Cleveland, was supported by the ethnographic data as well as by our examination of the early career histories of our informants. We criticized those who rely wholly on quantitative analysis of career trajectories at the start of the chapter and our examination of early careers was meant only as a starting point for the ethnography. The qualitative interviews also confirmed the significance of unemployment. It was found to be for many an enduring fact of post-16 life which shadowed the critical choices made and steps taken through the labour market into adulthood. Few jobs, an eagerness to work and the desperate experience of worklessness were all significant in pushing many people towards self-employment.

However, enterprise was undertaken by the majority for more than just survival. We should not forget that a minority of people had little experience of unemployment in the pre-enterprise period. (For them previous further education or employment were valuable experiences and often involved training closely related to their new enterprises). This group could be characterized as the most willing recruits to the ranks of the self-employed.

Becoming your own boss generally held positive attractions, even if the initial or prime motivation behind starting a business was the negative push of worklessness. Finn (1986) reports research which found that when asked why participants had joined the EAS the predominant answer was their inability to find jobs. Further questioning produced answers which stressed more positive reasons for starting up in business, such as the desire for independence, the potential challenge and financial reward. These positive advantages of becoming your own boss were mixed with the negative influence of unemployment in providing the set of reasons explaining the majority of informants' decisions to become self-employed.

The second part of the chapter examined what happened once the decision to start up in business had been made. A quite considerable amount of effort and time was usually spent on preparing for enterprise. This was perhaps surprising given the often negative reasons behind the decision to go self-employed. It might have been expected that people would have a less than wholeheartedly enthusiastic attitude to the processes of forming a business if what they really wanted was not a business but a job. On the contrary, informants were typically highly committed to their businesses once the first steps had been taken. Several months, in some cases years, passed in the process of planning businesses. A great deal of energy was devoted to revising business plans, visiting banks, researching markets, searching for premises, raising finances and building up stock.

Occasionally the strategies developed by informants to launch their businesses conflicted with official benefit regulations and also with the rules of the EAS. A small number of enterprising informants piloted their embryonic businesses whilst living on unemployment benefits. These activities in the informal economy are best understood as good examples of enterprising behaviour in the face of adversity rather than as 'dole fiddling' or manifestations of the so-called dependency culture.

We examined the work of enterprise agencies indirectly, through the experience of informants. Business enterprise agencies were reported in a generally positive manner, with support for the business advice and training given. Informants tended to name particular advisers as helpful and the one-to-one counselling given in the early stages of business preparation was welcomed.

Complaints were received, however, about the lack of medium- and long-term help, lack of specialist business advice and the perceived remoteness of agencies. In a small number of cases serious complaints were received about particular advisers who were perceived as having jeopardized grant applications for instance. Some informants also criticised the 'political' complexion of enterprise training in these enterprise agencies. It tended to omit reference to what one informant called 'the other side of things' (trade union membership and rights, Health and Safety regulations, etc.) in their emphasis upon the details of capitalist business development. Also little attention was given in the Awareness Days or enterprise training courses to forms of enterprise structure other than sole tradership or partnerships (for example, co-operatives).

The vast majority of our informants (85 per cent) used the Enterprise Allowance Scheme. Of course, the purpose of entering this scheme was to qualify for the allowance of £40 per week for their first year in business. Only a minority found it hard to gain acceptance on to the scheme (they either found difficulties in raising the necessary £1,000 or in qualifying for unemployment benefit for eight weeks). We drew attention to the undercapitalization of young businesses. Even those on EAS often only had the £1,000 for a limited period (if at all). Banks seemed to be operating ambiguously in respect of young entrepreneurs. On the one hand, potential EAS participants frequently benefited from banks' practice of lending on a very short-term basis. Some young men also received quite considerable bank loans (admittedly with the collateral of their parents' houses). Others, however — particularly it seemed, young women — found it much harder to raise even three-figure sums from banks. Issues of gender, age and class operated in the differential success of informants in winning business capital from banks. There was an apparent reluctance on behalf of some banks to deal positively with these non-traditional entrepreneurs. Young adults, particularly the unemployed sample, were also reluctant to risk debt. These could be important obstacles in the creation of an enterprise culture amongst the young and unemployed, particularly when other sources of finance previously used by our informants (e.g. the Regional Development Grant programme) have been discontinued. Undercapitalization emerged as a major problem for young entrepreneurs, as we will see in the next chapter.

The relationship between young entrepreneurs and their parents provided some surprises. Parents gave considerable support to their children in business. Material help was given, but perhaps most common was help-in-kind, for instance in the form of free board and lodging, which helped many people struggling with businesses in the early days. We found that, contrary to much research in this area, self-employment did not seem to be an experience shared by entrepreneurs' parents. Less than 10 per cent of people had parents who were or had been self-employed, a considerably lower figure than in other studies (e.g. Blythe et al., 1989a).

These informants seem to be non-traditional participants in the enterprise culture; many would have taken employee jobs if they had been available. Many take up enterprise, initially, as a way of surviving in a harsh economic climate. Most do not run innovatory businesses or exhibit enterprising competencies. The majority have no immediate family history of business ownership, and the area in which they live is one marked by a recent lack of an enterprise (i.e. small business) culture. It is feasible to argue, then, that these are a new breed of entrepreneur — exactly the sorts of people at whom government enterprise policies are aimed and who are represented in the increasing numbers of new entrants to self-employment in Britain during the past decade. Hakim, in an authoritative review of recent trends in self-employment, concluded: 'it appears that about one-third of the people entering self-employment in recent years are doing so primarily because of the job shortage' (1988:437).

If this new and developing interest in enterprise is to be sustained amongst people like our informants and in areas like Cleveland, some of the problems and issues we have identified here need to be addressed and remedied, and in the final chapter we present a fuller discussion of the implications our study has for youth enterprise policy. Perhaps the most immediate test facing government initiatives to foster an enterprise culture on Teeside lies in the experiences of young women and men who set up small businesses. If this new breed of entrepreneur can succeed, then there is every chance that the broader enterprise movement can. In this chapter we have explored why people become self-employed and the steps taken in preparing for enterprise. It is to the experience of young people actually running businesses that we turn in the next chapter.

Notes

1 In this chapter, we draw upon the comments and experiences of all those young adults who were some way along the self-employment trail, including those people who were intending to start up.

2 It is difficult to find another simple vacabulary to describe these processes, so we will retain this terminology but use this opportunity to state that neither a model of free will nor of career, in the senses we have described, is implied in our use of these concepts.

3 Some unemployed entrants to the world of enterprise characterized their move in terms of 'having nothing to lose', especially with the temporary safety net of the EAS £40 per week. For others, however, who were married and had children the decision to become self-employed involved much greater financial risk. A range of welfare benefits could be jeopardized by the decision to start up in business.

4 In the following quotation 'party plans' are referred to. This is a system of merchandising whereby goods are sold through an intermediary who often arranges evening parties in her/his home for friends and neighbours. The intermediary receives discounts or commission, and the producers (Mary and Jane) sell their goods and develop their customer base.

5 A small number of female informants reported a similar dismissive, patronizing attitude from particular enterprise advisers.

6 Some informants, those who did not participate in the EAS, received no business training whatsoever.

7 One of the authors (RM) participated in a Business Enterprise Programme (BEP) course at a local enterprise agency and was able to observe directly the greater emphasis upon business practice and the lack of attention to what Roger calls 'the other side of things'.

8 Hakim argues that 'it is precisely because so little attention has been paid to self-employment until the 1980s that debates have so far been informed more by ideology than by empirical research' (1988:445). She calls for more case-studies of small business formation which elucidate motivations to become self-employed. Burrows and Curran (1989) also look forward to more small business research 'adequate at the level of meaning'.

Chapter 6

Risky Business?

In the last chapter we examined the process of starting up in business; in this chapter we report the experiences of the same group as they actually ran their new businesses. First, we provide basic information about the firms and examine some key issues (for example, business finance, premises, managerial style). Following this, we look more directly at the experience of entrepreneurship which will lead us to a consideration of the expectations people had and the likely future of their enterprises. The focus then switches to the experiences of those who no longer traded in the enterprise culture and looked back upon their earlier business practices often with a more critical eye. Before concluding the chapter, we offer an analysis of the success and failure of these small businesses based on a three-fold typology of the experiences of informants.

Selling and Serving: Types of Young Business

First of all, the types of business need to be described. Teresa Rees has characterized alternative work for young people in the enterprise economy as consisting, at the 'loonier fringe', of 'pet rocks, kissagrams and bootstrap enterprises' (Rees, 1986:15). A *Guardian* (6 January 1989) double-page spread on youth enterprise corroborated this picture of strange and unusual practices. It featured a pet-food supplier, a hat maker, a manufacturer of four-poster beds and a stick insect breeder. In Chapter 5, however, we hinted that much of the business conducted by this group lacked any obvious innovatory design or ideas, nor were they initiated by any real entrepreneurial zeal. These enterprises largely reflected jobs in the local economy, rather than being the weird and wonderful enterprises favoured by the media. As Curran says:

> The great majority of those who start . . . a small business should not be seen as 'entrepreneurs' in any strict sense . . . the term 'entrepreneur' . . . might more properly be reserved for those who

create a new successful enterprise based on a novel product or service and/or a novel organizational means for producing a good or providing a service and/or the novel marketing and distribution of goods and services. Most small businesses owners are simply cloning an existing, well proven form of enterprise. (Curran, 1986:17)

Moreover, the type of work carried out by individuals in new businesses did not challenge traditional gender stereotyping. This is perhaps not surprising given the difficulties in starting any business, never mind an enterprise which works against the grain of a labour market with strict gender divisions.

We decided not to group the businesses by occupation, nor by industrial division. This would tell us only that the vast majority of businesses formed by our sample involved retailing or some form of service business. Nationally the self-employed tend to be concentrated in the service, distributive and retailing sectors. Within the EAS, construction and retailing have always featured as the largest industrial categories, with approximately 65 per cent involved in service businesses (Allen and Hunn, 1985). Both our figures and those from national surveys support the view that enterprise policies may be (re)creating a nation of shop-keepers: 'with the high proportion of retail management among the occupations, the profile of the typical self-employed person is reminiscent of a certain Grantham shopkeeper' (*Labour Research*, 1986:15).

The classification below breaks the sample of those seventy-four informants, who were in co-ops or small firms at the time of the interview, into ten loose categories.[1] They are listed in declining importance of size, with, for instance, nearly twenty people in the first group and two in the last. Of course there are other ways in which these businesses could be classified, but in grouping them according to the relative frequency of particular business types, we hope to give an idea of the actual businesses owned and run by the informants:

1 the design, production and retailing of clothes
2 graphic design, illustration and art-related work
3 non-clothing related retailing — usually grocers or specialist food shops
4 beauty therapy and hairdressing
5 the servicing, retailing and programming of computers or computer-related products
6 photography or video production
7 skilled or semi-skilled manual work (cabinet maker, mechanic, welder and gardener)
8 technical services to the local music industry
9 printing and publishing
10 business and financial services

A number of people worked in areas difficult to fit into these categories. These included two young men who specialized in watch and clock repairs, a writer of historical novels, two picture framers, a signwriter, an interpreter, a man who imported and exported silverware, a man who ran a nappy delivery service and a mountain guide.

Defining the structures of the businesses is a simpler process. Well over half of the informants operated their businesses as self-employed sole traders, whilst one-quarter were in partnerships. Nine were still trading in co-operatives. One person owned a limited company and a handful of business people were preparing to 'go limited'. In this way our sample is broadly typical of EAS participants generally (Bevan *et al.*, 1989). Two-thirds of all self-employed run 'micro-businesses' or what a recent report calls 'microfirms' (Nabarro *et al.*, 1986) on their own, employing few if any workers (Hakim, 1988).

The time in business is perhaps the last piece of factual information we can provide as background information. Some (three) were very new and had only been running for a few weeks when the business owner was interviewed. Others had been in operation for several years. Ten informants had been in business for over two years, with one informant self-employed for five years. The majority fell somewhere in between. Over half were still in their first year and still drew upon the assistance of enterprise agencies and the EAS in the operation of their businesses. About one-fifth had been trading for between one and two years. Of those people who were no longer trading (eighteen) most had managed to remain in business for approximately a year at least, with the financial assistance of the EAS. This provided a £40 per week prop for new businesses, which, when withdrawn however, was often a contributory factor in businesses going bust at the twelve-month point or in the months following. Only three out of the eighteen who had closed down had managed to last beyond two years in business.

Although our method has not been longitudinal, we can still gain something of a long-term perspective on the experience of running businesses by drawing upon the accounts given by informants at these different stages of business development. In the next section we identify the key issues prioritized by informants in discussing how they ran their businesses.

Running Businesses

Premises

One of the first problems for any new business is to establish a working base. Informants ran their businesses from three types of location: home, enterprise start-up units, or rented business premises (shops, offices, factory units) in the towns of Teesside. Each of these types of premises brought both advantages and disadvantages. Although working from home (usually the parental home) cut the cost of renting office or work-shop space, other potential expensive overheads (telephone, heating, lighting) and time and money spent on travel, it was also reported as having a number of drawbacks. Space was often cramped, interruptions and distractions frequent and people felt isolated from the 'real world' of business.

Renting premises overcame some of these problems but brought new ones. Of course, the main cost is financial with the price of a retail outlet near the centre of Middlesbrough or Hartlepool being quite pro-hibitive for most informants. Those that were in any way affordable were in great demand and highly sought after. One informant had searched for nearly a year to find appropriate premises at a reasonable rent. Even when premises became available to young entrepreneurs, the majority could not afford anything but the most basic accommodation. Premises were often poorly heated, scruffy and hidden away in the back streets — all negative influences, particularly when relying upon custom coming to these busi-ness locations.

Many new enterprises were poorly located, situated some distance from central commercial areas and lacking the shop-front needed, in particular, by retail outlets. Two young women, Felicity and Vivien, complained vigorously about the location of the shop unit they finally rented. It was upstairs in a small complex of business units about one mile from the centre of Middlesbrough. The distance from town, the lack of passing trade and the invisibility of their business were perceived as the reasons behind its eventual failure.[2] They regarded the building as jinxed and reported that several new businesses located there had folded during their tenancy.

Further problems associated with premises included difficulties in meeting legal and insurance requirements, given particular business prac-tices. For instance, Trevor spent several hundred pounds and many weeks modifying his already expensive industrial unit to meet health and safety requirements (to allow spray painting). These changes had not been anticipated by Trevor and set his business back considerably. Shops, in particular, were often old and in poor physical repair. A number of the shop traders reported this as having made them vulnerable to the burglar-ies they had suffered. One young man, Carl, had his shop in Hartlepool burgled twice in six months; the second time he had been physically attacked. (When last visited he had bought a Rottweiler dog, baseball bat and starting pistol for protection.)

Despite the various dangers and difficulties experienced by those young entrepreneurs who had taken premises for their businesses, locat-ing young enterprises in a 'real' economic environment, rather than at home, sometimes proved beneficial. If young businesses can give the appearance of being a credible, commercial organization (e.g. by having modern, smart, accessible offices), it is more likely that they will be treated positively by potential clients.[3] Location was important for one final reason. Lesley was self-employed as a beauty therapist and ran her business from a small complex of similar businesses (health foods, hairdressing and fitness centre). The location of her enterprise, in the immediate vicinity of these other related businesses, generated a lot of spin-off trade. Customers would come and use several of the services, including hers, in one visit.

Working either at home or in rented commercial premises both brought problems, albeit of different kinds. A half-way house between a home-based business and location in a more commercial setting is a starter unit provided by local enterprise agencies. These can, to some extent, overcome the isolation, the lack of credibility and the distractions associated with working from home, and they avoid the sometimes crippling rents charged in the market place. One of the key activities of the enterprise industry has been the provision of low-cost, supervised workshop and office space. Many of the informants were contacted through local enterprise agencies and some were interviewed in these start-up units. The general message gained from this group was that working from such locations was beneficial, with only a few drawbacks.

The major advantages over working from home were that start-up units provided reasonable physical space, heating, lighting, telephone-answering and reception services at a low cost. Obviously the cost of these units was cheaper than similar premises available in the market place, and they were run on subsidies to help young entrepreneurs establish themselves. Rents here varied from about £12 to £20 per week in 1989. Coupled with the advice available from counsellors, and the community support generated by working alongside other young entrepreneurs, these cheap rents provided the main attractions of start-up units.

Relatively minor complaints were received about such premises; these often boiled down to personality clashes and apparently petty squabbles between clients and the staff of the centres. The main issue seemed to be the atmosphere of the enterprise centres, particularly those specializing in advice and help for young business people. Some complained about 'being treated like kids' and that it was 'just like school, full of petty regulations and attitudes'. Access to the buildings was difficult at times with one informant having to argue long and hard for the right to come to work in her unit over a two-week period at Christmas time (when the centre's staff were on holiday). In short, a minority felt that they were not being treated as serious business people running serious businesses.

A more important planning problem in the provision of start-up units was identified. Tenancy of such premises is restricted to a time duration of usually between one and two years, the reasoning being that subsidized rents cannot be offered to all Cleveland's young entrepreneurs. So facilities are provided for a limited period of time which allows businesses to establish themselves before moving out into premises charging market rents. A fresh batch of tenants can then take the opportunities provided by start-up units.

The problem comes when they have to move out at the end of their allotted tenancy. It would be a backward step to move the business home so young entrepreneurs started to look for premises to rent in the local towns. The difference between the costs for these clean, modern, subsidized workshops and the costs for much less attractive accommodation at market prices was considerable. Two young men in a partnership run from an enterprise agency paid £8 each per week for their unit. Contrast this with one informant who was paying nearly £70 per week for his shop in Middlesbrough. The step from subsidized units to 'real' premises was made even more difficult by the timing of the move. Often tenancies expired at the same time as EAS allowances ran out (i.e. after a year).[4] People who had been struggling to set up a business for a year were now faced with the problem of losing both essential financial support and premises in one fell swoop. It is no wonder that many of those who go out of business do so at this point or shortly afterwards.

Business Capital and Equipment

A second significant element in running a business is the amount of capital available to the new entrepreneur. This group appeared to be very undercapitalized in the business start-up stages. Unfortunately the general picture did not change once businesses were up and running.

Some individuals were successful in securing quite large bank loans or overdraft facilities (up to £25,000) and these often became crucial in the early stages of businesses. They were used to locate enterprises in suitable commercial properties, to purchase necessary equipment and stock, to advertise products or services and to employ workers. Basically, funding of this sort at an early stage enabled new businesses to develop themselves comparatively quickly, which in turn generated the necessary business to repay bank debts and, in some cases, to start to expand. As we suggested in the last chapter, funding at anywhere near this level was quite rare and was restricted to a handful of informants. A number of key factors influenced the securing of early capital investment.

Firstly, the attitude of bank managers was important. They seemed to favour applications from more educated, middle-class, older males. Secondly, and relatedly, parents and family occasionally donated funds directly into their children's businesses. Help was also given indirectly in the form of collateral (e.g. the parental home) for their offsprings' bank loans. The third main influence on the level of early business capital was the availability of Regional Development Grants.

These three sources of help — banks, parents and government grants — amounted to considerable sums of investment in a small number of the businesses studied. One young man had offices, telephones, heating and all other business overheads paid for by his parents for his first year in business. Additionally, he lived at home and only paid £10 per week board and lodging. This level of family assistance was very rare but could provide a dramatic head start in enterprise.

Two successful informants working in a partnership had managed to invest £2,000 of personal savings, £6,000 in grants, a £3,000 bank loan (secured with their own house as collateral) and a £1,000 overdraft in their business. They had thus been able to rent a large factory unit, take on a small number of employees (some on government schemes) and advertise their products. Running their business on a reasonable financial footing from the outset had allowed them to compete successfully in the market place for business. For some businesses large scale capital invest-ment was crucial. Necessary equipment, in a small publishing/ printing firm, cost nearly £100,000. Regional Development Grants, before their demise, were particularly useful in funding the purchase of machinery and other equipment. The only problems involved the bureaucratic de-lays in the arrival of grants once they had been allocated, which could sometimes mean disaster for businesses on very tight budgets.

Beyond these sources there was little financial backing for young entrepreneurs. Typically, businesses were run on a shoestring with per-sonal savings (perhaps of a few hundred pounds) and £40 per week from the EAS. The majority of young entrepreneurs had little or no money in the bank. Most of the enterprises involved very little in the way of elaborate or expensive production processes. They tended to rely on the services and labour of the informants rather than on capital or equipment. Lillian, from Stockton, ran a business as a photographer from home. The only equipment she needed was a camera which cost her £135. Others might need a sewing machine or a computer in a front room to run their businesses, which were frequently the extension of teenage hobbies and often these items were already owned.

Finding Markets and Managing Businesses

Curran (1986) provides a neat review of research upon managerial styles in the small enterprise. Firstly, he identifies a boom in 'how to do' books, which has accompanied the rise of the enterprise movement generally: practical guides for the new business person covering particular aspects of business practice. These manuals tend to emulate practices identified in the success of big business and pay little attention to the realities of running small firms and micro-businesses.

One of the major findings of the second, more academic part of this large body of research literature draws a causal relationship between the owner-manager's personal characteristics (for instance, his or her 'entrepreneurial personality') and ensuing managerial style. It is argued that, for instance, the desire for autonomy inhibits delegation of managerial tasks and business growth. Curran reports that many owner-managers are found to be unwilling to innovate, delegate, borrow, or lose independence. Intuitively this would seem to make some sense; however, we would suggest that a factor of equal importance in determining entrepreneurial styles and practices is the local economy. If many people display a similar managerial style, this may be because they operate in similar, severely competitive markets, not because of similar personality traits. Curran also notes that business style is often characterized by 'fire-brigading' — attempts to solve a constant stream of crises, and that growth takes second place to 'steady state', independent existence.

The ways in which businesses were run were seemingly not out of the ordinary. There was little in the way of new, dynamic, enterprising business practices here. This is not difficult to understand. The motivation to start businesses lay not in the desire to make or market new products or to develop new methods of business proprietorship, but in more mundane reasons (see Chapter 5).

Generally, businesses ran close to debt, insolvency and potential closure. They had to compete with other small firms (new and old), with established larger firms and with the informal economy. Profit margins tended to be very low and new businesses often tried to establish themselves in the market place by competing on price. In this way older businesses or last year's crop of EAS businesses were undercut and customers could be attracted. This business strategy, reported by many, continued as follows. Good service and products would then ensure that the customer base was maintained and hopefully expanded. In time young entrepreneurs would start to charge nearer the 'going rate' for their work. The support of Enterprise Allowance money and subsidized premises in part permitted this strategy. With a guaranteed £40 per week young business people could afford to cut their charges to a minimum, in some cases barely covering the costs of materials.

There were other clear problems in this type of business management. Underpricing of goods or services was occasionally reported as a bad commercial move. It apparently suggested to customers that the businesss was not serious or credible and was therefore unreliable. Helen, the fine artist, sold her pictures at shows and to galleries. She found that initial attempts to sell at very low prices met with little success, but that when she raised her charges business increased. This point reflects one we made earlier about business premises: the more commercial and real they appeared, the more credible and potentially successful the business.

Competing on cost, with the help of the EAS, also generated difficulties in the second year of business when the allowance stopped. Once informants had started trading in cheap services or products, this practice became expected by customers in the long-term. If young business people could not afford to offer such bargains in their second year, customers could simply switch to more commercial, high street shops. In this way young entrepreneurs became trapped in a business practice they could neither afford to carry on nor to give up. Terry made a similar point. When he began trading unofficially as a joiner, whilst still working for his employer, he could afford to do weekend jobs 'on the side' very cheaply. After all, this was just a lucrative supplement to his weekly wage. Once he set up in business, however, customers expected him to charge the same rates as previously, making it very difficult for him to earn a wage similar to that previously earned as an employee (especially as he was unsuccessful in gaining entry to the EAS). The displacement effect of new, small firms like these has been recognized officially (National Audit Office 1988) and was of concern locally. In an interview with Training Agency staff in the area we were told:

> The Small Business Club on Teesside are not happy with EAS. They see small businesses being pushed out by the next EAS person that comes along. That's their moan. It's the crunch time just after twelve months, but there's always another EAS person to come along and take their place.

Some of the arguably more successful entrepreneurs were operating less usual businesses. They offered products, but more frequently services, which were quite specialized and drew upon uncommon skills and areas of expertise. One young man had a business offering a specialist repair and maintenance service for a very particular type of machinery. His market was national and his work was in great demand. In his first year of business he had a turnover of more than £50,000. Seemingly he had very few competitors, even within the wider, Northern region. The only problem he faced was a product of his success. Constant demand resulted in incredibly long working hours, with little room for a social life. He was not keen to take on employees and he had to ensure that he did not over-trade (i.e. take on too many customers) which would have resulted in poorer quality work, jobs being done late and dissatisfied customers.

Some businesses, though offering specialist work likely to capture a good slice of the market (e.g. two informants who learnt the watch repair business from their grandfather), were limited by that very specialism.

The work was highly skilled and of a rare sort. Hence, it was unlikely that they could employ someone with the same skills to help them without having to spend time training them. This time was not available — they had a business to run. Furthermore, the demand for specialist skills and products is probably limited on Teesside, compared with more prosperous areas. Middlesbrough does not have markets to compare with Covent Garden or Camden Lock in London, nor the same numbers of young, middle-class customers keen to buy stylish, specialist and unusual goods.

The problems of success, of over-expansion and over-trading, were not ones shared by most of the other informants. The potential for growth of these businesses was probably very limited. The vast majority employed nobody but the owner and most anticipated that this would remain the case. The majority simply could not afford to take on employees and the conditions of the local labour market ensured that growth was an unlikely prospect.

As has been reported elsewhere (Curran, 1986; Scase and Goffee, 1987), there was also an aversion to expansion. Independence, autonomy and flexibility were key positive factors influencing the move into self-employment in the first place and most preferred to keep their businesses very small. This allowed continuing personal control over the day-to-day running of the enterprise. Young entrepreneurs enjoyed being involved in all aspects and stages of their businesses. Being an employer, rather than a self-employed sole trader, was perceived as presenting unnecessary bureaucratic difficulties. Even the thought of taking on a trainee through a government scheme was daunting to most informants. The rules, regulations and relative costs and benefits were unclear and deterred sole traders. The unwillingness which in some became opposition to taking on employees, acted as a severe break to the growth of these concerns.

A minority of new businesses employed staff other than the owner. More often, though, young entrepreneurs received assistance from their family. In some cases wives became quasi-employees doing secretarial, delivery, book-keeping and other tasks for the entrepreneurial husband. This sort of help was also given by parents. The families of young business people provided essential physical, financial and emotional support. Their sacrifices and contribution to the success of new businesses often goes unrecognized in practitioners' guide books to starting and running businesses. But without their help many of the informants we studied would not have been able to set up in the first place.

The majority of business people ran firms which traded in a very local, confined market, and in a market which already offered many of the products and services they hoped to sell. As Ashton and Maguire argue 'opportunities for individuals to develop their own initiatives for creating employment are closely linked to the level of economic activity in the local labour market' (1986:45). In every sense these businesses were *small*. They had few if any employees, operated on miniscule budgets and profit margins, worked within a very restricted geographical area, and were run with low expectations and with limited entrepreneurial flair. What they lacked in size they made up for in sheer hard work and perseverance. Youth enterprise in Cleveland could be argued to be a prime case of 99 per cent perspiration, and 1 per cent inspiration.

Despite their efforts, custom was often very hard to develop. They were in competition with much more established, well-known and successful companies. They had the advantage of various types of support from the enterprise industry, but in general this only served to get them going in the early stages. As soon as they set up and began trading (advertising, buying stock, renting premises, charging for work) they were at the mercy of the market place. In becoming self-employed they did not suddenly become liberated from the demands and pressures of bosses; rather, young entrepreneurs found themselves at the command of their clients. Every (potential) customer was now the boss. Terry, the joiner, said:

> You're never your own boss. It's a fallacy that. You get your arse kicked by more people. When you're working you've only got your boss to worry about. When you're working for yourself you've got everybody else to worry about. Customers on your back. Bank manager after you. DHSS after one thing or another. Tax man chasing you. Everybody's taking their bit.

A handful of young business people managed to secure highly valuable contracts from much larger companies in the area. An informant in a video-production company earned £500 for one day's work for a local engineering firm. Contracts like these were crucial in the process of trying to establish a precarious young business. Not only did they bring in much-needed finance, they gave the chance to develop reputations and further contracts. Working for the local 'big fish' did present problems for these entrepreneurial minnows, as Jonathan, who had a company in Middlesbrough, described:

> RM: Would you describe yourself as successful?
>
> *Jonathan:* I could probably answer that at the end of the second year. We're successful-ish. We can pay our way...//
> ...Something could happen next week and we could go bankrupt. There's always that chance with any small business. If our one big client pulled out we'd be totally jiggered. We've got that hanging over us all the time. And the problem is — the bigger the client, the longer it takes them to pay up, and the longer we've got to put the money up. They know we need them. They don't need

us. If we get an £8,000 job, we maybe have to pay out £4,000 to get it done. If you've got three of those sort of jobs floating about that's £12,000 you've got to find from somewhere. You've already spent up and you're waiting for the money. It causes immense cash-flow difficulties.

Jonathan's company had been successful in getting a big order which continued to bring in the bulk of money and work. The profits from each completed job were reinvested in financing the next one. Success of this sort was, however, a double-edged sword. He had become reliant on this contract which could be lost at any time. He acknowledged that his business would most likely fold if this happened. Even 'successful-ish' enterprises involved risky business. Moreover, large companies demanded up to ninety days to pay for work done, but usually gave no credit or time to pay to new, small businesses in return. Apart from presenting severe cash-flow problems, meeting big orders demanded that work be carried out to a highly professional level very quickly, equalling more hard work and longer hours for these struggling entrepreneurs. Occasionally these business people ran into problems of non-payment, resulting in considerable time and effort trying to recoup money owed. Ray ran a sign-writing business, and had had one or two 'big jobs' with local firms:

Because my work might cost them £1,000 and they might have bills of £20,000 to pay to someone else, they just forget about me. They just treat people like me like dirt. They don't think twice about not paying you. They don't think you are trying to make a living as well. I'm sick of it.

Despite these problems, which are experienced by all sorts of small businesses, not just young entrepreneurs, big money contracts were highly valuable to these informants. Getting them, and more importantly keeping them, was a vital part of building a business likely to survive in the long-term. Most operated businesses which had to rely on a wider and variable range of customers, usually individuals purchasing personal products or services.

One aspect of business practice which was interesting and quite common involved networks of trade between young entrepreneurs. Many of the informants knew, and traded with, each other. A good proportion of them had been based in local enterprise agencies at some time and perhaps shared neighbouring start-up units. A business services agency might use a graphic designer who might in turn employ a self-employed photographer. In this way new firms run by young adults supported each other and spread work around.

Again there were some drawbacks to this style of enterprise. These informants were engaged in a form of sub-contracting. One business would gain work, which it was unable or unwilling to complete on its own, and then pass parts of it to other new businesses. For instance, one firm of leisure-wear manufacturers (run by young people who were not interviewed) provided most of the work for two small firms that we did study. Orders for these garments brought the majority of their work. Initially, however, they had set up to make specialist, original designer clothing for the fashion market. Now they had to sacrifice their independence, creative control and grander plans for these subcontracted, 'bread and butter' jobs. Some of our informants thus became cheap and reliable out-workers for other small companies.

Particular businesses were in some cases only part of the wider work in which young adults were involved. Informants, as well as running businesses as self-employed sole traders, were occasionally employed elsewhere. One man, a self-employed hairdresser, additionally worked in a newsagents from five o'clock to nine o'clock every morning. A self-employed woman who ran a design business also taught one day a week in a local technical college. In this way extra money could be earned from jobs outside the business. This employment could provide vital financial support for the self-employed business person.

Income and Hours: 'If I don't make it, I can't take it'

Whilst the enterprise industry provided help, the major reason why these new enterprises functioned at all was due to the hard work of young business people and the fact that they took very little in the way of financial rewards from their enterprises. The following extract is from an interview with Gary, who had run a graphic design business for a year in Middlesbrough. He had been unemployed for several years before attempting to join the enterprise culture and was unemployed again at the time of interview. His wife Shirley was present and also contributed to the discussion.

Shirley:　Nothing happened in the last quarter — he made no money at all in the last twelve weeks . . . he was disillusioned — it just sickened you a bit, didn't it?

Gary:　Well, it was a pleasure to go out to work. You wonder whether you are going to make any money. Tax your brains if you didn't — 'how could you make any money?'. It got a bit lonely, just sitting around. But it wasn't bad because you wonder whether you are going to make £15 during the week or whether you are going to make £20. You've got it in the back of your mind that things might pick up and you'd make £70 a week.

RM:　Did you manage to take a regular wage from the business?

> *Gary:*   I never took a penny from the business apart from the odd cash job which might have been up to £5 or £6 . . . I was taking the £40 and that was it. I gave that to the wife. I got a rise in my pocket money from £5 to £7 per week. I had to pay for my own petrol and cigarettes.
>
> *RM:*   It's not a lot, is it?
>
> *Gary:*   It's not a lot to earn.

Gary's case is not dramatically different from many of those investigated. He was one of the lowest paid, but some reported taking less money home as a wage, and he did at least have the EAS to help support his wife and two young children.

Personal finances are a particularly difficult subject to enquire about. It is also a subject which can attract greater attention than more qualitative research findings. It may be that in some research informants may choose to exaggerate (or underestimate) the pay they receive. One or two young men in our sample seemed to be rather wild in their claims for success. However, we feel that the information we gathered about money earned through enterprise is fairly reliable. The ethnographic method allowed reasonably in-depth discussions of often sensitive issues. In a small number of cases informants were hesitant about providing financial information. After reassurances about anonymity and the purpose of the questioning, only four out of the group of seventy-four people decided not to divulge the pay they took out of their businesses. It should be added that the pay of self-employed people is doubly difficult to estimate. Informants sometimes actually took very little money which could be described as pay from their businesses. Income from the business was confused and uncertain. We have attempted to arrive at a figure which could be regarded as income after business expenses had been paid. These problems aside, we were able to estimate reasonably accurately the pay of young entrepreneurs as follows.

When considering the income figures it should be remembered that many people were still receiving £40 per week from the EAS. This amount has not been deducted from the following figures. Over half were earning £40 per week or less and seven people reported taking home less than £25 per week. Two-thirds of the informants who gave informantion were working for less than £50 per week. Overall three-quarters were earning £80 per week or less for themselves. Three people made over £100 per week, with the highest paid informant earning £250 per week himself. These figures are lower than in other surveys of EAS participation (e.g. Allen and Hunn, 1985).

Like pay, the hours spent working in enterprises every week were usually highly variable. One male informant, for instance, was involved in the publication of a magazine. Immediately preceding publication he would work over seventy hours per week, but the following week he might not work at all. Thus, the figures we present for both pay and hours are average estimates. The clear majority were working for forty hours per week or more, with a concentration of people working around forty-five to fifty hours per week. Nine people usually worked for over sixty hours per week, with the highest average reported being 110 hours per week (this informant was one of three mentioned above who earned over £100 per week).

Youth enterprise, then, means low pay and long hours. The average pay of individual entrepreneurs was divided by the average hours worked to arrive at an average rate per hour. Again this paints a bleak picture. Only six people reported earning more than £2 per hour. Over two-thirds were working for £1 per hour or less. It is not surprising that a majority clustered around this figure given the heavy reliance upon EAS money by businesses in this first year. What it also indicates, though, is that very few managed to increase their earnings above EAS levels in the second and later years of business. Additionally, those that were earning comparatively high amounts were working long hours in order to do so.

We should remember when considering the money earned through self-employment that our sample of informants, though young, were predominantly in their early twenties. Pay at this sort of level has been reported amongst other people in the 16–19 age group. By comparison our sample were not teenagers but young adults (with the average age of twenty-one) who might, quite understandably, expect to be earning more than this. Many of those toward the older end of the age spectrum in our sample had families to support and mortgages to pay.

The Experience of Entrepreneurship

If enterprise for young adults in Cleveland means long hours and little money, why do they carry on? One immediate answer is that for many, as we illustrated in the previous chapter, there is simply no alternative. For some self-employment was an answer to unemployment, and to give up their new businesses would mean a return to the dole queues. However, the answer is not as straightforward as that. The practice of entrepreneurship did have its own attractions and these provided some reward on a more social and psychological level.

The first example is a section from an interview with Joanne, from Middlesbrough, who ran a knitwear business:

RM: So it's going well?
Joanne: Very well, I can't believe it.
RM: How many hours do you put in?
Joanne: It varies. The two months after Christmas was the least which was about forty hours per week. We will be more

busy from now until Christmas. It's well over forty hours. Sometimes I am knitting until ten or eleven at night, it depends how urgent it is.

RM: Do you give yourself a steady wage or does it . . .

Joanne: (interrupts) . . . No, it's just a steady wage. £40 per week. It's just literally to keep me going more than anything else.

RM: Some people might say it's an awful lot of work for little money?

Joanne: Well, that is it. I understand it's only business, just starting off. That you can't claim a big wage — I mean, literally, I'm struggling by, but it's a case of, well, waiting for the business to build up, and then I'll be able to claim a higher wage . . . // . . . money's not that important to me really, so long as I can keep my car and go out one night a week, I'm happy.

Few anticipated earning much money through enterprise, in the early days at least. A dominant theme which emerged from the interviews was this phlegmatic realism. Phrases such as 'struggling by' and 'plugging along' characterized a determined and hopeful, but also stoical attitude to the practice of enterprise. Hard work and long hours would not be rewarded by large sums of money immediately or even in the near future. One day businesses might blossom and then higher wages could be taken. In the meantime informants were happy with the minimal money earned and other less tangible rewards.

The second passage is from an interview with Fraser who had previously been self-employed as a joiner specializing in home improvements. He was asked about the advantages and disadvantages of running his own business, in comparison to being an employee:

You know that you are responsible for the money you get in the bank, whereas if you are working for somebody else, like I was before, I made so much of a product, someone else made so much and someone else painted it. So that was one [advantage] — job satisfaction. Another thing was that you didn't have someone on your back all the time. When I was at work if you stopped and blew your nose, they would crack the whip. Disadvantages? Well, when it isn't going too good you're directly responsible. Security is one of the main things. I always had the feeling that I hope the next six months go as well as this six months and you never quite know. You can see about ten feet in front of you but after that, it's a bit hazy. That's one of the disadvantages. In certain phases, yes. It does get a bit depressing because you start to think to yourself 'What am I doing? Where am I going?' and you've got nobody looking after you — it's a one-man band . . . .

// . . . it is very easy to keep flogging a dead horse. You are very enthusiastic and you can go up the wrong road and keep putting in 100 per cent plugging away and plugging away when really you should be taking a step back and thinking about what you are doing.

For Fraser, the disadvantages of being self-employed included the uncertainty of business and the (sometimes) disheartening pressure to find work. His trade was very seasonal, with plenty of work in the summer months but little in the winter. Opportunities to structure and manage his own time were positive benefits in comparison to previous employment. Relatedly, job satisfaction was higher. He became more of a craftsman involved with several stages of production, rather than only dealing with one part of a job. He finally gave up the business, a decision he should have taken earlier, because he was only just surviving and not making a decent living. At the time of interview he was employed part-time by a local firm and was being paid a similar wage to that he earned for very long hours in self-employment.

The insecurity of earnings, week by week and month by month, was reported more generally. Demand for products and services fluctuated quite markedly, with boom times before Christmas and a slump in trade afterwards. Helen, the artist, did very well in December making a record £340. In January, however, her income was £4 for the whole month. Poor budgeting compounded this insecurity, with pre-Christmas earnings being spent quickly leaving little for the leaner months. Increasing demand was, of course, welcomed but it also meant increasing working hours. Helen, to earn her bumper takings, had been getting only three or four hours sleep per night. One woman reported working for nineteen hours a day for a month to meet pre-Christmas orders for her knitwear products.

The unpredictability of work and income also meant that informants found it difficult to make social plans for the future. Holidays were particularly rare. Even if these could be scheduled, most informants reported that they could not affort to spare the time or potential earnings lost by taking two weeks off. Jonathan, with the graphic design business in Middlesbrough, said:

Jonathan: It's probably the best job satisfaction you'll ever get in the world. Everything you create is for yourself . . . // . . . We work together more or less like a family. We look after each other. You don't get that working for someone else . . . // . . . I might only earn £50 but I've earned it myself and maybe I've done five or six things to get that. You're actually producing something. Half of it, most of it is the job satisfaction.

RM: What are the disadvantages?

Jonathan: It's a bit risky. With a job you know you've got so many years and x amount of salary and you can plan things and get a mortgage. There's not much security. In six months you might be earning £20 per week, the next six months — £100 per week. It might be five or six years before it's going to be secure.

Carl also identifies both positive and negative aspects of entrepreneurship. He ran a clothes shop in Hartlepool.

RM: What are the best things about self-employment?

Carl: Freedom, money and being the owner of your business. If you go wrong, there's only you to blame. If you want money you can take it out of the business. It is there, if you want it.

RM: Disadvantages?

Carl: Pressure and bills. There is a hell of a lot of pressure on you. I can't sleep some nights worrying about bills. You never get any time for yourself. If I was working for somebody nine to five, I could go home and forget about it. With being self-employed I go when the work is finished. When I was doing the shop up I was working from eight in the morning until two in the morning. Now I finish at six unless there is people in the shop. Sometimes I work 'till two in the morning making up garments. But it's doing me more harm than good.

Freedom and ownership of a business, it will be recalled, were key elements in the positive reasoning behind starting businesses (see Chapter 5). Carl also mentions money. Unfortunately he was one of the few who avoided the question about his earnings. It is possible that he was already reaping reasonable rewards for the hours he was putting into his business. However, he had only been trading for a few months and was paying a large rent for his shop premises. It is more probable that, like other informants who stated that money was 'a good thing' about being self-employed, he felt that *in the long term* enterprise would financially reward his efforts.

Johnny ran a fashion design business. He had a very mixed attitude to self-employment and was one of the few people who would have actually preferred to be employed by someone else:

It's difficult to say what I like. I like the studio. You feel good actually coming into work and having your own place. You feel like King of the Castle. And the actual recognition — that people know I am a designer. I'm on the market now. People see your style of work. The flexibility of working hours — you don't have to bow down to any big boss. The challenge — to find gaps in the market and sell your work. Disadvantages? Well, the paperwork, if you're working for somebody else, you don't have to worry about that. You don't get a steady wage. It's lonely. When I was at college I was working with maybe forty other people. Now it's just me ... // ... all I need is one big break. It is getting better, even though the work really isn't coming in. It's a very difficult life, really ... // ... I don't think it has changed my attitudes. I'm still not a cut-throat businessman. If someone paid me £100 per week to work, I'd go for that. I'd be happier.

For Johnny, working in the enterprise culture meant a 'difficult life'. He specialized in a particular kind of fashion design and had not been successful in finding employment. After nearly a year on the dole he had set up in business. Trade was very slow, money extremely limited and only compensated for by less material rewards, like a feeling of pride in the work he did, in his studio and in knowing other people now regarded him as a designer and not as one of the unemployed. Working for himself had not overcome the feelings of isolation and loneliness previously encountered in unemployment. He and others felt cut off from a normal working and social life. Like a number of informants he was pleased to be interviewed — he enjoyed the unusual chance for social contact and the opportunity to talk to someone about his business.

Pressure from bills was the main drawback for many. Not sleeping at night because of business worries was mentioned by a lot of the informants. The ability to 'switch off' and forget the business once you went home was a key quality recommended for those anticipating starting businesses. Young entrepreneurs experienced considerable and continuous stress. When and where were the next orders coming from? How were the bills and bank debts to be paid? Would the business become successful? These were the worries for a highly stressed group of young business people. We cannot agree with Hakim's recent finding that 'becoming self-employed and running a business turns out to be a great deal easier than most people expect' (Hakim, 1989:292). Gordon, who was comparatively successful in his computer-related business, had received medical attention for migraine attacks caused by overwork and stress.

A number of these young entrepreneurs, although identifying several rather negative dimensions of running a business, still referred to the experience of self-employment *overall* as a positive one. Being your own boss was very highly valued. Informants rated their job satisfaction highly (one woman described feeling 'absolutely ecstatic' when she pulled in business). Pride and self-achievement were feelings often previously denied to these young adults. One young man described himself prior to setting up as 'a lost person'. His friends and family were continually

147

encouraging him to enrol for government schemes to help him out of his long-term unemployment. He became listless, depressed and aimless. In self-employment he had 'found his vocation'; he was happy, optimistic and hard-working. The personal psychological boost provided by owning and running a business compensated for the lack of financial rewards.

Some young men and women could find little to complain about in their self-employment. For them the move into the enterprise culture seemed an easy and straightforward step. We have reported the usual and typical difficulties in the passages above. Others, admittedly only a handful of people, had to rack their brains to think of 'bad things' about self-employment. They gave the impression that running their own businesses was a natural, unremarkable way of earning a living. Bob was twenty-five years old, lived in East Cleveland with his parents and had been running a one-man business as a freelance forestry worker:

RM: If someone came along and offered you £100 per week to do this as a job, but he would be the boss, would you take it?

Bob: No. There's no point working for someone else when you can do it yourself. There is a clear attraction in self-employment. Definitely. Basically I do what I want. I make all the decisions. I like running it all myself. It's all down to me if anything goes wrong. I like the responsibility . . . // . . . on a small scale like this it is pretty straightforward. There aren't any financial risks. I've not borrowed loads of money or anything like that. If it doesn't work out I don't stand to lose anything . . . // . . . I like getting paid for doing what I enjoy. If I was on the dole, I would be doing it anyway. It is as simple as that.

RM: What about the insecurity of it? Is that one of the drawbacks?

Bob: No. I've never had any sort of security in my life — it's not something I'd be interested in. There's no such thing as security. I've never had a nine to five job since I left school. I don't know what security is . . . // . . . I don't think I'll ever be a millionaire doing this but I'm pretty sure I can make a living at it. A job for a few years at least. I'm not complaining. I'm quite happy with it and the way it's going.

Bob was an interesting informant. He seemed completely at ease in his situation as a self-employed worker and spoke contentedly of his life, despite the fact that he realized he had little security and was earning relatively little money. Two points help explain his positive attitude to running businesses. First, he actually enjoyed the work and had been doing it for many years prior to practising it as a business. As he said, he was now being paid for doing what he would be doing if unemployed.

Second, his career to date had not consisted of a series of jobs which he could compare to self-employment. He had never worked nine to five and had never known the security and material bonuses of permanent employment. The experience of growing up with a mixture of life on the dole, government training schemes or further education could be argued to prepare people for enterprise. In many ways in *practice*, rather than in theory, the experience of enterprise in an area like Teesside is not dissimilar to that of unemployment.

One informant described her prior life on the dole and in education as essential training for her new life of enterprise. She was now twenty-five years old and was adept at living a life of little money, low personal security and high stress levels ('There hasn't been anything else in my life, really'). In reading the accounts of informants, the ability to cope with this sort of life emerged as a major quality which they needed. Perhaps the key enterprise skill can be summed up in one word — resilience — rather than in the extravagant lists promoted in practitioners' and academics' publications (see Chapter 2). Coping with little money, relying on parents for financial support and accommodation, living with uncertainty and low expectations for the future, structuring and managing time and generally learning to get by in a harsh economic climate, are all skills demanded of young adults like these. It is perhaps not surprising that people who had picked up these skills informally, like Bob, should continue to display a pragmatic, coping, stoical and even sometimes optimistic attitude when they take on the mantle of the young entrepreneur. Perhaps, then, we should talk less of enterprise skills and more of the skills needed to survive unemployment.

So, for the majority of informants the disadvantages of enterprise, which started with the long hours and low pay and continued through insecurity of work, stress, isolation, lack of social life and holidays, were, in the main, just outweighed by the advantages of being self-employed. Certainly the impression given by informants was one of enthusiasm, dedication and diligence. These people were not just playing at business; they had a realistic and level-headed view of their situation and prospects. For them working in their own businesses brought self-esteem, feelings of achievement and pride, enjoyment in actually making things and giving service, excitement, flexibility, independence and control of their working days and life. Overall it provided work, which for many was a prime motivation behind their earlier decision to set up in business. Some were more successful than others and managed businesses which would probably run for some time. Others seemed to be doing less well and were involved in very risky enterprises. Shortly, we will examine the experiences of those who were no longer running businesses. Before that, however, we will turn to a discussion of the expectations informants had for their businesses.

From Little Acorns . . .

One of the main political aims of government enterprise policies is to reduce unemployment, at least temporarily, and to rejuvenate local economies in the longer term. New, small firms are seen as at least part of the answer to economic decline in areas like Cleveland (we will consider the success of these aims in detail in the final chapter). We have already demonstrated how the majority of these young entrepreneurs were providing employment for themselves only. Only a handful of new businesses had created jobs. However, it could be argued that enterprises like these may be more successful in generating new employment in the long term. Consequently, informants were asked about the future of their enterprise as they saw it.

Some informants expressed what could be described as the expected view. They had big plans and expected their hard work to be rewarded by big money in the future. Adrian had a 'crazy dream' about retiring at the age of thirty and sailing the world in a yacht. Stewart felt that his business would be running itself in a few years at which time he would have made enough money and satisfied his personal ambitions. He then intended selling the business and taking on a new challenge. Shane expected to be employing fifty people in five years' time. Others hoped to get shops in Paris, New York, London *and* Middlesbrough. Carl typified these ambitions for the future:

> I want to be very rich. I've got ambition. There is no way you'll get rich by working for somebody else. I'd love a job that was paying me £100 a week but there's no future in it. In ten years' time I want a 9/11 Turbo and a big massive house — that's where I want to be. This [his shop] is just a stepping stone, a start. Next I want a factory.[5]

Far more common, though, were less glorious views of the future. 'Muddling along', 'plugging away' and 'plodding along' were the usual ways of describing the prospects of new businesses. Lillian compares her likely future with popular views of entrepreneurship:

> I'm just keeping my head above water, I think. I mean, I'd love to be Richard Branson and the rest but you've got to be realistic. Unless I hit upon some brilliant money-making scheme . . . //
> . . . you've got to face it that you're not. You're never going to be a millionaire, like a big film star. It's easier if you come to terms with it. I just see it as keeping my head above water. Just being my own boss really.[6]

Enterprise proved to be far less glamorous than some, like Carl, suggested. It was not a life of flash cars, massive houses and big bucks. In short, the reality of enterprise was rather harsh and contrasted markedly with popular images of 'budding entrepreneurs'. When asked what informants saw themselves doing in one or two years' time, a very frequent answer was that they would be on the dole. Despite the effort, hard work, determination and sacrifices of young adults in enterprise, inevitably many will not succeed and many do not expect to.

Between the Devil and the Deep Blue Sea

We interviewed a number of people who had gone out of business. For them the attractions and benefits of being your own boss were short-lived. The first passage we present in this section is from an interview with Duncan. He had run a business for just over a year as a freelance cartoonist from home in Middlesbrough. Previously he had been at art college for several years followed by thirteen months' unemployment.

RM: What caused you to close down? What were the main problems?

Duncan: The isolation — people not even knowing you're there. I struggled a lot. If this job hadn't come along I don't know what would have happened . . . it got dispiriting. You thought, well, there is no point in packing it in 'cos there's nothing there [to do] if you do. But you wonder whether it is worth carrying on with nothing [when the £40 per week finished]. You were putting a hell of a lot of hours in and getting nothing back at all. Some days I was working from eight in the morning till eleven at night. Some weeks nothing at all. Nobody expects to pay for anything and everything's supposed to be done yesterday. If I haven't been living at home, I wouldn't have survived as long as I did.

RM: How do you feel emotionally about being in business now?

Duncan: I wished I could have got a job straightaway, with good pay — something I enjoyed doing. Straightaway when I left college. It was just unfortunate. It seemed the only option at the time. I wouldn't recommend it to anyone, having done it. There's a few people said to me 'I'm thinking of starting up'. I've said: 'Really make sure you can get the work in'. I've said: 'I've struggled myself, make sure you don't end up like me'. My advice would be: don't do it.

Duncan closed down because of the insecurity of his enterprise. The pay was low and getting worse and he resented the stress and humiliation of continually scratching around for work. He had been supported by the EAS and by his parents but still he found that his time in business consisted of very negative, dispiriting and depressing experiences. Following his self-employment he was back on the dole for a further fourteen months. At the time of interview, however, he was much happier working in a job employed by a local company as a graphic designer.

Belinda had been engaged in running a small co-operative:

> I was putting everything I had into it and getting nothing at all back. I was leaving the house at 5.30 am and not getting back in 'till 5.30 pm. And all that for £40 per week which to me was peanuts. When we were doing outside work we would be work-ing 'till the early hours of the morning as well. I would come home and just sleep. I thought as though we were just flogging our guts out for nothing at the end of the day ... // ... I didn't realize how much it can kill you. We were absolutely shattered. It was just a nightmare. I used to be seething that we were up to our eyeballs in so much debt ... I used to cry all the time. I used to say 'I'm not going back — it's awful'. I used to be like that about twice a week. Worried about how much debt we were in and what we would do if we closed down — how we would survive.

Belinda's efforts to leave the ranks of the unemployed through her own enterprise in a co-operative had met with problems similar to those experienced by Duncan: long hours, low pay, high levels of stress and worry, mental and physical exhaustion. The final crunch came when, out of the blue, they received a rent and rates demand for the premises they had been occupying. The £1,000 bill, which they thought the bank had been paying by standing order, arrived at the same time as their EAS money ran out. Bailiffs arrived to seize what little equipment and assets they had and they were forced to close their business virtually overnight with, in all, £7,500 in outstanding debts. Belinda did not know to whom she owed money and whether these bills had been paid off by the co-operative organization which had supported their enterprise. Her time in the enterprise culture was in a sense not yet complete. She still worried about having failed and the stress of being in debt remained with her.

The final, long extract we present to illustrate the almost wholly negative experience of closing down businesses and leaving the enterprise culture comes from an interview with Lynne. She was one of our oldest informants and looked back on her experiences of running a small busi-ness in her early to mid-twenties. She was a single mother with one young child. Since leaving school she had participated in a number of government schemes, had been employed in various part-time and temporary jobs and had had several periods of time unemployed. She had started a business as a market trader in fruit and vegetables in Stockton:

> *RM:* Why did you go into self-employment? How do you feel about it now?
>
> *Lynne:* It was something I had to try. I was getting nowhere. I couldn't see any future in what I was doing. I'd levelled off and I wanted to climb. I wanted self-esteem. Looking back it's been totally the opposite. I'd had two relationships that'd failed. My life has been a failure since leaving college to now. I needed something to succeed. As it happens, I failed in that as well. Perhaps I'm just a born failure. But at least I've had the experience. I haven't just sat back moaning on the dole. I've tried to get out of the poverty trap. Fine, it didn't work but at least I've gained the experience ... //
> ... So now a year later I have about £10,000 debts and I can't afford to declare myself bankrupt so that amount is rising with the interest. I got taken to the High Court by a supplier for £1,300. Then I had the County Sheriff on my doorstep with a possession order. Because he was a nice chap, and he could see I had a kid, he left the furniture but he had possession of them so if I took anything out of the house or sold it, I would be charged with theft. So he owns the furniture and I'm being charged interest on that at twenty seven pence a day and fees of fifty eight pence a day and that has been going on since last year. The taxman has also caught up with me and he wanted to take the furniture, but he couldn't 'cos it belonged to the County Sheriff. I'm between the Devil and the Deep Blue Sea. I'm totally in the dark at the moment about what I owe people but I can't phone them to find out in case that reminds them about it. I'm stuck — just waiting for the axe to fall. I could have the £10,000 hanging over me for the rest of my life ... // ... I went through hell mentally with it. Straitjacket time, St. Nicks' here I come ...[7]

During the interview Lynne tried to retain a detached and dispassionate perspective on her experiences and there is perhaps little we can add to her account. Prior to setting up she had been unemployed for a year and following her business failure she had returned to the dole queues for another eight months. At the time of interview she was working part-time 'on the side' as well as claiming unemployment benefit: nothing more than a survival strategy.

She appeared resilient in her defeat even though she had experienced more personal failure.[8] Like many of those in business who had gone bust, she had persevered heroically to keep her business afloat (running up bigger and bigger debts). Some may argue that she should have ceased trading earlier than she did. With little professional advice on closing businesses (see Chapter 5) and with few remaining alternatives, 'failures', like Lynne, kept on going. Their keen determination to make a success of something led them to start up in the first place and delayed them from closing businesses even when they had reached a parlous state. Rees (1986) describes the troubles and failures of young adults in the enterprise culture as 'blaming the victim, mark two': unemployment is 'caused' by the unemployed themselves (mark one); business failure is 'caused' by young business people themselves (mark two).

Though young entrepreneurs may make mistakes in running their businesses, the blame for entrepreneurial failure should not rest with them: we should not blame these young victims of business failure. Rees and Thomas studied the potential for successful small businesses amongst redundant coal miners in South Wales (a locality with economic problems similar to those of Teesside). They identified cultural and economic factors, rather than individual reasons, behind the low entrepreneurial potential of their informants:

> Not only are they ill-equipped in terms of the requisite 'resources', but also they are culturally predisposed to avoid risk-taking and indebtedness, which are necessary prerequisites to small business development. Moreover, and perhaps most fundamentally, the same local economy which so cruelly restricts their opportunities of satisfactory employment, also acts to block the potential for the development of innovation in new business enterprises. (1989:16)

We asked those who had left the enterprise culture why they had done so. The answers collected are not surprising and reflect problems identified by those still running businesses and in other research (e.g. Bevan *et al.*, 1989; Rees and Thomas, 1989; Hakim, 1989a; Smallbone, 1990). Reasons for closing most often stemmed from very basic business failure. There was general lack of capital (which was by far the most frequent response) and the market for goods and services was felt to be swamped and highly competitive. Informants identified lack of trade (and seasonal downturns in what business there was), fear of increasing debt and the threat of being entangled in legal proceedings as further, related elements of their decision-making. Advertising proved cripplingly expensive or simply unaffordable. Premises were often very poorly located and too costly. Businesses often lacked the basic finances or equipment necessary to survive (one mobile catering firm and one mobile hairdresser had no transport, for instance). Young business people struggled to keep their enterprise afloat under very difficult conditions. Business did not expand and withdrawal of support from the enterprise industry (e.g. start-up units and EAS) after a year or so proved disastrous for many who had to close down. The low pay, long hours and high risk resulting from these efforts were also given as prime reasons for closure.

As one young woman said, the reason for her business failure was 80 per cent financial and 20 per cent personal. She, like many others, used the word 'disheartening' to describe the whole experience. She found that it was 'not glamorous, not a big romantic dream'. Loneliness and the desire to work with other people rather than in isolation were given as further reasons. Physical and mental health suffered and these disheartening experiences led to declining motivation and commitment to the business. It was often when all or many of these problems came together that businesses were closed and the informants decided it was time to abandon the enterprise culture.

Our group of informants may, like other recent entrants to the ranks of the self-employed, be particularly vulnerable to business failure. Capital, or rather lack of capital, was the most pressing issue during the start-up phase, through the period of running a business and was foremost amongst causes of business failure. Rees argues that: 'the single most frequent direct cause of folding is insufficient capital — young people are at a particular disadvantage given their high risk status in the eyes of potential investors' (1986:18).

Allen and Hunn (1985) and Finn (1986) suggest that it is amongst those groups, for instance women and younger people whose participation in EAS has recently increased, that the survival rate is likely to be the lowest. Although we cannot, by the nature of our research methodology, offer any estimation of survival rates for this sample, what we can draw attention to is the quality of the experience of enterprise (as above) and a description of the location of self-employment in this sub-group's career trajectories. In our sample, eighteen people had ceased trading. Of these, thirteen had been unemployed immediately preceding start-up, with the average length of unemployment being nine months. Immediately following closure, fourteen of this small group of people returned to the dole, two went on to government schemes and two found jobs of some sort. The majority of the small group who seemed to be successfully running businesses (see the next section) had not entered self-employment from unemployment. These figures support our argument that self-employment was being pursued by many as a response to unemployment, but also that for this group it turned out to be an unsuccessful or short-lived bid to lift themselves out of the ranks of the unemployed. Those that did not enter self-employment from unemployment appear to be more successful in running businesses. Bevan *et al.* (1989) found that only 38 per cent of their lapsed self-employed sample had found full-time employment: 54 per cent were unemployed at the time of their survey.

In the same survey it was also found, however, that two-thirds of these 'failed' entrepreneurs would give self-employment another go. That finding, given the sort of evidence we present here, is perhaps rather surprising. However, some of our failed entrepreneurs (admittedly not two-thirds of them) also said they would consider re-entering the enterprise culture. What we found was that, despite the often crushing experience of presiding over the closure of a failing business, the resilience and doggedness of some of these young entrepreneurs pushed them towards thinking about new business ideas. We gained the impression that part of the reason for this was to have the chance to correct the mistakes they felt they had made. They thought that they had learnt what had gone wrong and knew the realities of entrepreneurship and, hence, they would now be better suited to running a business.

We met one young man, Trevor (who had closed his business that week), in a local enterprise centre. He was in debt to the tune of several thousand pounds and was now seeking medical assistance for the depression and stress-related ill health he had been experiencing. He was unemployed but visiting the advisory staff there to rework and develop his original business plan. It is unlikely that he would actually start up a second time (particularly as he was unlikely to receive bank credit ever again). For Trevor, this was more a matter of pride. He wanted to learn for himself what had gone wrong and put this right in written form (in the original business plan).

Against the odds, even some of those who had run disastrous new businesses saw some positive outcomes of their enterprise (see Chapter 8 for a discussion of the concept of 'positive outcomes'). This also helps explain the ambivalent attitude of young entrepreneurs to their own personal failures. Even the darkest clouds could hold a silver lining. Whilst they clearly failed to develop a successful small business, they could draw attention to some more hopeful outcomes of their activities. Typical was the comment 'Well, at least I've tried'. They could look upon their own efforts to leave the so-called dependency of unemployment as evidence of their own self-worth, and, additionally, this could be offered as evidence of commitment, self-motivation and hard work to future employers. Gary (who ran a graphic design business for less than a year) said:

I knew where I'd gone wrong, so the *success* was finding that out. That I didn't have enough experience. I learnt lots of things: to be my own salesman, my own receptionist, my own planner, my own time-keeper. At the end of the day it was worth it because I know now where I went wrong. I know what I need to do to make a success of it in the future ... // ... I need better premises, capital behind me, the right advertising — basically that's it.

Though, for an outsider, it may be difficult to identify anything positive in the experiences of people like Duncan, Belinda and Lynne, it seems that some informants can describe at least a few positive aspects of business failure. This stands as testimony to their sheer determination, pride and resilience — characteristics which carried informants into starting businesses and were drawn upon and much needed when young enterprises collapsed.

Fallers, Plodders and Runners: Success and Failure in the Enterprise Culture

Though informants like Lynne, above, had apparently little difficulty in labelling themselves failures, attempting to define success and failure in enterprise more generally is a very difficult task. We had little access to definitive financial data (e.g. bank accounts) and we relied wholeheartedly upon less quantifiable data. Great care was taken in broaching this subject in interviews. To ask informants whether they considered themselves to be a success or failure, after they had, for instance, described the emotional pains of closing businesses would be insensitive in the extreme. Nevertheless, success in new small businesses lies at the heart of government enterprise policies. We feel it necessary, therefore, to try to classify the success or failure of our informants.

Success and failure in youth enterprise are particularly ambiguous terms. What are the criteria by which we judge whether a new business is successful? Official Training Agency evaluations of the EAS, for instance, generally use jobs created and 'survival' rates as indicators of success in self-employment. By the latter they mean the length of time people remain in business. Recent Department of Employment-sponsored surveys have found survival rates of 73 per cent at eighteen months and of 65 per cent still trading three years after starting in business (RBL Research International, 1987; Department of Employment, 1988b).

However, an evaluation of the scheme conducted by the National Audit Office (NAO) concluded that only 57 per cent of EAS participants were still trading two years after the scheme had finished (NAO, 1988). Part of this difference can be explained by the fact that the former reports exclude those who drop out during the first year from their calculations whereas the latter includes them. Finn (1986) found that 10 per cent of EAS participants drop out of the scheme during the first year (which was confirmed as the figure for Cleveland by local EAS staff). There are apparently no figures of local survival rates available for the county but we were told by Training Agency officers that 'there is no reason to doubt that these equate favourably with the national figure'.[9]

Even these levels of success must be weighed against what is called 'deadweight' (those who would have set up in business anyway, without the help of EAS) and 'displacement' (the amount of jobs in existing businesses which are lost through competition with EAS participants). The NAO estimates that deadweight can be estimated to be 44 per cent (i.e. nearly half would have set up in business without the EAS). It also suggests that about half of all jobs created simply displace other already existing jobs.

Even by these official criteria enterprise, through EAS, seems to have limited success. We would argue, however, that this quantitative analysis of self-employment only provides a bare, numerical sketch of success and failure in youth enterprise. A fuller picture can only be gained by drawing upon a qualitative understanding of these experiences. In this chapter we have already provided much ethnographic data to suggest that simply staying in business is not the only dimension by which youth enterprises should be judged. There may be a particular *quantity* of people still trading in new enterprises but what is the *quality* of their entrepreneurial experiences? We have tried to develop a broader understanding of success and failure, drawing upon a more in-depth appreciation of what counts as success in youth enterprise. We suggest that a number of further interlinked issues can be identified in the difficult job of trying to assess success and failure.

First, and perhaps obviously, given our stress upon ethnographic methods, attention needs to be paid to informants' own definitions of their success. Self-report data of this sort is tricky to analyze because people work with different personal criteria. Nevertheless, this sample of young entrepreneurs had apparently little difficulty in answering our questions in this respect. A few said they definitely were successful. One informant classified himself so. When asked why or how he could say he was successful, he leant back in his chair (in his modern, high-tech office) pulled up the matt-black window-blind and simply gestured to his and his partner's cars standing in the office car park. He owned a Porsche, his colleague an Audi Quattro, both new and bright red.

However, it became clear from the interviews that very few of the informants would describe themselves as successful. They were weighed down by the pressures of day-to-day business survival and thought that success, if it came at all, was a long way off. 'Getting by', 'keeping their heads above water' and 'plodding along' were the images they used to describe their status as young entrepreneurs.

A second and related criterion for judging success is the likely future of young businesses. We have already shown that the majority were rather gloomy about their prospects. Their businesses were felt to run a high risk of collapse or decline in the long term. Uppermost in their mind was keeping themselves afloat, rather than business growth.

Third, we should take note of the employment potential of new businesses (an aspect of official criteria). Again few imagined actually expanding their businesses to the point where they could take on extra workers. Keeping businesses as they were was difficult enough for this sample and only a small minority had or intended to take on any employees.

A fourth related issue in judging business success is length of time in business. This criterion, used by the Training Agency, is supported by those we have described already. Our method does not allow a direct estimation of business survival rates. For this we would need a larger, longer-term, longitudinal survey. What our evidence suggests, though, is that many businesses will not last beyond two or three years. It was difficult to locate young entrepreneurs in Cleveland who had traded for this long. Most of our sample were in the first year or two of business. They reported that the twelve-month point was, or was anticipated to be, a particularly testing time. Indeed, some thought it highly unlikely that they would be able to continue after a year. This is supported by the evidence from those who had already closed down businesses. Twelve of the eighteen people in this sub-sample ceased trading before the thirteen-month point. Finn (1986) has also found that two-thirds of the closures he studied happened at exactly the twelve-month point.

A fifth point in assessing success, which we have not yet mentioned, concerns dependency upon the EAS. If these new businesses are success-ful, they should be able to operate happily without government grant assistance. Generally, this was not the case. EAS money was crucial in supporting these firms. The withdrawal of £40 per week after twelve months was the major factor in explaining the actual or potential collapse of businesses after a year. Indeed, three of the more prosperous businesses never received this support. One of these informants actually said that EAS invited dependency amongst young entrepreneurs and that part of his own success could be explained by the fact that from the outset he had had to operate along real commercial lines.

Sixth, the money earned through enterprise, especially as it relates to the hours worked is a simple and clear indicator of success. The fact that about three-quarters of the sample were working long hours for as little as £80 per week or less must tell us that success was a long time coming.

To summarize, we can see that even official, scanty surveys tend to question the potential success of enterprises like those carried out by our informants. We have considered six more criteria for assessing youth enterprise and found that on all counts it would be difficult to characterize the majority experience as one of successful entrepreneurship. Equally, though, the experience of entrepreneurship cannot be described as com-plete failure. Overall the fortunes of our informants were mixed. Below we develop a three-part typology of entrepreneurial experiences based on the above criteria.

Some, as we have described, left the enterprise culture after one or two years of disheartening and wearing troubles. In terms of our sample these amounted to a minority (eighteen). However, it is likely that some of those we talked to who were trading as self-employed would join the enterprise fall-out. Cases of absolute disaster — crippling personal financial debt and severe emotional strain — were relatively rare. More common was a general feeling of failure, disappointment and dismay. Many had hoped to leave the ranks of the unemployed through their endeavours in enterprise only to find themselves back on the dole after giving all their commitment and effort to new businesses. Perhaps two in ten of our sample can be characterized in this way. These were the *'fallers'* in the enterprise sweep stakes who failed to make it over the first or second hurdles.

About one in ten seemed to be doing well in self-employment. They were the winners in the enterprise stakes. They had businesses which appeared to be commercially viable, soundly-based and managed, reasonably financed and likely to expand to some degree. These we call the *'runners'* — those who had established successful new firms.

The majority fell somewhere between these two extremes. Roughly seven out of ten of our informants were running business on a shoestring with little intention or hope of expansion in the foreseeable future. These were the *'plodders'* who ran businesses day-by-day on hard graft; who were 'just surviving nicely'. Enterprise in the majority of cases meant risky business; failure was close at hand, and even new firms which were in their second year and employing people could go out of business overnight if a single important contract was lost. On the other hand, over a period of years, through a combination of good fortune, hard work and low pay they may be able to work themselves into a more secure, successful position.

This middle group of young entrepreneurs is particularly interesting. Not only are they the most significant in terms of numbers, they also inhabit a generally ignored part of the entrepreneurial world. Young people in business are usually absent from small business research anyway. Popular media accounts of young entrepreneurs usually focus on the success stories (in the 'local boy made good' vein).[10] More radical critiques of government enterprise policies tend to highlight the horror stories of enterprise, reporting business failures and disasters. We would suggest that neither perspective does justice to the more complicated world of youth enterprise as related by our informants. Of course, as we have shown, enterprise *can* bring glorious success or painful failure. But far more typical is a middle road of neither complete success nor complete failure but one of almost herculean effort, determination and stress rewarded by low pay, new-found feelings of pride and achievement, and other intangible personal attractions of being the boss of risky businesses. Most informants operate not in a shining, new, glamorous enterprise economy but 'just plod along' in a twilight world of casualized, peripheral, poorly paid work.

This is, of course, just one way of typifying and analyzing the experiences of youth enterprise and as such it is not meant as a hard and fast classification. We are, for instance, quite certain that there will be movement up and down the three categories. In the next chapter we will examine these three types of youth enterprise more directly by discussing several case studies. One story we present is that of Dawn, a young woman who, had she been interviewed a year earlier, would probably have been eligible for inclusion in the successful, 'runners' category. At the time of the interview, however, she was unemployed and looked back on her failed business and very mixed experiences of the enterprise culture.

Summary and Conclusions

Small business owners themselves have become the centre of much media attention and their activities are described in flattering terms by all the major political parties. The state and national economic policy have rediscovered the small enterprise and have offered it a central role in the restructuring and revival of the economy needed to take Britain into the next century. (Curran, 1986:43)

Neither the political promotion of the enterprise culture nor, indeed, the academic research on small business have at their roots any deep or clear understanding of the complex world of youth enterprise. Policies to encourage the movement of young adults into the enterprise culture through self-employment tend only to evaluate schemes and initiatives (e.g. the EAS) quantitatively. Hence, success is estimated simply by survival rates and job generation. Moreover, very few official studies focus on youth enterprise or upon particular localities. These, we would argue, are also serious omissions in the tradition of small business research.

This body of research has grown remarkably over the past decade but still tends to be dominated by national questionnaire surveys of the self-employed population as a whole. In this chapter we have attempted to illustrate that youth enterprise has a cultural meaning for the majority of informants which contrasts sharply with more popular images or political versions of enterprise. Growing up in Cleveland still means for many people a life comprised of government schemes, unemployment and lowly, impermanent jobs. This was certainly true of our sample.

Most had started in self-employment because it seemed to offer a reason-ably attractive way of making a living when few jobs were available. These are exactly the people at whom government initiatives to reverse the 'dependency culture' are aimed. Even official data suggests that these efforts to create an enterprise culture are limited in their success. Most enterprises are short-lived and our own investigations have drawn atten-tion to the critical problems faced by young business people, especially after a year or so in business when they lose various forms of enterprise assistance. Moreover, very few of these young entrepreneurs actually employed other people or planned to expand. We would agree with a recent finding of a study of local enterprise policy for the unemployed:

> Very few small firms ever get to employ significant numbers and the typical picture is of small units 'getting by'. The 'archetype' of the competent businessman [sic] spotting a new opportunity and making a success of a new venture clearly exists. It is not, however, typical in terms of the numbers involved. (Nabarro *et al.*, 1986:3)

In terms of the economic transformation of areas of high unemploy-ment through job generation from new small firms like these, our evi-dence supports the growing research (e.g. Curran, 1986; Storey and Johnson, 1987a) which suggests that small firms are *not the* answer to unemployment. We will return to the broader question of the economics and politics of enterprise promotion policies in the final chapter. We conclude, here, that judging by the ethnographic accounts collected, most young entrepreneurs could not be classed as successful. The majority, however, did enjoy enterprise, and the more positive dimensions of entrepreneurship (in comparison with unemployment and working in jobs) at least partly compensated for poor pay and hard work. Few, though, were optimistic about the future. Miller says: 'The irregular economy of small enterprises with low wages, hustling, job insecurity . . . is an important component of the small business sector. The individuals involved in the irregular economy largely comprise the working poor' (1986:157).

The conditions of work for self-employed people like these are very poor. They are generally not entitled to a range of benefits afforded employees (e.g. maternity leave, sick pay, paid holidays, pension schemes, Unemployment Benefit), and employment is often dependent upon the whims of local big business. The majority of these people, in choosing to run new, small, capitalist enterprises, are not taking a step up the class ladder into the *petit bourgeoisie* (the traditional home of the self-employed) but rather remain in a casualized world of insecure work founded upon lower-class, poorly paid jobs, government schemes and the constant threat of unemployment. Rees sums up well the position of entrepreneurial young adults like ours:

> what we are seeing is a further segmentation of the labour market, with the ranks of those in the low paid, insecure, prospectless secondary labour market being swelled by a new breed of casual labour, the 'self-employed'. This is a far cry from the economic miracle anticipated through the rebirth of Britain's 'enterprise culture'. (1986:20)

In the next chapter we will examine further the successes and failures of this group of newly self-employed young people. Six cases are presented more fully to illustrate the experiences of 'runners', 'fallers' and 'plodders'.

Notes

1   In other parts of the book we have disguised the identity of informants by sometimes changing the type of their business slightly (see Chapter 1). In this paragraph, however, we describe the actual businesses run by our sample.
2   The inaccessibility of many new businesses run from both home and rented premises can be confirmed by one of the authors (RM) who on several occasions spent considerable time trying to locate them.
3   During the research the interviewer (RM) found himself taking a more positive attitude to those businesses which had attractive, business-like premises.
4   Even if tenancies in enterprise centres were available over a more extended period charges could soar markedly. One yound woman faced a jump in accommodation costs from £79 to £140 per month after a year in business, just as she lost her enterprise allowance.
5   Carl went out of business in the summer of 1990, about a year after he was interviewed.
6   Interestingly, Lillian refers to Richard Branson, Chairman of the Virgin Group Limited. He was the only individual ever named by informants when they discussed their self-image and status. Usually they compared themselves negatively with this self-made man, preferring more modest self-descriptions. This contrasts very sharply with a recent market research report on the views and ambitions of self-employed people in the region (see *Middlesbrough Evening Gazette*, 12 September 1990) which carried the title: 'In Branson's Footsteps — the North's whizzkids go for gold'.
7   'St. Nicks' is a local mental hospital.
8   The comments of Sir Geoffrey Holland, made at the meeting of the Public Accounts Committee investigating EAS, and when placed next to the stories of people like Lynne, suggest how close the Permanent Secretary at the Department of Employment is to the practice of enterprise. He said:

we do not think that anybody has been damaged by joining the EAS. Even of those who left quite a few go into employment with other people, having been given the confidence, after some considerable period of unemployment sometimes, to face a new future. (House of Commons Public Accounts Committee, 1989:3)

9   We tried repeatedly to find out the official 'survival' rate for new firms on EAS in Cleveland. These were not available, but we find it hard to understand how it is that a regional figure can be published if county-wide figures (from which a regional aggregrate is calculated) are not collected. However, we were given the view of one local Training Agency official: 'the actual figures, the real figures are very encouraging. We believe that in Cleveland people tend to stick at it more, really because there is no alternative. They tend to stick at it because the only real alternative is the dole'.

10   For example, see Note 6 above. Our own press release to local newspapers, which gave a more realistic view of youth enterprise, was given a very upbeat and positive treatment and was printed under the title of 'Whizzkids Win the Survival Stakes'.

Chapter 7

Runners, Fallers and Plodders: Case Studies of Youth Enterprise

So far we have developed our analysis of youth enterprise in Cleveland by drawing upon material from a large number of ethnographic interviews. The whole sample of young business people has been drawn upon to support, illustrate or develop our argument. In this chapter we will focus more intensively on a small number of cases. We try to illuminate the themes which have emerged by presenting fuller accounts of the experience of starting up, running and closing down businesses. We deliberately give more room to the accounts of informants and provide less in the way of supporting analysis or discussion. In all we draw upon six case studies: two from each of the three categories ('runners', 'fallers' and 'plodders'), which we developed towards the end of the last chapter.[1]

Runners

Barry

Barry was one of the most successful young business people that we talked to. He was twenty-five years old and, as such, fell at the older end of the age range of our sample. He was interviewed at his business premises in Stockton — a factory unit cum warehouse that was much larger than most of the premises that we visited. The impression that we gathered of Barry was of a young man who had built up his sportswear business from scratch and who, in short, could be classed as a typical, successful entrepreneur: a 'runner'.

Barry left full-time education at the age of eighteen with three O levels (he was unsuccessful in his attempt at A levels). Until his early twenties he worked in various temporary jobs: as an insurance salesman, as a petrol-pump attendant, as a musician with a local group, and as part of a company producing a music 'fanzine'. The ways in which he described these earlier years gave the impression that he had a generally 'enterprising' attitude to work and employment. He was, to use his phrase, a 'wheeler-dealer', picking up jobs and taking opportunities where he found them.

His first involvement with business ownership was at the age of twenty-one:

> I started getting involved in the clothing scene. I started buying bits and pieces of second-hand clothes from jumble sales and instead of just turning them out cheap and cheerful on a market stall, like most people were doing, I used to concentrate on the vintage American stuff. At the time all the younger kids were getting into it. I used to do reasonably well. I used to buy a shirt for 5p and sell it for £3 and marketed it in a different way. I got a little permanent shop.

This was all with the help of the Enterprise Allowance Scheme. After a year of trading in second-hand clothes from a shop in Stockton, he realized that a number of factors were combining to limit the potential of his business. Firstly, the location of the shop (with no shop frontage and lack of passing trade) was restricting the numbers of customers. Secondly, 'it was such low margin stuff, such a low unit cost'. Even though the percentage profit he might make on a particular garment was very high, overall the prices he was charging for his goods were still very low:[2]

> All right, if you are in Covent Garden on a stall or some other affluent area, you can get away with it. But you can't charge a premium price up here. With that in mind and with the fact that we couldn't really afford to move to a bigger unit because you were talking rents of £150/200 per week, and you know, some of the more designer shops have to sell only three shirts and they've got their rent covered. We would have had to sell 100/150 garments to do it . . . // . . . so we actually sold it as a going concern. I didn't get much for it, about £600, but I'd started it with nothing and just built it up.

Barry then got a job as an employee of a fashion clothing company in Newcastle and commuted daily to work there. He travelled up and down the country selling clothing and building up customer lists for the firm he now worked for. After a year he branched out and started trading in his own name again. He hired a Ford transit van and, using the customer list retained from his last employment, went on the road, drumming up custom for his new line of sportswear products. He started with a £1,000 overdraft from the bank and bought, on a sale or return basis, that amount of sportswear from a supplier in Leeds. He was wheeling and dealing again: spending from early morning to late at night on the road, visiting previous clients as far apart as London and Glasgow:

> I drove to Scotland once a week and I shifted about three and a half kilos of swag and maybe got a twenty per cent margin on it. The stuff was worth nearly £3,000 — so then you are starting to make a reasonable profit. It was the three weeks before Christmas so I picked up quite easy amounts. I'd accumulated about £2,000 by this point. I then took a lease out on a van and things went from there.

Business started to grow and he bought an answering machine to take business calls at home (he owned a detached house in one of the more prosperous parts of town, where he lived with his wife). He was very aware, he reports, of not wanting to over-trade and of 'doing business for business's sake'. This would have resulted in him letting down customers in the South when he was on business in the North. By this stage he was beginning to create demand for the goods he had been selling and was able to employ his first worker — a student on placement from the local polytechnic:

> And, you know, it just starts to build, you know, it's like by this time you've started to give some credit, [and become] less van-sales oriented. Starting to take orders rather than selling. In the December of the first year's trading we turned over nearly £10,000. In the following December I turned over nearly £30,000 ... // ... It was physically very, very hard.

We asked Barry about his income — whether he was taking a large salary:

> Oh no, it went back into the business. I worked for eighteen months on £50 per week. Because I firmly believe the more money you keep in the pot the more you can keep in stock. The stock can turn over once — you start off with £50, you buy and sell and turn it into £75. You buy and sell and turn that into £150 and at the end of the year — instead of drawing £100 per week with those extra £50s, those £50s you've left in — the business has turned out at £2,500. If you've turned that over six times you might turn that £2,500 into £9,000. But then again, when you are working so hard what the hell do you want money for? Because literally there are two ways that I can see that you do business. You either invest money or you invest labour. I literally did not have the money to invest. Maybe if I sell this [business] in five years' time and get half a million for it, I'll let someone else do

the donkey work next time. And anybody who starts a business with no capital and just does a meagre ten in the morning till four o'clock in the afternoon will not stay in business very long. Rigidly, for the first eighteen months, I started at six in the morning and worked until eight, nine, ten o'clock at night. Even now I'm still putting in twelve-hour days — you've got to.

Barry's business plan and his managerial style were firmly aimed at expanding the business and developing its profitability. He worked incredibly long hours and travelled the length and breadth of the country selling sportswear. By the second year he employed three workers: machinists to make up the sportswear now designed by one of his employees. Rather than simply selling other people's merchandise to outlets around the country, he branched out into producing his own designs under his company's name.

By the third year of trading, business had begun to 'snowball', partly as a response to the growing popularity of sports-oriented clothing in youth styles during the late 1980s. Banks were pressed for further overdraft facilities, more workers were taken on at production, design and administrative levels, enabling the customer base to be broadened. Two of the people Barry employed were young women (both informants to our study) who had recently closed down their own business. We found that Barry provided a further link between the informants in our sample: not only was he employing two of them directly, he also subcontracted a considerable amount of basic machining work to Cath, whom we introduce later in the chapter.

Additionally, Barry began to dabble in the export market. He simply phoned up contacts abroad (which he had developed in his previous job) and asked whether they would like to take some new lines, cash on delivery: a cheeky way to operate, as he himself admits. However his enterprising strategy was a success and the 'Stellar Styles of Stockton' label can be found on sportswear sold in Sweden, West Germany, Finland and the Netherlands. Thirty per cent of Barry's trade is now in the export market.

Throughout the interview Barry laced his conversation with phrases from the vocabulary of enterprise and business. He seemed fully acquainted with the language and concepts of profit and loss, unit costs, fixed assets, turnover and balance sheets. He had attended one or two enterprise training courses which he had found generally useful. His business know-how had, however, been learned largely through his experience of building up businesses from scratch. The biggest problem he found lay in the tasks of delegation. He 'never wanted to be an administrator, an accountant', yet with the growth of his business he found it impossible to keep control of all the day-to-day aspects of his business. Much of the earlier challenge and excitement of travelling the roads and clinching new deals had to be delegated to his sales staff whilst he was forced to become more of an administrator and manager. By the end of the third year the business had reached a plateau; it was successful, well established, but unlikely to grow any further given the limitations of the premises they occupied.

At this point Barry chose to take the next step in the growth of Stellar Styles and purchased a factory/warehouse unit. This was the next challenge and, according to Barry, a career in business was best viewed as a series of challenges; he disliked the feeling that business was becoming too easy.[3] Barry described two attitudes or motivations behind entrepreneurship:

> Now, I think you make a decision, you want to be quite OK immediately. You want to be: (a) self-sufficient; and (b) personally better off. Or you take the other course, if you want to build up a bigger business, for two reasons: (a) the challenge of it; (b) because you can imagine that at some stage in the future you are really going to cash in. I would say I fall into this second category ... // ... I certainly made a very conscious decision about a year ago where I could have just stayed where I was and drawn a salary of £25,000 a year and taken on two or three people. It would have been OK. But the other aspect is that, and we're not there yet, but if I can steer it on to the next level, where the profits are consistently £2,000 a week, and then maybe start to acquire other small businesses and maybe diversify a bit, you know, then, maybe, we can take the sales up to ... I mean I'm certainly targeting sales of over a million quid in the fifth year. Although we're becoming increasingly profit-oriented, you know, 'sales is vanity, profit is sanity'. I stand to make a lot more money than if I'd decided to stand still. In three years' time I could take my personal money out and go for a flotation or sell the business completely, say for half a million quid, and live off the interest for the rest of my life. It's up to me ... // ... I do have this vision in the back of my mind of being able to own a reasonable property abroad, maybe in the South of France and live a more relaxed sort of life. Lots of sitting around in the sun.

Certainly the upward spiral of growth and expansion experienced by Barry's business meant that this idyll of early retirement into relaxed, luxurious surroundings may not, for Barry, be too far-fetched. He was now employing over a dozen people as well as training people through YTS and ET. His new premises were large and allowed growth. His customer list continued to grow as did his credit with the bank. His business, in its fourth year, was already making several hundred thousand pounds a year profit and he was preparing to 'go limited'. The dual motivations behind his efforts in the enterprise culture had been the potentially large financial rewards and the challenges of business. He had managed the latter successfully, to the point where he had felt bored with the business, and was now looking forward to reaping handsome profits.

Barry described the qualities which he felt were needed, and that he had displayed, for enterprise:

> You've got to be pretty enthusiastic and sharp first. You've got to be confident. You've got to be knocking on doors. You've got to establish your customer base. You have got to have extreme discipline. You lose all sorts of freedom and your health suffers. You've got to sacrifice late nights or nights in the pub. The basic thing is that you've got to be very enthusiastic, you've got to be very, very hard working and determined. You've got to keep striding on.

That these personal characteristics and attitudes alone can account for success and failure in youth enterprise is unlikely. However, it does appear that individual characteristics or styles can contribute to business success. Barry was extremely confident and business-like in his manner and speech (believe it or not, he even wore a watch with 'Time is Money' emblazoned across the face). Coupled with his great determination and capital investment in his firm, these factors must have contributed to the success of Stellar Styles of Stockton. We will return to a broader discussion of success and failure in small firms in Chapter 10. Here we aim to present particularly interesting cases.

Shane

Shane was one of the youngest of our informants and also one of the most successful. He was only nineteen and had been trading from a business start-up unit in Middlesbrough for nearly eighteen months when he was interviewed. He ran a busy small firm providing desktop publishing facilities for local companies. Indeed, the interview with Shane was relatively short: he could spare less than an hour away from his business. Furthermore, Shane was not much of 'a talker', and consequently we present fewer long passages of direct quotation.

He left school at sixteen and then enrolled at the local technical college in Middlesbrough ('as a last resort'); he was hoping to find a job straightaway. Before leaving school he had written to a number of computer firms about vacancies as a trainee programmer. After three weeks at college one firm wrote back saying that they had a job for him. He took it and worked for them in their Stockton base for eight months before the company went into liquidation. Next he spent two months on the dole ('just sort of developing my computer and graphics skills') before getting another similar job for three months. After another three months' spell of unemployment, he went to work for the engineering firm where his uncle worked, training further in computer programming. Here he learned various aspects of the business and started to become more interested in the potential of desktop publishing. He reported that he had always considered working for himself and after only a few months at his uncle's firm, he left to start up in business.

Since his early teens he had been interested in and owned computers: playing games, developing programmes, experimenting with computer graphics. His business was an extension of this earlier hobby and he had always been keen to work for himself. He was offered a job 'down South' in a computer software house but: 'doing this really appealed to me. I wanted the freedom and I thought I would enjoy working for myself, which I do. I enjoyed working at my uncle's company but it still wasn't exactly what I wanted to do.'

After attending an evening course over eight weeks in enterprise training in Middlesbrough (covering book-keeping, advertising, grants, etc.), he started trading in a partnership with a friend. He did not join the EAS ('we had work lined up straightaway so we couldn't go on the dole for thirteen weeks, or whatever'). They did, however, apply for the Regional Development Grant (RDG) before the grant expired and re-ceived, eventually, £12,000 for creating four jobs (the two partners and two employees). At the earliest stage they registered themselves as a limited company on the advice of an accountant. Shane said that he knew little about the details of 'going limited' only that 'it just means that if you do go bankrupt, I don't think you have to pay off all your debts'.

Shane was one of only a small number of people who did not use the EAS. On this and other criteria he ran an unusual business. He had several important orders even before the business was properly estab-lished. These had been secured thanks to the reputation and contacts he and his friend had built up by working for local companies, especially the firm for which Shane's uncle worked. The jobs Shane had been employed in were stepping stones on the way to self-employment. They provided extra training in the technical skills needed, further knowledge of compu-ter systems and, perhaps most importantly, highly lucrative contacts with potential customers. Immediately on setting up, they had an abundance of work to do for big firms in the locality and they now provided specialist desktop publishing services for several large firms on Teesside. In a sense, they were now acting as subcontractors for larger firms who no longer had publishing, printing or graphic services in-house. In turn, they were in the happy position of being able to contract work out to other new small firms in Cleveland. Our introduction to Shane came through another informant who had been given work by Shane's firm.

Business was going well for Shane and his partner and he had no hesitation in classing himself as successful:

A lot of businesses are just scraping by with the skin of their teeth using the EAS. We've been doing better than that over the last year. We've recently come to the end of our first financial year and the turnover was nearly £20,000 but it should be a lot better this year. We're doing alright. And the grant [RDG] helped a lot.

The two partners attributed their success to the early capital injection of several thousand pounds (from the RDG) into their company which allowed them to employ the necessary staff to exploit fully the early orders they had won. These contracts had been essential to their fairly rapid development into an established, commercial company. They did acknowledge, however, that these first orders had not been won on purely commercial grounds. Their technical expertise and experience were important but so was Shane's personal relationship with a high-ranking employee (his uncle) of a big, local firm. Without that order they admitted that they would 'still be struggling'. Having said this, nepotism was a necessary but not sufficient condition to explain their success story. They had very little local competition and had been able to offer new, rare and 'hi-tech' skills and services to companies. They had cornered the local market and were now expanding to offer their services on a regional and even national basis. Demand for their services was growing and they continued to have little problem securing contracts.

A further reason underlying their success (though not one that differentiated them from less successful young entrepreneurs) was the hours they worked. Both Shane and his partner (though not their employees) worked, on average, fifty to sixty hours per week. Additionally, their success had not yet brought great financial rewards though they earned a higher income than most informants. They were able to pay themselves a regular wage which amounted to about £90 per week. They felt optimistic about the future, felt the company was safe with the growing level of business, enjoyed being their own bosses and looked forward to the future which they thought would bring greater financial rewards and greater security. They planned to be employing up to fifty people within five years.

Fallers

Dawn

Like Ronnie, whom we discuss next, Dawn was counted and publicized as a success story by enterprise professionals and we were directed to her by a youth enterprise agency in Cleveland. However, by the time we came to interview her she was unemployed and rather more level-headed about her experiences than some of those employed to deliver the gospel of enterprise in the county ('it's not all what it's cracked up to be'). She was interviewed at her parents' bungalow in Middlesbrough where she lived.

She was better qualified than most of our informants and had left school at the age of sixteen with nine O levels. She found a clerical job straightaway, working for a national company with a branch in Teesside. This lasted for two years. Next, Dawn moved to London to study at art college. Whilst she was there, she supplemented her educational grant by designing and making shirts and selling them to her friends. On returning to Teesside at the age of nineteen (she 'wasn't suited' to college), she signed on as unemployed and started to think about her employment prospects. She wanted to avoid further mundane, clerical jobs. She had ambition and wanted a challenge, especially one which might earn her money. On the day she was turned down for a job with a travel company her father suggested self-employment and she saw an advert for 'Live-wire' (see Chapter 5) and decided to turn her hobby and previously small-scale shirt-making enterprise into a new business: 'I thought *I* could do that. I could be independent. There will be nobody telling me what to do and I will also be able to make some money. It just seemed the perfect alternative to being unemployed.'

She was allocated a Livewire adviser who encouraged her to enrol for the EAS and to submit a business plan for the Livewire competition. She began to work from home supplying local shops on a sale or return basis and selling at local craft fairs.

After eight months or so she started looking for premises. She had applied for an RDG and had been promised £3,000 for job creation. She eventually found a small unit in an arcade of shops in Billingham and signed a two-year lease. At this point Dawn's business was building up according to plan. She re-entered the Livewire competition, passed interview tests on marketing and finance, and this time won several hundred pounds. Additionally, she entered and won a national competition for young entrepreneurs; the prize being a year's free first-class travel in Britain. This was put to good use in visiting suppliers, designers and fashion houses in London. Here she managed to pick up £1,000 worth of orders. Soon afterwards she won another business competition and was successfully nominated as delegate to an international conference of young entrepreneurs held in Paris.

She, unlike many informants, had been able to secure premises and a reasonable level of early capitalization. Furthermore, she developed a number of different styles of marketing her products: direct retailing through her shop; wholesaling; selling through commissioned agents on a party-plan basis. It is understandable that, by looking at Dawn's performance in the first two years of business, she could easily be classified as a success story by local enterprise agencies. So what went wrong? Why did she close the business to rejoin the ranks of the unemployed?

Dawn: I would carry on doing it but I have no money and I have lost heart. I loved doing it.

RM: You have obviously been very successful in the business and winning all these awards. When did the lack of money and being disheartened come in?

Dawn: Well, there has been quite a few different factors. One of the main things is I want stability. Right through self-employment I thought I can't spend that money cos it's not mine. I haven't dared take any money out and it has been on my mind for three years that I cannot take any money out. I felt guilty about it if I did . . . // . . . Going to Paris kept me going a bit longer and meeting all the people but I came back and was just sitting in the shop day after day, not very many people coming in, knowing the shop was going to be demolished and I just got very disheartened.

RM: The arcade was going to be knocked down but was the shop in a good position?

Dawn: No. I had a few regular customers but very little passing trade. Fair enough, I could have worked from home but that's not very professional, is it?

RM: When you talk about being on your own was that being overworked or were there other issues as well?

Dawn: It was very lonely. That's one of the main things. When people think about self-employment they think about the money but you miss the stupid things like Christmas staff parties. You have nobody to talk to. You become very independent, but you get in a rut. It gets very disheartening. There's nobody there to chat with.

Dawn had typically been working over forty hours every week for three years, but even after this amount of time she was unable to take a regular wage. Usually she took between £20 and £30 per week for herself, sometimes less. Her business went reasonably well and she could have imagined closing down a lot sooner had she not been making money. The constant 'just getting by' (supplemented by kindly parents at home) was a drain upon her enthusiasm. Official recognition and rewards for her entrepreneurial efforts were outweighed in the long term by loneliness, insecurity and poverty. She knew she would lose her shop premises in the near future. She had had no holidays in three years. She became disheartened. Losing heart for the continuous struggle of running new small businesses was a common way of expressing the reasons for closure. She now wanted to be employed so that she had the security and a regular wage coming in ('although I want a job that has responsibility, I want a job that I know at the end of the day I can go home and forget about').

She identified a number of problems with initiatives to encourage youth self-employment which bear great similarity to those discussed in Chapter 6:

> The EAS is excellent for people who want to get off the dole but there is no proper back-up. Nobody to say 'have you got this and this, have you got this amount of money?' There's nobody like that. The EAS come and visit you but they just say 'Are you okay?'. They just want to know if you're still doing it. To keep giving you the money. You're on your own, really. That is just one more number off the dole on to the EAS. There should be more back-up.

Despite the closure of her business after three years, Dawn did not consider herself a failure: on the contrary, she described her business as a success. This illustrates further the essential precariousness of our informants' involvement in youth enterprise in areas like Cleveland. We said in Chapter 6 that the categories (runners, fallers, plodders) are flexible and overlapping. Had Dawn been interviewed six months earlier no doubt we would have classified her as a runner and one of the winners in Cleveland's enterprise stakes. She said:

> If you are working-class, you are brought up to believe that you can just be that, you cannot be anything higher. The way I have been brought up is that you can get anything if you go for it . . . // . . . I wanted to be very big. Some people might want to be chugging along, with a garage business or something like that, which is fine. I wanted to be well known around the country for Dawn Sanderson Designer Shirts . . . // . . . I was unemployed and to get off the unemployment register, somebody offered this incentive to become self-employed. I have gone from being dependent on the state to total independence to being dependent again . . . // . . . I didn't want to but it just happens that I've had to.

She came fairly close to her ambitions, certainly closer than most of those who start up new one-person businesses. Self-employment was enjoyable and rewarded her with feelings of independence and pride for three years. Finally, the pressures and drawbacks experienced by very many of our informants took their toll and she closed the business. In terms of our analytical framework for understanding the process and experience of youth enterprise, she fell from the upper reaches of 'success' into the group of people who no longer traded but now, instead, were again looking for employment in a depressed labour market.

Dennis

At the outset we must stress that Dennis's story is not typical of youth enterprise. His attitude to self-employment and his strategies for running a business were not to be found elsewhere in the sample and his story contrasts sharply with Dawn's. However, we think that there should be room in ethnographic accounts for unusual cases and the issues highlighted in the following case study should perhaps be confronted by all those delivering enterprise policies to non-traditional entrepreneurs.

Dennis was well known to those working in Teesside's youth enterprise industry. He was suggested as a possible contact for our research both by enterprise advisers and other young entrepreneurs who knew him or at least knew of him. Having said this, we took several months to track him down. He had been in business with his wife, selling office equipment. They had operated from a start-up unit in a local enterprise agency for a few months (in the interview he was rather vague about how long he had actually been in business). Prior to setting up, at the age of twenty-two, he had been unemployed for a period of several years broken only by a spell on Community Programme and one or two casual part-time jobs.

Dennis had lived in bed and breakfast accommodation for a number of years before getting a council house (with his wife and her children). His attitude to working and state benefits was rather roguish. He talked gleefully about how he had been claiming supplementary benefit at the same time as working on CP (and receiving roughly £50 for four days' work). He avoided getting jobs for a couple of years because this would have jeopardized the money that he received to pay for his bed and breakfast lodgings.

He decided to set up in business after being called in for a Restart interview. They suggested the idea of starting a business to him and he reports that they threatened to stop his dole unless he found an alternative to unemployment. At the time he had been getting bored with the dole and saw people he knew apparently making a success of their small businesses (one person in particular, again one of our informants, apparently inspired Dennis to set up). Restart directed him to a local enterprise agency where he attended a short enterprise training course in the hope of setting up a business to rival those in the town. His long period of unemployment was not the motivation behind his entrepreneurial plans, rather he was attracted simply by the potentially large sums of money to be earned.

He spent a long time preparing his business: revising a business plan, attending short enterprise courses, learning about cash-flows, opening 'business accounts' and so on. He joined the EAS and had little trouble in raising the necessary £1,000, though he accomplished this through a rather unorthodox method:

RM: Was there any problem with the £1,000?
Dennis: Not really because I walked straight into 'Pallisters' [a high street store] and got £1,600 worth of equipment out of there and I had the receipt for it and that actually classed as my £1,000.
RM: Did it? But it wasn't your money — you owed it?
Dennis: Yes, I still owed Pallisters but I still got the £1,000 which got me the £40 per week.

After we finished recording the interview, Dennis went into more detail about how it was a good idea for RM to work a similar fiddle on 'Pallisters' in Newcastle. He had been able to get over a thousand pounds worth of goods from the Teesside branch by simply walking in, showing evidence of his address and that he possessed a bank account and signing a credit agreement. The receipt for the goods was apparently satisfactory proof that he had £1,000 (and could therefore enter the EAS). Many high street stores operate such easy credit schemes but they rely on the good intentions of customers to pay them back:

RM: In the beginning did you have any intention of paying for these things?
Dennis: Well, I did and I didn't. Put it this way, the repayment was supposed to be £60 per month. If I'd had the money I would have done, but I didn't. If the business had worked or the big RDG grant had come in, I would have paid it with that.

Dennis applied for the RDG, and expected to receive £6,000 (for creating two jobs) with which he would pay off some of his early business debts. This money never arrived. He got a cheque for £175 a year after he closed down. He started trading from a local enterprise agency but things started to go wrong almost immediately:

I asked for help with the book-keeping [from the enterprise agency staff] and in the end I didn't get it. I wasn't writing anything down. I was ringing companies up, ordering stuff and then not paying for it. That's what let me down. I was also advertising in the local newspapers. I mean, I even advertised in

177

newspapers in Newcastle and places like that. People kept phoning me up and asking me if I wanted to advertise with them. Some I did. Some I didn't. But I didn't even pay for them! (laughs). With the *Evening Post* the account was either £1,000 or £2,500 when I finished, I can't remember which. It was their fault — I mean we were getting phone calls every day asking if we wanted to advertise that night. I think for the first two weeks I just said no and after that I'd had enough [and started advertising]. I mean I knew, in the long run, that they would have to come off worse in the long run — not me. But they shouldn't hook people and I've told the enterprise people and they've passed it on.[4]

He did not require any business capital to start trading, he said, because he had established credit accounts with various national suppliers of office equipment. He simply ordered goods and then resold them to customers on Teesside, initially repaying his debts to suppliers and keeping any profits. Trade was reasonably brisk after a month or so of heavy advertising and he reported making up to £300 per day from his business at the peak time. Much of the earnings was spent immediately. Unfortunately, he now realized that some of his business practices lacked real commercial sense. For instance, he used to sell a lot of ribbons for typewriters — but made less than ten pence profit on each sale. On some of his deals he realized that he was losing money. Additionally, his book-keeping went awry: 'it was the accounts — when they started asking for their money back'. He was getting goods on credit from suppliers but had stopped paying for them. He felt that he was only given any real help when his business was collapsing; enterprise advisers helped his wife write letters to suppliers informing them of their closure. Dennis estimated his total debt resulting from his period in business to be 'well over £20,000'.

We asked about this rather astounding figure (he operated in business for less than six months) and he added that this included unpaid rent on his house, the money he still owed Pallisters and local newspapers, unpaid VAT and Income Tax, as well as the money he owed to numerous suppliers. Letters demanding repayment were simply thrown away.

RM: Did you get into any sort of trouble?

Dennis: Oh yes, we had the Sheriff. I mean we have been through the courts. But with me and my wife being separated, everything was in my name. So they can't actually touch our lass [and all their possessions were in her name] because nobody knows she was actually a partner. None of the companies did. So she virtually got off with it. So it's when they catch up with me — I'm done for! (laughs).

RM: I don't like to be too personal but aren't you actually living
          with her at the moment?

Dennis: Yes.

RM: But you're separated?

Dennis: Yes. But not really (laughs). I have two addresses. One
          where she is and one where the dole is sent . . . my business
          address (laughs). But nobody's found us. The first com-
          pany that came after me dropped the account as a bad debt.
          And I think that's what might happen with the rest of
          them. Some of them still send me letters — bills, I never
          get proper letters, but I mean I've finished now. It was over
          a year ago now that I did it . . . // . . . we had fellas coming
          round to the house trying to frighten us. I wasn't worried I
          just turned round to our lass and said 'look get the telly and
          get the video and take it round to Dave's or take it over the
          road when they come'.

Apart from his rather lax attitude to his business accounts, his
expensive overheads (mainly advertising costs), and his lack of business
sense, Dennis reported being 'ripped off' by customers. One, who happened to be one of his enterprise advisers, never paid him for an expensive electric typewriter. When he closed the business and pursued the
money (£600), he claimed that the enterprise adviser said 'If you want
your money, get a solicitor'. As Dennis said, it would have been difficult
to take this person to court at the same time as he was being pursued for
unpaid debts.

After continual efforts by debt collectors to locate him and reclaim
money owed, Dennis left Teesside for a while:

RM: Why did you decide to go to Milton Keynes?

Dennis: To get away, literally.

RM: A midnight flit? (laughs)

Dennis: What's that?

RM: When you run away under the cover of the night.

Dennis: It was, actually (laughs). It was a spur of the moment
          thing. We just decided to get a taxi down there to see my
          mate, who could get us a place to live. I got the taxi at
          twelve-thirty at night and he said 'Where are you going?',
          and I said 'Milton Keynes' and he said 'Where's that?' and I
          said 'Do you know London?' and he said 'Yes' and I said
          'It's near there'. It cost £90 but I had the money to show
          him. There was me, our lass, the kids and the cats.
          We were knocking at our friend's door at five in the
          morning.

Unhappily, Dennis's escape to the South was short-lived. The accommodation he had been promised fell through because the landlord did not rent properties to unemployed people. However, his now technically homeless family did have an enjoyable few days over Easter staying in a bed and breakfast paid for by the local council, before returning to Teesside. He, however, remained 'out of the way' in Milton Keynes for a few months before returning home.

Throughout, Dennis's attitudes to what many would find rather worrying circumstances remained relaxed and unflustered. To say that he had a cavalier approach to his predicaments would be an understatement. Indeed, it would be fair to say that he did not really feel that his experiences amounted to much of a predicament. Since the age of sixteen he had learnt an enterprising and quick-footed way of getting by. He simply didn't care about his debts and the financial pressures upon him. Self-employment for him had been a very enjoyable interlude in his longer-term ventures.

RM: So how do you feel about it all now — that's the big question? I mean I've got debts of a couple of thousand pounds and they give me enough headaches. You seem to be taking it all very calmly, being £20,000 in debt.

Dennis: Well Rob, you shouldn't worry. It's only money. I look at it and I think, if I think about it, I'm going to make myself really bad [ill]. So I think, why worry? It's only money. The worst that anybody can do is decide they want to take it back off me . . . // . . . I mean they can actually send me to prison and I know what that's like 'cos I've been in before. So I've got nowt to lose there. I'll spend probably at the worst six months inside. That's if they find me. I mean what's six months inside for £20,000? In the long run they'll either give up on us or find us . . . // . . . I don't think it'll come to going back inside again. The worst is getting made bankrupt. Which is what I wanted to happen anyway. After a few years you can set up again [in business].

RM: This is not a question I'm asking but that some people will ask — don't you feel guilty about it?

Dennis: About ripping people off? No. I take into consideration that these companies are insured against it. I mean if a company sends you a pamphlet through the door every month saying you can order all this stuff, just ring this number . . . . I mean it's been coming though my door for nearly three years. And I decided to ring up to see if I could actually get it.

RM: So you just exploit other people's mistakes?

Dennis: Yes. If they're pushing things at me, I take them. Like Pallisters.

When Dennis was interviewed, in a local pub, he was on an Employment Training scheme run by the enterprise agency which had helped him set up previously. The scheme specialized in helping unemployed people into business and he now had further entrepreneurial plans. After some months of trying to find him in Teesside (he had been in Milton Keynes), he was eventually located by chance in this local enterprise agency. He had changed his name ('I'm still keeping my head down') and it took a little time to ascertain that this was the man we wished to talk to. He had been using the agency as a base from which to develop a second business. He did say that he would be more careful with his accounts in future and that he would aim to secure enough capital to make his new business a success. Under his new name he had received verbal agreements from a bank and a number of trade suppliers for several thousand pounds' worth of new credit to support his entrepreneurial ambitions. He said that the enterprise agency were keeping a closer eye on him but 'if I want to start up again nobody's going to stop me — I could always go to a different place where they don't know me'.

Plodders

Ronnie

Ronnie was the first person we interviewed. He was twenty-one years old and ran a small business as a self-employed motor mechanic. Since leaving school at the age of sixteen he had been on YTS, experienced a short period of unemployment and started his business at the age of seventeen with the help of EAS. He was one of the youngest to start a business and he was now in his fourth year of trading. He was contacted through a local enterprise agency and was claimed as a 'success' by at least two such organizations (see our discussion of multiple auditing in Chapter 4). In terms of the length of time he had survived in business he could perhaps be judged to be successful in comparison with the sample in general. However, Ronnie's story will illustrate that successful entrepreneurship is a complex, ambiguous phenomenon which involves experiences and commitments which outside observers might find difficult to interpret quite so easily as a new form of successful, thriving, profitable economic activity.

During the summer holiday, after leaving school at the end of his fifth year, he tried to find a job through the Careers Service and the Job Centre. He applied for a course ('It was a proper job, you know, an apprenticeship') in motor mechanics based at Hartlepool, along with 380 others. The course had seven places available and he was unsuccessful. He applied for a number of other ordinary jobs (e.g. shelf-stacker in a supermarket, warehouseman) before joining a YTS offering workshop-based training in a variety of manual skills. This suited his interest in skilled, technical work. Whilst on the scheme it was suggested to him that he could develop his long term hobby of working on cars by taking a course in motor mechanics. Here he learned a wide range of technical skills and started ordering parts and materials for the scheme from suppliers. He also began to provide a cheap and small-scale motor repair service for staff and trainees on the scheme and, later, for the local public. By working in and outside of YTS time, and by sharing costs and profits with the scheme, Ronnie was able to start making a profit (a few pounds a week) from his embryonic business. Towards the end of the scheme Ronnie took part in an enterprise training course provided for a few of the scheme trainees, and it was suggested to him by the scheme organizer that he set up in business properly when his YTS finished.

After initial apprehension about getting into debt and great difficulty in finding suitable premises which he could afford, Ronnie started trading from a workshop attached to a nearby youth drop-in centre. The rent was very low (only £5 per week) compared with prices more usually paid, but as Ronnie says:

> My profit was OK. I was making 100 per cent profit on some jobs . . . // . . . but it was all small-scale stuff. That was the problem. I was covering my costs but not the £5 rent. It's only a fiver, but a fiver is a fiver when you're not actually earning. I mean the business was going OK. It's not a sob story, you know, it's the truth. I was getting about £20 in at that time: £10 lodge and the rest back into the business. Well, I had nowt for myself, you know. I thought I'd have to go back on the dole unless something was sorted out.

Two things were eventually sorted out which eased these early struggles. Firstly, Ronnie, after many bureaucratic battles, finally managed to gain access to the EAS and £40 per week. His early application had been rejected (he was deemed to have already started the business whilst on YTS and was therefore ineligible for EAS support), but with the help of a local enterprise adviser he was made a special case. Secondly, after numerous problems with his original premises (thefts, lack of visibility and poor access, skinheads from the drop-in centre urinating in his workshop and frightening off potential customers), he managed to find alternative accommodation for his business nearby:

The first week I moved in I had a customer every day. This was the first time it had ever happened since I started business. I swear going into the drop-in centre was the worst decision I ever made. It put me back a year. I lost so many customers.

Ronnie also secured an RDG of £2,500 (for creating a job for himself). He was unable to use these finances to secure any further loans or credit with the bank because he had no personal security to offer (a house or car); Ronnie lived with his father in a council-rented house. He used the RDG to purchase machinery and to pay the higher rent at his new premises. After four years of business and working, on average, for fifty hours per week, Ronnie said:

> I've got about £500 in the bank now. The rest has been spent. I'm not making enough profit to pay the rent and pay myself wages. I can see month by month that the money is getting lower . . . //
> . . . I'm just sitting here plugging along working but the money in the bank is getting less and less. I've picked it up to about two customers a day now . . . // . . . I tried advertising in the paper again: I got two customers and that cost me £30 . . . // . . . I make about £50 per week for myself but I don't actually take that out. I only take what I need. I'm not on a wage. I can't do it like that. I don't know if you can understand that? I've got to put money away for the bad months when there's nothing coming in . . . I can't spend money at Christmas. I can't pay the bills if the money isn't there. I'm not like my friends. They can go and buy a pair of trousers at the weekend. If I want a pair of trousers I have to save up for months to buy them . . . // . . . If I can hold on, I'll get there. You've got to not be greedy, though it's not being greedy. You've got to think about later in time — is it worth my while to hang on?

Ronnie's vocabulary of enterprise, the words he uses to describe his experiences in business, seem a long way from the official rhetoric and ideology of the enterprise culture (see Chapter 2). So why does he continue to 'plug along' working fifty hours a week for £50 (which he doesn't actually draw from the business)? His answer is typical of many others:

> It's a positive choice, in a way. I wanted to be self-employed . . . //
> . . . In this business you are your own boss. But, you see, you're stuck 'cos you've still got to tell yourself what to do. You get these people who say 'Oh well, you're self-employed you can do

whatever you want'. You can't. You're committed to the business. You know what it wants, what needs doing. In some ways it is better than working for an employer. I'm still working but it's all mine, isn't it? At least you've got a job, haven't you? You're still working for someone but it's yourself, see what I mean? You've got some freedom but it's only limited. It's not the money, but it could be later on. In a few years' time, in three or four years maybe, it could take that long, I could be in a place on every high street . . .

Self-employment provides work, a job, which is better than being on the dole and better in some ways to being an employee. Limited freedom and flexibility, and a feeling of ownership and autonomy partly make up for his low income. The motivation to keep him plodding along comes from a glimpse of possible future success:

Ronnie: I've got a way of looking at it. It might sound funny this. Self-employment is like a corridor, like a tunnel, and I've made the decision to step into that corridor and I'm just at the start of it and it is pretty dark, but, you know, there's light at the end of the corridor. There's loads of doors off the corridor, but, you know, if you can just keep on going, like one day you'll get to the end.

RM: And what's at the end?

Ronnie: Well, I don't know, you know, success. Maybe a pot of gold! (laughs).

Very briefly, then, this is part of Ronnie's story of his efforts to become an established member of the enterprise culture. The general experience he describes — of struggling to make a living through enterprise — was typical of the majority of informants. Most plodded along neither obviously failing nor succeeding in their businesses. Of course, all cases, though sharing common patterns and themes, are unique and some aspects of Ronnie's experiences are perhaps not typical of the sample of informants generally. For instance, he moved into self-employment at a younger age and had been in business for longer than most. He had day-to-day help with his business from his unemployed girlfriend and from a YTS trainee he had taken on. It was more usual for people to be working alone.

Cath

Cath was twenty-two years old and was involved in running a small business partnership as a clothes designer and manufacturer in Stockton. She had been self-employed for virtually a full year. Prior to this she had done many things including: varying lengths of time unemployed, work in a local textile firm, a brief spell at FE college and part-time work in the evening as a bar maid and as a 'kissagram girl'.

Cath's experience of doing 'kissagrams' had been demeaning and risky. She stressed that this was something that she did not enjoy doing; she found it threatening and always took a friend with her for emotional and physical support. Literally, she did it to pay the rent. Unfortunately, she thinks she must have 'done a kissagram' on her signing-on officer (from the Unemployment Benefit Office) because she was soon penalized by the DHSS (as it was) for doing undeclared work while claiming benefit. The unpleasant phenomenon of being 'grassed up' by anonymous informants to the authorities for working while claiming was reported by several of our sample who had dabbled with 'work on the side'. Cath would not let her unemployed boyfriend take any 'fiddly jobs' because of her own experiences.

She had intended staying in education past the age of sixteen but, unfortunately, she had to leave college due to family rows about her boyfriend. She moved out of her parents' house and into a rented flat in Stockton and consequently could not afford to study at college. She found a job, after a year and a half on the dole (which she hated), as a machinist with a local firm 'Boro Textiles', where the work was 'really boring'. She says: 'I had to sew 1,500 seams down the back of jeans a day, and I was only coming out with about £60. By the end of the day I was falling over, tired'. She left this job voluntarily (she made her employer sack her by frequently being absent) and then returned to the dole for eight months before she officially started self-employment through the EAS.

She decided on her own business after seeing an advert for EAS and on realizing her hobby of making dresses could be turned into a source of money. She started designing, making and selling clothes while still on the dole (and working at her evening jobs). She attended a short enterprise training course at the Polytechnic and prepared her business plan with the help of a local enterprise centre. The main emphases of this training were cash-flow forecasting and the revision of general business plans.

Cath described the way she felt about the business she ran with her partner:

I know it's mine. Everything in it is ours. Even if we go bust at least I know that we've tried. I'm hoping to get a shop eventually — full of my own designs. It is a lot of responsibility but I feel proud. If I do eventually make a lot of money at it, I know I've done it myself. There is a sense of achievement. There hasn't been anyone else apart from me. I do it my own way. I don't have to listen to anyone else.

There were, however, drawbacks:

> Not making enough money. Being skint — I'm absolutely broke. With renting a flat I daren't take any more than £40 per week and that finishes soon. When I first started out I was thinking of packing in a few months later because I wasn't getting anything in. Everything was being paid out. I got a £3,000 grant from the Regional Development. But most of that got paid out on stock. Then I started getting big orders — just before Christmas. After Christmas I wasn't making anything at all. It's picked up again over the past two weeks. If I can keep the orders coming I should be OK when the EAS finishes... // ... the hours are bad. Some weeks there's nothing to do. Today I'll probably be working till ten and eleven o'clock. 5.30 am is my record. Those are the things I hate — the money and the hours.

The 'big orders' Cath refers to were from two local firms, the owner of one of which was Barry, the first case study in this chapter, and the other was also run by young people. In Chapter 6 we drew attention to the practice of networking whereby young entrepreneurs traded between themselves. In this instance, Cath was subcontracted to produce not her own designs but those of rival small firms. In this way her work in enterprise bore many similarities to her work as an employee of Boro Textiles. She simply had to make up patterns given to her, rather than creating and selling her own designs. Moreover, she could not clock off at 5 pm like an employee but had to work into the night in order to ensure that the order was completed on time. For this work she received no more income than the £60 per week she previously earned as an employee.

Cath could not afford to advertise her products and services and, though the start-up unit she occupied was cheap, she lacked any passing trade. She was, thus, very dependent upon these 'bread and butter' jobs from other young entrepreneurs. She enjoyed her work even if she was not creating her own designs. However, the success of the business was perceived as hanging in the balance. In a year's time she imagined herself either back on the dole or in a shop on Stockton High Street. At the time of interview she would have sacrificed her business and taken a decent job with an employer purely because she was continuously 'skint and down in the dumps' about her business.

Sometimes she felt bitter about government enterprise policies. She was ambivalent about the EAS: on the one hand it had helped her set up in business; but, on the other, it provided very little money to cover rents and other business costs and was going to be badly missed when it stopped. She realized that part of the problem with her business was the sheer level of competition on Teesside. There is no shortage of specialist shops selling designer clothes for young people but there was, she felt, a general lack of cash in people's pockets. Sometimes she felt that the movement of people like herself into self-employment was 'just a big con':

> It's good because you get the £40 per week but I think they stop it too soon. They give you help for a year and then you are just dumped. It's like all the schemes to get people off the dole. I mean I still feel like I'm on a scheme. One of Mrs Thatcher's little diddles to get me off the dole, you know what I mean? I hate this Government. All they do is fob us off with schemes. You know: 'You've got a job for a year — be happy with it'.

With this final passage we are branching out into more political understandings of youth enterprise — the subject of a much fuller investigation in the Chapter 9.

Summary and Conclusions

Most of the themes and issues referred to by informants in this chapter are not new. Elsewhere in the book we cover much the same ground but in less detail. The people we describe here were selected to illustrate, and enliven further, various aspects of the wider realities of youth enterprise. In focusing upon just six cases we are able, however, to highlight some of the contradictions and inconsistencies in the general movement to promote an enterprise culture on Teesside.

Particularly striking are the similarities between those we class as runners and fallers. It might have been imagined that those who were successful in their businesses would display characteristics or attitudes that would set them apart from their less successful contemporaries in small businesses. This was not the case. Indeed, it has proved very difficult to identify many factors which could be characterized as determinants or explanations of relative success. For instance, it could be hypothesized that intelligence or educational achievement (as signified by qualifications) might relate positively to success in the business sphere. Dawn, who was unusual compared with the rest of the sample in that she had gained as many as nine O levels, failed in the long run. Contrast her case with that of Barry who, though having three O levels, failed to achieve any further qualifications in his two years of post-compulsory schooling but still made a success of his business. Shane, also a 'runner', had fewer qualifications and quickly abandoned college at the age of sixteen to enter the world of work.

Furthermore, virtually all our informants shared a diligent, determined and serious attitude to their businesses. Only Dennis displayed a brazen, casual attitude to his tasks and financial responsibilities. Neither effort nor income could be selected as variables to explain differential success and failure. All worked hard for little money. Perhaps these can be identified as necessary, but not sufficient, conditions for success in small business.

Possibly of more importance in the progress of new small firms are structural and material factors. The importance of suitable premises was confirmed by these cases. Dawn suffered from having an 'invisible' shop with little passing trade and Ronnie's initial workshop 'set him back a year', whereas Barry's new premises were perfectly suited to his plans for expansion. Contacts and contracts with bigger established firms were again crucial to the runners in their first months in business. This early commercial trade provided an absolutely critical financial boost to Shane, for instance. In the final chapter we will argue that the job of predicting who will win out and who will fail is difficult, if not impossible. To conclude the examination of these six cases, however, we wish to make one final point.

In separating out the experience of youth enterprise into three analytic types (runners, fallers, plodders), we should be careful not to forget that the similarities in the day-to-day experiences of all informants tended to outweigh most differences. Our typology is presented as an analytical tool for understanding and categorizing experiences of success and failure, and we should reiterate that the boundary between the successful 'wheeler dealing' of Barry and the disheartening, day-to-day drudge of Ronnie (or the unpredictable failure of Dawn) is a very thin and shifting one. Perhaps this is the main conclusion of this chapter. The cultural and economic world that these people inhabit is, after all, just a new and politically fashionable part of the wider over-arching capitalist economy. The essence of this economic system is one of individual success and failure. The market will allow some businesses to grow and prosper (affording the Barrys of this world the dream, and probably the reality, of lazy, hazy days of youthful retirement). Such success, however, is underpinned by competition — competition which in turn demands that some, like Dawn, will fail. All (most) cannot succeed in the enterprise game by the very nature of the economic rules. Some make it, most don't: this is the secret trick of enterprise. For every Shane, with his desktop publishing and potentially fifty employees, or Barry with his exports, business-speak and 'Time is Money' watch, there are, according to our evidence, another nine people (like Ronnie, Cath, Dawn and Dennis) who will either fail or 'willingly' plod along hoping that they too will eventually clear the hurdles in their way and reach the winning-tape and glittering prizes afforded by business success.

Notes

1   Three of the six were involved with the clothing industry (at different levels and with differing degrees of success), reflecting the high proportion of people who designed, manufactured and sold clothes in our sample (see Chapter 6).
2   In this passage Barry uses the term 'we.' He was, however, working completely on his own at this stage. We noticed that on occasions some informants would use the 'royal we' to refer to themselves and their business operations. Perhaps this was accidental or perhaps it was a semiconscious attempt to suggest that their businesses amounted to more than a sole tradership.
3   This bears similarity with Stewart, who traded in imported Turkish rugs. Stewart intended to close his business once the challenges it posed had been overcome. Perhaps this is a characteristic of a more successful entrepreneurial attitude.
4   Apparently local newspapers no longer pursue such a hard-sell policy with young entrepreneurs, largely due to their experiences with Dennis.

Chapter 8

Beyond Small Business:
Alternative Forms of Enterprise

In Chapter 4 we described how the small business model dominated the local enterprise scene. Alternative interpretations of what constitutes youth enterprise were rare and very much overshadowed by self-employment in sole traderships, both in terms of the numbers of young people we found that were following each path and the numbers of organizations that promoted them. However, we did identify other agencies that are significant in the different view they take of what it means to be enterprising. In this chapter we examine, firstly, community enterprise and secondly, co-operatives.

Problem Solving and Community Enterprise

Our discussion of community enterprise is quite short, compared to our examination of risky businesses in the preceding three chapters. This is because, in the first place, although community enterprise operates along quite different lines (to small business), it is quantitatively far less significant for young people on Teesside. Secondly, we had great difficulty in locating even small numbers of people who had participated in community enterprise projects. The discussion in this section, then, is necessarily preceded by a cautionary note about the size of the sample we are referring to here. We were able to talk to only nine people who fitted the bill of being from Cleveland, being aged under 25 and having taken part in community enterprise ventures with Problem Solvers, the organization promoting this type of enterprise in the county (see Chapter 4).

The number of possible contacts provided by this agency was very small (despite giving the early impression that hundreds of people had benefited from their services) and their records seemed to be patchy and/or out of date. Consequently, we found it difficult to contact some of the people suggested to us; some of those whom we did speak to on the phone could not recall having anything to do with Problem Solvers. After interviewing some of those who had, we realised that this was probably not because they had been wrongly classed as clients, but rather that they had forgotten their involvement with community enterprise.

Problem Solvers was established in 1988 with the aid of a substantial MSC/TA grant. To recap from Chapter 4, it aims to provide facilitators and working capital to young and unemployed people so that they can design and manage projects of benefit to the community but 'not for profit'. The agency works across different sectors and with different client groups: school-pupils, YTS trainees (particularly, it seemed to us, young women on care courses), the unemployed and FE college students. Consequently, the average age of informants was younger than the sample as a whole: about nineteen years old at the time of interview.

Our interview and questionnaire survey of the local enterprise industry uncovered a good deal of resentment and criticism of Problem Solvers; some of which we would argue is probably well founded and some of which is perhaps unfair. Part of the unease felt about Problem Solvers stemmed from the large grant they received from the MSC. This was public knowledge and it provoked considerable animosity amongst competing enterprise organizations.

The aims and objectives of Problem Solvers also seemed to inspire quite scathing comments from those working in more mainstream enterprise agencies. It was not that they were necessarily opposed to broader conceptions of enterprise, but that the aims and methods of Problem Solvers appeared to them to be confused and obscure. We can sympathize with this criticism to some extent. We take the liberty of repeating a quotation we used in Chapter 4:

> Enterprise is about making things happen. It refers to the willingness and ability of people to be self-determining and flexible, influencing, shaping and taking control over their own lives in any sphere, be that social, personal, economic or political. (Problem Solvers promotional material)

At first sight this definition of enterprise can be read as a description of the political outlook of the Anarchists, which some might argue, would serve as nice balance to the free market principles inherent in most enterprise programmes. However, an inspection of the activities flowing from this mission statement shows that the definition bears little resemblance to the reality of the practice. The objective of Problem Solvers is to 'foster an enterprising environment in Cleveland which will encourage new ideas and creative responses to change'. It aims to do this by instigating projects in the local community to be run by members of that community which will be of social benefit. The benefit should run in two directions: those running the projects will learn new skills and gain in personal experience, and disadvantaged groups will be helped directly by the projects.

The concept of 'positive outcomes', the range of possible outcomes of enterprising activities facilitated by Problem Solvers, is pertinent here (see also Chapter 6). Unlike other agencies, they aim to generate a wider range of outcomes which can be defined in some way as symbolizing personal improvement. For instance, a positive outcome of a Problem Solvers project may be an emergent new community or co-operative business, but equally it could be an increased feeling of self-worth. The beneficial effects of these enterprise projects are measured by self-report forms which participants fill in before and afterwards. These aim to measure the sorts of enterprise skills identified by Dave Turner (1989) and listed by us in Chapter 2, by asking whether respondents feel self-confident, whether they enjoy facing challenges and so on. Responses given afterwards are compared with those given before the enterprise project, and the improvements in the personality of the young or unemployed person are interpreted as evidence of the social psychological efficacy of the Problem Solvers' approach.[1]

The types of projects instigated by Problem Solvers to foster these positive personal and community results include: supporting a group of young people who aimed to set up a music co-op by helping fund market research; the establishment of a school 'tuck shop' by pupils; a photographic project set up by local unemployed people for schoolchildren; a camping trip run by YTS trainees for disabled children; theatre outings for elderly people; and school-pupils making bird boxes for an old people's home.

Spike, who had been involved with the music co-op, and Gill, a YTS care trainee, summed up what we found to be the common interpretation of Problem Solvers' objectives:

> It's for unemployed people to run projects to benefit the community. Like running trips out for disabled people. They'll provide the money to hire a minibus. It seems to be to get people more involved in community-based things ... // ... rather than giving someone money to make a profit for themselves (Spike).

> To give people on the outside, like in hostels, that haven't got the money, to give them times to go out and do things which they wouldn't be able to otherwise (Gill).

It was common for informants to view the aim of Problem Solvers as purely community improvement, with little understanding of the objective of promoting enterprise amongst those taking part in the projects. We found that informants in this sub-sample had quite prosaic views of Problem Solvers' enterprise projects compared with its grand aims.

Graham was in his mid-twenties when we interviewed him and he had been unemployed for over five years since leaving school. Graham was part of a project to set up a week-long training session in photography for local schoolchildren. He was approached by a Problems Solvers facilitator when he was participating in a Community Programme scheme in Middlesbrough. The work he was employed to do on the scheme involved photographing the local area and his skills and those of his work colleagues were drawn upon by Problem Solvers to help younger people learn about photography. Their job was to train eight schoolchildren and set up a week-long exhibition of their collective work. This involved organizing trips to photograph museums and galleries ('We called it giving them inspiration').

The organizational part of their project also included finding out about the equipment they needed, planning the visits, arranging transport and so on. Problem Solvers provided the funding for the project. Graham was unsure of the total cost but he thought it was about £500. His group was supposed to have handled the financial arrangements (in order to instil experience of budgets, money management and account-keeping), but the responsibility for this had been taken over by Problem Solvers because of delays caused by their lack of organization (according to Graham).

Graham and his colleagues filled in forms which enquired into their levels of self-confidence, orgnizational skill, managerial ability, etc. They were told that they would be given forms to complete after their participation in the Problem Solvers project but 'we haven't actually filled in the "afterwards" form yet. I think they've forgotten about us'. This was nearly a year after their first contact with Problem Solvers and it had taken both parties the best part of ten months to organize the week-long exhibition. We decided to do Problem Solvers' job for them and asked him whether he now felt personally developed by his participation in the project; whether he felt more self-confident, enterprising or organized:

> *Graham*:   I would say that I have . . . a bit more out-going. Before I would have had the idea to see the gallery and to think about the exhibition, but I wouldn't have done anything about it. I also learned more about writing business letters, organizing, budgeting . . . // . . . it has helped. It has given me more confidence as a photographer as well.
>
> *RM*:   Although I know it's not directed to trying to get people into jobs, do you think it helps people to be more employable?
>
> *Graham*:   It's useful . . . it's possible . . . I don't know. It's a bit more to stick in my c.v., I suppose. But it's gone back to the

'we don't want to know you' stage from people I apply for jobs to.

Colin and Sharon were interviewed in a community centre in an area of very high unemployment in Middlesbrough. They were both on the dole and had, between them, experience of all the government schemes recently available to unemployed people (apart from EAS). They had also participated in a Problem Solvers project:

Colin: First of all Problem Solvers came. I don't think they really knew what to do when they started. They wanted us to put in an application for funding to Problem Solvers and we had to decide what we wanted to apply for and so we decided on camping equipment for kids. To take kids camping. We went through the stages of putting the application in.

RM: Was this everybody?

Sharon: Oh yes. We were put into teams and had to find out how much it would cost — camping equipment costs.

RM: How long did this process take?

Colin: Six months, I think.

Sharon: Something like that.

RM: And did you get the money? How much?

Sharon: Yes. I can't remember.

Colin: I think about £2,500, I think. All the equipment we asked for we got the money for. We got grants off other people for buses and petrol and that.

RM: And what was the purpose of Problem Solvers? Did you learn much through it?

Sharon: Well, they just sort of came here and we did role-plays and played games and things. I mean some people, after the first week or so, were more open, brought them out. One lad, he was quiet . . .

Colin: He talks to anybody now. Brought him out of his shell with the games and role-playing.

RM: So it worked on that level?

Sharon: Yeah, I can talk to people now. Before I just sat there and was quiet.

RM: Is that due to Problem Solvers?

Sharon: Partly.

Sarah Louise, who was on a YTS care scheme at the time, became involved with organizing a holiday for elderly people from a residential home:

RM:	What did you do with Problem Solvers?
Sarah Louise:	Played daft games (laughs).
RM:	Anything else?
Sarah Louise:	They said if we could come up with some ideas that would help the community and that, providing it wasn't too much, they would fund it and it would go towards our course at the time. Because everybody was just doing day trips and taking them to panto-mimes and that we decided to go away for a week.
RM:	As far as you understand it, what was the idea behind Problem Solvers?
Sarah Louise:	I don't know — they didn't tell us very much to start off with. Just played these daft games and nobody knew what was going on (laughs). We didn't know what they were on about or anything . . . // . . . we had this camp and they turned up and played these games. It was like being back at nursery school. It was terri-ble, dead embarrassing.

She became involved in the planning of the trip to the holiday camp at Skegness for eight elderly or disabled people at a total cost of £1,000. It was 'brilliant fun'. Sarah Louise had to negotiate transport and arrange bookings with the holiday camp and overcome problems with Social Services. All this took nearly a year in all to finalize and she and her friends filled in forms to say that they had learnt things: initiative, problem-solving, organizing and letter-writing. She admitted that she had 'done things I would never have done if it weren't for Problem Solvers'. She was unemployed for a few months after her YTS finished before getting a job as a receptionist. She was adamant, however, that this definitely did not have anything to do with her enterprise project.[2]

To summarize, it would seem that community enterprise projects were reasonably well received by this small sample of their clients. Most reported that they could see some improvement in themselves (increased self-confidence and organizational ability) as a consequence of taking part in these projects. They were not particularly demanding, they were free, they could be good fun and they afforded the opportunity to take part in enjoyable activities away from the dull routine of YTS or unemployment (holidays, theatre trips, shopping expeditions to the Gateshead Metro-centre). Additionally, these projects certainly seemed to benefit the community, for instance, by providing recreational trips for elderly and disabled people.

Whether these ventures taken together amount to, or will lead to, 'people taking control over their own lives', politically, economically, socially or personally, we doubt. That they are creating an 'enterprising environment' on Teesside, we also doubt. To us, they seem to be worth-while but small and short community projects which have a limited role in improving either the lot of the young unemployed or some of the elderly and disabled people in depressed areas. Admittedly, they play a role in building the confidence of those suffering the harsh experience of unemployment (and the projects do give some informal and minimal training in such things as writing business letters), which cannot be bad.

Though we are sure that the objectives underpinning Problem Solvers are worthy, we gained the definite impression that the consequent activities were unfocused and ambiguous in their aims and strategies. Informants were, in the main, unable to specify what the point of their participation had been or when the project had actually started and finished. They also complained about disorganization. The original objectives of this form of community enterprise are certainly interesting and constitute a much-needed, liberal counterweight to the prevailing small business ideology. However, the projects as translated into everyday practice certainly fell short of the weighty and radical ambitions contained in their mission statements.

One of the main differences between this version of enterprise and small business is that success in the latter is far easier to quantify. The numbers of clients counselled, businesses started, jobs created and firms surviving at various lengths of time, can be used to justify to funding bodies the existence of agencies working in this sphere. It is much harder to measure the positive outcomes of community enterprise ventures, which can, as we have described, range from a heightened feeling of self-worth to an extra item for a curriculum vitae, to an emergent idea for a collective business. Consequently, Problem Solvers was frequently criticized, partially unfairly in our opinion, by others working in the local enterprise industry. Its aims were said to be vague, its philosophy cloudy, its methods and results unproven, and its organization unreliable.

The main criticism that can, in our opinion, be levelled at the Problem Solvers' community enterprise ventures is that they provide activities which fill in time, which may contribute to personal and community development, but which really act as a poor substitute for a job. We accept that this may be perceived as another unfair criticism, but the major morale boost for young and unemployed people comes not from arranging camping expeditions or nights out at the panto for old people, but from securing a decent job with decent pay and decent prospects. We have shown how such youth opportunities are few and far between and that economic recovery is taking a long time coming to Cleveland. In the meantime, it is possible that Problems Solvers can step into the breach and lay on activities which may contribute in relatively small ways to preserving personal dignity and feelings of being wanted by the community. It is also possible that these community enterprise ventures may lead to improved chances of finding employment or self-employment.

However, this was not a positive outcome reported by these informants and we feel that this aspect of the work of Problem Solvers remains to be proven.[3]

Working the Co-operative Way

Co-operatives are a second form of economic activity, promoted locally, that have less overtly capitalistic motivations than small business. Throughout the book we have made little effort to distinguish the comments and experiences of those working in co-operatives from those in more straightforward small firms. This is because in most respects they were little different. Motivations underlying movement into both these non-traditional avenues of economic activity were similar, and the negative and positive aspects of running a small business or a co-operative shared much in common. Thus, we felt it suitable to collate these experiences in Chapters 5 and 6. Here, though, we aim to investigate briefly the more specific elements of co-operative work.

We also had difficulties in locating and interviewing people who were, or had been, co-operative workers. In this case, though, it was not due to any problems of over-exaggeration on behalf of the enterprise agency we used to help us gain access to informants (NECDA), but rather to the simple fact that there were very few young people in co-ops on Teesside. We talked to thirteen people and we have been assured that this number probably represents most, if not all, of the total population in our target group at the time.

Given this, we do feel able to comment on some aspects of the experience of co-operatives even from such a small number of cases. Furthermore, the operation and meaning of co-operative work will be more familiar to readers than community enterprise ventures, and far more has been written about them. Attention has typically been drawn to: the historical origins of co-ops in the labour movement and philanthropic organizations of the last century; the liberal, middle-class origins of many co-operative founders; the lack of business skills and commercial acumen of co-op workers; how often weak financial capital structures can be compensated for by high levels of worker commitment; success and failure rates in comparison with other types of small firm; the level of state and political support for co-operative development: and, comparisons between the co-operative movement in this country and in Mediterranean Europe (e.g. Coates, 1976; Campbell *et al.*, 1977; Cockerton *et al.*, 1980; Thornley, 1981; Hughes, 1984; Hunt and McVey, 1984; Thomas and Cornforth, 1989; Ball, Knight and Plant, 1990).

Jenny Thornley's examination of worker co-operatives in Britain and in Europe begins with the following definition and comment:

A co-operative is a particular kind of firm which has grown up around a set of ideological beliefs in response to external econo- mic and social circumstances ... // ... the basic features of a workers' co-operative are that it is owned and controlled by those working in it ... [they] have to compete alongside other firms in the capitalist market and at a superficial glance appear to suffer many of the same problems that face most small firms. However, any analysis of how co-operatives function in the market must contain an examination of the ideology of their supporters, and the political and economic background to their formation. (1981:1–2)

The political, economic and social context in which our co-operative informants started, has, of course, been described earlier in the book. The same economically depressed locality, and the same broad enterprise movement structured the movement of young people into co-operatives and self-employment in one-person businesses. Here we will concentrate on the ideology and politics of those entering co-operative work, particu- larly how they started up, and how this compares to those starting more conventional forms of business. In the next chapter we develop a much broader discussion of the political and economic attitudes of our infor- mants. In general those running co-ops were found to be very similar, in their political views and voting preferences, to the rest of the sample.

The people we talked to who had been involved in co-ops went through many of the processes in starting up that we described in Chap- ter 5: they had completed a round of enterprise agencies, counselling sessions, visits to bank managers and so on. They participated in EAS and attended an Awareness Day:

RM: What was the Awareness Day like?
Tony: They are not too hot for co-ops. They tell you about all three — sole ownerships, partnerships, co-operatives — but the co-operatives and partnerships were about 15 minutes long, but the other was all day. But we kept asking him about co-ops. We went away and thought about it and picked people's brains and decided co-ops were for us.
RM: Would you say that there were any political (with a small 'p') reasons for you setting up as a co-operative, rather than going into a small businesses? Or was it just a practical thing?
Reggie: I think it was more the practical side ...
Tony: I don't know. It's got a lot of aspects ... // ... When I worked in the factory I'd get a chit of paper from upstairs saying what wanted doing. But as a co-operative I can see things working a lot better than sole ownerships. When I

was working there a chap two grades above me in the
stores was getting £35 a week more. He sat on his bum all
day and I slogged my guts out.

Reggie: I think the main thing with co-ops is that everyone's doing
the work not just you and someone sat in an office giving
orders out. It's the whole lot of you. You're in charge of
your job.

Tony: I think if you did a survey of everybody in the North of
England, besides business, sole ownership, there's nobody
wants to make a profit. People just want to make a living
wage . . .

Reggie: (interrupts) Not thousands.

Tony: From my point of view — just a decent living where you
can turn round to the wife and say: 'We'll have a night out'.
Maybe if it's only once a month. Profit? No. A living
wage? Yes.

Reggie and Tony were both unemployed, married men in their
mid-twenties who were still in the process of establishing a construction
co-operative, with others, in Middlesbrough. Their comments are quite
typical: they wanted a more equitable working arrangement where jobs
and income were shared evenly. In some ways, though, they were driven
by the same motivations as the sample in general: their enterprise was not
inspired by the desire for financial gain and they would be satisfied with
'a living wage'; and at least part of their reason for starting up lay in the
fact that both had experienced long-term unemployment. As we argued
in Chapter 4, they found effort in the enterprise industry to be directed
toward starting up small business enterprises, rather than other forms
such as co-ops. However, one organization, NECDA, does much to
encourage the development of co-ops on Teesside. All the people we
talked to had used NECDA's services. We think it highly unlikely that
young people would set up co-ops either without their assistance or
without them knowing about it. They provided the main stimulus for
many choosing the co-operative way of working:

It was simply the fact of the help he [a NECDA adviser] gave.
That he got in touch with you. He was saying that they're better
cos no-one's the boss and this kind of thing. We thought it was a
good idea. We did agree with him, but it made no odds to me
whether there was a boss or not. I worked for plenty of bosses
before. It was mainly the help we were getting from them
(Donna).

Some set up in business in a co-operative because they did not really
know anything else. By chance Donna (above) and Belinda her

co-worker, met a NECDA officer who impressed them with his discussion of co-ops so they started up in that form rather than any other. They both said that the help they received in planning, setting up and running the business was invaluable and this assistance continued throughout the year they were trading (as a catering co-op). The political and ideological essence of the co-operative movement was, in the main, absent from the primary reasons given by informants for why they set up co-ops. Louise and Alex were two young women from Billingham who were part of a group that set up a small-scale printing co-operative:

> RM: People talk about co-operatives in terms of common owner-
> ship of the business. Did you have any political beliefs that
> co-operatives would be a better way of going about things?
> Louise: No. You've got to remember that I was only twenty at the
> time and I'd never heard of a co-operative. All I knew was
> that it was for people who wanted to set up in business and
> have an equal amount of say. That was it. Full stop.

Informants like Louise, and Reggie and Tony, did express a deeper understanding of the larger philosophy of co-operation when they talked about equality in income, decision-making and work responsibilities. They approved of equality in these spheres but they had been introduced to the meaning and aims of the co-operative movement by people working for this organization. Had they not come into contact with NECDA it is probable that they would have started up in more traditional small business structures.

Having said this, informants did talk highly of their involvement with this enterprise organization and of their co-operative experience. The only problem that was identified with co-operatives *per se* was that if those who started co-ops wanted to employ other staff at a later date then the johnny-come-latelys would have equal rights, income, etc. We are not sure that this is necessarily always the case, but this was reported by a few people as being unfair given the amount of effort expended by the founder members. NECDA, as we reported in Chapter 5, operated a much more personal and extensive advice and help service than the small business enterprise agency we studied. Co-op members would be paid personal visits at home and at their businesses, assistance extended right through the course of the co-op's life, often until after it had closed down. Guidance was not restricted to the start-up stage and close attention was given by NECDA advisers to co-ops in the stages of going bust. Belinda and Donna's co-op went out of business after a year or so with quite large debts (see Chapter 6). NECDA oversaw the closure of the firm and dealt with most of the financial, legal and other tasks left outstanding.

Additionally, NECDA, unlike all the other youth business start-up agencies we studied, was able to give grants and loans to new co-operatives. Informants mentioned this fact, that 'it was easier to get funding as a co-op', as often as they referred to the politics or philosophy of co-operatives.

The advantages of co-operative work (as opposed to employment) were similar to self-employment in a small firm (flexibility, 'being your own boss') but Hannah (from a wholefood co-op) also reported that she encountered less discrimination and more equality as a young woman. She felt co-ops were 'definitely a good idea. I haven't really thought about the politics of it, but it is a good way of working'. In her previous employment she had often done all the 'gofer' jobs often given to female office juniors: 'go for the sandwiches', 'go for the post', 'go for' this and that. In her new co-op she found much more equality between older and younger workers, and between men and women in the group.

We interviewed two men and two women who had established a co-operative offering services to the local music scene in Hartlepool. They too talked about the greater freedom and equality they experienced working together without any bosses: 'It is nice not to have bosses and that it is for ourselves and the community — not for business profit'. All these co-ops had become limited companies which they saw as a distinct advantage if, or when, they went bankrupt (see Chapter 5).

Co-operatives, like community enterprise ventures, provide an alternative model of enterprise. Historically they have offered a different politics of economic production and their importance over the last fifteen years has certainly grown. It has been estimated that in 1986 there were around 1,000 worker co-ops in Britain compared with 50 only a decade earlier. Cross-party political support, economic recession, mass unem-ployment and local authority expenditure all contributed to the expansion of this potential 'third sector' of the British economy during the late 1970s and early 1980s (Jefferis, 1989).

Our evidence shows, however, that in the reality of day-to-day survival on Teesside, many of the grander aims and objectives of the broader co-operative movement are replaced by more pragmatic concerns (e.g. availability of help and grants). In addition, the experience of co-ops contains shades of a more communal approach to making a living and hints of more equal working relationships. It has been suggested that the wheel is turning full circle for co-operatives and that we now face a likely decline in their number as local authorities (which have done much to encourage local co-operative development) come under the greater finan-cial and political control of central government, and as many of those established in earlier periods collapse in the face of long-term competition from large-scale, capitalist companies (Jefferis, 1989).

Our evidences suggests, and can do no more than suggest, that the types of co-ops we examined probably have the same chance of survival as the small firms we studied. Survival rates in co-ops nationally have been shown to be similar to other sorts of small firms (Thomas and Cornforth, 1989). The problems which threatened survival and caused closure in these co-ops (particularly lack of business capital, income and trade) paralleled those we discussed in Chapters 5 and 6 in relation to more mainstream, small enterprises. We have focused only on the differences and consequently this section has been kept deliberately brief.

Overall, the experience of running co-ops bore a striking resemblance to those of the much larger group of people we interviewed who were running risky businesses. The reality of working the co-operative way falls a long way short of the brighter dreams and ideals associated with the co-operative movement. The degree of self-exploitation matched that found in the rest of the sample. Louise and Alex said that their friends presumed that they would have lots of money and 'Dallas style' offices but really they 'were scrimping and saving all the time just to keep going', a comment typical of the majority of the sample. There was *no* easy route out of unemployment for young people in Cleveland.

Notes

1   Obviously there are a number of immediate problems with this methodology: for instance, how do we know that any improvement in these respects can be attributed to participation in an often quite short course of activity? Surely there are a host of other likely factors (such as changes in personal circumstances, health, family bereavement etc.) which could intervene and influence the changes in the way people feel about themselves, over the quite long period between the completion of the two sets of forms?
2   One of the less positive and unintended outcomes of Sarah Louise's participation with Problem Solvers was that she ended up having a fight, to which the police were called, with one of the other young women involved with the holiday trip, about who had done the most to organize it.
3   Since we first became involved with Problem Solvers in 1988, its focus and activities have become redirected towards more mainstream enterprise activities. This has resulted from the sorts of criticisms that we have mentioned here and from the need to find new sources of revenue. Initial MSC funding has now expired and the organization, like many other local enterprise agencies (see Chapter 4), has been forced into searching for new sources of finance. A perusal of recent promotional material shows that this has led Problem Solvers to complement its original broad community-based enterprise ventures (with the unemployed) with private training contracts to provide a commercial consultancy service delivering courses on management, selling and leadership skills to business people.

Chapter 9

Maggie's Army?

Having explored the experiences of young men and women in small business, community ventures and co-operatives, we now turn our attention to the political and economic understandings of our informants, particularly their views on the initiatives to develop an enterprise culture on Teesside.[1]

Young entrepreneurs are often held up, especially by the media, as evidence of an ideological revolution brought about by the Conservative Government. As Hakim says 'entrepreneurial activity and self-employment are thought to entail a distinctive set of attitudes, values, motivations and ambitions, which together make up an "ideology" of self-employment and the enterprise "culture"' (1988:433). 'Thatcher's children' are popularly considered to be more ambitious, individualistic, money-minded and less concerned with youthful rebellion and opposition to authority than, for instance, their 1960s predecessors, and in Chapter 4 we heard how economic regeneration in the North-East demanded 'nothing less than a cultural change amongst young people' (Harrison, 1988a).

Here we examine the ways in which these young adults made political sense of their experiences in the enterprise culture. We will illustrate primarily that there exists a clear gap between the official rhetoric of enterprise, as promoted by government ministers, for instance, and the political attitudes of young people at whom enterprise policies have been aimed. Although our informants would seem, at first glance, to be converts to the enterprise culture, our evidence suggests that, on the contrary, young adults in business display quite critical and oppositional attitudes.

All Aboard the Enterprise Express?

The following discussion between Gary, his wife Shirley and the interviewer contains many of the different elements that constitute the general political outlook of our informants. Gary, to recap, had run a small business in graphic design which he had closed down after about a year.

RM: You could say that Maggie Thatcher has helped you a lot setting up these schemes. Do you think anybody can do it? Do you think it will help solve the unemployment problem?

Gary: It's going to help because obviously there are going to be people who are successful. Everybody's not going to be a failure. Even though I had to fold the business, it doesn't mean that I'm a failure because I learned things by it. It's going to get the figures down — the guys who make it will give other people jobs.

RM: Are you interested in politics?

Gary: Not really.

Shirley: We just shout at her when she comes on the telly.

Gary: It's no good blaming Mrs Thatcher. It's no good blaming whoever was in power before Mrs Thatcher, because they all make promises and they all break them.

Shirley: It's no good saying don't blame Mrs Thatcher. It was Mrs Thatcher that's got these young kids working for £25 per week. Whereas the likes of us, when we were leaving school you could walk straight into a job.

Gary: But you learn something.

Shirley: Well, you learn while you're working in a proper job. What happens when they come off YTS — there's nothing there for them even though they've learned.

RM: If there was a general election tomorrow, would you vote?

Gary: I wouldn't vote for Maggie Thatcher — probably Labour.

RM: Why?

Gary: I'd vote but I'd probably be wasting my time.

One might have expected intuitively that informants involved with enterprise might display some of the attitudes expressed by Gary. He had some faith in enterprise initiatives and felt that future business successes (even of a minority) would help generate jobs and so help combat unemployment. Even his attitude to his own business closure was not totally negative: he had learned something and felt his time had been spent positively. His support for such initiatives stretched to incorporate YTS. Although he would probably vote Labour he did not condemn Mrs Thatcher out of hand — she was not to blame for many of the problems they discussed. His wife Shirley (who was not strictly part of the interview sample as she had been uninvolved with enterprise) was far more critical.

In this case it would seem that, whilst the enterprise culture may not have wholly transformed Gary's thinking, he at least showed a generally positive attitude to small business and training initiatives. This, it must be said, was a rare occurrence. In the first part of this chapter we will consider the few informants who seemed to be political supporters of enterprise and the policies of the Conservative Government.

It was impossible to find anyone who was willing to wave the enterprise banner unreservedly. Some backed the Conservative Party generally and particular policies of the Thatcher Government. Barry, below, came the closest to being a young Thatcherite. He was the sportswear 'whizz-kid' — one of the 'runners' discussed at the start of Chapter 7:

> *RM*: Are you interested in politics at all, Barry?
> *Barry*: Mmm . . . yes.
> *RM*: What is the deliberation about?
> *Barry*: Well, I'm quite well spread. I suppose I want the best of all worlds. I'm definitely a Tory because their monetary policies suit me . . . // . . . I want to see tax go down as low as possible. But there again I think some of their policies are absolutely bloody diabolical. From the business angle I support them but my values aren't . . . I don't think it is a case of everybody should get off their backsides and set up businesses like me. I don't think I accept the sort of Tory enterprise values . . . // . . . and, to be quite frank, I wouldn't like to think that another 100 companies like this will spring up. The less competition we have the bigger the market and the easier it should become.

Adrian, who could be described as one of the 'runners', had a busy small firm supplying specialist engineering equipment. He voted Conservative but claimed no special knowledge or reason for doing so:

> Well, I've always voted Conservative. Don't know why — just have. It's just one of those things. I'm not interested in politics — very, very little. I don't care. I just let everybody get on with their own lives. As long as I am happy, I just don't care.

We had some trouble in locating wholehearted supporters of the Government and their policies regarding youth enterprise. Even these two young men could hardly be classed as hard-line free-marketeers. They were two of the more successful of our informants and perhaps could be expected to feel happy with the broader political values underlying enterprise. Certainly Barry's business, he felt, had benefited from Tory taxation policies and he would continue to vote Conservative in the hope that this would help the profitability of his company. However, on a wider level he found some policies 'diabolical'. These tended to be policies relating to less economic and more broadly social issues (the particular political issues highlighted for concern are discussed later in the chapter) Even his attitude to small business formation could be argued to be at odds with enterprise philosophy. More small business meant more competition which meant (potentially) less profit. There exists a tension between right-wing emphasis upon a laissez-faire, free market of unbridled economic competition and the perhaps equally strong capitalist motivation to maintain high levels of profitability by keeping competition under control.

Adrian had always voted Conservative but claimed to be uninterested in politics. The latter point was a very common one; the former was rarely found in our sample. He seemed to be displaying an 'I'm alright Jack' view of the political world which could be seen to mesh with the stress on individual effort contained within the official rhetoric of enterprise. These three extracts from interviews with Gary and his wife Shirley, Barry and Adrian were the only real evidence we could identify to support the idea that young entrepreneurs have accepted the ideology of enterprise, as promoted by the present Government and the proponents of the enterprise movement; Curran (1980) and Hakim (1988) also question the myth that the owners of small businesses are invariably conservative. Later in this chapter we will turn to a brief examination of voting intentions which confirm this finding. In the following section we will explore the more common, critical views of the enterprise culture.

Anti-enterprise

Lynne closed down her business (market trading in fruit and vegetables) with quite severe financial and emotional consequences (see Chapter 6).

RM: What is your view of the government's enterprise policy?
Lynne: The way I see it is that they think something's got to be done about all these people who are unemployed. We've got these massive figures — we'll have to get them down. We don't want a true figure of how many people are out of work. So we dream up these schemes and one of them is called enterprise and one of them is called ET.
RM: You have had some fairly extreme experiences of the things that Tories are promoting and yet you say you are not interested in politics?
Lynne: I am not interested in it because it is above my level of understanding. I don't understand how it works. If I don't understand it, I avoid it. I can talk about the issues that affect me, like being a single mother.

RM: I would say that what you have talked about and the way you talked about it is very political.

Lynne: I would say practically.

In this passage Lynne relates two themes which were typical of the political consciousness of the sample. Firstly, enterprise policies were roundly condemned as simply a way of dealing with embarrassingly high levels of unemployment in the locality. The motivation behind enterprise schemes was not interpreted as a positive or genuine attempt to help the unemployed and the local economy, but rather as a more cynical attempt politically to *manage* unemployment by artificially lowering the figures. One informant described the removal of people on schemes from the unemployment register as 'juggling the figures and keeping a million in the air at one time'. Lynne coupled her criticism of schemes like EAS with other 'special measures' such as ET.

Secondly, despite this clear view, Lynne professed a profound lack of interest in politics. This again was a very common response from informants. They said that they knew little or nothing about the subject, were not interested in it anyway and found it an immensely boring topic of conversation. Often interviews would grind to a sticky halt when these questions were broached with informants. This is interesting given, as in the above extract, that very many of the informants *in our view* talked in a moving, informed and political way about their experiences, often immediately preceding our question about their interest in politics.

In the following pages we will explore these themes by drawing on the comments of other young entrepreneurs. Firstly, we return to the interview with Belinda (from Middlesbrough, who had run a failed co-operative with her friend Donna):

RM: You say your advice to a young person would be to stay at school because there are no jobs, but aren't things looking better? I thought unemployment was going down?

Belinda: It's going down 'cos they've brought out a thing called Employment Training and they'll pay you £10 extra a week to go on it. So you go on this ET for a year and say 100 people out of 500 unemployed go on it, they say their statistics are down by 100 'cos there is 100 who has got jobs. But they haven't — they're on ET and at the end of their training they're going to get finished and they'll be unemployed again. So I mean it's rubbish, it really is — it's absolute rubbish. Nearly everyone you talk to around here, families round here, you talk to them and they say 'Oh, my daughter's on a scheme and our Bill's on a scheme'.

RM: Do you agree with the move toward self-employment?

> *Belinda*: I agree, but I think it's got to be a person that has got that in mind. I don't think it's right pushing somebody on the dole into it. You've got to be a bit business-minded and there is an awful lot of work if you are going to succeed. And a lot of people out there want to work the general nine to five and come home and go out and enjoy themselves. You can't do that if you're self-employed.
>
> *RM*: Have you heard of this phrase 'the enterprise culture'?
>
> *Belinda*: No.
>
> *RM*: Are you interested in politics at all? Would you vote?
>
> *Belinda*: I just honestly wouldn't know who to vote for. As I say I don't agree with the way she [Mrs Thatcher] has gone on and what have you. I mean I know she has done the best that anyone has ever done — she's totally changed the world all over. She's done a really good job, but she's also done a lot of harm. I wouldn't vote for her. I mean she's brought all the schemes out but they're just an excuse for full-time employment.

Again, Belinda argues forcefully that government schemes, particularly ET, are aimed at reducing unemployment *figures* rather than at seriously tackling the lack of jobs. She generally supports the idea of self-employment as an option for young unemployed people, but does not think that they should be encouraged, if they lack the commitment and skills necessary. One question that was asked of many informants was direct and simple: 'Have you heard of the [phrase] enterprise culture?'. Predominantly the answer was 'no'. People had not heard of it even though they were busily running small businesses and carrying out all the activities of this most popular, politically fashionable version of enterprise. Belinda was typical. Furthermore, she did not know whom she would vote for and displayed a good deal of ambivalence in her attitude to the Thatcher Government.

Sharon was from Southbank in Middlesbrough — one of the areas with the highest levels of joblessness. She was unemployed at the time of the interview but had participated in a community enterprise project. She was asked about her political views and voting intentions:

> I'd support Labour 'cos they'd abolish all the schemes and then they'd see how much unemployment there really is. I mean you don't go for jobs round here — you go for schemes. My dad's on a scheme, my mum's on a scheme and my brother is on a scheme. My sister will be when she leaves school...//...the dream is really that a big factory might move here and we'll get a thousand jobs — that's the dream really (laughs).

Sharon reiterates Belinda's view that the main aim of government schemes is to disguise the true nature of the unemployment problem; a problem which forces all her family to make a living through some government scheme or other. Belinda and Sharon conjure up an image of Teesside as 'scheme land', where whole families exist on ET, EAS and CP. Sharon would like to see these schemes scrapped if only to reveal to 'them' how much unemployment there really was. Many of the informants saw the solution, even if it was talked of as a vain, laughable dream, as the establishment of new factories in the locality. One young man added: 'They talk about a boom economy. Well, it might be down there, but it's not a boom economy up here'.

Implicitly, and in a few instances like this, a geographical dimension informed political views. 'Us' versus 'them' was not expressed in terms of upper and working class but rather in terms of the poor North-East/ Teesside versus the prosperous South ('down there'). Informants had a sense of their area, even if this was a generally negative one,[2] which was expressed as a sense of marginality and isolation. Even within the North-East, people from Cleveland often think of themselves as the poor relations — overshadowed by better known Tyneside (particularly Newcastle). Economic solutions were perceived as being remote possibilities and involving macro-industrial development — 'setting up factories'; they did not really *depend* on anyone for economic salvation (because they did not expect it) but also, quite realistically, they did not see their own efforts as the key to a local boom economy. They wanted 'a decent bit of support for the North-East and support for people who aren't so well off' (Danny, Middlesbrough).

Like people interviewed in other studies of youth, our sample often drew upon individualistic interpretations of unemployment (e.g. Coffield *et al.*, 1986; Hutson and Jenkins, 1989). We would generally agree with the following conclusions:

> The combination of individualism with, on the one hand, a daily experience of inequality and relative powerlessness, and, on the other hand, a localist frame of reference which reflects limited geographical mobility and social networks, limits the possibilities of working-class political action and is an important buttress for the status quo of the class system. Individuals are typically blamed — by themselves and by other people — for their own misfortunes and held responsible for their own lot in life; where responsibility is allocated elsewhere, it falls generally upon vague stereotypes, the distant 'them' which is the other side of the local 'us'. (Hutson and Jenkins, 1989:114)

Individualism was an important part of the political consciousness of our informants and, as Hutson and Jenkins argue, they were limited by it in their understandings of youth enterprise. Occasionally individuals involved in youth enterprise would criticize young entrepreneurs (in general) for being lazy, unmotivated and seeking an easy option (on EAS). We were unable to locate anybody, apart from, possibly, Dennis (see Chapter 7) who pursued enterprise as an 'easy option'. In this way some informants, to some degree, were accepting dominant ideological attitudes to unemployment and the unemployed which held sway over more realistic, empirically-based explanations. Additionally, political or economic solutions were framed in terms of a vague 'us' and 'them'. This polarity has also been noted in much earlier studies of working-class culture (see for instance, Dennis, Henriques and Slaughter, 1956; Hoggart, 1957). We would argue, however, that individualism only partially limited the development of more collective understandings of their experiences. Later in the chapter we will argue that many of this group *shared* aspects of a political consciousness which clustered around anti-enterprise views and distrust of formal political structures and parties.

Fraser, who had owned a home improvements/joinery business (now closed down), was asked about the enterprise culture:

RM: What do you think of this enterprise culture idea — you know the idea that you can help get rid of unemployment by getting people to set up businesses?

Fraser: I don't think it's the answer. No. I think more companies should be set up with a better structure and more stability and I don't think it should always be left to one person. I think it is good for the North-East to have all these businesses set up but I think it's a bit misleading and I think it's trying to get the unemployment figures down.

RM: Are you interested in politics at all?

Fraser: Not really, no. I'm becoming more so. Now I sit and watch the news.

RM: Would you like to be seen as part of Mrs Thatcher's booming Britain?

Fraser: No. I wouldn't like to be seen as part of her Government's Britain. I did it regardless of her input into it. I couldn't have done it without the EAS but I don't support her . . . // . . . I didn't vote at the last election but I would now — for the Green Party.

We present this extract both as a final example of the main theme we have been discussing so far — that enterprise schemes were seen as part of a cynical attempt to lower unemployment statistics — and as introduction to a second theme: that self-employment and one-person businesses, as a solution to local unemployment, were considered to be ill-conceived and impracticable. Furthermore, Fraser at least hints at his opposition to

Thatcher and to being seen as part of her drive towards enterprise. This was a further dominant theme: these people were certainly not happy volunteers to Maggie's army, nor were they happy to be seen as living tokens of entrepreneurial revival.

The enterprise culture was seen to be ill-conceived because the movement toward the setting up of myriad busy small firms would inevitably lead to competition and saturation of the market. This level of competition would not be healthy and would demand that some firms closed with workers returned to the dole queues. It is, of course, argued that all business competition is healthy and that such competition leads to a generally 'fitter, leaner' economy and a more favourable deal for customers: that redundancy might be painful in the short-term but in the long-term the workings of the market will guarantee a stronger economy. We do not intend to enter into such debates here (See Chapter 10). Rather we report the views on this subject expressed by informants: they opposed the enterprise culture in this respect. Reggie and Tony, who were involved with a co-operative in Middlesbrough, were typical:

RM: Have you heard about the enterprise culture? You know, moves to help local unemployment with small businesses? Do you agree with it?

Tony: No, I think you just flood the market with too much of the same stuff. There's not enough work to get that many people off [the dole]. Our co-operative, if it gets to full strength, should hold between twenty and twenty-five people. But what if another firm doing the same thing set up? There wouldn't be enough work. Too much competition in a local area. They would knock us on the head or we'd knock them on the head. Then what would we do? They're ramming down your throat to do self-employment — 'it's the easiest thing in the world to do' . . .

RM: Are you interested in politics at all?

Reggie: Not really.

Tony: I am just lately — that's because my views are that the Conservatives don't do things right.

Reggie: Even if Labour got in, I don't think they would change a hell of a lot.

Tony: True. No government would.

Ranjeet, who owned a shop in Middlesbrough, expressed the same critical view of small business generation and general antipathy to being classed as one of 'Thatcher's children':

RM: Can everybody make a success of self-employment?

Ranjeet: No, not everybody can make a success of it — how can you make a success on £80 per fortnight in business? How can anybody on the dole set up a business with that? And the more they push the more they fail. You know, there is only a certain amount of money around and everybody can't have a bit. Like there's a shop here, and there could be a shop over there in the corner and each area can only support a certain amount. The more shops there are, the less well we will each do.

RM: Are you interested in politics at all?

Ranjeet: Not really. I try not to be.

RM: But wouldn't you be a perfect example of what Mrs Thatcher goes on about?

Ranjeet: I don't think so somehow! (laughs) . . . I don't know. I try and stay neutral. I tend to keep out of it — it causes lots of arguments.

Whilst Ranjeet was still trading and was quite happy with the way her business was going others had ceased trading and had left the enterprise culture. They shared very similar criticisms of the politics of enterprise.

So far we have illustrated that, despite claiming not to be interested in politics, nor to know the meaning of the phrase 'the enterprise culture,' many informants did have interesting, critical and cogent comments to make about their lived experience of enterprise. These criticisms tended to cluster around particular issues (e.g. the effect on the unemployment count, market saturation and too much competition) but one or two informants developed slightly more thorough and sophisticated critiques. We present two fairly lengthy examples below. The first is from an interview with Bob, the freelance forestry worker from rural East Cleveland:

RM: One of the things behind this idea of the enterprise culture is that people have become too dependent upon the dole . . .

Bob: That's the Government's policy — to get people off their backsides, to make people get on with it themselves, to be dependent upon themselves. It's not something I go along with.

RM: Why not? People might look at you as a perfect example of a very enterprising young man, a young Thatcherite . . .

Bob: I don't agree. I think the Government should put more money into this area and put more factories up and get people back into work. I think it's more the Government's responsibility to create work, not individual people.

RM: But you said earlier that anybody could do it?

Bob: Yes, if they *wanted* to and if they had some skill, fair enough. Why not? But it shouldn't be left down to them, should it?

RM: Why not? People might say if *you* can do it, why can't everybody?

Bob: Everybody can't be self-employed can they? It's ridiculous. There's 50,000 unemployed people in Cleveland. You couldn't expect all of them to become self-employed all of a sudden. Some people have families and mortgages to consider. I'm different. I live with my parents. I don't need a lot of money to live on. I don't have the worries. Other people have. It should be more the Government's responsibility.

The second is from an interview with Jack, the artist from Stockton.

RM: This enterprise culture thing — what does it mean to you?

Jack: Well, we were told [by his enterprise trainers] that enterprise culture, it didn't necessarily mean forming a business, that it meant doing something for the community or setting up a business, that anybody can make their own way — I suppose that's what it meant.

RM: Did you see yourself as being part of the enterprise culture?

Jack: No.

RM: Why not?

Jack: I think it's just one of these late-1980s phrases.

RM: You don't believe in it?

Jack: I'm all for people getting up and doing something for themselves, setting up their own businesses, or if they want to do something for the community, that's OK, but I don't think the politicians should make such a big deal of it.

RM: Do you think this enterprise culture idea can — economically, by setting up small business — turn things round in places like Stockton?

Jack: No, not really. I think the people who can turn things round are people who work for big companies — British Steel, ICI — people who have a good education or whatever. They can maybe set up companies and come up with a good idea that could beat the Japanese. They are the people who can turn the economy around. People like myself can only make up about 2 per cent. A lot of them [politicians] are hoping for tourism, which is never going to come to this town. You've got to sell yourself, sell your local culture off to a tourist scheme ... //
... There was all this talk at the enterprise agency about how BSC and ICI were on their way out and the only way forward was for self-employment, and that young people might have to face a life of schemes, periods of unemployment and self-employment. I think, to be honest, that it is wrong to tell people who are in their late teens that sort of thing, to try and

213

make them believe that. Because I think if that is the case —
well, pack your bags and go to Australia or somewhere.

RM: What did you mean by saying that enterprise culture was one
of the late-1980s phrases?

Jack: Well, they even say it themselves. Firstly, it was if you want
to please the MSC use the word 'community' in everything:
'community care', 'community' this and that. Then along
came 'enterprise' — the MSC want to hear 'enterprise'. Stick
enterprise in the title somewhere. They [the enterprise agency
with which he trained] said with 'enterprise' and 'community'
in the title we can wangle our way around the MSC and do
whatever we want, you know. I think it was to figure out
what the powers that be want and then sort of give them
it . . . to get the money to keep them in business.

RM: Are you interested in politics at all?

Jack: A little bit — I can't really be bothered with it.

Jack and Bob pointed to many of their political worries about enterprise initiatives and the enterprise culture. These can be summarized as:
its trendiness and vacuity as a fashionable political catch-phrase; the
enormity of the economic problem addressed by (what they describe as)
an inadequate political and economic response; the over-emphasis upon
individual effort and responsibility for job creation at the expense of more
macro-level, industrial development; and, relatedly, the unfair way in
which the weight of responsibility for local economic rejuvenation is
placed upon the shoulders of some of the least qualified and least able to
cope with such a burden.

Graham, who had been unemployed for several years and had taken
part in a community enterprise project, highlighted this last point quite
clearly and candidly:

RM: Are you interested in politics?

Graham: No, not particularly.

RM: Is there high unemployment in the area?

Graham: Well, there was, but I presume it must be going down
because you don't hear much about it [on the news] now.

RM: Have you heard of the phrase 'the enterprise culture'?

Graham: No.

RM: You know, the idea that you should try and help the
unemployment problem by encouraging people to set up
in business? Don't you think that is a good idea?

Graham: I suppose it had its good points . . . It depends on the
person — whether they've got the confidence. It's no good
trying to force people to do it. Every time I go to Restart
they're on about me setting up my own business. But I

just don't have the confidence. I'm more confident now —
I'm talking to you, aren't I? — but not to set up my own
business. It's not the answer for people like me. It would
soon become saturated with people doing various things.

RM: If there was a general election tomorrow, would you vote?

Graham: I'd vote. SDP or Liberal. The other two seem too extreme
either way. SDP seem to be taking the best out of the
other two and putting them together. Middle of the road.

Graham seemed to be quite a shy man, spending much of his time in
the house with his mother, and he took some persuading to take part in
the interview (we discussed his experiences of community enterprise in
the preceding chapter). He lacked confidence and the idea that he could
set up a business was, to him, almost preposterous. However, Restart
officials still encouraged him to follow this course out of his long-term
unemployment.

Youth, Politics and Voting

What were the voting intentions of the sample? Although we would
argue that such information gives only a limited view of the political
knowledge or views of young people, we still feel that how people say
they would vote in a general election may provide *some* insight into their
experiences of, for instance, youth enterprise. We were able to ascertain
the voting intentions of all but ten of the whole sample (i.e. ninety-four),
including those in the unemployed and community enterprise categories.
All those directly involved with small business or co-operative enterprise
gave their preferences. The results from our small opinion poll are contained in Table 9.1. The sample is, of course, very small and we accept
that the business of opinion-polling is a complex and technical one. We
do not intend to read too much into these results and we provide only
brief commentary upon these figures.

The party gaining most support is Labour, with over a quarter of the
sample saying they would vote for them in a general election. This is
perhaps not surprising given that the area is one which, though not
totally dominated by Labour, has a large bedrock of working-class,
Labour support.[3] Furthermore, it is often claimed by opinion pollsters
that younger people (the eighteen to twenty-five age group) tend to be
more likely to support Labour than older age groups (e.g. White, 1990).
The period during which most of the interviews were carried out (Spring
to Autumn 1989) was also a period of increasing Labour support.

The Conservative Party does rather badly, claiming little more than
ten per cent of the intended vote. This finding adds weight to the
conclusions from our interviews: young entrepreneurs in Cleveland tend

Table 9.1   *Voting Intentions of Sample*

Party	Number
Conservative	10
Labour	27
SDP/Liberal	4
Green	6
Don't Know	26
Won't Vote	21
Total	94

not to be supporters of the Thatcher Government.[4] It also supports other studies of youth politics which have found little support for the Conservative Party and its present leader (McRae, 1987; Banks and Ullah, 1987; Hollands, 1990).

Two other parties (perhaps three) together received ten votes of support. Six people said they would vote for the Green Party in a general election, reflecting a much wider movement towards enviromentally-conscious politics (and illustrated in the level of support received by the Green Party in the 1989 Euro-elections). Four people said they would either vote Liberal or for the SDP. The interviews revealed that, in the minds of such informants, the two parties were virtually synonymous. Typically, support for the Liberal and Social Democratic Parties resulted from a dissatisfaction with the two main parties. Graham, earlier in this chapter, for instance, said he would vote for the SDP because they took the best elements of Tory and Labour policy and combined them. There was a sense that informants were unsure about politics and chose a 'middle of the road' party in order to play safe and 'hedge their bets'. Informants sensed that, whilst they may not understand or feel at ease with older, established political structures and parties, the Greens and the centre parties provided a simple appeal and a fresh, younger image.

The most interesting groups in our opinion are, however, those which make up exactly half of the given responses: those people that would not vote and those whom we call 'Don't Knows'. The latter category covered only one less person than would support Labour. The 'Don't Know' category, as employed in our analysis, includes not only those who said that they did not know whom they would vote for in a general election, but also people who expressed a doubt about whether they would vote at all. Typical was the answer: 'Well, I don't know if I'd vote — I didn't last time, but even if I did I don't know who it would be for'. In addition to these 'don't knows' there were twenty-one people (more than the Conservative, Green, SDP/Liberal supporters combined) who said they would *definitely* not vote. Many opinion polls or, to be more exact, analyses of opinion polls, exclude groups which do not indicate a preference and concentrate on the balance of support expressed for the major, and sometimes minor, political parties. What this misses is, in this instance, the particularly high level of potential abstention, indecision and unclear political support.

This finding is supported by other research on youth which has pointed to an *apparent* political indifference, ignorance and apathy amongst their samples of young people (e.g. Stradling, 1977). Coffield *et al.* found that: 'men and women slumped deeper in their chairs, rolled their eyes to convey utter boredom, groaned and muttered at the very mention of the word politics' (1986:191).

Furthermore, this finding relates to some of the themes which emerged in interviews and which have been presented so far. We would argue tentatively (tentatively, because a whole interview would need to be devoted to the exploration of political issues like these) that when these people say they would not vote, or that they are not interested in politics, what is meant is that they are not interested in one particular model or interpretation of politics.

Politics for most young people means a drab world of grey, be-suited, middle-aged, middle-class, male MPs, compulsory party political broadcasts and strange, heated arguments about which they know little. Informants in this and other studies saw politics as an arena of discussion to be avoided not only because it was boring, but also because it was something which they *felt* they knew nothing about: 'If I don't under-stand it, I avoid it'. It was a potentially threatening subject and some informants were obviously embarrassed to admit they had no interest or view. They felt they *should* know something about it.

Most people receive no direct education at school under the title of politics (Bynner and Ashford, 1990; see Harber, 1987, for a fuller dis-cussion). Traditional avenues for learning working-class politics (e.g. apprenticeships into not only skilled factory work but also, simultaneous-ly, trade unionism, and versions of socialism and collectivism) have virtually disappeared (Cohen, 1983; Hollands, 1990). This is not to argue that these informants are not interested or politically ignorant, rather that in asking simply 'Are you interested in politics?' or 'Would you vote, if so, who for?', we are only tapping a very limited part of their political consciousness and we receive the standard reply of most young adults. We are asking narrow questions about formal politics and political struc-tures and we employ the dreaded word 'politics' itself, all of which are alien to this group. Roberts and Parsell make this point neatly in talking about respondents to the *16 to 19 Initiative* surveys:

> it is important to be clear about the senses in which most young people are 'not interested' in politics. We can demonstrate that what our sample was 'not interested' in was the politics of party

politicians as presented through the media. Most were not avid readers of political journalism. Party political broadcasts and current affairs were not their favourite television programmes ... Needless to say, our young people's lack of interest in these matters was not setting them apart from most adults. And it is important to recognize that young people's professed disinterest does not necessarily mean that they are unconcerned about the issues that politicians consider important. (1990:21)

We have illustrated how the same people who talk at length about the ways in which they have experienced government initiatives, and how they now critically assess such schemes and experiences, can, in the next breath, claim to be uninterested in politics. We follow Clarke and Jefferson's view of 'politics':

Our use of 'political' is a broad one, but one we feel is all the more justified by the increasing narrowness of its normal usage. We wish to emphasise that this attempt to define and express one's own situation and to break with dominant cultural representations is a very real, political struggle. (1973:9)

The method we have adopted, being ethnographic in nature, is one that has enabled insights to be made into the political consciousness of these young adults. Only more exploratory, speculative, flexible research questioning can reveal the gaps and contradictions between researchers', politicians' and informants' understandings and definitions of enterprise. Using a standardized questionnaire would have entailed the researcher coding most of these informants as uninterested in politics (see Chapter 1). More qualitative interviewing can at least pursue responses actively and imaginatively, probing and challenging the professed lack of interest in politics and exploring actors' own appreciations of the politics of enterprise.[5] We would accept the point made by Theo Nichols and Huw Beynon in their introduction to *Living with Capitalism*:

so much of what passes for 'theory' (even Marxist theory) fails to connect with the lives that people lead, whereas most descriptive social surveys too often fail to grasp the structure of social relations and the sense which people make of them. (1977:vii)

And we suggest that this apparent contradiction (the gap between a keen disavowal of political interest on the one hand and yet quite acute political commentary on the other) can be explained by the vocabulary employed — these informants *are* politically educated and have their own political theories (such as the anti-enterprise views recorded above) but they do

not call them political. The 'P word' is one used by the more academical-
ly educated and privileged sections of society (or perhaps, more accurately, those privileged with education). Lynne, earlier, makes this point
neatly. When asked about whether she was not in fact talking politically,
she responded that no, she was talking *practically*.

Gramsci's theories of philosophy and common sense are pertinent to
this discussion. He argued that 'philosophy is not just the abstract cogita-
tion of a few professional intellectuals but a concrete social activity in
which, implicitly, all men (sic) are engaged' (1971:321). Thus, Gramsci
maintained that philosophy was not a practice restricted to the academic
ivory towers but an everyday, practical activity undertaken by us all.

He argued that within the historical life of the working class, people
will develop their own political views (their own philosophies, folk-
theories) of the world *and* of their collective experiences of living under
capitalism. These may contradict more dominant ideologies or they may
take the shape of, and reflect, ruling-class interpretations of social reality.
What we have in the political accounts we collected are, we would
suggest, working-class, theoretical responses to the collective, cultural
experience of youth enterprise. In a sense they are what Willis (1977)
(perhaps unfortunately) calls 'cultural penetrations': insights into the real
motives and workings of an economic/educational system, culled from
collective experience. They are generally oppositional and highlight the
ideological contradictions experienced and identified by young entrepreneurs. In this way they are what Gramsci might call 'good sense':
practical, critical ways of understanding the economic conditions under
and through which they live. These anti-enterprise views are not what
they would call political — they are good sense, working theories (and
theories which work) which emerge 'organically' (to borrow Gramsci's
terminology again) from the practices of trying to survive economically,
through youth enterprise in Cleveland.

In this way, young adults in business carry out the activities of youth
enterprise but develop political understandings of the enterprise culture
quite at odds with more official ideologies and rhetorics. Although many
millions of pounds have been spent on the ideological project to transform Cleveland into an enterprise culture, and to jolt the young unemployed from 'dependence' to 'enterprise', the project seems to have failed
to incorporate these young people politically. They resist the gospel of
enterprise as passed down from on high (or from the MSC's offices in
Moorfoot, Sheffield) but find, in the *practice* of enterprise, alternative
elements of their experiences (e.g. feelings of pride and self-achievement)
which they value and celebrate and with which they construct their own
understanding of the politics and economics of enterprise.

And although one of the unintended consequences of the enterprise
movement has been to consolidate anti-Conservative views amongst this

Risky Business?

group of people, we cannot yet see any real positive signs for political parties on the Left. To use Willis's terms again, these 'cultural penetrations' are very much 'limited' and do not begin to threaten seriously the prevailing ideological status quo. Philip Cohen has drawn attention to 'the failure of the [Labour] movement to construct a popular form of youth politics' (1983:28), and the political outlooks that we have described in this chapter should provide little encouragement to those who would look to the young working-class as a source of political opposition to the present Government or, indeed, to the political system as a whole. Although they opposed enterprise and the Thatcher Government, this was just part of a broader disenchantment with 'political' solutions in general. No parties really appealed to them. Even those saying that they would vote Labour in a general election did so with little enthusiasm or conviction. They lacked information about politics and economics, and sought the bases of their own 'theories' in their collective, local experiences. Whilst many resented their present situation and recent encounters with government schemes, they could provide no real solutions to the problems and there was little in their political views that militated for change. Political action (even at the low level of voting) was rare. They were unconnected to parties or organizations which could provide ideas or programmes for change. Cohen argues that to understand why:

> the old political culture [of the Left] . . . cuts no ice with a generation of school-leavers headed for YTS or the dole, it is necessary to look both at how the links between growing up, working and class have changed, and at how these hubs of identity have become disconnected from each other, and from the transmission belts of organized ideology. (1983:35)

Although we have no space to enter the historical investigation of working-class culture and politics here, we can draw upon Hollands' (1990) ethnography of YTS, which aims to explore the problems set out by Cohen. He concludes that the lengthened transitions (through YTS) being followed by large sections of the working-class pose a serious test to the Labour Party and the Left more generally. The cultural inheritance of collectivism, trade union membership and Labour Party support, traditionally bound to apprenticeships into manual labour, are swiftly being eroded by the new cultural identities constructed over the past decade through youth traineeships. He argues that the challenges posed by 'the youth question' are of critical importance for any future Labour Government, but it would seem from our (admittedly limited) evidence and the evidence presented by writers such as Hollands, that the Labour Party (and the Conservative Party) have not as yet found a way of reaching this part of the electorate. In these passages all we have hoped to do is recognize, rather than romanticize, the real political knowledge and views of these young women and men, and highlight the failure of the Labour Party to construct a form of politics that appeals to, and reflects, the experiences of some of its traditional sources of support, amongst the young and working-class of the North-East.

Summary and Conclusions

Although we think it would be fair to say that the politics of young people has not, in itself, been an area of prolific, theoretical speculation, we can identify two broad and separate trends.[6] One has been to examine political attitudes to formal political structures and parties (e.g. as manifested in voting intentions) and how these relate to personal characteristics, for example, education, class (e.g. Roberts and Parsell, 1990) and particular psychological variables (e.g. Dowse and Hughes, 1971; Furnham and Gunter, 1989). We do not wish to enter into a critical review of this body of research apart from saying that the methods (generally positivistic) and conception of politics (tending towards the narrow and formal) are not ones which we feel are appropriate for uncovering an insightful understanding of the broad and complex meanings of politics for youth.

A second, more interesting approach has focused upon politics in the form of sub-cultural resistance to the dominant culture (e.g. Hall and Jefferson, 1976; Willis, 1978; Hebdige, 1979). Sub-cultural styles are 'read' for their symbolic opposition and participation in various working-class youth groupings (Teds, Skinheads, Punks and so on) is interpreted as offering some form of 'magical' solution to collective inequality and alienation in a society run by the middle-aged and middle-class. This influential form of youth study has been the subject of considerable criticism over the past fifteen years (e.g. Waters, 1981; Brown, 1987; Hutson and Jenkins, 1989; MacDonald, 1989; Hollands, 1990) and we can draw attention to two particular problems as they relate to our present discussion of youth politics.

First, in drawing upon participant observation as their main methodological tool these studies tend not to employ more direct methods of enquiry such as asking young people about their politics. Instead, political stance and attitudes to the social and political world are interpreted through observation of styles of dress, posture, argot and gang activities. Young people's own interpretations and analyses tend to be left out in this sub-cultural tradition as does discussion of what could be termed 'real politics'. 'Real politics', like the organization of Asian youth against fascist attack during the late 1980s, or the anarchic activities of many thousands of young people in the 1990 Trafalgar Square riots against the

Poll Tax, are marginalized in the emphasis upon resistance through rituals.

Second, even if the sub-cultural tradition managed adequately to capture the politics of Punks, Mods and all the other spectacular youth cults of the post-war period, it would still ignore the mass of ordinary young people. Elsewhere it has been argued that part of the academic emphasis upon the most glamorous (or glamorizable), visible and media-hyped youth stems from the search (by greying and left-wing, male sociologists) for exotic, youthful and rebellious sections of the working-class (e.g. Clarke, 1982). This tradition provides fascinating case studies and valuable theoretical development but it does ignore the majority of young people who never enter any of the sociologist's youth sub-cultures (see Chapter 1). By implication most of these people are regarded as somehow dull, conforming, 'cultural dopes' (the 'earoles' in Willis's *Learning to Labour*, for example). In our sample perhaps only one or two could be identified as belonging to a particular youth sub-culture.

These are but two of the difficulties we have with the once dominant sub-culture tradition. There are others and these have been tackled more fully elsewhere (e.g. Hollands, 1990). To conclude our criticism: we prefer to explore the cultures of a wider section of youth and to examine the politics of youth, not in how they dress or behave, but in what they say about their lived experiences of, in this case, youth enterprise.

Our sample were not young Thatcherites and were annoyed to be described as such. They felt that their attitudes had not become more individualistic, right-wing or conservative. If anything, their views had become less conservative. Part of the explanation for this can be traced to cultural reasons behind starting up in business and their material circumstances. Most did not enter the enterprise culture because they were attracted by the values that self-employment represented, nor did they hold in their minds a positive (self)-image of the entrepreneur.

Furthermore, if, by any chance, they did make it big in enterprise and started to earn larger amounts of money, they, like Barry, might start to consider the financial (e.g. tax) benefits of supporting the Conservative Party. The vast majority of our informants, however, were a long, long way from having to weigh up such matters. Most were earning very little, were still dependent upon government grants and were closer materially to the unemployed than to the famous entrepreneurial role models (Richard Branson, for instance). Their lives were still intertwined with families, friends and a local community that relied heavily upon welfare state benefits. Their lives were ones in which poverty remained real and close at hand. Issues surrounding housing benefit, the Poll Tax, changes to the Health Service, YTS allowances and educational reforms were all important to this group and generally influenced them towards more welfarist points of view (hence greater electoral support for Labour compared to the other parties). Sometimes informants would deny an interest in politics in general but would be very interested in particular issues (e.g. the NHS, support for single parents, the environment, nuclear power, the Poll Tax).

Our final conclusion is that the politics of young people like these are probably not too dissimilar to older sections of the (local) population. We do not think that our evidence points to a particularly youthful interpretation of, or attitude to, the political world, but that these people share common, cultural perspectives with people over the age of twenty-five. Indeed, it would perhaps be surprising if the opposite was true. After all, the categorization of 'youth' that we have employed has drawn upon fairly arbitrary criteria. Why should a twenty-one year old be more or less 'political', more or less conservative or rebellious than, say, a thirty year old?[7] We suspect that the lack of interest in 'politics' is not restricted to teenagers and people in their early twenties, and we expect that we would uncover a similar antipathy to formal politics had we asked the same questions of older groups of people.[8] Young adults like these learn their politics (or lack of it) in the same social, geographical and cultural settings as older people, like their parents (indeed, often from their parents). We would suggest that much of the politics that we have discussed in this chapter is a combination of that learned from personal experience (e.g. of being a young entrepreneur) and that learned from more shared history (e.g. of being working class, of living on Teesside, of surviving unemployment, of looking for work and getting places on schemes, and of listening to relatives and friends recount similar stories).

Admittedly, there are some likely areas of difference between younger and older groups. This particular sample obviously had more than most to say about enterprise and other government schemes. A further point relates to the particular historical period of which we are talking. A typical member of our sample, being twenty-one (in 1989), would have been only eleven years old when the Conservative Government began their period of office in 1979. Few could remember anything but Thatcher's Government and perhaps this influenced the lack of political hope, idealism and imagination expressed: to coin a phrase, 'there is no alternative'. It seemed to them that the political world that they inhabited was the political world that there would always be. But these are areas of debate that require much further questioning. We can only speculate about the ideas that we are developing here; intuitively we might have expected the sample to be more optimistic about the political world as a whole. This group was anti-politics (in its formal sense) rather than simply anti-Thatcher. Although they *were* frequently anti-Thatcher, their attitude was generally more ambivalent: 'She's done a really good job, but she's also done a lot of harm' (Belinda, Middlesbrough). They distrusted all political parties (even if they could not remember the Labour

Party in power) and politicians: 'They all make promises and they break them' (Tony, Middlesbrough); 'No government would change things' (Gary, Middlesbrough).

Their cynicism regarding politics and politicians in general should not, we suggest, be interpreted as ignorance, apathy, fatalism or necessarily as a 'bad thing'. Too often the political 'apathy', or 'passive alienation' (Ridley, 1981), of young people (i.e. their non-voting or lack of interest in 'political' questions) is treated as a cause for liberal concern — something that needs remedying by better education or the provision of more information. Bynner and Ashford draw upon questionnaire survey data from the core studies of the *16 to 19 Initiative* to examine questions similar to ours. They identified high levels of political apathy, disaffection and alienation amongst those who left school at 16 compared with those who stayed on for longer periods:

> The significance of educational attainment in the development of political alienation and the significance of self-efficacy in the formation of intention to vote points to the importance of the post-16 period in the development of an orientation to the political system and consequently political identity. If the young person remains in the education system then political interest and activity is likely to increase . . . // . . . if the young person leaves school to become unemployed or to go into a dead-end job or YTS scheme then this critical stage in political socialization is likely to be lost. (1990:13)

We would wish to make three points regarding this thesis. First, we suggest that in leaving school and experiencing (un)employment and government schemes young people do not *lose* a stage of political socialization, rather they undergo different class cultural experiences (to their peers who have remained in school) which they interpret politically. To use Bynner and Ashford's terms, they undergo a different type of 'political socialization' (which *may* lead to *apparent* apathy, disenchantment etc.).

This takes us to our second point; politics (and political socialization) are interpreted too narrowly and Bynner and Ashford argue, implicitly, that 'good' political socialization leads to readily expressed political interest and involvement, voting and support for the mainstream parties. Elsewhere in the paper they refer to a 'fully participative democracy' (14) without really examining critically what they mean by this or whether, in fact, we have one.[9] It could be argued that in Britain we are some way from such a level of democracy and that the political disenchantment, boredom and lack of involvement of young people (especially the unemployed and those on YTS) reflect this, rather than a lack of education or feeling of self-efficacy on their part. In short, we feel that disenchantment with political structures and lack of interest in the main parties can be interpreted in themselves as political. Hollands, in examining transitions through training schemes, makes a related point. He argues that if we define politics as party and institutional politics then the conventional wisdom, that young people are not interested, holds true, but:

> if, however, we take politics to mean an awareness of what is happening in society, a concern over the forces and events shaping everyday lives and anxieties about the future, then surely young people must be viewed as political beings.

Hollands goes on to question:

> the limitations of a politics based around purely party or even traditional labour movement concerns. The whole issue of youth politics must be turned on its head and we need to ask how relevant existing parties are to young people's everyday concerns. (1990:180–1)

Our third contention with Bynner and Ashford regards their implied remedy for the 'problem'. The task of increasing the numbers of people who stay on at school is not a simple one and such a problem would need much more debate than they allow or we can afford here. Suffice it to say that we think that wider, powerful and more pressing contingencies than the socialization of youth into formal party politics (e.g. local labour markets, cultural traditions and the impact of recession upon the household's finances) determine the school-leaving age of working-class youths. Even if all were to stay on until the age of eighteen, would this mean that all would become politically empowered? We think not. Political consciousness, however well developed, reflects personal and collective understandings of economic and social reality. Just because working-class youths would be leaving school to, say, join the dole queues at the age of eighteen rather than sixteen does not mean that they would somehow become more socialized into liberal, mainstream, consensual politics.[10]

Although we are not opposed to political education in schools and sympathize to some extent with Bynner and Ashford's worries about the state of British youth politics, we feel that it just may be the case that what needs remedying is not young people and their supposed lack of interest in politics, but a political system which does little to involve the mass of people *of all ages* and which provides little in the way of real (perceived) choice.[11] Bill Williamson adds a final twist to the argument: 'Behind a thin democratic veil, [Britain] is a society which relies on apathy and self-interest and ignorance as the conditions for its political stability'. (1990:16). To reiterate, we suggest that the politics of young adults like these should not be interpreted as necessarily an outcome of either their age or their entrepreneurial activities. Their lack of interest may be more an outcome of their political realism and political disenchantment — their realization that formal politics had little to offer them — than the result of simple apathy. Trevor puts it neatly:

> *RM:* Are you interested in politics at all?
> *Trevor:* Mixed. I am of the view that I have been poor under this lot and I will under the rest. No matter who gets in I will be poor. It's as simple as that.

Part of our concluding discussion in Chapter 10 will aim to move from informants' political and economic understandings of their experiences to a broader critique of government enterprise policies.

Notes

1 We would like to thank Karl Jankowski for suggesting the chapter title.
2 Cleveland's image was very poor, in the eyes of informants. Terry, the joiner, said: 'All this child abuse! It's though Stockton and Middlesbrough are Sodom and Gomorrah. Come to Cleveland and turn into a pillar of salt! That's all it's famous for: child abuse and unemployment'.
3 At the time of writing, the county has two Conservative MPs and four from Labour. The County Council is controlled by Labour (with forty-eight councillors, to the Conservative's nineteen and ten for the Social and Liberal Democratic Party).
4 None of the interviewees expressed an intention to vote for far right parties such as the National Front or British National Party. This was perhaps surprising given the racist views expressed by a significant minority of young people in other studies (e.g. Coffield *et al.*, 1986; Roberts and Parsell, 1990). Racism, a political expression largely unsupported in the interviews, was, however, an important negative factor pushing informants from the Pakistani culture on Teesside into business (see Chapter 5).
5 Fife-Schaw and Breakwell (1989) raise an interesting methodological point in their discussion of the potential non-voting of 16 to 19 Initiative respondents. They accept the problem of trying to interpret discrete, coded questionnaire items, in this case trying to separate analytically those who ticked the box saying they would not vote from those that did not know whom they would vote for. Fife-Schaw and Breakwell have to assume that these are clearly different groups of people whereas we were able to explore these responses ethnographically (and found, for instance, that there was overlap in such responses).
6 More has been written on the relationship between schooling, the educational system and politics (e.g. Harber, 1987; Walker and Barton, 1989) than on youth culture and youth politics directly. The ESRC's 16 to 19 Initiative holds as one of its central foci the political socialization of young people.

Research emanating from this source (e.g. Roberts and Parsell, 1990; Connolly and Torkington, 1990), and particularly from some of the more qualitative research projects (e.g. Quicke, 1990; Corr, Jamieson and Tomes, 1990), is beginning to expand the base of our empirical knowledge as well as develop more interesting theoretical perspectives on the political consciousness of youth.

7   Of course, the idea that 'youth', as a period of time (i.e. adolescence), can be equated with psychological turmoil and emotional conflict and that 'youth', as a social category, can be equated with 'trouble', alienation, rebellion, etc., has a well established history (Stanley Hall, 1904; Cohen, A.K., 1955; Coleman, 1961; Musgrove, 1964; Erikson, 1968; Willmott, 1969). Stan Cohen (1973), Michael Rutter *et al.* (1976) and Dick Hebdige (1979) have produced valuable critiques of these ideas.

8   Heath and Topf (1987, quoted in Bynner and Ashford 1990) argue that as many as two-thirds of potential voters in Britain could be classified as disaffected from the political system.

9   A 'fully participative democracy' could be, hypothetically, full, local, political control by workers' soviets, or five-yearly parliamentary ballots. Lenin suggested that: 'the oppressed are allowed once every few years to decide which particular representatives of the oppressing class shall represent and repress them in parliament' (1976:107).

10 Bynner and Ashford refer to the appeal of extremist groups to disaffected, uneducated youth. Whilst we accept that support for the National Front and British National Party comes in the main from working-class males, their efforts to recruit higher education students should not be overlooked. However, we would also argue that revolutionary groups of the extreme left (the Socialist Workers Party and Socialist Organizer provide obvious examples) gain much, if not most, of their support from highly educated young people (students in higher education). This would seem to contradict Bynner and Ashford's thesis that more education means closer involvement with, and attachment to, present political structures and parties.

11 We would suggest that, if we accept a broader conception of politics, it is not difficult to argue that much of what pupils learn in schools (through both the formal and the hidden curriculum) is highly political, even if political education is not used as the title for particular lessons (see Bowles and Gintis, 1976, and Willis, 1977 for two contrasting, neo-Marxist versions of this general argument). Hargreaves talks of how 'the hidden curriculum exerts on many pupils, particularly but by no means exclusively from the working-class, a destruction of their dignity which is so massive and pervasive that few subsequently recover from it' (1982:17).

Chapter 10

A Culture of Enterprise or
a Culture of Survival?

In this final chapter we aim to do four things. First, we summarise the main conclusions and findings of the preceding chapters. Second, we draw out what we feel to be the implications of our study for research into small business and the sociology of youth. Third, we spell out the conclusions of our research for public policy in the realms of youth education, training, employment and enterprise. In particular, we will focus upon recommendations for the Enterprise Allowance Scheme and local enterprise industries. Finally, we attempt to broaden our perspective to explore the values and politics of the enterprise decade and to explore an alternative agenda for Britain in the 1990s.

Youth and the Enterprise Culture

In the introduction we located the *Teesside 16 to 25 Initiative* within the ESRC's research programme and described how our interests in youth and enterprise had arisen. The project was based in the county of Cleveland which, owing to its recent history of unemployment and because of the traditional dominance of big business, poses a severe test of Government policy. If the enterprise culture could be shown to work in Cleveland, it would probably work anywhere. Following a description of our research methodology, we set ourselves a number of questions to be answered and tasks to be completed.

The first of these was to examine the enterprise movement and the concept of enterprise (Chapter 2). Britain in the 1980s witnessed the rise of a broad enterprise movement including such initiatives as Enterprise in YTS, the Training for Enterprise Programme, the Enterprise Allowance Scheme, Enterprise in Higher Education, and several hundred Local Enterprise Agencies. We argued that it would be reasonable to suppose that there would need to exist a well-researched and well-thought out philosophy of enterprise on which to base and sustain all this endeavour.

We studied the concept of enterprise and the curricula of enterprise courses. Instead of the consensus claimed by some of the leading academic exponents of enterprise, we found that the term 'enterprise', like 'intelligence' before it, had as many definitions as contributors to the literature, that there were as many as 50 'core' skills of enterprise, and that conceptual confusion pervaded the field. Ball, Knight and Plant sum up our position neatly: 'The 1980s saw the word "enterprise" suffer the same fate as the word "community" suffered in the 1960s and 1970s. Both are widely used, much abused and poorly understood' (1990:3).

In Chapter 3, we described and analyzed the Cleveland labour market. We illustrated how Middlesbrough, the 'infant Hercules' of the nineteenth century, had grown spectacularly in size through the entrepreneurial genius of the Victorian ironmasters and industrialists, only to become dependent upon a small range of industries — chemicals, iron and steel, and heavy engineering — after the Second World War. Since then a local culture founded upon skilled, male, manual employment, often lasting a lifetime, has been shaken by rationalization and redundancy. The processes of retrenchment pursued by, for example, ICI and BSC were inspired by declining profits, sharper international competition and a trade recession in the 1970s and early 1980s and resulted in massive unemployment for the people of the county.

The employment prospects for school-leavers and young adults in the county became, and remain, particularly grim. Despite partial economic recovery locally, reflecting an upturn in the national economy during the second half of the 1980s, the numbers of school-leavers entering full-time jobs in Cleveland in 1988 was the lowest ever recorded. Moreover, we raised serious questions about the accuracy of government unemployment figures in recording the true level of joblessness. The impact of various government schemes and changes in the method of counting the unemployed were shown to have combined to reduce the visibility of the unemployed. Although unemployment slipped down the list of national, political concerns, young people in this locality still faced transitions to adulthood severely restricted in opportunity by the impact of ten years of high unemployment on Teesside.

In September 1990, however, at the time of writing, unemployment is once again beginning to make the national headlines. Mainstream bodies, like the CBI, are increasingly forecasting recession and even the Government's figures, which only a year ago were being heralded as the statistical manifestation of an 'economic miracle', show unemployment to be rising after over forty months of decline. In the late 1980s the economic recovery experienced by more prosperous areas to the south was just beginning to make a (limited) impact upon Teesside. Declining numbers of school-leavers, inward investment, indigenous company expansion and job creation all combined to give the future a rosier glow (e.g. Teesside TEC, 1990), even if, as Robinson (1990) argues, the economic base of the region remained vulnerable and recovery was only partial. Now it seems that the dark cloud of unemployment has only been temporarily dispelled and it would take a brave (or foolish) person to predict a prosperous future for the county. The recently announced redundancy of 640 workers at ICI's Billingham plant can only add to our concerns about the continuing dependence of the local economy upon a few industrial giants.

Through these past ten years of economic decline, limited recovery and impending recession, young people have been making transitions from school into the labour market. Through the historical and economic landscape that we painted in Chapter 3, young men and women have struggled to get on and get by. For many, the post-school years of early adulthood have consisted of a seemingly endless round of government schemes and dead-end jobs punctuated by often lengthy periods of unemployment. In Chapter 9 informants conjured up an image of Teesside as 'scheme-land', with whole families struggling to make a living on one or another of the government-sponsored unemployment measures.

In Chapter 4 we examined one of the proposed solutions to this so-called 'dependency culture'. Here we investigated how the concept and philosophy of enterprise was translated from theory and initiatives at a national, macro-level into local practice. We illustrated the way in which the enterprise industry in Cleveland had mushroomed during the early 1980s using a combination of public and private funding to finance a maze of activities under the banner of enterprise. Many millions of pounds, usually in the form of MSC/Training Agency grants, poured into the county to oil the wheels of the 'enterprise express'. One of the unintended consequences of the promotion of an enterprise culture, we argued, was the provision of jobs, not for the unemployed youth of the area, but for a new tier of bureaucrats and enterprise trainers. Although many worked extremely hard for their clients, they often did so in very difficult circumstances. Job security was minimal, frustration and internal politicking were rife, and broader enterprise aims were quickly abandoned as the pressure to meet numerical targets intensified in order to keep or win new funding contracts. What surprised us was the speed with which new courses and types of enterprise training kept arriving on the scene: what has been called 'policy on the hoof'. Pilot schemes were hurriedly introduced at the first whiff of a possible Training Agency grant, and these in turn became established as central elements in new training regimes, even if there was little or no continuity with an organization's original objectives or philosophy. In short, large sums of public money were used to underwrite a sprawling industry which promoted an incoherent and uncoordinated set of initiatives and activities.

We witnessed, within the space of two years, the rise and partial fall of this young empire of activities, schemes, courses and organizations, all devoted to the promotion of youth enterprise. Indeed, our own investigations were hampered by the mergers (the word 'takeover' was not used) and closures that were set in motion as those involved with funding (and those working in) the enterprise industry began to realise that there were too many organizations dealing with the same client group. The advent of Teesside TEC helped this process of rationalization along, and we hinted in Chapter 4 that the path of the enterprise industry in Cleveland seemed to be following the pattern set by local manufacturing industry of speedy growth and even more sudden contraction, with the same human consequences of unemployment, albeit on a smaller scale.

Having said this, the enterprise industry on Teesside remains relatively lively even if incorporation of the buzzword 'enterprise' into funding proposals and training programmes is now less likely to guarantee success. A central element of youth enterprise work is still business start-up. The dominant model of enterprise promoted on Teesside was that of small business, and *very* small business at that. The development of self-employment in sole traderships was the primary objective of the majority of organizations that we surveyed, by far outweighing the work that was done in the locality to promote enterprise in co-operatives or in community ventures.

In Chapter 5 we began the discussion of our ethnographic data by examining the motivations and decision-making of the informants who had started, or were intending to start, their own businesses. We explored the two main influences that they described: unemployment and entrepreneurship.

Following recent practice in the sociology of youth, we attempted to plot the 'career trajectories' of our informants. Our ethnographic perspective led us to criticize the notion of career trajectory and we identified a number of problems which we feel are pertinent to the wider task of mapping youth transitions (see Chapter 5). Nevertheless, we concluded that labour market experiences preceding (and following) youth enterprise could throw light upon youth enterprise itself and unemployment was found to be a major factor influencing people to start up in business. This was, in a sense, not surprising given the recent history of worklessness amongst young people. To gain access to the Enterprise Allowance Scheme (EAS), people must be unemployed and in receipt of benefit for eight weeks. Again it is not surprising, therefore, that the clear majority of our informants had been unemployed prior to start-up. However, the average duration of this period of unemployment was approximately a year, suggesting that for many self-employment was being pursued as a solution to personal unemployment.

This finding was fully supported by the more qualitative data: unemployment, with its associated material, psychological and social deficits, *pushed* people into self-employment. This was not, however, the whole story. 'Become your own boss' is a popular phrase encapsulating the appeal of self-employment (and employed by the Training Agency to encourage youth business start-up); it was also a phrase used by our informants to explain the *pull* of entrepreneurship. For people like these, often previously denied the chance to gain personal pride, control, independence and feelings of achievement in their working lives, self-employment seemed an attractive option compared to a continued existence on the dole.

Whilst the push of unemployment and the pull of entrepreneurship provided the *main* incentives to start a business, other factors also played their part. Issues of gender, race and class were important here; for instance, the small number of people we interviewed from the Pakistani culture on Teesside all described racist exclusion from the decent jobs in the locality as a major reason for setting up in business. We also discussed in some depth the impact of gender on reasons for starting up. We found, confirming other studies, that self-employment was being taken up by some women as a way of working which enabled them to maintain a degree of flexibility (in hours and place of work) and independence (e.g. financial and symbolic). Enterprise constituted part of a broader working life in which part-time jobs, household work and child-care also featured.

The majority of our informants joined the EAS and some drew upon other sources of financial assistance (bank loans, government and enterprise agency grants, family support, personal savings) in setting up businesses. For some, this process was simple, but for others it proved a complicated and frustrating undertaking. A particular difficulty was the severe lack of finance available to young people intending to set up in business. Even the £1,000 necessary for EAS entry sometimes proved elusive (some young women in particular had difficulties, reporting a sexist attitude from bank managers). Despite the considerable amount of advice and help available from the local enterprise industry, many of those who set up did so as a result of sheer hard work, determination and considerable family support, and in a few cases, sacrifice.

Most businesses were formed in the service sector, for example in retailing (e.g. clothes shops) or personal services (e.g. hairdressing), as we described in Chapter 6. Only one or two were inspired by unusual or innovatory business ideas, with most mirroring jobs in the local area. Of those trading at the time of interview, the majority were in the first eighteen months of business, with only a small number having businesses more than two years old. After a year these embryonic businesses lost the support of the EAS and other props, such as subsidized start-up units, and this point in the life span of new enterprises proved particularly critical. Of those who were no longer trading the majority had gone out of business between eleven and thirteen months after starting up.

Finding commercial premises suitably located and at reasonable rents was an initial hurdle to be cleared. A second problem involved the securing of business capital. Most new businesses were severely under-capitalized and these two issues combined to make the practice of running new enterprises a very risky one. Institutional support certainly helped and most informants talked in generally positive terms about their experience of enterprise agencies, but most businesses survived through the diligence and determination of people keen to escape unemployment and make a living through their own endeavours. The pay earned was extremely low and the hours worked long. More than half were paying themselves £1 per hour or less.

Informants were partly compensated by less tangible rewards: feelings of pride, self-achievement and enjoyment, for example. However, mixed with these feelings were further more negative consequences of entrepreneurship. Long hours, low pay, insecurity, isolation and loneliness, mental stress and financial worries were all part of running risky businesses. The fact that many ran at all was largely due to the low expectations and stoical attitude of young entrepreneurs. Informants who had closed down businesses usually emphasized the stress, lack of money and trade and the disheartening nature of their experience as the reasons for so doing. Some had gone bust with severe financial and emotional consequences.

The conclusion of Chapter 6 was based around a three-part typology of our informants' experiences and their relative success and failure, which was supported by a series of case studies in Chapter 7. Around 10 per cent fared well (the '*runners*') and were in charge of successful money-making, employment-generating, long-term business ventures. A further 20 per cent (the '*fallers*') failed, often disastrously. These two groups, and particularly the former, often make the headlines (e.g. 'Whizzkids Win the Survival Stakes') and distort what we found to be the majority experience of enterprise. About 70 per cent of the people we interviewed (the '*plodders*') fell between these well-publicized extremes and were neither successful nor failures; they struggled hard and long to make a living through self-employment and for them risky businesses had as much to do with a culture of survival as a culture of enterprise. This was the cold reality of youth enterprise for the clear majority of our informants.

In Chapter 8 we examined directly the experience of people involved with alternative forms of enterprise in community ventures and co-operatives. These models of enterprise tend to be overshadowed by the promotion of more conventional small business, but offer a broader concept of enterprise to the young and unemployed. Although community enterprise ventures did seem to provide activities which contributed to the confidence and skills of their unemployed participants, we found that their grander aims were often not realized. In short, they often consisted of short-term, disorganized activities which were very much second best to the personal developments to be gained through decent jobs. Similarly, although those in co-operatives were introduced to egalitarian principles, more pragmatic motivations frequently underlay the movement of young people into co-ops (e.g. the funding benefits of starting up in business through the auspices of the local cooperative agency). We found that the experiences of running cooperatives were strikingly similar to those reported by informants in more mainstream, capitalist small businesses.

In Chapter 9 we focused upon the politics of young men and women with experience of business. Perhaps contrary to the popular view, these young entrepreneurs were not ideological followers of the Conservative Government. Just over 10 per cent reported that they would vote Conservative in a general election. To us, more interesting was the fact that nearly half would either not vote at all or were unsure for whom they would vote. Many studies of youth have come to the disappointing and hackneyed conclusion that young people are apathetic, bored and fatalistic in their responses to questions about politics. We argue, to the contrary, that our informants were politically vocal, but that the narrow definition of 'politics' (e.g. the world of Westminster), usually employed by sociological investigators, did little justice to the critical views expressed by our informants, for instance, in relation to the enterprise movement and the Thatcher Government. These people did not share the philosophy or political ideology of enterprise and were able to provide often quite damning critiques, even if these were not recognized by them as being political.

Small Business and Youth Transitions

Before turning to the substantive issues and policy implications which stem from our research, we feel that we should repeat from Chapter 1 some of its limitations (and our response) so that readers can estimate for themselves what weight they may wish to attach to our conclusions. Because of constraints placed upon us by time and funding, our informants were, in the main, interviewed only once (but in some depth); the sample was not systematically random (but still considered, however, valid and appropriate); observational methods were under-used; the approach was not longitudinal (interviewees were, however, at different stages of setting up and running businesses); the emphasis was on economic and political issues (rather than a holistic treatment of all the main issues in the lives of young people) and, as a result, some theoretical questions (for instance, those revolving around 'race' and gender) received less attention than we would have liked. Having admitted these weaknesses, what implications does our research still have for research into small business and youth transitions?

We came to the study of youth enterprise from the fields of education and sociology of youth. We felt reasonably confident that we knew something about 'youth', but were less happy with 'enterprise'. Consequently, much of our early academic efforts were geared to understanding the concept of enterprise (see Chapter 2) and the now quite established body of work which seeks to investigate the dynamics of small business (see Chapter 5). We would not claim, however, to be experts in this field by any means. We would, though, like to suggest a number of ways in which our project has started to extend the possibilities of research in these areas.

First, we found much of the methodology underpinning small business research to be overly quantitative, psychological and positivistic. Little attention is paid to the meanings people attach to the experiences they undergo in business and samples tend to be large, eschewing more small-scale studies. Our perspective has enabled an examination of more qualitative aspects of business start-up, management and closure. Furthermore, most small business research tends *not* to be about micro, one person businesses like those we studied. 'Small business' can mean quite large operations and service sector businesses are often missed out (see Curran, 1986; Burrows and Curran, 1989, for a fuller debate about the size of small business). We hope to have gone a small way to adding to empirical knowledge of these important sorts of firm.

Second, we hope to have demonstrated the usefulness of focusing upon a particular age group, and in this case, a previously overlooked one.[1] Whilst many of the issues that we relate in this book bear relevance to older groups of people, we still feel that it is important to examine youth enterprise directly. During the 1980s young people were the subject of considerable popular press condemnation as work-shy 'scroungers'. By illustrating the almost heroic efforts of young men and women in enterprise we hope to have helped to dispel this persistent myth. Relatedly, young people in particular have been the focus of government measures to alleviate unemployment in depressed areas of the country. Young entrepreneurs are often highlighted and held up to be the guardians of the economic future of localities like Cleveland (see Chapter 4). They receive glowing praise in the newspapers for their entrepreneurial success (see Chapter 6). We hope also to have challenged some of the inaccuracies and half-truths surrounding this popular view of youth enterprise. The majority experience consisted neither of wholehearted success nor of complete failure (see Chapters 6 and 7).

Third, we incorporated a form of local labour market analysis, in which we described and analyzed the history of Cleveland's economy. This reflects a growing interest in the significance of locality in social research generally (e.g. Cooke, 1989). It is true that some small business studies have focused on particular localities, and a few have also been based in the county of Cleveland (e.g. Storey, 1982). None to our knowledge, however, have as yet investigated the structure of opportunities prevailing in local labour markets for particular groups of workers as fully as labour market sociologists like Ashton and Maguire (1986). Burrows and Curran (1986, 1989), in calling for strengthened sociological research on small business, isolate, in particular, the need to develop a fuller understanding of locality. We fully accept the importance of dis-aggregating national or even more regional labour market statistics in order to understand properly the often quite specific social processes operating at a local level (e.g. Coles, 1988; MacDonald, 1989). The *history* of Teesside's economy that we developed in Chapter 3 provided an additional perspective to our discussion of policies to promote youth enterprise and small business revivalism in the 1980s.

Fourth, we have examined the broader politics of the enterprise movement, for instance, by debunking the concept of enterprise and by tracing critically the development of the TECs. Too often we found small business studies to be written in an historical and political vacuum. Few incorporate any discussion of the wider structural forces or policy initia-tives which shape and direct the ebb and flow of people into and out of self-employment.

In these four points we have tried to describe some of the ways in which we feel our work could add to small business research. The academic direction of the project has, however, not been one-way. We continue to work within the now quite enormous field which is con-stituted by the sociology of youth, education, training and (un)employ-ment. The ESRC's *16 to 19 Initiative* is at present, perhaps, the main programme of research into British youth (see Chapter 1). Our focus has been ethnographic, reflecting our interest in youth cultures. The scope of our study, in terms of who was included in the sample, was reasonably wide in the sense that the young entrepreneurs that we talked to were from a variety of socio-economic backgrounds, there were roughly equal numbers of men and women and they had pursued varied post-16 career trajectories prior to starting businesses.

Unlike studies of youth in the 1970s (e.g. Hall and Jefferson, 1976; Hebdige, 1979) we were not preoccupied with subcultural style, but rather the cultural responses of a wider range of young people to the structure of opportunities facing them in a particular locality. Our infor-mants could be described as 'ordinary kids' (Jenkins, 1983; Brown, 1987) two or three years after leaving school, FE college or YTS. We believe these people were representative of their age group, but were different to their peers in the steps they took as they struggled to find decent jobs on Teesside. They took the enterprise path and it is their experiences of working in the enterprise culture which form the backbone of this book.

Having mentioned the ways in which small business research could be developed, it is now time to make similar comments in relation to the sociology of youth. If small business studies have ignored youth, studies of youth have certainly ignored small business. The examination of transitions into the labour market has included virtually all aspects of labour market activity except self-employment. Why should this be the case?

We are not certain of the complete answer but we think that part of the explanation can be found in the artificial age boundaries that are employed to categorize youth in sociological investigations. 'Youth' tends not to be defined in many texts and it is almost implicitly held to be that period after minimum school-leaving age (i.e. sixteen) and the end of the teenage years (i.e. nineteen). This short span does, of course, cover a period of great significance not just for individuals of that age but for society as a whole. Perhaps the sociological interest in these years results mainly from the fact that they cover a crucial time in the reproduction of class, gender and other inequalities. For instance, during this period school-leavers are placed at various levels within the class/occupational hierarchy, and young men and women begin to take steps to form new families, sharing unequal burdens of responsibility in the household economy. (The latter element of social reproduction still remains relatively under-theorized, however). It is the significance of youth in these respects that has led to the now dominant interest in youth transitions.

The question that we would like to raise is: although we accept the importance of transitions during this period of youth, why does the study of such transitions terminate at the age of nineteen? We would argue that interesting and controversial aspects of youth tend to be left out by retaining such a narrow definition. Our study of youth enterprise would have been very short-lived if we had restricted ourselves to the sixteen to nineteen age range.

We found that young people tend to take up the option of enterprise after they have had experience of Youth Training Schemes, jobs, unemployment and other government schemes (Community Programme, Employment Training), even if the seeds of enterprising ideas were laid earlier in youth (see Chapter 5). Often the impetus to start up businesses came from the negative experience of searching for decent jobs in a depressed area. Moreover, legal constraints, bank lending policy and the regulations of the EAS all act to delay the possibility of self-employment until the age of eighteen or after. The average age of our informants was twenty-one years old. In a sense, then, we are studying both the sorts of people that the *16 to 19 Initiative* dropped a few years earlier in their lives and aspects of youth economic activity not included in such investigations. Other commentators have argued for a more extended study of youth transitions in order to incorporate a fuller investigation of the impact of family formation, household careers, sexuality and romance upon economic transitions and some have followed young people as they enter their twenties (e.g. Wallace, 1987; Hutson and Jenkins, 1989). We welcome this widening of perspective and hope that our study of youth enterprise has illustrated the empirical and theoretical importance of continuing the study of youth beyond the arbitrary cut-off point of nineteen that is so often used.

Part of the reason why self-employment and enterprise have been largely absent from studies of youth may also be found in the general distaste of social scientists for the politics and economics usually associated with enterprise and commerce. Although not wishing to align ourselves with the attacks made upon sociology by David Marsland (e.g. 1988a and 1988b), there may be some truth in the view that sociological critiques of work in capitalist societies have highlighted the position of the working-class and have tended to pay less attention to the experiences of capitalists or owner-managers themselves.[2] However, Burrows and Curran (1989) provide an authoritative rebuttal of Marsland's criticism, based on a number of examples of studies which run counter to the general case.

Besides, self-employment has traditionally been a relatively minor aspect of British labour market activity. Researchers interested in the sociology of work have tended to concentrate their attention upon employment and particularly aspects of the labour process. During the early 1980s unemployment became a major focus of research. Sociologists of youth have latterly followed this lead and the experiences of youth in the labour market (on schemes, in jobs and on the dole) now comprise the major avenue of investigation. The core studies of the *16 to 19 Initiative* are typical in this respect. As we argued in Chapter 5, however, self-employment over the past ten years has come to constitute a far more significant part (both quantitatively and qualitatively) of overall labour market activity. The numbers 'becoming their own boss' have risen by over one million during the past decade (Hakim, 1989a) to the point where the self-employed now comprise well over 10 per cent of the labour force (Burrows and Curran, 1989). And, although a recent review of prospects for the small firm over the next decade concluded that the conditions for small firms will be less favourable than in the 1980s, this was balanced with the statement that:

> there are few indications of any real decline as happened after the
> last revival in the fortunes of the small firm sector in the 1930s.
> Given the exceptionally favourable combination of circumstances
> in the 1980s some downturn is to be expected but the evidence
> still points towards a continuing importance of the small enter-
> prise. (Curran and Blackburn, 1990:8)

We would conclude that present economic conditions make small firms particularly precarious (as we will argue further, later in the chapter) but we think that enterprise and small business, as substantive topics for sociological investigation, will continue to grow in importance. And although self-employment is still a minority experience for British youth as a whole, we suspect that the numbers setting up small firms will also continue to grow. Burrows and Curran (1989) trace the links between sociology and small business research and conclude their article with a call for greater collaboration and cross-fertilization between the two domains. During the second half of the 1980s enterprise was something of a political 'hot potato' which tended to be either unconditionally supported or condemned out of hand. The next decade should see more balanced, sociologically informed and critical appraisals, and we hope to have made a small step in this direction.

One fashionable avenue of sociological debate in which small business is already well established is that which focuses upon macro-level, economic restructuring in Western capitalist societies. The link between our study of youth enterprise and topical developments in the sociology of work can be found in the growth in the qualitative and quantitative significance of enterprise and small business. Participants in the 'flexibility debate' (for a critical discussion see, for example, Pollert, 1988; Wood, 1989; Burrows and Curran, 1989; Rainnie, 1990a, 1990b; Amin and Robins, 1990; Amin, 1990; Penn, 1990) have drawn upon evidence of rising levels of self-employment to argue that capitalist societies like Britain are witnessing a radical change in the direction of industrial production. Very briefly, it is argued that the decline of mass production and the rise of 'flexible specialization' in what are termed post-Fordist forms of production, results in greater numbers of smaller, craft-based firms (Piore and Sabel, 1984). Whilst this thesis has been the subject of much criticism, it is generally accepted that the organization of work in late-twentieth-century Britain is undergoing substantial change and that one of the biggest single elements in the movement away from employment in large-scale, manufacturing industries can be found in the large and increasing numbers of people in self-employment (Hakim, 1988, 1989a).

As such, our study supports those writers who claim that the growth of self-employment is part of a changing culture of work in late-twentieth-century capitalist economies (e.g. Beynon *et al.*, 1985; Hakim, 1988). It is argued that central to these changes is an increasing divide in the organization of work between the employment of a core, skilled, highly-paid work-force and more casual, disorganized, often subcontracted forms of labour. Youth enterprise, as we understand it, forms a new and important segment of the poorly paid, casualized, insecure and peripheral economy.

It is this changing culture of work, constituted by self-employment in new small enterprises, co-operatives, voluntary jobs, work in the domestic economy, part-time jobs and migratory work, which we will be investigating in our continuing research.[3]

Youth Enterprise and Social Policy

So far we have done no more than summarize the contents of the preceding chapters, to remind readers of the empirical thrust of our work, and we have appraised these findings in relation to, first, small business research and, second, the sociology of youth. Now, however, we need to take a step beyond these empirical findings to tease out their implications for social policy. Obviously, this is a more tentative task than, for example, analyzing the ethnographic interviews collected. Whilst we inevitably have to take an analytical step away from the experience of youth enterprise in interpreting the ethnographic material, we have to take an even greater stride away from the 'raw' interview data in suggesting the direction of future policy. If we failed to draw even tentative conclusions, however, we suspect that our research would be interpreted by different sectional interests as support for different policy initiatives and, as such, we now with to place our own conclusions on record.[4]

Our findings and conclusions are pertinent, we think, both to those who formulate and deliver enterprise policies (and other initiatives in the realm of youth education, training and employment). We shall begin by discussing issues which stem directly from our fieldwork (for example, concerning EAS) and then gradually broaden the perspective to more macro-level issues (for example, the future of the TECs) in the final section of the chapter.

The Enterprise Allowance Scheme

Nationally, the EAS remains the main policy mechanism for moving unemployed people into self-employment. At a local level, Cleveland's enterprise industry centred much of its activities upon this scheme during the 1980s. In response, we have focused much of our attention upon the experience of young women and men who have entered the enterprise culture using the EAS.

Indeed, it could be argued that the existence of the EAS largely shapes the type of enterprise pursued by young people. It demands that businesses be new, that they are aimed at making profits, and the structure and content of advice offered in conjunction with the scheme (the EAS Awareness Day, enterprise agency counselling, enterprise training courses) do much to promote enterprise as self-employment in sole traderships at the expense of broader models of enterprise (e.g. in co-operatives). The £40 per week available through the scheme may not be much but it is, for many of these previously unemployed young people, better than nothing. The simple existence of a well-publicized scheme coupled with this financial incentive pulls many into starting businesses of this type and in this way. Alternative ways of being enterprising in the local economy are marginalized (see Chapters 4 and 8). Thus, the workings of the EAS demand special scrutiny. First, we will discuss entry to the scheme.

The EAS has a number of criteria which must be met before participation can begin. These are listed in full in Chapter 2. Foremost amongst these are that the intending business person must possess £1,000 to contribute to the business, that he or she must have been unemployed and in receipt of benefit for eight weeks and that the business must be new. We found evidence that calls into question the usefulness of such rules.

Many of the people that the EAS is aimed at simply do not have £1,000 or access to such a sum. The comment that 'I've never had £100, never mind £1,000' sticks in our minds. Many of our informants had come from the ranks of the long-term unemployed or were ex-trainees of various sorts. They had little money, and less savings and in many cases came from poor families. Yet they were keen to start businesses. This dilemma was resolved in one of three ways; first, the money could be borrowed from friends, relatives or banks. This is perhaps the intention of the scheme — participants will then have an increased sense of responsibility for the success of their business. Second, we came across a small number of informants for whom the money was a real problem. Mary and Jane (intending to set up a partnership) were offered half the necessary money and worked (in 'fiddly jobs') for a year in order to raise the remainder. Together with their savings they managed to earn enough money to enter the scheme, in an arduous and drawn-out way. Third, this condition could be circumvented by borrowing money, from banks for instance, for a very limited period (a day or a week). Bank statements then could be shown to EAS staff and, yes, on a given day intending participants would have the £1,000. This was a widespread practice. We heard of one amount of £1,000 (originally a loan from a parent) being passed between nearly twenty people in Newcastle, affording them all access to the scheme before it was returned to the original owner. A version of this method was pursued by Dennis (Chapter 7) who 'borrowed' over £1,000 in credit from a high street store which was acceptable to the EAS (even though he never paid it back).

A further problem is that informants must be in receipt of benefit for eight weeks and that the business must be new (i.e. involving trade not carried out before entering the scheme). We found some evidence of informants 'going unemployed' (i.e. voluntarily signing on the unemployment register) in order to meet this demand, though it would not be accurate to say that this was common as many more were unemployed for several months through no fault of their own. Those who pursued this strategy argued that it would be unfair if they did not receive the same support in self-employment as their peers (on EAS). It was a risky way of joining the EAS because, in order to receive unemployment benefit (part of the conditions), claimants must be deemed not to have made themselves voluntarily unemployed.

A further risk involved working at the business before applying for the EAS. In effect this was what Mary and Jane (above) had done to raise finances. They were forced into illicit, undeclared, part-time work whilst at the same time receiving unemployment benefit in order to fulfil their intention of participating in a government scheme. In Chapter 5 we described how Terry the joiner began his trade in a casual way after leaving employment and whilst signing on (in order to spend eight weeks unemployed). He became entangled in a bureaucratic and legal wrangle with the DHSS and EAS staff and was eventually rejected from the EAS because his business was not deemed to be new.

One of the motivations behind some business start-ups was the ambition to turn teenage hobbies into enterprising ways of making a living in early adulthood. The condition that business ideas be new hinders the efforts of some young people to become self-employed. It can act as a barrier between previous activities (whether hobbies, casual work, jobs 'on the side', previous employment) and the establishment of new businesses.

Finally, we must draw attention to the models of enterprise promoted. We can see no real advantage in limiting the types of business structures promoted by enterprise agencies. The model of enterprise which interprets small business to mean exclusively the sole-trader may fit more neatly with the political values of the present Government, but we are sure that some intending entrepreneurs would benefit from participation in enterprise as it is more widely defined. Partnerships, co-operatives, limited companies, community businesses and community enterprise ventures all have their own advantages and disadvantages which should be presented and discussed to allow applicants to choose which model best suits their circumstances. For instance, starting a business demands a good degree of confidence which many, escaping from long-term unemployment, may not have. Starting up in the company of a friend or friends in a partnership or co-op *may* increase the chances of business success.

A second set of problems with the EAS was uncovered when we examined the experiences of young people once they had started businesses. One widespread complaint was that, once businesses had been started, there seemed to be little help given or checks made on their progress. Those involved with co-operatives reported quite long-term involvement from NECDA (see Chapter 8), whilst the majority who were running sole-traderships reported being left very much on their own. EAS staff impose no test of commercial viability upon proposed businesses and do little to follow up participants once they have set up. In discussions with Training Agency staff we were told that the minimal visits carried out through the year were 'a very loose, shallow check that the person is still alive' and that these had resulted in nobody being ejected from the scheme, that they could remember.

Informants confirmed this story. Visits from EAS personnel were rare and brief, usually involving a passing glance at the accounts books (if businesses had them). Sometimes people did run into trouble with particular aspects of their businesses, but these were usually not the sort of thing that could be solved in a fifteen-minute visit. We received complaints about the lack of any thorough help or guidance with, for instance, book-keeping, advertising and marketing, which should be provided free of charge.

Whilst it is true that there are myriad organizations offering such advice in Cleveland, there is no compulsory business training attached to the EAS (apart from one Enterprise Awareness Day). To expect young people starting businesses to appreciate the potential pitfalls, to recognize the impending problems and to seek appropriate advice at the appropriate stage, is to ask a lot of this new breed of entrepreneur. Moreover, informants were sometimes unaware of the help available to them or too busy to search it out. Miller (1987) has drawn attention to the need for more outreach work by enterprise advisers and counsellors. Questions need to be asked, then, about the degree of informational support available to those starting businesses through the EAS and the non-compulsory nature of that which exists. At present enterprise policies operate with a 'black box' design: there are inputs at the start-up stage and examination of the later consequences (survival rates), but less attention is paid to the intervening processes and problems. Clearly there is a need for greater policy responsibility; responsibility for the management, growth and development of enterprises (and their owners) encouraged by government policy.

Having said this, we did receive many positive comments about particular enterprise agencies (TYE and NECDA, for instance) and we should reiterate that, without the support of the local enterprise industry and the EAS, very many of these people would never have set up in business. The advice and information functions of the enterprise industry were welcomed and we reiterate our conclusion that these provide a very valuable source of help for intending business people. These need, however, to be better organized and there is a case for more accurate targeting of enterprise guidance to those who most need help. This form of support must continue to be free and greater effort should be made to make this form of support available after the initial start-up stages. 'Crisis help' should be more easily available and advice on closing down businesses with the minimum of emotional and financial distress should be part of the standard range of activities offered to young business people.

The *Calouste Gulbenkian Foundation* have reported on local enterprise policies for the unemployed and many of their conclusions are confirmed by our study (we recommend Nabarro *et al.*, 1986, for a complete discussion). The provision of reasonably priced, centrally located start-up units run in a professional way on an 'easy in and easy out' basis would help many young businesses. In Chapter 5 we illustrated that organizations like TYE were already offering such support but we would recommend greater flexibility in the duration of leases for start-up units so that they do not terminate after twelve months and so coincide with the withdrawal of Enterprise Allowance after a year. The simultaneous loss of these two crucial props caused great problems (see Chapter 6).

Thus, we support the call of the *Calouste Gulbenkian Foundation* for greater organization of the existing services so as to increase coordination rather than competition, and to clear the maze and ease access for clients to the available enterprise support. In particular, there is a need to simplify and make some processes more 'user friendly'. One issue that arose on a number of occasions was the lack of coordination between Housing Benefit and Enterprise Allowance; informants had difficulties in finding out beforehand whether or not they would still be eligible for help with rent money, and consequently whether or not they could actually afford to set up in business. Once they started in business some reported severe delays in getting Housing Benefit.

We have shown how EAS was viewed positively by some young women who were able to retain some independence, avoid low paid and dead-end, part-time jobs, work from home, make some money, and start a business which could be extended and developed at a later date when other commitments lessened. We suggest that, in the absence of improved working conditions and opportunities for, in particular, young mothers in the local economy, that use of the EAS in this way should be encouraged. Constructive and flexible self-employed work through the scheme should be supported and, hence, we would like to see less strict conditions on the numbers of hours worked per week by EAS participants. Additionally, we question the regulations that bar married women (who are not eligible for unemployment benefit) from the EAS. This enterprising way of combining different kinds of work should be fostered even if this requires the abandonment of the condition that all entrants must be in receipt of unemployment benefit. This relatively minor policy alteration would also allow people on disability benefit access to the EAS.

An obvious issue in assessing the EAS concerns the weekly allowance. Though there were surprisingly few negative comments about the £40 per week, we feel that serious questions need to be asked about the level of material support given to young businesses. The weekly allowance has not been increased since it was set at £40, in 1982, to be analogous with a married person's supplementary benefit (which was approximately £55 in 1988). We can see little reason, following the Government's own logic, why the allowance should not at least be kept in line with other inflation-linked state benefits. We have shown how the vast majority of people had little to contribute financially to their businesses and how they relied primarily upon their own labour to trade in micro-businesses, usually in the service sector.

We suggest that the very limited financial support provided to new businesses does much to limit their potential development in areas like Cleveland. As one enterprise adviser put it to us, if a young person intends to set up in business as a window cleaner, perhaps £40 per week will suffice as early business support. But if a young person wants to further an interest in computer technology by setting up a business to develop and manufacture sophisticated micro-technology, how far will £40 per week go? Some of our informants had benefited greatly by the receipt of Regional Development Grants (see Chapter 5). This was, however, recently discontinued and in one fell swoop a major source of government backing for new, small businesses was removed. Moreover, a recent analysis of the RDG scheme in Cleveland (Wren, 1989) argues that the reasons why it was withdrawn (that it was associated with high levels of 'deadweight' spending) are highly debatable.

Again it seems that the type of support provided by the EAS works to restrict new business start-up to labour-intensive work in the service sector; for example in retailing, where initial costs are comparatively low, where capital investment is marginal and where enterprise is founded upon long hours, low pay and hard work. There is much effort by all concerned in the enterprise industry and much rhetoric from politicians behind the enterprise movement, but, to put it bluntly, is it not time to provide a decent level of support for young business people, if the rhetoric is to be taken seriously?

Part of the ideological rationale underpinning the enterprise movement in Cleveland is that in the past the county has been too dependent upon a small number of large manufacturing firms. The proposed solution is the creation of a large number of very small firms in the service sector. This seems to us to be putting all our economic eggs into one small, cheap ideological basket. If we are to avoid repeating the mistakes of the past by becoming less dependent upon one form of economic activity, should we not begin to give more critical consideration to the type of economic activity that is being promoted through schemes like the EAS? Who believes that an increased number of hairdressers, fashion retailers and picture framers will turn the Cleveland economy around?

Given the problems that we have identified, we now call into question the seriousness of the policy underlying the EAS. If the Government were really committed to helping young people set up firms in depressed areas like Teesside, why is there not more long-term 'hand-holding' of young businesses? Why is there no real, compulsory training in business management? Why is there no test of commercial viability? Why has the allowance paid not been increased in the eight-year history of the EAS? Can the Government really expect an enterprise culture to be forged with an investment in enterprising individuals of only £40 per week for one year?

Given that many professionals working within the local enterprise industry privately acknowledge many of these same problems and, we suspect, that Training Agency officials are probably aware of these inconsistencies and difficulties, should we not conclude that the policy underlying EAS has other motivations? In a meeting with officials in the North-East we were told, after enquiring about the possibility of increased progress checks and support for young business people, that:

> These are good criteria, but the main government criterion [by which the scheme should be assessed] is the register effect... //
> ... EAS is really an outlet from unemployment and the Government's main interest is in the register effect. Department of Employment and Training Agency staff believe that Ministers are only concerned with the register effect of EAS.

By the 'register effect' the interviewee meant the impact the EAS had upon the numbers registered and thus counted as unemployed. In other words, EAS was seen by those working to promote it at a local level to be designed primarily to reduce the unemployment figures. In a letter from John Cope, then a Minister at the Department of Employment, we were told, however, that:

> We believe that by encouraging the wealth of talent, ideas and abilities that can be found amongst the unemployed, particularly the under-25's, many will find their own way out of unemployment and create flourishing new businesses which will go on beyond the time of the allowance. I am glad to say that in the majority of cases they actually succeed in not only creating jobs for themselves, but, even better have created jobs for others. (Personal communication, July 1989)

In Chapter 6 we cast doubt on the employment generation potential of the businesses we studied and drew upon the publications of the National Audit Office to question the survival rates claimed by Government for EAS businesses. What we highlight here is the apparent disparity between the professed aims of the scheme at the highest, national policy level and the way the scheme is viewed by the civil servants delivering it on Teesside. On the one hand, we have a Government Minister triumphantly declaring the success of the EAS in creating jobs and, on the other hand, we have officials working at a local level claiming that Ministers are only really interested in the 'register effect'; further confirmation that ideology can be still be powerful even when its logic is internally fractured, contradictory or inconsistent (see Chapter 2).

We concluded Chapter 6 by arguing that our evidence supports growing research (e.g. Curran, 1986; Storey, 1982, 1986a, 1986b; Storey and Johnson, 1987a, 1987b; Binks and Jennings, 1986; Bannock, 1986) which suggests that policies to encourage the start-up of small firms, whilst perhaps being a welcome and necessary part of economic policy, are not *the* answer to unemployment in depressed areas of Britain. Elsewhere, it has been argued that much of the growth of the small business sector is accountable in terms of economic recession rather than in some upswing in entrepreneurial zeal (Storey and Johnson, 1987a). David Storey estimates that the 'seedcorn' role of new, small firms has been very much exaggerated and that the probability of a new firm starting up now, employing more than 100 people in ten years' time, is as low as less than 1 per cent (Storey, 1986b). His research findings come even closer to our interests in a separate paper where he provides a very convincing but pessimistic picture of the possibilities for job generation in small firms in Cleveland:

> If we make the extremely optimistic assumption that public policy could raise overnight the rate of the new firm formation in Cleveland to that of the East Midlands [his comparison area], in those industries where comparison can be made, this would create a maximum of 1,000 new jobs over an 11 year period ... // ... this has to be placed in the context of the net loss of 16,704 jobs, over the same period, through in-situ decline. (1986a:18–19)

We now see clearly the horns of a public policy dilemma. Should government support new, small firms or larger, existing firms, or both? All the options have their attendant dangers given the historic failure of big business on Teesside to safeguard jobs and the likely chances of small firms (Storey, 1982). Binks and Jennings conclude, however, that:

> There is little justification for the implementation of policies, the design of which is based upon the assumption that new and small firms can lead to economic recovery. This merely distracts attention from more realistic sources of economic change. (1986:35)

Our relatively small-scale study of self-employment in Cleveland cannot provide detailed or reliable 'success rates', but we can use our qualitative data to give some indications of the *likely* success or failure of new businesses (see Chapter 6). We found that success was restricted to a small number of firms and that failure seemed close at hand for others who at the time were just managing to keep their businesses afloat. The National Audit Office (1988), drawing upon a much more extensive set of official data, confirms our impressions: less than 4 per cent of entrants to the EAS accounted for more than 60 per cent of all jobs created, whilst the clear majority (43 per cent) failed two years after EAS or continued to employ only themselves (approximately 40 per cent again). Claims for even this limited level of success of schemes like EAS have to be balanced against the officially acknowledged effects of 'displacement' and 'dead-weight'. These issues were spotlighted in a recent TUC appraisal of the EAS:

> The TUC's attitude to EAS is that it can provide help to unem-ployed people wishing to set up small businesses, but that the creation of small businesses is no solution to the existence of mass unemployment. The TUC has expressed concern . . . // . . . about the lack of training for participants and high failure rates . . . // . . . Of even more concern to the TUC has been the past indica-tions that many jobs and businesses created through the EAS have either replaced other existing firms (displacement) or would have been created whether EAS was available or not (dead-weight). (TUC, 1988:2)

One of our main conclusions, moreover, is that as important as the rates of business start-up, survival and job-generation, is the *quality* of work and entrepreneurial experience reported by young women and men in business. An ethnographic perspective on business formation and man-agement is very rare in policy reviews of enterprise. Our study of youth enterprise indicates that other dimensions of success are important (e.g. work satisfaction, future prospects, psychological benefits, income). We must conclude, however, that on all the criteria we developed most of our informants could not be deemed successful, even if a minority had established profitable enterprises.

To summarize, at the level of policy our research calls into question the whole premise upon which enterprise policies are based. Even accord-ing to official figures most new, small firms will not succeed. Our research shows that even those who survive face a very difficult struggle. We do not want to under-estimate the importance of success for those individuals who make it but wish to emphasize that there are only a handful of people in this category. The sheer scale of the problems facing areas like Cleveland make self-employment initiatives to combat un-employment rather insignificant: like 'rowing up a waterfall'. On a more detailed level enterprise schemes and agencies seem to provide only limited help to counter the problems highlighted by informants (e.g. lack of business capital, saturated markets, high street competition). Even changes to schemes like EAS (e.g. the provision of longer-term advice, the development of tests of commercial viability, greater funding), would not make youth enterprise an option likely to rejuvenate such a deeply depressed local economy.

Selectivity

One of the most direct possible recommendations for policy concerns the implementation of measures to introduce greater *selectivity* in the funding and promotion of new firm start-ups. David Storey, in particular, can be identified with this line of argument and the reader is referred to texts in which he and his co-writers present detailed and comprehensive assessments of public policy towards small firms and their arguments for selectivity (Storey *et al.*, 1987; Storey and Johnson, 1987a, 1987b). In short, Storey concludes that blanket support for new firm start-ups is inefficient in the medium-term and that it *is* possible to 'pick winners'. Storey studied the growth and failure of manufacturing firms in the North-East of England and concluded that a firm likely to generate jobs can be distinguished at an early stage from firms with less potential. The factors identified in a firm with high growth potential include: by the two-year point, it is generally three times larger, in terms of assets and employment, than a typical competitor; that it is likely to be owned by experienced directors rather than, say, previously redundant, skilled workers starting up a firm in their trade; and that it started relatively large. Moreover, he has found that out of every 100 small firms, the fastest growing four firms will create half the jobs in the group over a decade (Storey *et al.*, 1987). This leads to a call for:

> a reversal of current policies for promoting 'the enterprise culture' in which every redundant worker is encouraged to gamble his or her redundancy money in starting a business. Instead it means a policy of selectivity in which only a few chosen firms are eligible for support, but where the support makes a significant contribution to the growth and development of the business. (Storey and Johnson, 1987a:41)

The movement toward greater selectivity has also been tentatively backed by the National Audit Office in their assessment of the EAS: 'there may be potential for improved value for money if support was more closely targeted to those most likely to benefit' (1988:4) and hinted at by Government Ministers (see Woodcock, 1990). The growing emphasis on the expansion of already existing firms rather than business start-up (for instance, as embodied in the Business Growth through Training scheme), and the reduction in the relative importance of business start-up activities promoted by local enterprise organizations, also indicate that more focused policies towards the small firm are being pursued. It appears that the enterprise industry at the local level is moving away from the 'numbers game' of so many business start-ups, at such a cost, in a given amount of time (Coles and MacDonald, 1990), to a more targeted and selective approach. The advent of TECs should add impetus to this movement toward selectivity, as fewer organizations are forced into unhelpful competition, and fewer wild and exaggerated claims need to be made in order to justify survival.

Indeed, we have recently been made aware of pilot schemes set up to evaluate such changes in practice. In an interview with managers of a local enterprise agency we were told that the Department of Employment is, at the time of writing, examining, through these pilots, a change in entry requirements to the EAS wherein applicants must show that they have gone through the *process* of preparing a business plan (although they do not actually have to have produced one). These same professionals suspected that this was a move inspired, not by an increasing concern for the welfare of people in EAS businesses, but rather a method for reducing costs and the numbers of people using the scheme at a time when unemployment was seen as less of a problem nationally. They also thought that this new demand would probably mean that the numbers taking up Employment Training would increase, as aspiring entrants to the EAS were forced to attend recognized courses in business planning (e.g. through the 'Enterprise in ET' option). Local enterprise centres, as ever, were busily arranging new courses (and applying for appropriate funding) to meet these new requirements.

Although more efficient targeting of the EAS and other support would certainly fit in with the overall political ideology of the present Government, and would possibly help save public money (by not funding those firms likely to fail), this must be weighed against the increased costs of administering the scheme if more rigorous tests of commercial viability are to be introduced, and the need to help those in need (i.e. the unemployed) who wish to set up businesses (NAO, 1988).

Furthermore, it is by no means certain that it is, in fact, possible to select at an early stage those new firms bound for commercial glory. Gill studied the factors affecting the survival and growth of smaller companies and concluded that 'there is no golden rule or formula which will identify future success however measured' (1985:207). 'How to succeed' handbooks aimed at aspiring entrepreneurs may well offer sensible advice about pitfalls to be avoided. But there are numerous influences of different sorts which can be part of the complex mix of economic, social, psychological and other factors that result in failure or success; and, as Gill says, to proffer one prescription for success to an intending or practising business person would be to fall into an easy and attractive reductionist trap.[5] Whilst psychologists, in particular, have sought the personality trait which is the magic key to entrepreneurial success, we should not attempt to distil the wide variety of experiences of enterprise into simplistic rules.

In our own project it proved very difficult to isolate factors which might explain the success of some and the failure of others (see Chapters

6 and 7). The similarities between those who fell and those who were the winners in the enterprise game outweighed the differences that we observed. Virtually all the 'fallers' displayed the same level of commitment, hard work and motivation to enterprise as did the 'runners'. Admittedly, material factors seemed to play a part. For instance, a reasonable level of business capital in the earliest days of business start-up was found to be important for success. But then again, one informant, Stewart who imported and exported Turkish rugs, started his successful business with very little money. What advice could we offer here? Not to start businesses unless you have lots of money? While this may, after reading the accounts in Chapters 5, 6 and 7, appear to be sound advice, it would also appear bland and unhelpful to the people who start new businesses in order to escape the poverty and depression of unemployment. (This is not to say that practical advice cannot be offered to young people thinking of starting their own business. In Appendix 1 we have *attempted* to collate some 'advice for the intending entrepreneur' passed to us by our informants).

The task of picking winners in this way has been described to us as a 'minefield' by researchers with more experience of small business research than ourselves. Although we feel unable to contribute to the selectivity debate with any real degree of authority, what we can draw attention to is the need to remain flexible in deciding enterprise polices. On the one hand, it would be easy to call for greater selectivity in the public funding of new business start-ups, but, on the other hand, it would appear difficult to isolate the criteria by which such funding should be allocated. Virtually all our informants would appear to have few objective factors in their favour. They were working with very low levels of capital, they had very marginal market locations, their businesses were very small, they had to compete on a very local basis with well established firms, their experience of business management was non-existent, they had minimal support, training or backing, and, in the main, they did not manufacture products.

They are further disadvantaged by their age and by their area. Recent surveys of the EAS have shown that 'survivors' were more likely to be older than 'non-survivors' and more 'non-survivors' than 'survivors' were aged under 35 (Department of Employment, 1988b). Although it has been argued by us and others (Finn, 1986; Bevan *et al.*, 1989) that young people are likely to play a bigger part in the small business sphere in the future, they face more problems than other age groups. These are documented in Chapters 5, 6 and 7 but we draw attention to just two here. Firstly, young people are less likely than older people to be warmly received by banks. They usually have little collateral or finances of their own (or the appropriate cultural capital) with which to generate necessary business capital. Secondly, they often have minimal skills or little experience of important aspects of business management.

We would argue that young people in Cleveland are placed at further disadvantage by the local labour market and the cultures of work which have developed on Teesside. The small business literature shows that one of the biggest boosts to a new business is family experience of small business ownership. We have illustrated how this was quite rare for this new breed of entrepreneur and that unemployment was the major factor influencing business start-up. Again surveys of the EAS have identified problems associated with areas of high unemployment; 'survivors' are less likely to have experienced long spells of unemployment than 'non-survivors' (RBL Research International, 1987). The high levels of unemployment in Cleveland, and in the career trajectories of our informants, suggest, then, that they are likely to be less successful than their counterparts in other parts of the country.

This may help explain the skew in self-employment and EAS take-up away from areas like the North-East (Finn, 1986; Bevan *et al.*, 1989). Only 6.2 per cent of EAS entrants come from the Northern region compared with 23.6 per cent from London (House of Commons Public Accounts Committee, 1989). There are many possible reasons for this: for example, the relative size of the population and client groups, or the level of previous demand for the scheme. But we would argue that local unemployment rates and local demand for goods and services play a large part in limiting the development of self-employment on Teesside. Given the types of businesses likely to be helped by measures like the EAS (i.e. microfirms operating in the service sector with minimal potential for growth) the contribution of such firms to local economic regeneration is likely to be small. Moreover, such firms are likely to be more successful in the areas which need them the least — the more prosperous parts of the country where there are potentially more customers with higher disposable income (Nabarro *et al.*, 1986). A policy of assisting the small firm (at the expense of the large firm) runs the risk of being regionally divisive (Storey, 1982); the areas with the greatest take-up of such assistance are likely to be the more prosperous regions with high levels of employment.

Given these general disadvantages of age and area and the more specific characteristics we described earlier, it is highly probable that the vast majority of our informants would *not* have received funding had selectivity measures been in place when they started up. These young men and women from Teesside stand right on the bottom rung of the small business ladder. If anybody was to be excluded from enterprise in the increased targeting of support to likely winners, it would be our informants.

Yet around 10 per cent became successful, generated a small but significant number of jobs and were likely to grow and trade in the future. Selectivity measures may well have thrown these entrepreneurial babies out with the bath water. Others, whilst not being what we could call particularly successful, had not failed and continued 'to plod along', quietly providing themselves with a job and a living after support from the EAS had stopped. Too often, we feel, analysis of small business policy is based on studies of atypical samples. Until recently very little work had been done on service sector businesses and most studies tend to focus on quite large, manufacturing concerns at the expense of one-person, service businesses (which statistically dominate self-employment), as Burrows and Curran have pointed out (1989). We suspect that the dynamics of really small businesses (like those we studied) are still not properly understood. As such there may be a tendency to translate unproblematically the criteria by which, say, a manufacturing firm in London employing 250 people is judged successful or not, to the assessment of a mobile hairdressing business run by a young woman in Hartlepool. What counts as success or potential will be very different in each case, as will the problems that each faces.

Despite the persuasive arguments of those lobbying for greater selectivity in funding, we feel unable to come to the conclusion that people like Cath, Ronnie, Shane, Barry and Dawn (see Chapter 7) should not have been allowed the chance to set up in business (and the majority of informants would not have done without the EAS). Many saw their own business as the last chance to achieve something (some pride, recognition, money), and to escape the dispiriting round of unemployment, government schemes, dead-end jobs and more unemployment. After all, £40 per week is not a lot of money and (to repeat the 'register effect' argument), it compares favourably with what it would cost to keep someone unemployed on benefit for a year.

A different interpretation of the selectivity debate would turn this discussion on its head to argue that if this new breed of entrepreneur has all these disadvantages compared to larger businesses and to some other, more favourably situated small businesses, why not provide more, rather than less, support? This presents us with a possible recommendation of greater assistance to those firms wishing to start up in more depressed areas, especially to those firms begun by young people and other disadvantaged groups. Differential, regional scales of EAS support could be implemented, with depressed areas like Teesside targeted for greater levels of business start-up funding. Also there is no reason why funding should be limited to one year in areas starved of jobs (or indeed for as long as one year in areas deemed to be advantageous to new firm formation). We strongly recommend that policy-makers consider the introduction of other sources of grants to young business people to replace the now abandoned RDG. The job creation potential of this sort of funding has been supported in a recent analysis of the scheme (Wren, 1989).

In concluding this section, we find it difficult to go beyond listing the strengths and weaknesses of the case for greater selectivity; what can be said more definitely is that there are more moral, social, economic and political questions raised by the selectivity debate than there are answers.

Youth, Enterprise and Policy for the 1990s: Final Remarks

In 1975, Sir Keith Joseph laid bare the ideological foundations for the enterprise project of the coming Thatcher government:

> We are debating a very important subject — nothing less than the prospects for the prosperity of the country and the solidarity of our liberties . . . The convenience of our daily lives and the functioning of our economy depend upon a pulsing fabric of more or less vigorous enterprise, the self-employed and small businesses. The very seedbed of our economy is composed of medium and small businesses . . . The vitality of our economy, the vitality of our country as a whole, and the vitality of individual towns and cities depends not upon large establishments but upon the untidy growth of small, constantly adaptive competing businesses . . . There is a close link between economic, social, cultural and political liberties, and at the heart of that link is the small business man and the self-employed. (House of Commons, 13 March 1975, quoted in Ritchie, 1984)

We have traced the practical outcomes of this aggrandizement of enterprise and charted the helter-skelter of new programmes and schemes that followed. Enterprise education can be seen as ideological training for some of the nation's youth. The Victorian values of Samuel Smiles have been prioritized, propagandized and passed into local practice in areas like Teesside and accepted without much critical debate or opposition, transforming swathes of educational and training policy with beguiling Training Agency grants as they go. Courses and initiatives are steeped in quite explicit, free market ideology. We wonder what the reaction would have been if courses were set up with public money to train young people, not in the dynamics of capitalist business management, but in how to start unions, to raise wages and to fight for better conditions for workers. After all, these activities and concerns are no more or less political or ideological than the advice given to young people on how to start small businesses, and how to make profits.

Given our conclusions about the mixed motivations of the EAS (to reduce the embarrassment of unemployment and at the same time to stimulate the economic vitality of depressed areas), it is difficult to avoid the conclusion that the real objectives behind the enterprise movement are defined more by political ideology than by a realistic and credible set of social and economic plans.

Fifteen years after Sir Keith Joseph's speech, Lord Young, in his autobiography, reflected as follows: 'the need for enterprise, for small firms, for self-employment, the simple acceptance of the necessity to create wealth before we spend it, has become generally accepted' (1990:326–7). Peter Morgan, who is currently Director General of the Institute of Directors, returned to the same themes but he concluded that 'the enterprise culture has not yet won the battle for Britain'. In an address to the Institute of Directors Annual Convention at the Royal Albert Hall on 27 February 1990, Peter Morgan set out to produce a 'coherent vision' of the enterprise culture and then discussed 'the obstacles which are in the way of that vision'. We quote at length to give one possible scenario for Britain in the 1990s:

> An enterprise culture is one in which every individual understands that the world does not owe him or her a living, and so we act together accordingly, all working for the success of UK PLC... successful companies, which regularly make profit and grow, are the flagships of the enterprise culture. Directors who lead those successful companies are heroes of the enterprise culture... In an enterprise culture the whole nation understands that we are locked in competition with other nations. We are all soldiers in a global economic war... Some competitors are disturbingly professional about these issues. The West Germans in business behave uncomfortably like the East Germans in sport — they pick their players while they are still in school and then coach them meticulously until they are old enough to compete ... The sorry state of education and training means, that in effect, we [in this country] confront panzer divisions with the home guard ...

He goes on:

> But we've come far enough to identify the obstacles to progress. There are three main problems: establishment attitudes, the middle class salariat; and what the dictionary calls the lumpen proletariat ... It is obvious that responsibility for the 100 years of decline of UK PLC must be laid at the door of the 'establishment' which purported to guide the affairs of the nation ... What do I mean by the term 'middle class salariat'? I mean our vast body of state employees who don't have to worry where the next pay check is coming from: in nationalized industries, in central government, in social security, in local government, in schools and

universities, and in health, where Kenneth Clark is confronting one million of them almost single-handed . . . What do I mean by our third obstacle, the lumpen proletariat? I mean the mass of the population we choose not to educate . . . Less educated people are less able to profit from the enterprise culture. Because they cannot profit from enterprise, they are thrown into the dependency culture . . . Our task is to deliver the goods — create the wealth — and win more hearts and minds for capitalism and enterprise . . . The government must keep the faith.

Given the military metaphors which litter this passage, Peter Morgan's title of Director General seems most appropriate. The military analogy is employed to celebrate the triumph of the free market and it is sustained for fifteen pages of high-blown invective which also contains the admission that 'in preparation for our global economic war, many officers have not been to Sandhurst' (11). It is tempting to dismiss the brutality and the intemperate nature of the language as ridiculous, but as Richard Roberts (1990) has argued, this powerful rhetoric has for the last eleven years been translated into social reality and the lives of millions of people have been adversely affected as a result.

Roberts has further pointed out that this form of rhetoric denies that it is rhetorical. Sentences which begin 'Enterprise people know that . . . ' or 'It is obvious that . . . ' are trying to persuade us to accept some simple and obvious truths established by practical men of business and to forget alternative explanations. In Roberts' words, what is avoided most of all is 'the ethical void at the heart of capitalism' (1990). Peter Morgan's notion of social responsibility, for example, consists of handouts by the rich to their favourite charities: in his own words, 'we are now in a position to share our good fortune with causes in which we have a personal interest, whether the arts, the environment or the disadvantaged' (14).

In relation to our informants and their attempts to enrol in the army of successful entrepreneurs, what is missing from Peter Morgan's vision is the realization that in any battle, economic or otherwise, there will be victors and vanquished and casualties on both sides ('fallers' as well as 'runners'). As society becomes increasingly more sophisticated, technical and specialized, we all become more and more dependent upon one another; and as the ratchet of international competition is constantly twisted upwards, company after company, together with the communities which provide them with workers, will fail, with all the attendant pain and poverty. The consequence for any society, as Richard Titmuss argued (1963:55) 'which invests more of its values and virtues in the promotion of the individual, is individual failure and individual consciousness of failure' (quoted by Bill Williamson, 1990:287). Certainly, some of our informants, like Trevor and Lynne, felt the pain of individual failure acutely and, in a culture which stresses individual achievement, are left blaming themselves rather than, say, the low level of economic activity in the local economy.

Some of the central mechanisms of free-market capitalism produce not only dejected and despairing individuals who have been thrown out of work but depressed and marginalized regions like the North-East. The international nature of trade and commerce whereby jobs do not disappear off the face of the earth but are switched to Japan, South Korea and the Philippines means that there are strict limits to what can be achieved by any one economy through the constant drive for competitive advantage. As Raymond Williams put it:

> It may seem for a time to make sense, until you realize that *everyone*, every economy is doing this. I know that I have gone from reading the English newspapers on these familiar themes and then read... the French or the Italian or the German newspapers only to realize, beyond the differences in language, that the same analyses were being applied, the same remedies proposed, as if each were the only people in the world. This talk is described by its practitioners as tough and realistic, but even where it is benevolent it is a fantasy... Yet most of this talk is by smooth men in sleek offices taking no significant risks. The real toughness is all at the other end... (1983:96, emphasis as in original)

What we need now is an alternative vision, another set of values to replace the violent, divisive future advocated by Peter Morgan. Increasingly over the last ten years, the idea of freedom has become narrowed to the freedom to make money, the only form of wealth which is now publicly acknowledged is the accumulation of private possessions, and enterprise has, in the main, been reduced to self-employment in small business.

Bill Williamson has caught the current mood of the British people as they search, at an individual level, for ways of coping with Thatcherism; 'It is not that people have become more selfish: rather it is that selfish behaviour has become more necessary' (1990:231). And nowhere more necessary than in education where, as Ruth Jonathan (1989) has argued, the introduction of market forces will intensify competition among parents over places in maintained schools thought to be desirable and will put pressure on parents to behave selfishly to protect the interests of their own children, whether they believe in the ethics of a market in education or not. In a highly competitive market, where economic and cultural capital are unequally distributed among the competitors, 'freedom for the pike is death for the minnow' (Tawney, 1964:164). We need to rekindle the notion that the education, the training and the employment of *other people's* children is a collective responsibility which cannot be left to

257

chance or to a market where the strong, the informed and the wealthy ensure the success of *their* children and politely wring their hands about the plight of those left behind. There is a need for a broader, more fraternal and more generous vision of society where freedom and equality are seen, again in Tawney's words, 'not as antagonists but as allies' (1964:26).

It is, however, all too easy to produce a list of alternative values — solidarity, justice, freedom, equality, hope, social cohesion and so on — but it is another matter entirely to translate such replacement rhetoric into a substantive programme of action.

We have decided to contribute to the policy debate partly because the task is so often ducked by social scientists and partly because our study of the concept and practice of enterprise has, perforce, involved us in the evaluation of political initiatives at a local and national level. We do, however, acknowledge at the outset that our suggestions are not so much rooted in our ethnographic research with young adults, as in our interviews with key professionals, our reading of the relevant literature and our understanding of the current political scene. Criticism, however, is easy and construction difficult: we end with a few suggestions for national policy.

Beyond Exclusive Reliance on the Market

The free market is still seen by the Conservative Government as *the* solution to the very problems which the inefficiencies of the market created in the first place. As a result of their faith in market forces, a faith which has proved impervious to evidence or argument, the TECs are likely to be given more and more responsibilities (now that the Training Agency has been transformed into the Training, Enterprise and Education Division of the Department of Employment, the transfer of non-advanced further education is under active consideration at the time of writing), but no real power to stimulate local economic development. The present Government's professed opposition to central planning and its belief in the magical power of markets has led and will continue to lead it to hand over more and more of the responsibility for (and the cost of) training to employers. As ever, business and commerce are likely to concentrate on making profits in the short-term and their response to a squeeze on profits or a recession will be to cut their training budgets, just as happened in the 1970s. But the leaders of the business world have been entrusted by the Government not just with attending to the needs of today's markets but also with the task of creating a new culture of continuing education, training and enterprise to meet the needs of tomorrow. Our first conclusion regarding policy, then, is that the dogma of the efficiency of unregulated markets must be abandoned before it does more harm. Lee *et al.* conclude their six years of research into the workings of Youth Training Schemes in a prosperous town in the South-East, by arguing that:

> the Government is going in precisely the wrong direction in equating the behaviour of individual employers with the public good. It is useless in a system whose whole rationale is based on short-term competitive individualism to expect hard-pressed employers to behave altruistically with an eye to the long-term public interest. Investment in British industry as a whole suffers the disease of 'short-termism'. And as our findings confirm, individual employers will only invest in workers they intend to use for their own production needs. (1990:192)

One wonders for how long the chief executives of British companies will continue to serve on the Boards of TECs if government funding is continually being reduced, if employers generally are expected to contribute more and more to the costs of training and if their remit to develop local economies remains as constricted as at present. TEC chairmen (and nearly all are, of course, chair*men*) are also concerned lest the TECs become, in effect, the Training Agency operating under yet another name; they are worried about the former staff of the TA, who found employment in their local TEC, bringing with them their administrative procedures and hierarchical ways of thinking, which are considered to be overly-bureaucratic by business executives used to seeing their decisions acted upon speedily.

The Role of Government

The retreat by the Thatcher Government from the setting of national targets for education and training is creating a vacuum of leadership at the top which will not be easy for eighty-two local TECs to fill. Norman Fowler, the former Secretary of State for Employment, listed a number of objectives for the training of young people and adults in a speech in December 1989, but the Government has since argued that it does not make sense to set targets if it cannot deliver them. That stance has not prevented the Government from making the defeat of inflation its primary economic objective. Attending conferences of educationists and employers over the last few years has convinced us that both groups have now become aware of Britain's precarious economic future and how this rests on our comparatively weak education and training base. Both parties have begun to articulate the wish to be part of a national campaign to improve our knowledge and skills base, but they will look in vain to this Government for a long-term vision which would set out the objectives of a national plan for education, training and employment (ETE), or stress the urgency of the timetable and seek national consensus for its implementation.

Over the past year, we have also witnessed the development of a remarkable consensus over the need for such a national strategy, a consensus which has been supported by the CBI in their report *Towards a Skills Revolution* (1989) and the TUC in their document *Skills 2000* (1989). Both sides of industry have come to realize not only that there is an appreciable gap between the competence and qualifications of British workers and those of our competitors, but also that the gap is steadily widening. The Government, trapped by their reliance on market forces, continues to abrogate its responsibilities.

But what should the role of government be in the production of a national strategy for ETE? Apart from the leadership function mentioned above, government could help to jack up the whole system by setting national targets for education and training and so raise the expectations of both employers and employees, as the French Government has done so successfully over the last twenty years (Steedman, 1990). In addition, if a high tech/high value added economy is to be created in the United Kingdom, then strategic guidance needs to be issued and premium funding targeted at the key areas where success is considered to be vital. A single, national system of vocational qualifications needs to be established, with renewed emphasis on access, progression through the system, and evaluation to ensure quality. The National Council for Vocational Qualifications was established by the present Government in 1986. It has since introduced a National Record of Vocational Achievement, but more recently its funds have been cut and it has been set the unrealistic objective by Government Ministers of becoming self-financing. If, as the Government believes, responsibility needs to be pushed down the line to local decision-makers, then the question becomes: are the short-term tactics of the eighty-two TECs in England and Wales likely to constitute a national strategy for the future? In sharp contrast, the Japanese who have built the most successful economy in the world since the Second World War, believe that:

> the state has a vital role to play in raising the nation's standards of vocational competence ... Japanese Ministries are active in testing for the additional purpose of raising standards of competence — of plumbers and printers, cooks and computer-programmers — in the interest of national efficiency. (Dore and Sako, 1989:ix, xiv)

A Strategy for the Regions

Government intervention is needed to prevent Cleveland and the North-East as a whole slipping further behind the more prosperous parts of the South of England and of Europe. Without devolution of power to the regions, the Single European Act of 1992 and the opening of the Channel Tunnel will exacerbate the difficulties of regions like Scotland, South Wales, the North-East and the North-West of England. In our view, the infant Hercules of the nineteenth Century has become the 'shackled Hercules' (Saunders, 1983:2) of the late twentieth century and will not be able to struggle free without government intervention.

In 1986, one of us was writing:

> the North has in recent decades been transformed into a 'global outpost'. It has neither the economic resources nor the political clout to solve its own problems. There is no-one to speak for the region in Whitehall, Brussels or beyond, in the way that the Secretaries of State for Scotland and Wales represent their areas'. (Coffield *et al.*, 1986:218)

Since then there has been no advance towards creating a tier of regional government which would allow more strategic decisions to be taken in the North-East and which would play on its considerable strengths (see Osmond, 1988). The rhetoric of government, which has come to dominate every aspect of policy, has stressed individual choice and increased freedom for consumers: the reality has been *not* creeping, but galloping, centralization of power.

A New Education, Training and Enterprise Culture without Legislation?

Let us for a moment do what social researchers are so notoriously bad at — taking a risk and making a prediction. We are of the view that TEC Board members are unlikely to succeed in persuading sufficient ordinary, British employers to invest in their own workers, that they may be dispirited and frustrated by the number and the significance of the responsibilities handed down to them by government, that their entrepreneurial and reforming zeal may become dampened by the deadening bureaucracy of seconded TA staff, and that they finally become angered by being asked to pick up the lion's share of the tabs. As they become increasingly exhausted and defeated by their efforts to create a new education, training and enterprise culture by persuasion, they will tend to resign from the TECs and return full-time to their own firms.

At that point another approach will be necessary to clear up the mess — the TECs could then be reconstituted with adequate representation from the trades unions, education and perhaps even young people and clients generally. Such a move would re-establish the tripartite arrangements (government, employers *and* trade unions) for the planning of training which were abandoned when the Training Commission was abolished in 1988; the cooperation achieved by the 'social partners' in France and Germany is often cited as one of the major reasons for their industrial prosperity. Legislation could then be passed which encouraged employers to train their own workers or pay someone else to do so and they would forfeit around 1 per cent, say, of their profits, in taxation, if they failed to comply. The law would also be used to ensure that employers complied with nationally agreed training standards. Legislation on both these issues has been in operation in the Federal Republic of West Germany and France for many years and could with advantage be introduced into this country, perhaps avoiding much of the bureaucracy with which the German system is enmeshed.

Proposals for legislation are bound to be opposed by some employers, especially by the 20 per cent of British employers who 'had not given any training to any of their employees during 1986/87' (Training Agency, 1989d:81). The findings of the report *Training in Britain* (Training Agency 1989d), for example, that one in three individuals of working age have no qualifications (p. 55), that 'one-third of 19–34 year olds, and almost one-half of those aged 35 and over, said they could not imagine any circumstances in which they would seek to undertake any further education or training' (p. 80), show very starkly the mountain that has still to be climbed. The next few years will test both the good intentions of all employers and the Government's reliance on voluntary action, and our prediction is that legislation will prove to be necessary sooner rather than later.

After the above had been written, the House of Lords Select Committee on the European Communities issued a report in September 1990 on *Vocational Training and Re-training*. This cross-party committee has produced an admirably concise and incisive report which proposes the establishment of a 'national strategic framework for vocational training' for all age groups in the United Kingdom. Its ten recommendations are worth quoting in full because they are comprehensive in nature and because they summarize and go beyond the discussion of the previous pages:

1 analysis of future national training requirements, particularly those resulting from technological change;
2 clear objectives and detailed targets for improving training performance;

3   plans for installing and maintaining a single national system of vocational qualifications and standards;

4   the provision of individual records of achievement prepared for all young people;

5   arrangements for providing individuals with access to the information they need to make informed training and career choices;

6   proposals for monitoring and improving training quality;

7   ways of improving access to training, including policies designed to ensure equal opportunities;

8   specific proposals for increasing women's access to training, particularly returners to the labour market;

9   specific incentives to be used to encourage employers and employees, including small businesses, to improve training;

10   plans for monitoring and evaluating national training performance.

(1990, para. 92)

The Committee concluded that this framework would need legislative underpinning to act as a catalyst for change 'given the scale of the gap between the United Kingdom and its main industrial competitors . . . and given the long history of failure which has marked the voluntary approach to training in this country' (para. 118). It also considers that 'legislation should be introduced which would ensure that all 16–18 year olds are provided with education or training' (para. 119).

The history of the Thatcher years of the 1980s had begun to be written as the journey down an epic road to economic recovery, a new ideological vision of a bright, shining world of enterprise turned into an economic miracle of declining inflation, rapidly falling unemployment and a record number of jobs created. The beginning of the new decade has already shown that much of this story has been written in sand. Whilst we are sure some jobs have been created and some parts of the country have become prosperous, other areas, like Cleveland and other people, like the majority of those we talked to, have been by-passed by the enterprise express to recovery and prosperity.

During the short lifespan of our project — from October 1988 to September 1990 — we have seen quite a dramatic change, if not reversal, in the economic climate of Britain. At the time of writing, unemployment, which had been falling fast according to the figures, has now, as adjudged by the same figures, started to rise again. The word recession is on the lips of politicians and economists and the CBI have warned of a high interest rate 'crisis' for small firms (Halsall, 1990). Inflation is back in double figures, the balance of payments is in record deficit and there are now roughly 600,000 more people (officially) unemployed than in 1979

(Elliot, 1990). Company failures have soared to their highest level for ten years (Beavis, 1990). Indeed, the Forum of Private Business has argued that high interest rates 'robbed' Britain of nearly one million jobs in 1989 as small firms were forced to cut back on plans for expansion (Wood-cock, 1990a). We know from our evidence that it will take much to defeat the ambitions and hopes of the young women and men we talked to. But it is also true that, when the economy tightens, it is often the smallest businesses who are the last to be paid by clients (often larger businesses) and the first to go bust. The collapse of one large firm can take with it, in a domino effect, several dependent smaller ones. Hard times for young business people seem set to continue.

We have found that young people in business are not the shock troops of the government's ideological programme but just ordinary people finding new ways to survive when times are hard, or if they are the lucky few, running successful small firms through working long and hard in the 'enterprise culture'. Our informants have no real faith in enterprise, they do not expect to become millionaires or even to become comfortably off; rather they ask only for the chance to make a decent living. Their resilience and their perseverence keep them going through the poverty they face in running risky businesses and, in the absence of a more coherent and sustained programme for economic renewal, we wish them the best of luck.

Notes

1   Very few studies in Britain (e.g. Rees, 1986; Hobbs, 1988; Blackburn and Curran, 1990) have examined youth enterprise with a sociological eye.
2   The image that Nicholaus (1968) conjured up in the 1960s of sociologists raising a palm up to the ruling-class for funding but casting their eyes down to the activities of the working class, comes to mind.
3   The main aim of our new research project, which has been funded through a grant from the ESRC, is to extend our examination of youth enterprise and new careers by investigating changing patterns of work for older groups of people. The project *Adults, Enterprise and New Forms of Work in a Depressed Area of Britain* will widen the scope of our investigations to include people over the age of twenty-five. A three-year research period will allow a much more in-depth analysis of theoretical and policy-related questions. We will employ a broadly qualitative approach and focus upon the following five critical 'non-traditional' forms of work and employment:

  1   self-employment and enterprise initiatives
  2   co-operatives and community based projects
  3   voluntary work
  4   migration and moving away from Teesside for work
  5   the informal economy

4   In September 1990 we held a seminar/workshop at the University of Durham at which we presented our research and conclusions to many of the key people working in the fields of education, training and enterprise in Cleveland. The main purpose of the meeting was to enter into a dialogue with the participants in order to check the relevance and applicability of our policy suggestions. Our thanks, for their helpful and constructive comments, is acknowledged here, even if they do not recognize their contributions in this final version of our conclusions.

5   However, we recently discovered a list of six 'golden rules for the entrepreneur' (Robinson, D., 1990:113) which included advice ranging from 'know yourself' (golden rule number one) to 'be prepared to change' (number six).

Appendix

Advice for the Intending Entrepreneur

The *Unemployment Unit* (1990) has recently published a short booklet providing practical information to prospective 'entrepreneurs' (available from The Unemployment Unit, 9, Poland Street, London, W1V 3DG). The thrust of the guidance it offers is summed up in its title *In With Your Eyes Open*; it aims to provide detailed advice about entrance requirements to the Enterprise Allowance Scheme, benefit entitlements, different methods of running businesses and it describes the likely chances of success and difficulties that can be encountered. It makes welcome reading and certainly acts as an antidote to some of the more gung-ho approaches to youth enterprise to be found in the training materials and curricula of the enterprise industry. We recommend it to any person considering starting up a business.

Whilst we are hesitant about offering our own guidance to those thinking about starting up in business (that was not, after all, one of our objectives) we feel that it is, on balance, a worthwhile task. We hope that this book will find its way into the hands of people working in local enterprise industries and be useful to them. It is not designed to be a purely academic text, though we expect that some practitioners working in youth enterprise will feel it to be overly abstract, theoretical and (we hope) critical. We do not presume to do their job for them but what we attempt to do in this Appendix is to spell out some of the issues that our informants raised as important for others intending to become self-employed. These are not 'golden rules' for business success, but issues to be borne in mind when embarking upon the enterprise path. The points covered are by no means exhaustive and can only supplement the professional advice available from workers in the youth training, education and enterprise arena.

Perhaps more importantly, academic texts on youth tend to do little to address themselves directly to their subject group. The following points have been written for people aged between 16 and 25 and it is hoped that this Appendix will be used by enterprise advisers working with young women and men who are considering enterprise.

1 First, and most importantly, we would urge prospective business people to consider their options fully before embarking upon the enterprise path. We uncovered many depressing stories of business failure or, more frequently, simply disheartening and unrewarded effort. Whilst the media often contains upbeat images of 'whizzkids winning the survival stakes' we found that these do not convey the reality of youth enterprise. From the outside being your own boss can appear glamorous and financially lucrative. From the inside it often becomes very mundane, badly paid and arduous. However, there are less tangible rewards — feelings of pride, self-respect and self-achievement, for instance — which can make it a more attractive option than, say, a dead-end job or unemployment.

2 If you do decide to start your own business, we strongly recommend that you seek as much advice and help as possible in the early stages of thinking about your enterprise. There are now numerous agencies and organizations offering such guidance. These range from initial one-to-one counselling, to enterprise training courses of various lengths and the provision of cheap workshops, offices and start-up units. To find out the addresses of such agencies, contact your local Training and Enterprise Council.

3 Spend as much time as possible researching and planning your business idea. This can often appear to be pointless, frustrating and diversionary, especially when you really want to get your business on the rails. However, a number of the people in our study told us that they wished they had worked out their plans more thoroughly in the early days. This helps prevent mistakes and problems in the long-term. For instance, one man set up as a freelance photographer only to find later that the local phone book listed dozens of people doing the same thing. His business collapsed in less than a year due to the high level of competition. Assess your local market to see if there is a niche in it for your business, a niche which has not been already filled by others.

4 Investigate the different ways that businesses can be run. Many enterprise agencies tend to promote self-employment in terms of sole-traderships (i.e. setting up a business to work on your own). This may be what you want but it is wise to consider the other options. We came across a number of young people who were involved in their own enterprises in different ways from this most common method. Co-operatives and partnerships are two other possibilities which we suggest you explore before coming to a decision.

5 In choosing a type of business activity (i.e. the sort of job that you will be doing in self-employment) try to pick an idea that is relatively novel, original or uncommon. Most new businesses are simply copies of

ones already existing and they have to compete with larger firms doing the same thing in the local area. Avoid over-crowded markets, if you can.

6   One of the main issues that people raised was their lack of money (business capital). Those with finances to inject into their new businesses, not surprisingly, tended to do a lot better than those who ran their enterprises on a shoestring. Lack of business in the early stages did much to restrict the development of many new firms. They could not afford to advertise properly, to rent decent premises, to buy necessary stock or to take on staff. Additionally, many people came to rely too heavily on the £40 per week from the EAS. When this finished after a year, a high proportion of people go out of business (or soon after). Our advice is to seek help with your finances from as many sources as possible (from parents, friends, banks, Prince's Youth Business Trust, Livewire and so on). However, be sure that you will be able to afford to pay it back (with interest if applicable). Whilst it always seems risky to borrow money, many firms will have no chance of success without it. Before you start up in business give some thought to how you will cope once the Enterprise Allowance ends at the end of the first year. As one person put it to us: 'It is OK to be earning £50 per week when you are eighteen, but is that going to be enough when you are in your mid-twenties?'. In other words, do not expect to become rich through enterprise and think about how your business might grow over time.

7   Be careful about where you run your business from. There are a number of options (home, start-up units, rented properties) and each has its pros and cons. One drawback associated with business premises that was mentioned by a lot of people was the lack of visibility of their businesses to their customers or potential customers. They had to compete with high street shops from out of the way and poorly located units and offices.

8   Once the business is up and running do not hesitate to request further advice, support and help from enterprise agencies. That is what they are there for and they are the experts, but they won't come to you unless you ask them to. Being self-employed can be a lonely business and occasionally people run into problems (e.g. with book-keeping or marketing) that they can't solve on their own. Do not be afraid to ask for help.

9   However, be careful about from whom you seek advice. There are plenty of free advice agencies to help young people into business, so be wary of individuals who charge for their services. One or two people we talked to reported being 'ripped off' by con-men who promised to help them get grants for a fee, only to find that they provided little useful or new information. The enterprise culture has its shadier side and young

people new to business are prime targets for less scrupulous business people or those who would wish to make quick profits at their expense.

10   Before you even begin, find out what is involved in closing down a business. This may be the furthest thing from your mind as you struggle to find outlets for your goods or services, but enterprise agencies are very good at starting people up in business (with plenty of advice in the early stages), but not so good in helping people to close down once they run into insurmountable troubles. In particular, find out about debts and who is responsible for them, about going bankrupt and about the legal situation you might find yourself in if the business collapses or you have simply had enough of it and want to quit. Ask about the differences between sole-tradeships and limited companies. Each has its disadvantages and advantages as a way of being in business, but sometimes having a limited company can mean less personal responsibility for debts incurred in closing a business. Knowing the worst possible outcome may help you to avoid it.

11   Running a business demands a lot of hard work, commitment and long hours for often little income in the first few years. Indeed, there is no guarantee that you will ever make much money. Some people, very much a minority, become very successful and can earn quite large amounts. Do not be fooled into thinking that these people are typical or that success comes easily. For every 'whizz-kid' or wheeler-dealer, there are another nine or ten people who will continue to struggle or fail (according to our evidence from Teesside). Consider the impact of such long hours and poor financial rewards on your social life.

12   Many people start businesses in order to turn a hobby or skill into a way of making a living if they are unemployed or have been made redundant. However, having your own business involves additional knowledge and skills (e.g. sales, time management, organization, communication) which many people may find challenging. In short, you may have to be a jack of all trades *and* a master of one.

13   Becoming your own boss will almost certainly have implications for your friends, family or domestic partner. They can provide invaluable (and unpaid) support to a new business, but you may also wish to consider the possible impact on them of the early years when your business is likely to be risky.

14   Informants to our study mentioned other more specific advice to us which ranged from the tip to avoid at the beginning expensive forms of advertising, such as local newspapers, which can bring little return in new

trade, to the advisability of employing an accountant to sort out book-keeping.

15 If you have parents, friends, or relatives who have experience of self-employment or working in a co-operative, spend time with them finding out what their experiences have been, what they have learned and what relevance they have to your plans.

16 If you decide to go ahead, after carefully considering all the above points and getting all the help you need, then good luck from both of us.

Bibliography

ABERCROMBIE, N., HILL, S. and TURNER, B.S. (1986) *Sovereign Individuals of Capitalism*, London, Allen and Unwin.

AINLEY, P. and CORNEY, M. (1990) *Training for the Future and the Rise and Fall of the MSC*, London, Cassell.

ALLEN, D. and HUNN, A. (1985) 'An evaluation of the EAS', *Employment Gazette*, 93, 8, pp. 313–17.

ALLEN, S. *et al.* (Eds) (1986) *The Experience of Unemployment*, London, Macmillan.

ALLEN, S. and TRUMAN, C. (1990) 'Women, business and self-employment: a conceptual minefield', *British Sociological Association Conference*, University of Surrey.

AMIN, A. (1989) 'Flexible specialization and small firms in Italy: myths and realities', *Antipode*, 21, 1, pp. 13–34.

AMIN, A. and ROBINS, K. (1990) 'Not Marshallian times', *British Sociological Association Conference*, University of Surrey.

ASHBY, P. (1989) *Citizenship, Income and Work*, St. George's House, Windsor Castle.

ASHTON, D.N., MAGUIRE, M. and GARLAND, V. (1982) *Youth in the Labour Market*, Research Paper 34, Department of Employment, London.

ASHTON, D.N. and MAGUIRE, M. (1986) *Young Adults in the Labour Market*, Research Paper 55, Department of Employment, London.

ASHTON, D.N., MAGUIRE, M. and SPILSBURY, M. (1988) 'Local labour markets and their impact on the life chances of youth', in COLES, B. (Ed.) *op. cit.*

AUSTRIN, T. and BEYNON, H. (1979) 'Global outpost: The working class experience of big business in the North-East of England 1964–1979', Mimeo, Department of Sociology, University of Durham.

BALDWIN, C. (1986) 'Young women and style in the 1980s', *Social Science Teacher*, 15, 3, pp. 96–7.

BALL, C., KNIGHT, B. and PLANT, S. (1990) *New Goals for an Enterprise Culture*, London, Training for Enterprise Limited.

BANK OF ENGLAND (1989) 'The relationship between employment and unemployment', Discussion Paper, 39, July, London.

BANKS, M. and ULLAH, P. (1987) 'Political attitudes and voting among unemployed and employed youth', *Journal of Adolescence*, 10, 2, pp. 201–16.

BANKS, M. and ULLAH, P. (1988) *Youth Unemployment in the 1980s: its Psychological Effects*, Beckenham, Croom Helm.

BANNOCK, G. (1986) 'The economic role of the small firm in contemporary industrial society', in CURRAN, J. *et al.* (Eds) *op. cit.*

BASTIN, R. (1985) 'Participant observation in social analysis', in WALKER, .R. (Ed.) *op. cit.*

BATES, I. (1988) 'Culture, curriculum and caring: an exploration of economic socialization of YTS girls', *ESRC 16 to 19 Initiative Occasional Paper Series*, No. 5, London, City University.

BATES, I. *et al.* (1984) *Schooling for the Dole?*, London, MacMillan.

BEAVIS, S. (1990) 'Company failures soar to highest level for ten years', *The Guardian*, 9 July.

BECHHOFER, F. and ELLIOTT, B. (1978) 'The voice of small business and the politics of survival', *Sociological Review*, 26, 1, pp. 57–88.

BELL, C. and ROBERTS, H. (Eds) (1984) *Social Researching: Politics, Problems and Practice*, London, Routledge and Kegan Paul.

BELL, T. (1985) *At the Works*, London, Virago.

BEVAN, J. *et al.* (1989) *Barriers to Business Start Up: A Study of Flow into and out of Self Employment*, Research Paper 71, Department of Employment, London.

BEYNON, H. (1973) *Working For Ford*, Harmondsworth, Penguin.

BEYNON, H. *et al.* (1985) 'Middlesbrough: contradictions in economic and social change', *Middlesbrough Locality Study*, No. 1, University of Durham.

BEYNON, H., HUDSON, R. and SADLER, D. (1986) 'The growth and internationalisation of Teesside's chemicals industry', *Middlesbrough Locality Study*, No. 3, University of Durham.

BEYNON, H. *et al.* (1987) 'Left to Rot? Middlesbrough in the 1980s', *Urban Change and Conflict Conference*, University of Kent, Canterbury.

BILLIG, M. (1989) 'Psychology, rhetoric and cognition', in *History of the Human Sciences*, 2, 3, pp. 289–307.

BINKS, M. and JENNINGS, A. (1986) 'Small firms as a source of economic rejuvenation', in CURRAN, J. *et al.* (Eds) *op. cit.*

BLACKBURNE, L. and JACKSON, M. (1988) 'Thousands of youngsters face penniless Christmas', *Times Educational Supplement*, 16 December.

BLUMER, H. (1956) 'Sociological Analysis and the Variable', in LAZARSFELD, P.F. *et al.* (Eds), *Continuities in the Language of Social Research*, New York, Free Press.

BLYTHE, S. *et al.* (1989a) *On Course for Business*, London, Small Business Research Trust.

BLYTHE, S. *et al.* (1989b) 'Causal elements in the development of enterprise culture — some empirical evidence', *12th National Small Firms Policy and Research Conference*, Thames Polytechnic.

BOARD OF TRADE (BoT) (1963) *The North-East: a programme for regional development and growth* (commonly known as The Hailsham Report), Cmnd. No. 2206, London, HMSO.

BONNETT, C. (1990) 'Who wants to be an entrepreneur? A study of adolescents interested in a Young Enterprise Scheme', Undergraduate Psychology Report, University College, London.

BOWLES, S. and GINTIS, H. (1976) *Schooling in Capitalist America: Educational Reform and the Contradictions of Economic Life*, London, Routledge and Kegan Paul.

BRAKE, M. (1980) *The Sociology of Youth Culture and Youth Subcultures*, London, Routledge and Kegan Paul.

BRAKE, M. (1985) *Comparative Youth Culture*, London, Routledge and Kegan Paul.

BRAVERMAN, H. (1974) *Labour and Monopoly Capital*, New York, Monthly Review Press.

BRIGGS, A. (1963) *Victorian Cities*, London, Odhams Press Ltd.

BRITISH BUSINESS (1989, 9 June) 'Vat registrations and deregistrations of UK businesses: 1980–1987', pp. 32–5.

BROCKHAUS, R.H. (1982) 'The Psychology of the Entrepreneur', in KENT, C.A. *et al.* (Eds) *Encyclopedia of Entrepreneurship*, New Jersey, Prentice Hall.

BROWN, J.A.C. (1971) *The Social Psychology of Industry*, Harmondsworth, Penguin.

BROWN, P. (1987) *Schooling Ordinary Kids*, London, Tavistock.

BULMER, M. (Ed.) (1975) *Working Class Images of Society*, London, Routledge and Kegan Paul.

BURGESS, R.C. (Ed.) (1982) *Field Research*, London, George Allen and Unwin.

BURROWS, R. and CURRAN, J. (1989) 'Sociological research on service sector small businesses: some conceptual considerations', *Work, Employment and Society*, 3, 4, pp. 527–39.

BYNNER, J. (1987a) 'Coping with transition: ESRC's new '16–19 Initiative', *Youth and Policy*, 22, pp. 25–8.

BYNNER, J. (1987b) 'Transition to what? ESRC's new '16–19 Initiative', *ESRC Newsletter*, 61, pp. 8–10.

BYNNER, J. (1991, forthcoming) *Careers and Identities*, Milton Keynes, Open University Press.

BYNNER, J. and ASHFORD, S. (1990) 'Youth politics and lifestyles', *ESRC 16–19 Initiative Occasional Paper Series*, No. 25, London, City University.

BYRNE, D. (1989) *Beyond the Inner City*, Milton Keynes, Open University Press.

CAMPBELL, A. *et al.* (1977) *Worker Owners: The Mondragon Achievement*, London, Anglo-German Foundation for the Study of Industrial Society.

CARTER, M. (1966) *Into Work*, Harmondsworth, Penguin.

CARTER, S. and CANNON, T. (1988) *Female entrepreneurs*, Research Paper 65, Department of Employment, London.

CHAMPION, T. (1988) 'Migration from the North-East: The need for a more positive approach', *Northern Economic Review*, Spring, pp. 8–16.

CHELL, E. (1986) 'The Entrepreneurial personality: a review and some theoretical developments', in CURRAN, J. *et al.* (Eds) *op. cit.*

CITY AND GUILDS OF LONDON INSTITUTE (1988) *Enterprise Skills Record of Achievement*, Portland Place, London.

CLARKE, G. (1982) 'Defending Ski-Jumpers: A Critique of Theories of Youth Subcultures', Paper No. 71, Birmingham, Centre for Contemporary Cultural Studies.

CLARKE, J. and JEFFERSON, T. (1973) 'The politics of popular culture', Paper No. 14, Centre for Contemporary Cultural Studies, University of Birmingham.

CLARKE, J., CRITCHER, C., JOHNSON, R. (Eds) (1979) *Working Class Culture*, London, Hutchinson.

CLEVELAND COUNTY COUNCIL (1987) *Unemployment Strategy*.

CLEVELAND COUNTY COUNCIL (1989) *Towards an Economic Strategy*.

CLEVELAND COUNTY COUNCIL, CAREERS SERVICE (1988–1989) Monthly *Reports of the Principal Careers Officer* to Careers and Youth Employment Sub-Committee.

CLEVELAND COUNTY COUNCIL, EDUCATION DEPARTMENT (1984–1988) *Education Statistics*.

CLEVELAND COUNTY COUNCIL, ECONOMIC DEVELOPMENT AND PLANNING DEPARTMENT (1983) *The Economic and Social Importance of the British Steel Corporation to Cleveland*.

CLEVELAND COUNTY COUNCIL, ECONOMIC DEVELOPMENT AND PLANNING DEPARTMENT (1985a) *Manufacturing employment change in Cleveland, 1976–1981*, Report 252.

CLEVELAND COUNTY COUNCIL, ECONOMIC DEVELOPMENT AND PLANNING DEPARTMENT (1985b) *Cleveland Structure Plan: Issues Report*.

CLEVELAND COUNTY COUNCIL, ECONOMIC DEVELOPMENT AND PLANNING DEPARTMENT (1986a) *Cleveland Structure Plan: People and Jobs*.

CLEVELAND COUNTY COUNCIL, ECONOMIC DEVELOPMENT AND PLANNING DEPARTMENT (1986b) *Cleveland Structure Plan: Economy*.

CLEVELAND COUNTY COUNCIL, ECONOMIC DEVELOPMENT AND PLANNING DEPARTMENT (1987) *Unemployment in Cleveland: Unemployment Trends*, Report 286.

CLEVELAND COUNTY COUNCIL, ECONOMIC DEVELOPMENT AND PLANNING DEPARTMENT (1990a) *Changes in the Unemployment Count — the Effect on Cleveland*, information note 90/1.

CLEVELAND COUNTY COUNCIL, ECONOMIC DEVELOPMENT AND PLANNING DEPARTMENT (1990b) *Cleveland Employment Projections*, information note 90/4.

CLEVELAND COUNTY COUNCIL, ECONOMIC DEVELOPMENT AND PLANNING DEPARTMENT (1990c) *Unemployment in Cleveland*, report 322.

CLEVELAND COUNTY COUNCIL, ECONOMIC DEVELOPMENT AND PLANNING DEPARTMENT (1990d) *Unemployment in Cleveland*, report 324.

CLEVELAND COUNTY COUNCIL, RESEARCH AND INTELLIGENCE UNIT (1983) *Why Cleveland is Different? Its Needs and Expenditure*, CR 401.

CLEVELAND COUNTY COUNCIL, RESEARCH AND INTELLIGENCE UNIT (1985) *Cleveland Economic and Demographic Review 1985–1989*.

CLEVELAND COUNTY COUNCIL, RESEARCH AND INTELLIGENCE UNIT (1986) *Survey of the Unemployed: Looking for Work*.

CLEVELAND COUNTY COUNCIL, RESEARCH AND INTELLIGENCE UNIT (1987a) *Cleveland 1987–1991: An Economic, Demographic and Social Review*.

CLEVELAND COUNTY COUNCIL, RESEARCH AND INTELLIGENCE UNIT (1987b) *The County Council's Response to Unemployment: an Update*.

CLEVELAND COUNTY COUNCIL, RESEARCH AND INTELLIGENCE UNIT (1987c) *Self-employment as an Option for Cleveland's Unemployed*, CR 589.

CLEVELAND COUNTY COUNCIL, RESEARCH AND INTELLIGENCE UNIT (1988a) *Cleveland 1988–1992: An Economic, Demographic and Social Review*, CR 626.

CLEVELAND COUNTY COUNCIL, RESEARCH AND INTELLIGENCE UNIT (1988b) *Cleveland Statistics in Brief — 1988*.

CLEVELAND COUNTY COUNCIL, RESEARCH AND INTELLIGENCE UNIT (1988c) *Unemployment in Cleveland 1960–1988*, information note 342.

CLEVELAND COUNTY COUNCIL, RESEARCH AND INTELLIGENCE UNIT (1990) *Cleveland Progress: Realising the Prospects of the 1990s*, CR 693.

CLEVELAND YOUTH ENTERPRISE NETWORK DEVELOPMENTS (1987), Spring Update, Occasional Papers.

COATES, K. (Ed.) (1976) *The New Worker Co-operatives*, London, Spokesman Books.

COCKERTON, P. et al. (1980) *Workers Co-operatives: A Handbook*, Aberdeen, Aberdeen People's Press.

COFFIELD, F. (1990) 'From the decade of the enterprise culture to the decade of the TECs', *British Journal of Education and Work*, 4, 1, pp. 1–19.

COFFIELD, F. and MACDONALD, R.F. (1989) 'Youth and enterprise in Cleveland', *British Educational Research Association Conference*, University of Newcastle.

COFFIELD, F., BORRILL, C., MARSHALL, S. (1986) *Growing Up at the Margins*, Milton Keynes, Open University Press.

COHEN, A.K. (1955) *Delinquent Boys: The Culture of the Gang*, New York, Free Press.

COHEN, P. (1972) 'Sub-cultural conflict and working class community', Paper No. 2, Centre for Contemporary Cultural Studies, Birmingham.

COHEN, P. (1983) 'Losing the generation game', *New Socialist*, 14, pp. 28–36.

COHEN, S. (1973) *Folk Devils and Moral Panics*, St. Albans, Paladin.

COLDWELL, B. (1990) 'A business view from a potential TEC in Teesside', *Regional Studies*, 24, 1, pp. 74–7.

COLEMAN, J.S. (1961) *The Adolescent Society*, New York, Free Press.

COLES, B. (1986) 'Gonna tear your playhouse down — towards reconstructing a sociology of youth', *Social Science Teacher*, 15, 3, pp. 78–80.

COLES, B. (Ed.) (1988) *Young Careers: The Search for Jobs and the New Vocationalism*, Milton Keynes, Open University Press.

COLES, B. and MACDONALD, R.F. (1990) 'From new vocationalism to the culture of enterprise', in WALLACE, C. and CROSS, M. (Eds) *Youth in Transition*, Basingstoke, Falmer Press.

COMMUNITY ENTERPRISE TRUST LIMITED (1988) *A Directory of Local Contacts for Youth Enterprise*, Hartlepool.

CONNELL, R.W. (1983) 'The porpoise and the elephant: Birmingham on class, culture and education', in CONNELL, R.W. (Ed.) *Which Way is Up?: Essays on Sex, Class and Culture*, London, George Allen and Unwin.

CONNOLLY, M. and TORKINGTON, N.P.K. (1990) 'Black Youth and Politics in Liverpool', *ERSC 16 to 19 Initiative Occasional Paper Series*, No. 33, London, City University.

COOKE, P. (Ed.) (1989) *Localities: the Changing Face of Urban Britain*, London, Unwin Hyman.

CORR, H., JAMIESON, L. and TOMES, N. (1990) 'Parents and Talking Politics', *ESRC 16 to 19 Initiative Occasional Paper Series*, No. 29, London, City University.

CROMIE, S. and HAYES, J. (1988) 'Towards a typology of female entrepreneurs', *Sociological Review*, 36, 1, pp. 87–113.

CROMPTON, R. and MANN, M. (Eds) (1986) *Gender and Stratification*, Cambridge, Polity Press.

CURRAN, J. (1980) 'The political world of the small firm worker', *Sociological Review*, 28, 1, pp. 75–103.

CURRAN, J. (1986) *Bolton Fifteen Years On: A Review and Analysis of Small Business Research in Britain 1971–1986*, London, Small Business Research Trust.

CURRAN, J. and BURROWS, R. (1986) 'The Sociology of petit capitalism — a trend report', *Sociology*, 20, 2, pp. 265–79.

CURRAN, J. and BURROWS, R. (1988) *Enterprise in Britain: A National Profile of Small Business Owners and the Self-Employed*, London, Small Business Research Trust.

CURRAN, J. and BLACKBURN, R. (1989) *Young People and Enterprise: A National Survey*, Kingston Business School, Occasional Paper, No. 11.

CURRAN, J. and BLACKBURN, R. (1990) *Small Business 2000, Socio-Economic and Environmental Factors Facing Small Firms in the 1990s*, London, Small Business Research Trust.

CURRAN, J. *et al.* (Eds) (1986) *The Survival of the Small Firm*, Vols. 1 and 2, Aldershot, Gower.

DALE, A. (1986) 'Social class and the self-employed', *Sociology* 20, 3, pp. 430–4.

DALE, R. (1985) *Education, Training and Employment: Towards a New Vocationalism?*, Oxford, Pergamon Press.

DEARDEN, R. (1984) 'Education and training', *Westminter Studies in Education*, 7, pp. 57–66.

DENNIS, N., HENRIQUES, F. and SLAUGHTER, C. (1956) *Coal is Our Life*, London, Eyre and Spottiswoode.

DENZIN, N.K. (1978) *The Research Act*, 2nd. ed., New York, Mcgraw-Hill.

DEPARTMENT OF EDUCATION AND SCIENCE (DES) (1988) *Statistical Bulletin 14/18*, December, London, HMSO.

DEPARTMENT OF EMPLOYMENT (1986) *Working Together — Education and Training*, London, HMSO, Cmnd 9823.

DEPARTMENT OF EMPLOYMENT (1988a) *Employment for the 1990s*, London, HMSO, Cmnd 540.

DEPARTMENT OF EMPLOYMENT (1988b) *Enterprise Allowance Scheme: Third Eighteen Month Postal Survey*, London, Research and Evaluation Branch, Report No. 11.

DEPARTMENT OF EMPLOYMENT (1989a) *North-East Labour Market Review*, Winter, Newcastle.

DEPARTMENT OF EMPLOYMENT (1989b) *North-East Labour Market Review*, Summer, Newcastle.

DEPARTMENT OF TRADE AND INDUSTRY (1988) *DTI — the Department for Enterprise*, London, HMSO, Cmnd 278.

DEPARTMENT OF TRADE AND INDUSTRY/NATIONAL WESTMINSTER BANK (1988) *Mini-Enterprise in Schools 1987/88*, London.

DORE, R.P. and SAKO, M. (1989) *How the Japanese Learn to Work*, London, Routledge and Kegan Paul.

DOWSE, R.E. and HUGHES, J.A. (1971) 'Girls, boys and politics', *British Journal of Sociology*, 22, pp. 53–67.

DUNN, J.H. (1977) 'The Language and myths of the New Right', *New Society*, 5 May, pp. 225–6.

DURHAM UNIVERSITY BUSINESS SCHOOL (1989) *Primary Enterprise: A Primary School Approach to Enterprise Education within the National Curriculum*, Durham, Casdec.

EDWARDS, T., FITZ, J. and WHITTY, G. (1989) *The State and Private Education: An Evaluation of the Assisted Places Scheme*, Basingstoke, Falmer Press.

EISENBERG, P. and LAZARSFELD, P.F. (1938) 'The Psychological Effects of Unemployment', *Psychological Bulletin*, 35, pp. 358–90.

ELLIOT, L. (1990) 'Dole Queue Spectre as Recession Looms', *The Guardian*, 1 August.

EMPLOYMENT SERVICE (1988) *The Enterprise Allowance Scheme: Information Paper*, December.

ERIKSON, E. (1968) *Identity, Youth and Crisis*, London, Faber and Faber.

FENNELL, E. (1990) 'Teesside TEC — Building for the Future', *TEC Director*, Issue 2, Moorfoot, Sheffield, Training Agency.

FIFE-SCHAW, C. and BREAKWELL, A. (1989) 'Predicting Intention not to Vote in Late Teenage: a UK Study of 17–18 year olds', *ESRC 16–19 Initiative Occasional Paper Series*, No. 16, London, City University.

FINCH, J. (1984) 'It's great to have someone to talk to . . . ', in BELL, C. and ROBERTS, H. (Eds) *op. cit.*

FINCH, J. (1988) 'Ethnography and Public Policy', in POLLARD, A., PURVIS, J. and WALFORD, G. (Eds) *Education, Training and the New Vocationalism*, Milton Keynes, Open University Press.

FILSTEAD, W.J. (1990) (Ed.) *Qualitative Methodology*, Chicago, Markham.

FINEMAN, S. (Ed.) (1987) *Unemployment: Personal and Social Consequences*, London, Tavistock.

FINN, D. (1986) 'Free Enterprise?' in *Unemployment Bulletin* Issue 22, pp. 5–10.

FINN, D. (1987) *Training without Jobs: New Deals and Broken Promises*, London, Macmillan.

FOORD, J. *et al.* (1985) *The Quiet Revolution: social and economic change on Teesside 1965 to 1985*, A Special Report for BBC North-East, Newcastle.

FOORD, J., ROBINSON, F. and SADLER, D. (1986/7) 'Living with economic decline: Teesside in crisis', *Northern Economic Review*, 14, pp. 33–48.

FOWLER, N. (1989) Speech to the *Business in the Cities* Conference, December, 1989.

FULLAN, M. (1982) *The Meaning of Educational Change*, Ontario, Oise Press.

FURNHAM, A. and GUNTER, B. (1989) *The Anatomy of Adolescence*, London, Routledge and Kegan Paul.

GIBB, A. (1987) 'Enterprise Culture — its Meaning and Implications for Education and Training', *Journal of European Industrial Training*, 11, 2, pp. 1–28.

GIBB, A. and RITCHIE, J. (1982) 'Understanding the process of starting small business', *European Small Business Journal*, 1, 1, pp. 26–45.

GILL, J. (1985) *Factors Affecting the Survival and Growth of the Smaller Company*, Aldershot, Gower.

GINZBERG, E. *et al.* (Eds) (1951) *Occupational Choice: an Approach to a General Theory*, New York, Columbia University Press.

GLASER, B. and STRAUSS, A. (1967) *The Discovery of Grounded Theory*, Chicago, Aldine.

GLASSER, R. (1988) *Gorbals Boy at Oxford*, London, Chatto and Windus.

GLEESON, D. (1983) *Youth Training and the Search for Work*, London, Routledge and Kegan Paul.

GODLEY, W. (1989) 'Economic disaster in slow motion', *The Observer*, 27 August 1989.

GOLDTHORPE, J.H. *et al.* (1987) *Social Mobility and Class Structure in Modern Britain*, 2nd edition, Oxford, Clarendon Press.

GOW, L. and MCPHERSON, A. (1980) *Tell Them from Me*, Aberdeen, Aberdeen University Press.

GRAHAM, H. (1984) 'Surveying through stories', in BELL, C. and ROBERTS, H. (Eds) *op. cit.*

GRAMSCI, A. (1971) *Selections from Prison Notebooks*, edited and translated by HOARE, Q. and NOWELL SMITH, G., London, Lawrence and Whishart.

GRAY, C. and STANWORTH, J. (1986) *Allowing for Enterprise: a Qualitative Assessment of the EAS*, London, Small Business Research Trust.

GRAYSON, D. (1989) 'At the roots of enterprise', *Employment Gazette*, 97, 10, pp. 534–8.

GRIFFIN, C. (1985) *Typical Girls?*, London, Routledge and Kegan Paul.

GUARDIAN, THE, (1989, 6 January) 'Youth enterprise'.

GUARDIAN, THE, (1990, 8 June) 'Where have all the unemployed gone?'

GUARDIAN, THE, (1990, 12 June) 'Protests as British steel looks abroad'.

GUARDIAN, THE, (1990, 20 July) 'Key indicators suggest UK economy is teetering on the brink of stagflation'.

GUARDIAN, THE, (1990, 27 July) 'City tumbles as ICI slumps'.

GUARDIAN, THE, (1990, 17 September) 'Doing it the British way helps trainers blaze an eastern trail'.

HAKIM, C. (1987a) 'Trends in the flexible workforce', *Employment Gazette*, 95, 11, pp. 549–60.

HAKIM, C. (1987b) *Home Based Work in Britain*, Research Paper 60, Department of Employment, London.

HAKIM, C. (1988) 'Self-employment in Britain: recent trends and current issues', *Work, Employment and Society*, 2, 4, pp. 421–50.

HAKIM, C. (1989a) 'New recruits to self-employment in the 1980s', *Employment Gazette*, June, pp. 286–97.

HAKIM, C. (1989b) 'Workforce restructuring, social insurance coverage and the black economy', *Journal of Social Policy*, 28, 4, pp. 471–503.

HALL, S. (1988) *The Hard Road to Renewal: Thatcherism and the Crisis of the Left*, London, Verso.

HALL, S. and JEFFERSON, T. (Eds) (1976) *Resistance through Rituals*, London, Hutchinson.

HALSALL, M. (1990) 'Small firms in high interest rate crisis, says CBI', *The Guardian*, 8 August.

HAMMERSLEY, M. and ATKINSON, P. (1983) *Ethnography: Principles in Practice*, London, Tavistock.

HARBER, C. (Ed.) (1987) *Political Education in Britain*, Basingstoke, Falmer Press.

HARDING, P. and JENKINS, R. (1989) *The Myth of the Hidden Economy*, Milton Keynes, Open University Press.

HARGREAVES, D. (1982) *The Challenge for the Comprehensive School*, London, Routledge and Kegan Paul.

HARRÉ, R. (1980) 'Foreword', in KITWOOD, T.M., *Disclosures to a Stranger*, London, Routledge and Kegan Paul.

HARRISON, R. (1988a) 'Enterprise education in Cleveland County'. Paper given at *Youth Enterprise Conference*, Middlesbrough, 8 July.

HARRISON, R. (1988b) *Going for Enterprise: Resource Materials*, BSC Industry/DUBS.

HEATH, D. and TOPF, R. (1987) 'Political Culture in British Social Attitudes', in JOWELL, R., WITHERSPOON, S. and BROOK, L. (Eds), *British Social Attitudes Survey, the 1987 Report*, Aldershot, Gower.

HEBDIGE, D. (1979) *Sub-culture — the Meaning of Style*, London, Methuen.

HENCKE, D. (1990) Article discussing Restart scheme, *The Guardian*, 12 January, quoted in ROBINSON, F., 1990. *op. cit.*

HOBBS, D. (1988) *Doing the Business*, Oxford, Clarendon Press.

HOGGART, R. (1957) *The Uses of Literacy*, Harmondsworth, Pelican.

HOGGART, R. (1990) *A Sort of Clowning*, London, Chatto and Windus.

HOLT, M. (Ed.) (1987) *Skills and Vocationalism: The Easy Answer*, Milton Keynes, Open University Press.

HOLLANDS, R.G. (1990) *The Long Transition: Class, Culture and Youth Training*, Basingstoke, Macmillan.

HORTON, C. (1985) *Nothing Like A Job*, London, Youthaid.

HOUGH, J. (1982) 'Franchising — An Avenue of Entry into Small Business' in STANWORTH, J. *et al.* (Eds) *op. cit.*

HOUSE OF COMMONS COMMITTEE OF PUBLIC ACCOUNTS (1989) *Assistance to Small Firms*, Eighth Report, London, HMSO.

HOUSE OF LORDS (1990) *Vocational Training and Re-training*, Select Committee on the European Communities, Session 1989–90 21st Report, HL Paper 78–1, London, HMSO.

HOWARD, M. (1990) 'Skills: the Buzzword for Business in the Nineties', *The Observer*, 11 March.

HUDSON, R. (1986) 'Sunset Over the Tees', *New Socialist*, September, p. 13.

HUDSON, R. (1989) *Wrecking a Region: State Policy, Party Politics and Regional Change in North-East England*, London, Pion Press.

HUDSON, R. and SADLER, D. (1985) 'The Development of Middlesbrough's Iron and Steel Industry, 1842–1985', *Middlesbrough Locality Study*, No. 2, University of Durham.

HUGHES, J. (1984) 'Community co-operatives as small business', in LEWIS, J., STANWORTH, J. and GIBB, A. (Eds) *op. cit.*

HUNT, D. and McVEY, P. (1984) 'Fishing co-ops — what are we really talking about' in LEWIS, J., STANWORTH, J. and GIBB, A. (Eds) *op. cit.*

HUTSON, S. and JENKINS, R. (1989) *Taking the Strain: Families, Unemployment and the Transition to Adulthood*, Milton Keynes, Open University Press.

INSPIRING SUCCESS (1989) *The Youth Enterprise Conference* 'Report and Feedback', University of York.

INTERNATIONAL JOURNAL OF URBAN AND REGIONAL RESEARCH (1982) Special Edition devoted to Enterprise Zones, 6, 3.

JAHODA, M. (1979) 'The impact of unemployment in the 1930s and the 1970s', *Bulletin of the British Psychological Society*, 32, pp. 309–14.

JAMIESON, I. (1989) 'Education and the economy: themes and issues', *Journal of Education Policy*, 4, 1, pp. 69–73.

JEFFERIS, K. (1989) 'Is the wheel turning full circle for worker co-ops?', *The Guardian*, 11 September.

JENKINS, R. (1983) *Lads, Citizens and Ordinary Kids — Working Class Youth Lifestyles in Belfast*, London, Routledge and Kegan Paul.

JENKINS, R. (1984) 'Ethnic minorities in business: a research agenda', in WARD, R. and JENKINS, R. (Eds), *Ethnic Communities in Business*, Cambridge, Cambridge University Press.

JONATHAN, R. (1983) 'The Manpower Service Model of Education', *Cambridge Journal of Education*, 13, pp. 3–10.

JONATHAN, R. (1987) 'The Youth Training Scheme and core skills: an educational analysis', in HOLT, M. (Ed.) *Skills and Vocationalism: The Easy Answer*, Milton Keynes, Open University Press.

JONATHAN, R. (1989) 'Choice and control in education: parental rights, individual liberties and social justice', *British Journal of Educational Studies*, 37, 4, pp. 321–38.

JOHNSON, C. *et al.* (1987a) *Key Skills: Enterprise Skills Through Active Learning, 14–16*, London, Hodder and Stoughton.

JOHNSON, C. *et al.* (1987b) *Key Skills: Enterprise Skills through Active Learning, 16–19*, London, Hodder and Stoughton.

JOHNSON, D. and ROGER, J. (1983) 'From redundancy to self-employment', *Employment Gazette*, 91, 6, pp. 260–64.

JONES, B. *et al.* (1988) 'Finding a post-16 Route — the first year's experience', in COLES, B. (Ed.) *op. cit.*

JONES, T. and McEVOY, D. (1986) 'Ethnic enterprise: the popular image', in CURRAN, J. *et al.* (Eds) *op. cit.*

JOSEPH, K. (1974) Speech during the debate on 'Small Business and the Self-employed', *House of Commons Official Report*, 888, pp. 10–21.

KETS DE VRIES, M.F.R. (1977) 'The entrepreneurial personality: a person at the crossroads, *Journal of Management Studies*, 14, 1, pp. 34–58.

KEYNES, J.M. (1936) *The General Theory of Employment, Interest and Money*, London, Macmillan.

KILBY, P. (1971) 'Hunting the Heffalump', in KILBY, P. (Ed.), *Entrepreneurship and Economic Development*, New York, Free Press.

THE LABOUR PARTY (1990) 'Unemployment Under the Conservatives — Miracle or Mirage?' *Labour Market Briefing*, No. 2, prepared by Henry McLeish MP, Shadow Employment Minister, London.

LABOUR RESEARCH (1986) 'The growing army of self-employed', *Labour Research*, 75, 2, pp. 13–15.

LAW, B. (1983) 'The colour-coded curriculum', NICEC *Training and Development Bulletin*, 23, pp. 2–3.

LEE, D., MARSDEN, D., RICKMAN, P. and DUNCOMBE, J. (1990) *Scheming for Youth: A Study of YTS in the Enterprise Culture*, Milton keynes, Open University Press.

LEE, R. (1985) 'The entry to self-employment of redundant steelworkers', *Industrial Relations Journal*, 16, 2, pp. 42–9.

LEES, S. (1986) *Losing Out: Sexuality and Adolescent Girls*, London, Hutchinson.

LENIN, V.I. (1976) *The State and Revolution*, Foreign Languages Press, Peking.

LEVITAS, R. (Ed.) (1986) *The Ideology of the New Right*, Cambridge, Polity Press.

LEWIS, J., STANWORTH, J. and GIBB, A. (Eds) (1984) *Success and Failure in Small Business*, Gower, Aldershot.

MACDONALD, R.F. (1988a) *Schooling, Training, Working and Claiming: Youth and Unemployment in Local Rural Labour Markets*, unpublished D. Phil. thesis, University of York.

MACDONALD, R.F. (1988b) 'Out of town, out of work: research on the post-16 experience in two rural areas', in COLES, B. (Ed.) *op. cit.*

MACDONALD, R.F. (1989) 'Youth, Unemployment and Locality', *British Sociological Association Conference*, Plymouth Polytechnic.

MACDONALD, R.F. (1990) 'Enterprising or surviving? Youth entrepreneurship and business start up in a depressed area of Britain', *British Sociological Association Conference*, University of Surrey.

MACDONALD, R.F. and COFFIELD, F. (1990) 'Youth Enterprise and Business Start Up in A Depressed Areas of Britain', *ESRC 16 to 19 Initiative Occasional Paper Series*, No. 28, London, City University.

MACKENZIE, M.L. (1989) *Scottish Toryism and the Union: A Phenomenological Approach*, Cambridge, Tory Reform Group.

MAIZELS, J. (1970) *Adolescent Needs and the Transition from School to Work*, London, Athlone Press.

MALINOWSKI, B. (1922) *Argonauts of the Western Pacific*, London, Routledge and Kegan Paul.

MANPOWER SERVICES COMMISSION (1981) *A New Training Initiative: An Agenda for Action*, Selkirk House, London.

MARSLAND, D. (1988a) Various articles in *Network*, Journal of British Sociological Association.

MARSLAND, D. (1988b) *Seeds of Bankruptcy: Sociological Bias Against Business and Freedom*, London, Claridge Press.

MAYER, K. and GOLDSTEIN, S. (1961) *The First Two Years: Problems of Small Firms Growth and Survival*, Washington, D.C., Small Business Administration.

McCALL, G.J. and SIMMONS, J.L. (1969) *Issues in Participant Observation: a Text and a Reader*, Reading, Mass, Addison-Wesley.

McCLELLAND, D.C. (1961) *The Achieving Society*, New Jersey, Van Nostrand.

McCLELLAND, D.C. (1971) 'The achievement motive in economic growth' in KILBY, P. (Ed.) *Entrepreneurship and Economic Development*, New York, Free Press.

McKIE, L., LLEWELLYN, T. and PEPPIN, T. (1989) 'Compatibility or Conflict? Teeside Development Corporation and Cleveland County Council', *British Sociological Association Conference*, Plymouth Polytechnic.

McRAE, S. (1987) 'Social and political perspectives found among young unemployed men and women' in WHITE, M. (Ed.) *The Social World of the Young Unemployed*, London, Policy Studies Institute.

MEAD, M. (1972) 'Research with human beings: a model derived from anthropological field practice', in FREUND, P.A. (Ed.) *Experimentation with Human Subjects*, London, Allen and Unwin.

MIDDLESBROUGH CAREERS OFFICE (1988, 28 November) 'The destination of middlesbrough school-leavers 1985 to 1988', Personal Communication.

MILLER, J. (1987) 'The self-employed: entrepreneurs, professionals and casual labourers', *Initiatives*, April, pp. 5–7.

MILLER, S.M. (1986) 'Notes on neo-capitalism', in Curran *et al.* (Eds) *op. cit.*

MILLS, C.W. (1970) *The Sociological Imagination*, Harmondsworth, Penguin.

MORGAN, P. (1990) Address to the *Institute of Directors Annual Convention*, Royal Albert Hall, 27 February, pp. 1–15.

MUSGROVE, F. (1968) *Youth and Social Order*, London, Routledge and Kegan Paul.

NABARRO, R. *et al.* (1986) *Local Enterprise and the Unemployed*, London, Calouste Gulbenkian Foundation.

NATIONAL AUDIT OFFICE (NAO) (1988) *Department of Employment/ Training Commission: Assistance to Small Firms*, Report 655, London, HMSO.

NATIONAL AUDIT OFFICE (NAO) (1988) *Department of the Environment: Urban Development Corporations*, No. 492, London, HMSO.

NATIONAL AUDIT OFFICE (NAO) (1990) *Regenerating the Inner Cities*, No. 169, London, HMSO.

NEARY, M. (1990) 'Youth Enterprise and local economic planning', *Youth and Policy*, 29, pp. 29–32.

NICHOLAUS, M. (1968) 'Fat Cat Sociology' — Address to the *American Sociological Association Conference*, New University Conference, Boston.

NICHOLS, T. and BEYNON, H. (1977) *Living with Capitalism*, London, Routledge and Kegan Paul.

NORTH OF ENGLAND COUNTY COUNCILS' ASSOCIATION (NECCA) (1986) *Towards a Stronger North, the State of the Region Report 1985.*

OSMOND, J. (1988) *The Divided Kingdom*, London, Constable.

PENN, R. (1990) 'Flexibility in Britain during the 1990s: evidence from the ESRC's social change and economic life initiative', *British Sociological Association Conference*, University of Surrey.

PIORE, M. and SABLE, C. (1984) *The Second Industrial Divide: Possibilities for Prosperity*, New York, Basic Books.

PITMAN EXAMINATIONS INSTITUTE (1987) *Enterprise Skills*, Surrey.

POLLERT, A. (1988) 'Dismantling flexibility', *Capital and Class*, 34, pp. 42–75.

PRING, R. (1987) 'The curriculum and the new vocationalism', *British Journal of Education and Work*, 1, 3, pp. 33–48.

QUICKE, J. (1990) 'Moral Career Continuities and Political Transformations', *ESRC 16 to 19 Initiative Youth and Politics Workshop*, University of Liverpool.

RAFFE, D. (1987) 'Youth unemployment in the UK 1979–1984', in BROWN, P. and ASHTON, D.N. (Eds) *Education, Unemployment and Labour Markets*, Basingstoke, Falmer Press.

RAFFE, D. (1989) 'Scotland v England: the place of 'Home Inter-Nationals' in comparative research', *Training Agency Conference*, Manchester, September.

RAINNIE, A. (1990a) 'Back to the future: The political economy of the new localism', *British Sociological Association Conference*, University of Surrey.

RAINNIE, A. (1990b) 'Labour market change and the organization of work', *British Sociological Association Conference*, University of Surrey.

RAVEN, J. (1989) 'Viewpoint: British culture and the enterprise culture', *Past and Present*, 123, pp. 178–204.

RBL RESEARCH INTERNATIONAL (For MSC) (1987) *EAS Evaluation Three Year National Survey*, RBL 65418, London.

REES, G. and THOMAS, M. (1989) 'From coal miners to entrepreneurs? a case study in the sociology of re-industrialisation', *British Sociological Association Conference*, Plymouth Polytechnic.

REES, T. (1986) 'Education for enterprise: the state and alternative employment for young people', *Journal of Education Policy*, 3, 1, pp. 9–22.

RIDLEY, F.F. (1981) 'View from a disaster area: unemployed youth in Merseyside' in CRICK, B. (Ed.) *Unemployment*, London, Methuen.

RISEBOROUGH, G.F. (1988) 'We're the YTS Boys!: An Ethnographic Explanation of Classroom Politics', *ESRC 16 to 19 Initiative First Findings Workshop*, Harrogate.

RITCHIE, J. (1984) 'Small business revival as cultural play and spectacle', Working Paper, School of Occupational Studies, Newcastle Polytechnic.

RITCHIE, J. (1987) 'Explaining enterprise cultures', *Tenth UK Small Business Policy and Research Conference*, Cranfield.

ROBERTS, J. (1988) 'Pie in the sky? or sharing the cake on the plate? Lessons from evangelical enterprise,' *Employment Gazette*, July, pp. 365–71.

ROBERTS, K. (1984) *Schoolleavers and their Prospects*, Milton Keynes, Open University Press.

ROBERTS, K. (1987) 'ESRC — young people in society', *Youth and Policy*, 22, pp. 15–24.

ROBERTS, K. and PARSELL, G. (1988) 'Opportunity Structures and Career Trajectories from Age 16 to 19', *ESRC 16 to 19 Initiative Occasional Paper Series*, No. 1, London, City University.

ROBERTS, K. and PARSELL, G. (1990) 'The Political Orientations, Interests and Activities of Britains 16–18 year olds in the late 1980s', *ESRC 16 to 19 Initiative Occasional Papers Series*, No. 26, London, City University.

ROBERTS, R. (1990) 'Rhetoric and the resurgence of capitalism', Lecture at Durham University, 19 March.

ROBINS, K. and WEBSTER, F. (1989) *The Technical Fix: Education, Computers and Industry*, Basingstoke, Macmillan.

ROBINSON, D. (1990) *The Naked Entrepreneur*, London, Kogan Page.

ROBINSON, F. (1990) *The Great North?*, A Special Report for BBC North-East, Newcastle.

ROBINSON, F. and GILLESPIE, A. (1989) 'Let the good times roll? The North's economic revival', in *Northern Economic Review*, 17, Spring, pp. 60–73.

ROSA, P. (1989) 'Family background and entrepreneurial activity in

British graduates', *12th National Small Firms Policy and Research Conference*, Thames Polytechnic.

ROTTER, J.B. (1966) 'Generalized Expectancies for Internal Versus External Control of Reinforcement' *Psychological Monographs*, 80, 609.

ROYAL SOCIETY OF ARTS (1987) *Enterprise Skills Profile 1987–88*, London.

RUTTER, M. *et al.* (1976) 'Adolescent Turmoil: Fact or Fiction?', *Journal of Child Psychiatry*, 17, pp. 35–56.

SADLER, D. (1986) 'The Impacts of Offshore Fabrication in Teesside', *Middlesbrough Locality Study*, No. 5, University of Durham.

SAUNDERS, J.W. (1983) *What Happened to a Town Without a University: Continuing Education in Middlesbrough*, Stockton, Harrison.

SCASE, R. and GOFFEE, R. (1987) *The Real World of the Small Business Owner*, 2nd edition, London, Croom Helm.

SCOTTISH VOCATIONAL EDUCATION COUNCIL (1988) *Enterprise Activity 1*, National Certificate Module Description, No. 81209, Glasgow.

SHILLING, C. (1989) 'The Mini-Enterprise in Schools Project: a new stage in education-industry relations?', *Journal of Education Policy*, 4, 2, pp. 115–24.

SHILLING, C. (1989) *Schooling for Work in Capitalist Britain*, Basingstoke, Falmer Press.

SILVER, H. and BRENNAN, J. (1988) *A Liberal Vocationalism*, London, Methuen.

SMALLBONE, D. (1990) 'Success and failure in new business start ups', *International Small Business Journal*, 8, 2, pp. 34–47.

SMITH, A. (1958) *The Wealth of Nations*, (2 vols.), London, Dent.

SMITH, R. (1987) 'Teaching on stilts: a critique of classroom skills', in HOLT, M. (Ed.) *Skills and Vocationalism: the Easy Answer*, Milton Keynes, Open University Press.

SPRADLEY, J.P. (1979a) *The Ethnographic Interview*, New York, Holt, Rinehart and Winston.

SPRADLEY, J.P. (1979b) *Participant Observation*, New York, Holt, Rinehart and Winston.

STANLEY HALL, G. (1904) *Adolescence*, New York, Appleton.

STANWORTH, J. and CURRAN, J. (1973) *Management Motivation in the Smaller Business*, Aldershot, Gower.

STANWORTH, J., WESTRIP, A., WATKINS, D. and LEWIS, J. (Eds) (1982) *Perspectives on a Decade of Small Business Research: Bolton Ten Years On*, Aldershot, Gower.

STANWORTH, J. *et al.* (1989) 'Who becomes an entrepreneur?', *International Small Business Journal*, Vol. 8, 1, pp. 11–23.

STEEDMAN, H. (1990) 'Improvements in workforce qualifications: Britain and France 1979–88', *National Institute Economic Review*, No. 133, August, pp. 50–61.

STOREY, D. (1982) *Entrepreneurship and the New Firm*, London, Croom Helm.

STOREY, D. (1986a) 'New firm formation, employment change and the small firm: the Case of Cleveland County', in CURRAN, J. *et al.* (Eds) *op. cit.*

STOREY, D. (1986b) 'Entrepreneurship and the new firm' in CURRAN, J. *et al.* (Eds) *op. cit.*

STOREY, D. and JOHNSON, S. (1987a) *Are Small Firms the Answer to Unemployment?*, London, Employment Institute.

STOREY, D. and JOHNSON, S. (1987b) *Job Generation and Labour Market Change*, London, Macmillan.

STOREY, D., KEASEY, K., WATSON, R. and WYNARCZYK, P. (1987) *The Performance of Small Firms*, London, Croom Helm.

STRADLING, R. (1977) *The Political Awareness of the School Leaver*, London, The Hansard Society.

STRATTON, C. (1990) 'The Interview', *Adult and Youth Training News*, Issue 1, Training Agency, Sheffield.

STRATTON, C. (1990) 'TECs and PICs: the key issues which lie ahead', *Regional Studies*, 24, 1, pp. 71–4.

TAWNEY, R.H. (1964) *Equality*, London, Unwin.

TEC DIRECTOR (1990) 'Teesside TEC-Building for the future', Issue 2, Employment Department, Training Agency, Sheffield pp. 28–31.

TEESSIDE DEVELOPMENT CORPORATION (1990) *Annual Report and Financial Statements*, Middlesbrough, Tees House.

TEESSIDE TEC (1990) *Corporate Plan: 1990–1993*, Middlesbrough.

THOMAS, A. and CORNFORTH, C. (1989) 'The survival and growth of worker co-operatives: a comparison with small business', *International Small Business Journal*, 8, 1, pp. 34–51.

THOMPSON, K. (1984) 'Education for capability — a critique', *British Journal of Educational Studies*, 32, 3, pp. 203–12.

THORNLEY, J. (1981) *Worker's Co-operatives*, London, Heinemann.

TITMUSS, R.M. (1963) *Essays on the Welfare State*, London, Unwin University Books.

TRADES UNION CONGRESS (TUC) (1988) *Government Assistance to Small Firms: National Audit Office Report*, Employment Policy and Organization Committee, London, TUC.

TRADES UNION CONGRESS (1989) *Skills 2000*, London, Twentieth Century Press.

TRADE UNION STUDIES INFORMATION UNIT (TUSIU) (1987) *Northern Economy Notes*, 10, pp. 1–4.

TRAINING AGENCY (1989a) *Enterprise in Higher Education*, Moorfoot, Sheffield.

TRAINING AGENCY (1989b) *Training and Enterprise: Priorities for Action 1990–91*, Moorfoot, Sheffield.

TRAINING AGENCY (1989c) *TECs: Guide to Planning*, Moorfoot, Sheffield.

TRAINING AGENCY (1989d) *Training in Britain — Main Report*, Moorfoot, Sheffield.

TURNER, D. (1989) *The Enterprise Factor: Community Enterprise in the Curriculum*, London, CSV.

UNEMPLOYMENT BULLETIN (1989) 'Developing TECs', 30, Summer, pp. 1–3.

UNEMPLOYMENT UNIT (1990) *In With Your Eyes Open*, London.

VARLAAM, C. (1984) *Rethinking Transition: Educational Innovation and the Transition to Adult Life*, Basingstoke, The Falmer Press.

WALKER, R. (1985) *Applied Qualitative Research*, London, Gower.

WALKER, S. and BARTON, L. (Eds) (1989) *Politics and the Process of Schooling*, Milton Keynes, Open University Press.

WALLACE, C. (1987) *For Richer, for Poorer: Growing up in and out of Work*, Tavistock, London.

WARD, R. and JENKINS, R. (Eds) (1984) *Ethnic Communities in Business*, Cambridge, Cambridge University Press.

WARR, P. (1983) 'Work, Jobs and Unemployment', *Bulletin of the British Psychological Society*, 36, pp. 305–11.

WATERS, C. (1981) 'Badges of half-formed, inarticulate radicalism: a critique of recent trends in the study of working-class youth culture', *International Labour and Working Class History*, 19, pp. 23–37.

WATKINS, J. and WATKINS, D. (1984) 'The female entrepreneur: background and determinants of business choice — some British data', *International Small Business Journal*, 3, 1, pp. 21–31.

WHITE, M. (1990) 'Labour woos student vote', *The Guardian*, 28 September.

WHITE, T. (1990) 'Special training needs and TECs', *Unemployment Bulletin*, 33, Summer, p. 24.

WIENER, M.J. (1981) *English Culture and the Decline of the Industrial Spirit 1850–1980*, Harmondsworth, Penguin.

WILKS, S. (1987) 'From industrial policy to enterprise policy in Britain', *Journal of General Management*, 12, 4, pp. 5–20.

WILLIAMS, R. (1983) *Towards 2000*, London, Chatto and Windus, The Hogarth Press.

WILLIAMSON, B. (1990) *The Temper of the Times: British Society Since World War II*, Oxford, Basil Blackwell.

WILLIS, P. (1977) *Learning to Labour*, Farnborough, Saxon House.

WILLIS, P. (1978) *Profane Culture*, London, Routledge and Kegan Paul.

WILLIS, P. (1980) 'Notes on method', in HALL, S. *et al.* (Eds) *Culture, Media, Language: Working Papers in Cultural Studies, 1972–1979*, London, Hutchinson.

WILLMOTT, P. (1969) *Adolescent Boys of East London*, London, Harmondsworth, Penguin.

WILSON, P. and STANWORTH, J. (1985) *Black Business in Brent: A Study of Inner London Black Minority Enterprise*, London, Small Business Research Trust.

WILSON, P. and STANWORTH, J. (1988) 'Growth strategies in small business Asian and Carribean Businesses', *Employment Gazette*, January.

WITHINGTON, J. (1989) *Shutdown: The Anatomy of a Shipyard Closure*, London, Bedford Square Press.

WITTGENSTEIN, L. (1987) *Philosophical Investigations*, Oxford, Basil Blackwell.

WOOD, S. (Ed.) (1989) *The Transformation of Work*, London, Unwin Hyman.

WOODCOCK, C. (1990a) 'Interest rates rob UK of 900,000 new jobs, says survey', *The Guardian*, 2 July.

WOODCOCK, C. (1990b) 'Government may pick winners in carve-up of aid to small business', *The Guardian*, 2 July.

WREN, C. (1989) 'The revised Regional Development Grant Scheme: a case study in Cleveland County of a marginal employment subsidy', *Regional Studies*, 23, 2, pp. 127–37.

WRIGHT, B. (1986) 'Cleveland's model of self-employment support for young people', *Business in the Community 5th Annual Conference*, Newcastle, 8–9 December.

YOUNG, LORD (1986) 'Enterprise — the road to jobs', *London Business School Journal*, 11, 1, pp. 21–7.

YOUNG, LORD (1990) *The Enterprise Years*, London, Headline.

Index